Supernatural Fiction
for Teens

SUPERNATURAL FICTION FOR TEENS
More Than 1300 Good Paperbacks to Read for Wonderment, Fear, and Fun

2d Edition

COSETTE KIES
Chair and Professor
Department of Library and Information Studies
Northern Illinois University
DeKalb, Illinois

1992
LIBRARIES UNLIMITED, INC.
Englewood, Colorado

LIBRARIES UNLIMITED, INC.
P.O. Box 6633
Englewood, CO 80155-6633

Library of Congress Cataloging-in-Publication Data

Kies, Cosette N., 1936-
    Supernatural fiction for teens : more than 1300 good paperbacks to
read for wonderment, fear, and fun / Cosette Kies. -- 2d ed.
        ix, 267 p. 17x25 cm.
        Includes index.
        ISBN 0-87287-940-2 (softbound)
        1. Bibliography--Best books--Young adult fiction.
2. Bibliography--Best books--Fantastic fiction. 3. Supernatural in
literature--Bibliography. 4. Young adult fiction--Bibliography.
5. Fantastic fiction--Bibliography. 6. Paperbacks--Bibliography.
I. Title.
Z1037.K485 1992
[PN1009.A1]
016.80883'937--dc20   91-45469
                                                                CIP

Contents

Introduction to the Second Edition

The supernatural encompasses a fascinating range of subjects, most of which provide intriguing themes for fiction. Teenagers, like other readers, have shown great interest in reading supernatural fiction in recent years, and a considerable amount of material is available at present. Since publication of the first edition of *Supernatural Fiction for Teens* in 1987, many more supernatural fiction titles have been published, some new and some reissued.

Very simply defined, the supernatural includes all subjects not explainable in terms of present-day science. In this particular compilation of titles for teens, the supernatural is organized in three major categories: (1) those subjects now included in parapsychology and psychic phenomena, such as ghosts and haunted houses, reincarnation, altered states of consciousness, levitation, time travel, fortune-telling, spiritualism, and alchemy; (2) tales and legends with strong magical and occult elements from various cultures, such as Arthurian tales and fairy tales as well as stories dealing with lost lands, heaven and hell, eternal youth, mythical beasts, shamanism, astrology, voodoo, witchcraft, and satanism; and (3) horror, both traditional and modern, from the supernatural gothic fiction tradition, which emphasizes the terrors of the heart, including vampires and werewolves, curses, science gone wrong, transformation, and monsters of all sorts. Works of pure fantasy are not included unless authors have strongly based their works on traditional mythic and/or occult themes. Science fiction, sword and sorcery, alternative (parallel) worlds, animals endowed with human attributes, and futurism work are generally not included.

Fictional works based on these fascinating themes provide all readers, including teens, with speculative books that excite, tantalize, amaze, and horrify. The wide range of subjects and fictional explorations provides a rich body of literature to share with young adults, and almost any reader should find something appealing in this book. This listing is not confined only to works of the highest quality, although some very fine pieces of writing are represented. Instead, the intent has been to give an idea of the various works available, from the humor of *Mad Magazine* through gross-out horror books full of violence and disgusting descriptions to gentle stories of ghostly maidens and a few classics that sometimes even teens will read. In the end, quality in this area is probably a very subjective judgment to be made by the teens themselves. Their interests are very likely to be piqued by what seems possible, yet they also love works that stretch their imaginations. They are not likely to analyze horror fiction such as the novels written by Stephen King in terms of literary criticism, yet they will sense the excellent pacing of King's work, for pacing is what makes a story move along and keeps the reader eagerly turning the pages. The archaic writing style employed by nineteenth-century authors will not necessarily turn teens off; instead, they may secretly like those works on occasion because they give the impression of being old arcane mysteries of some sort—because the books are written in the fashion of an earlier time, the supernatural becomes somehow more believable.

The books listed in the main body of the text are coded. Categories include (1) books written specifically for teens; (2) books written for younger teens that may appeal to high-interest/low-reading-level readers; (3) books written for adults, often including explicit sex, gore, violence, and vulgar language; and (4) books now considered to be classics. A letter designating the category is to be found in the main text under each main entry number as follows:

A   Written for teens

B   Written for younger teens

C   Written for adults

D   Classics

Selections were made somewhat subjectively, sometimes based on what books were available for examination. Some works judged to be unlikely to appeal to today's teens, such as works by James Branch Cabell, were omitted. Some new talents, as well as leading contemporary and classic authors, have been included. Because of the wide range of reading abilities and cultural sophistication of teens, books for younger teens include a few titles that might be considered more appropriate for younger readers. It is sometimes difficult to categorize titles in the supernatural, for paperback publishers are engaging in "cross-publishing," reissuing in adult paperback format many books originally written and published for children in order to take advantage of the current popularity of fantasy fiction. Included also are books written for adults; a number of these titles are in the horror genre, which is popular with some kids just because they love being "grossed out." Books beyond the American experience are included to provide a sense of the rich traditions of the supernatural in other cultures.

Availability of specific titles is always a problem, particularly with paperbacks, because books often go out of print quickly. In the area of the supernatural, however, high interest and brisk sales seem to keep some titles in print longer, and some titles are reissued, usually with new cover designs. Certain subjects and themes seem to be immensely popular at present, such as the legend of King Arthur, and many books are available on the story of Camelot. Vampires, also enjoying a vogue, are well represented in the bookstore racks, too. By keeping abreast of such trends, the wise librarian is able to stock up in certain areas while continuing to seek out worthy titles on less-popular themes.

In the following numbered list of more than 1,300 supernatural fiction titles for teens, the item number is followed by the author's name. Pseudonyms, such as Mark Twain and Saki, have been used if the author's name appears that way on the books. The author's real name is noted in parentheses. Following the author's name is the book title, along with the paperback publication data and reader code. A note regarding original publication information may be included, as is series information. SBNs and ISBNs have been included when available. Titles of sequels are listed, as are other works by the same author that might also find favor with teen readers. If a movie has been based on the book, brief information regarding the film is given. If there is more than one movie version, titles are listed chronologically. Titles that are novelizations of movie scripts are also noted. A brief annotation of the book title follows that is suitable for use in booklists. Contents of short-story collections are provided as well. The annotation concludes with a subject designation in brackets. Whenever possible, the most specific subject headings have been used. For example, the heading "Legends, Arthurian," is used for books about Camelot rather than the broader "Legends, English."

This compilation has multiple uses. First and foremost, it is meant to serve as a purchasing guide for librarians and teens; second, it serves as a reading guide. It may also be used for programming: films may be selected from the Movie List and book titles for booktalks from the Subject Index. Overall, this guide is meant to help librarians and teens find books of interest to them in the field of supernatural fiction.

Additional reference sources are available for avid readers. These include

1. Everett Bleiler, **A Guide to Supernatural Fiction.** Kent, Ohio: Kent State University Press, 1983.

A survey of more than 7,000 stories and books on the supernatural published between the mid-eighteenth century and 1960.

2. Everett Bleiler, ed., **Supernatural Fiction Writers.** New York: Scribners, 1985. 2 vols.

A survey of more than 140 major authors in the field of supernatural fiction. Each entry includes an essay about the author and his/her development and writings.

3. Cosette Kies, **Presenting Horror Fiction for Teens.** New York: Twayne, 1991. Young Adult Authors Series.

A discussion of some of the more popular American horror writers, including V. C. Andrews, Dean Koontz, John Saul, Robert McCammon, Robert Bloch, Stephen King, Anne Rice, and Chelsea Quinn Yarbro. Contains separate chapters on satanism and splatterpunk.

4. Jack Sullivan, ed., **The Penguin Encyclopedia of Horror and the Supernatural.** New York: Viking Penguin, 1986.

A compilation of more than 50 essays and 600 shorter entries dealing with authors, illustrators, moviemakers and stars, critics, television programs, and media involved in the production of supernatural entertainment.

5. Marshall Tymn, **Horror Literature.** New York: Bowker, 1981.

A source book on horror literature, with emphasis on its earlier years. Covers authors, books, periodicals, associations, poetry, awards, criticism, and reference sources.

6. Marshall Tymn, Kenneth Zahorski, and Robert Boyer, **Fantasy Literature: A Core Collection and Reference Guide.** New York: Bowker, 1979.

Similar in format and coverage to Tymn's *Horror Literature.*

As with any book of this sort, thanks are due to many people. Tom Bell and Linda Chesser gave particular attention to the Title Index, and Beverly Balster provided invaluable assistance in the overall production of the manuscript. Finally, I owe my thanks to colleagues at Northern Illinois University and elsewhere for their interest and moral support.

Supernatural Fiction
for Teens

1. Aaron, Chester. **Out of Sight, Out of Mind.** New York: Bantam, 1986. 181
A pp. ISBN 0-553-26027-8. (First published by Lippincott, 1982.)

Erin and Sean, twins with ESP powers, find themselves in a dangerous international episode when they try to deliver a speech vital to world peace. Their parents, originally scheduled to give the speech, have been killed by terrorists. Now the terrorists want Erin and Sean out of the way as well. [Paranormal abilities]

Aaron, Sidney. *See* Paddy Chayefsky.

2. Abbey, Lynn. **Unicorn & Dragon.** New York: Avon, 1988. 230 pp. ISBN
C 0-380-75567-X. (First published in hardcover by Avon, 1987.)
Sequels: *Conquest.*

Medieval England is a place of hardship and warfare. When their home is threatened by invaders, beautiful sisters Alison and Wildecent turn to ancient powers to protect their home and country. [Legends, Celtic; Witchcraft]

3. Adams, Richard. **The Girl in a Swing.** New York: Signet, 1980. 371 pp. ISBN
A 0-451-13467-2. (First published by Knopf, 1980.)
Other works: *Maia; The Plague Dogs; Shardak; Watership Down.* Movie versions: *The Girl in a Swing,* 1988. Director: Gordon Hessler. Stars: Meg Tilly, Rupert Frazer, Nicholas Le Prevost, and Elspeth Gray.

Alan Desland, an English dealer in porcelain, tries to ignore his talent for ESP, but when he meets the beautiful, bewitching Kathe, he finds his self-made logical world slipping away. [Ghosts; Paranormal abilities; Reincarnation]

4. Adkins, Patrick H. **Lord of the Crooked Path.** New York: Ace, 1987. 216 pp.
A ISBN 0-441-49036-0.

Before the ancient gods and goddesses lived in glory on Mount Olympus, there lived an even more ancient race of giants—the titans. These little-known beings led fascinating lives, and their adventures are spellbinding. [Legends, classical]

5. Adler, C. S. **Footsteps on the Stairs.** New York: Dell, 1984. 160 pp. ISBN
B 0-440-42654-5. (First published by Delacorte, 1982.)

Plump Dodie's new life in an old house on the salt marsh with a reserved new stepsister is difficult and soon complicated by the mysterious presence of two ghosts, sisters from an earlier time. [Ghosts]

6. Ahern, Jerry, and Sharon Ahern. **Werewolves.** New York: Pinnacle, 1990.
C   383 pp. ISBN 1-558147-335-8.

Adolf Hitler, a believer in the occult, decides to gamble on the superhuman abilities of werewolves. They might be able to win the war — and ultimately the world — for this man whose name has become synonymous with evil. [Nazi occultism; Werewolves]

7. Aiken, Joan. **The Shadow Guests.** Harmondsworth, England: Puffin, 1982.
A   167 pp. ISBN 0-14-031388-5. (First published by Jonathan Cape, 1980.)
    Other works: *Up the Chimney Down; A Bundle of Chill; All but a Few; Return to Harken House; Midnight Is a Place.*

Cosmo's mother and brother have been missing for a long time. When Cosmo returns to the old millhouse after years in Australia, he begins to see things that no one else seems to be aware of or even notice, things that can only be done by ghosts. [Ghosts]

8. Aiken, Joan. **A Touch of Chill.** London: Fontana Lions, 1981. 190 pp.
A   (First published by Victor Gollancz, 1979.)

Scary stories guaranteed to keep a night-light on, including "Lodgers," "Mrs. Considine," "The Sewanee Glide," "Listening," "The Companion," "The Rented Swan," "Jugged Hare," "A Game of Black and White," "Time to Laugh," "'He': The Story about Caruso," "The Helper," "Power-cut," "Who Goes Down This Dark Road?," "A Train Full of War-Lords." [Horror; Short stories]

9. Aiken, Joan. **A Whisper in the Night.** London: Fontana Lions, 1983. 189
A   pp. ISBN 0-00-672133-8. (First published by Victor Gollancz, 1982.)

Delightfully shivery and scary stories for teens, such as "Old Fillikin," "Miss Spitfire," "She Was Afraid of Upstairs," "The Birthday Party," "The Black Cliffs," "Finders Keepers," "The Hunchback of Brook Green," "Mrs. Chatterbox," "Sultan: A Friend," "Hanging Matter," "Picnic Area," "Merminister," "The Swan Child." [Horror; Short stories]

10. Ainsworth, Ruth. **The Phantom Cyclist and Other Ghost Stories.** New
B   York: Scholastic, 1974. 138 pp. (First published by Andre Deutsch, 1971.)

A collection of ghost stories with an English twist, including "The Phantom Cyclist," "Cherry Ripe," "The Whistling Boy," "The Cat Who Liked Children," "The Silent Visitor," "Mirror, Mirror on the Wall," "The White-haired Children." [Ghosts; Short stories]

11. Albert, Marvin H. **Goodbye Charlie.** New York: Dell, 1964. 157 pp.
C   Movie versions: *Goodbye Charlie*, 1964. Director: Vincente Minnelli. Stars: Debbie Reynolds, Pat Boone, Walter Matthau, and Tony Curtis. Remake, *Switch*, 1991. Director: Blake Edwards. Stars: Ellen Barkin, Jimmy Smits, and JoBeth Williams.

A novelization of a merry mix-up movie. It all starts when Charlie, a bit of a rat when women are concerned, dies in an accident. Charlie is reincarnated and rejoins his old buddies, but Charlie has changed. Charlie is now an attractive woman. [Reincarnation]

12. Alcock, Vivien. **Ghostly Companions.** London: Fontana Lions, 1985. 124
A pp. ISBN 0-00-672535-X. (First published by Methuen, 1984.)
Other works: *Monster Garden; Mysterious Mr. Ross; Travelers by Night.*

Some good ghost stories, including "The Sea Bride," "Patchwork," "The Strange Companions," "Siren Song," "A Change of Aunts," "The Good-looking Boy," "The Whisperer," "A Fall of Snow," "QWERTYUIOP," "Masquerade." [Ghosts; Short stories]

13. Alcock, Vivien. **The Haunting of Cassie Palmer.** New York: Dell, 1990. 149
A pp. ISBN 0-440-43370-3. (First published by Methuen, 1980.)

Cassie thinks psychic powers are silly, and even though she's the seventh daughter of a seventh daughter, she scoffs at the idea that she might be special. But one day on a dare, she raises an unpredictable spirit from the dead and finds it's not as easy to make ghosts go away as it is to make them come. [Ghosts; Paranormal abilities]

14. Alcock, Vivien. **The Stonewalkers.** New York: Laurel-Leaf, 1985. 151 pp.
B ISBN 0-440-98198-0. (First published by Methuen Children's Books, 1981.)

Poppy Brown, unpopular because of her lies, comes to view a stone statue, Belladonna, as one of her only friends. Then Belladonna comes to life and activates other statues as well. Soon Poppy is in danger, and she and her only human friend, Emma, must flee across the moors to escape the pursuing stone-walkers. [Magic; Transformation]

15. Alcock, Vivien. **The Sylvia Game.** London: Fontana Lions, 1984. 157 pp.
A ISBN 0-00-672138-9. (First published by Methuen, 1982.)

Emily Dodd's father, an impoverished artist, takes Emily with him when he goes to the country on "business." At first Emily is bored, but when she meets Oliver, she finds her recuperation after the flu becoming more and more intriguing. Things become frightening; Emily realizes that she is the center of a mysterious game, all because she looks like Sylvia, who lived and died in Mallerton House. [Ghosts]

16. Alcott, Louisa May. **Behind a Mask: The Unknown Thrillers of Louisa May**
C **Alcott.** New York: Bantam, 1978. 308 pp. ISBN 0-553-02575-9. (First published by William Morrow, 1975.)

Gothic ripsnorters by the author of *Little Women*, originally published under several pseudonyms in pulp magazines of her time. Contents include "Behind a Mask, or A Woman's Power," "Pauline's Passion and Punishment," "The Mysterious Key and What It Opened," "The Abbot's Ghost, or Maurice Treherne's Temptation." [Gothic romance; Short stories]

17. Alderman, Clifford Lindsey. **The Devil's Shadow: The Story of Witch-**
A **craft in Massachusetts.** New York: Archway, 1970. 182 pp. SBN 671-29299-4. (First published by Messner, 1967.)

A fictionalized account of what really happened so many years ago in Salem, Massachusetts. The frightened young girls who start the turmoil are confused, as is everyone else in the small community, and they react by destroying those accused of witchcraft and dealing with the devil. [Witchcraft]

18. Aldiss, Brian. **Frankenstein Unbound.** New York: Warner, 1990. 157 pp.
C   ISBN 0-446-36036-8. (First published in England by Cape, 1973.)
     Movie versions: *Frankenstein Unbound*, 1990. Director: Roger Corman.
     Stars: John Hurt, Raul Julia, and Bridget Fonda.

After being blasted to the past, Joe Bondenland, ordinary citizen of the twenty-first century, is amazed to discover that Frankenstein and his monster were not just products of the imaginative mind of Mary Shelley. [Frankenstein; Time travel]

19. Alexander, Jan. **Blood Ruby.** New York: Ballantine, 1975. 154 pp. SBN
C   345-24747-095. (Birthstone Gothic series).

The gorgeous, deep-red stone holds fascinating lights in its depths, and legend says that it will grant wishes. Yet it also is cursed, dooming its owners to a soulless life after death. Joseph Hanson owns the stone now, and his wife, Liza, is very afraid for her husband and herself. [Curses; Gothic romance]

20. Alexander, Karl. **The Curse of the Vampire.** New York: Pinnacle, 1982.
A   310 pp. ISBN 0-523-41874-4.

A modern American movie actress on location in Transylvania becomes a victim of the vampire legend. Sinister, moldering Vladimir Castle becomes her refuge as she leads a double life as actress by day and blood-sucking vampire by night. [Vampires]

21. Alexis, Katina. **Scorpion.** New York: Leisure Books, 1986. 287 pp. ISBN
C   0-8439-2400-4.

Odd things are happening to Dr. Nan Bristow and her two beautiful daughters, one in a strange catatonic state. In the nearby woods a fearsome ancient horror is being unleashed by legendary Cherokee rites, and the final outcome is frightening and awesome to contemplate. [Legends, Native American]

22. Alexis, Katina. **Young Blood.** New York: TOR, 1982. 283 pp. ISBN
C   0-523-48028-8.

At first Dr. Electra Karatassos is only concerned about the health of her patient, Ariadne, and doesn't wonder at the significance of Ariadne's name. Yet the doctor's Greek heritage should have triggered thoughts of the legendary Ariadne, a beautiful woman destined for an ancient sacrifice. [Legends, Greek]

Allardyce, Paula. *See* Charity Blackstock.

23. Allen, Derek. **Blood from the Mummy's Tomb.** (Based on Bram Stoker's
D   *The Jewel of the Seven Stars*.) New York: Barron's, 1988. 138 pp. ISBN
     0-8120-4074-0. (Fleshcreepers series).
     Movie versions: *Blood from the Mummy's Tomb*, 1972. Director: Seth
     Holt. Stars: Michael Carreras, Andrew Keir, Valerie Leon, and James
     Villiers. *The Awakening*, 1980. Director: Mike Newell. Stars: Charlton
     Heston, Susannah York, Jill Townsend, Stephanie Zimbalist, and Patrick
     Drury.

Margaret Trelawnney is no longer herself. Her father, a noted archaeologist, has disturbed the centuries -old sleep of an Egyptian mummy, and Margaret has become the pawn of the mummy's revenge. [Legends, Egyptian]

24. Allende, Isabel. **House of the Spirits.** New York: Bantam, 1986. 433 pp.
C   ISBN 0-553-25865-6. (First published by Knopf, 1985.)
   Other works: *The Secrets of Eva Luna; Of Love and Shadows.*

The Trueba family of South America possesses wealth and mysterious powers. The various members of the family pursue different goals and dabble in mystic matters, and they come to very different ends and find various degrees of happiness. An allegorical and mysterious book. [Mysticism; Spiritualism]

25. Almquist, Gregg. **Beast Rising.** New York: Pocket Books, 1987. 256 pp.
C   ISBN 0-671-63497-6.

There are many lakes in the north country, and most of them look calm and peaceful. But Woman Lake is different; it is evil. Somewhere beneath its still waters lies an incredibly foul beast, one Laird Menton comes to recognize as evil incarnate. [Monsters]

26. Amado, Jorge Luis. **Dona Flor and Her Two Husbands.** New York: Avon,
C   1969. 521 pp. ISBN 0-380-01796-2. (First published in the United States by Knopf, 1969.)
   Movie versions: *Dona Flor and Her Two Husbands*, 1979 (Brazilian). Director: Bruno Barreto. Stars: Sonia Braga and José Wilker. American remake set in New York, *Kiss Me Goodbye*, 1982. Director: Robert Mulligan. Stars: Sally Field, James Caan, and Jeff Bridges.

Gentle, pretty Dona Flor was enchanted by her first husband, a charming, irresponsible rake. She mourns his death but finally agrees to wed an upstanding dull citizen of the town. To her surprise and horror, her first husband returns as a ghost to be part of her life and jeer at her new spouse. Dona Flor turns to voodoo to help her out of her predicament but still cannot rid herself of her passionate love for her ghostly first husband. [Ghosts; Voodoo]

27. Ames, J. Edward. **The Force.** New York: Leisure, 1987. 400 pp. ISBN
C   0-8439-2480-2.

Young Matt has been having terrible dreams, as lots of kids do. But Matt's dreams are different; they are caused by an incredibly evil force, and they are possessing his mind. [Dreams; Evil]

28. Ames, Mildred. **The Silver Link, the Silken Tie.** New York: Scholastic/
A   Point, 1986. 254 pp. ISBN 0-590-33537-X. (First published by Charles Scribner's Sons, 1984.)
   Other works: *Anna to the Infinite Power.*

Tim and Felice are both haunted by tragedy from the past. When they meet, they discover a special mental ability to communicate on another level, which helps soothe their emotional scars and brings new wonderment to their lives. [Paranormal abilities]

29. Anderson, Mary. **The Leipzig Vampire.** New York: Dell/Yearling, 1987.
B   122 pp. ISBN 0-440-44719-4. (Mostly Ghosts series).
   Sequels: *The Haunting of Hillcrest; Terror under the Tent; The Three Spirits of Vandermeer Manor.*

The Ferguson twins, Amy and Jamie, are special. Jamie is superbright, and Amy is psychic. When a strange and famous German scientist moves to town, the twins decide that he is up to no good and it's up to them to stop his evil plan. [Paranormal abilities; Vampires]

30. Anderson, Michael Falconer. **Blood Rite.** New York: St. Martin's Press,
C   1988. 156 pp. ISBN 0-312-91115-7. (First published as *The Woodsmen* by Robert Hale, 1986.)

The dark forest is full of secrets. The ancient trees have seen much in their years. But these trees and this forest are not passive. They hold the ancient secrets of terrible evil. Karen is not aware of the danger — at first. [Witchcraft]

31. Anderson, Poul. **The Devil's Game.** New York: Baen, 1985. 251 pp. ISBN
C   0-671-55995-8.

Seven people are on an isolated island, but this is not a story from "Fantasy Island," for the people must play a terrible game with the devil. If they break the rules, all is lost. [Satanism]

32. Andersson, Dean. **Raw Pain Max.** New York: Popular Library, 1988. 260
C   pp. ISBN 0-445-20828-7.

Star of the Safe Sex Club, Trudy McAllen uses the stage name of Raw Pain Max. She seems to be a thoroughly contemporary woman, but then she meets a figure from the past, the real-life female Dracula, Elizabeth Bathody. (See *Countess Dracula*, entry 805.) [Vampires]

33. Andrews, Mark. **Satan's Manor.** New York: Leisure, 1977. 287 pp. ISBN
C   0-8439-0460-7.

When Miriam decorates her apartment as "Satan's Manor," she is not only celebrating Halloween with her friends but is marking the end of a struggling existence as a theater actress and the start of a new life as a movie star. But when Miriam arrives in Georgia at the old mansion to be used as a movie set, she finds she has arrived at a real Satan's Manor, one from which there may be no escape. [Legerdemain]

34. Anson, Barbara. **Golem.** New York: Leisure Books, 1978. 184 pp. ISBN
C   0-8439-1095-X.

Last Halloween the local Catholic priest died in an accident. This year on Halloween, it's David Demneck's father, the rabbi, who dies. David does not believe these deaths are unrelated, and he calls forth the dreaded golem, created by Rabbi Loew in sixteenth-century Prague. Once called, however, the golem's awesome power cannot be fully controlled. [Legends, Jewish]

35. Anson, Jay. **666.** New York: Bantam, 1982. 280 pp. ISBN 0-671-83126-7.
C   (First published by Simon & Schuster, 1981.)
     Other works: *The Amityville Horror*.

The house has a terrible history of brutal murder. The Olsons are not happy when the house is moved to their neighborhood, but they little realize the horror that will soon start and change their lives forever. [Haunted houses]

36. Anstey, F. (pseud. of Thomas Anstey Guthrie). **Vice Versa.** Harmonds-
A   worth, England: Puffin, 1981. 302 pp. ISBN 0-14-035067-5. (First
    published by John Murray, 1882.)
    Movie versions: *Vice Versa*, 1948. Director: Peter Ustinov. Stars: Roger
    Livesey, Kay Walsh, David Hutcheson, Anthony Newley, James Robertson
    Justice, Petula Clark, and Patricia Raine. *Vice Versa*, 1988. Director: Brian
    Gilbert. Stars: Judge Reinhold, Fred Savage, and Swoosie Kurtz.

Young Dick Bultride is in trouble at school, but his father, Paul, believes
that this is all nonsense. He'd love to be a carefree schoolboy again. Then,
miraculously, a switch takes place – Dick becomes Paul and vice versa – with
some hilarious results. [Transformation]

37. Appel, Allen. **Time after Time.** New York: Laurel, 1987. 372 pp. ISBN
C   0-440-59116-3. (First published by Carroll & Graf, 1985.)

Professor Alex Balfour, a history professor, is sure of his facts, sure that
Anastasia, daughter of the last tsar of Russia, was killed with her family during
the revolution. Then Alex begins to have dreams of another time and place, and
he finds himself in a position to find out what really happened to Anastasia.
[Time travel]

38. Armstrong, F. W. (pseud. of T. M. Wright). **The Changing.** New York:
C   TOR, 1985. 244 pp. ISBN 0-812-52754-2.
    Sequels: *The Devouring*.

A modern technology corporation like Eastman Kodak shouldn't be subject
to superstition and folklore. Yet something strange is happening to people in
Kodak Park: They're being ripped to shreds by something bestial and inhuman.
[Werewolves]

39. Armstrong, Sarah. **Blood Red Roses.** New York: Dell, 1982. 154 pp. ISBN
A   0-440-90314-9. (Twilight series).

Kate is delighted with her new mirror, an ornate antique that her rival,
Tracy, also wants. Yet Kate's pride in her new possession starts to diminish as an
increasing sense of doom and fear emanates from the mirror. [Possession]

40. Arnason, Eleanor. **Daughter of the Bear King.** New York: Avon, 1987.
C   239 pp. ISBN 0-380-75109-7.
    Other works: *To the Resurrection Station*.

Esperance is a typical, somewhat dissatisfied housewife in Minneapolis who
starts having dreams about another existence as the daughter of the bear king in
another time and place. The dreams are a wonderful escape at first, but then the
monsters from the other world invade her placid existence in Minneapolis, and
there are no longer any firm boundaries between reality and fantasy. [Dreams]

41. Arneson, D. J., and Tony Tallarico. **Ghost Horse Mystery.** Mahwah,
B   N.J.: Watermill Press, 1981. 96 pp. ISBN 0-89375-492-7.

At first it seems that cleaning up the old theater would be a pretty good job
for the members of the club; it would involve lots of work, but it might be fund as
well. Then strange things start happening, including the appearance of a ghost
horse seeking revenge. [Ghosts; Occult mystery/detective]

42. Arnold, Margot. **Death of a Voodoo Doll.** New York: Playboy, 1982. 220
C   pp. ISBN 0-867-21114-8. (First published by Jove, 1982.)

Amateur sleuths Penny Spring and Toby Glendower (an anthropologist and archaeologist, respectively) stumble upon a mysterious murder in exotic New Orleans during Mardi Gras. Voodoo rites and the mysteries of secret societies add exciting details to a classically styled detective tale. [Cults; Occult mystery/detective; Voodoo]

43. Arnold, Margot. **Death on the Dragon's Tongue.** New York: Playboy,
C   1982, 224 pp. ISBN 0-867-21150-4. (First published by Jove, 1982.)

Modern cults and ancient Celtic customs mingle in another Penny Spring and Toby Glendower mystery. This time the setting is the bleak coast of Brittany peopled with sinister cult members. [Cults; Legends, Celtic; Occult mystery/detective]

44. Arnold, Margot. **Marie.** New York: Pocket Books, 1979. 486 pp. ISBN
C   0-671-81919-4.

Marie Laveau was the most powerful voodoo queen of New Orleans, and her influence in this nineteenth-century city is incalculable. This fictionalized account of Marie's life provides a fascinating glimpse of her times and practices. [Laveau, Marie; Voodoo]

45. Arvonen, Helen. **The Witches of Brimstone Hill.** New York: Fawcett, 1971.
B   160 pp. SBN 449-02485-075.

Jamie has the power of second sight, but she fears her gift and has kept it secret. Now she must use it to save those she loves from the terrible evil of witchcraft. [Satanism]

46. Avi. **Devil's Race.** New York: Avon Flare, 1987. 118 pp. ISBN 0-380-
A   70406-4. (First published by Harper & Row, 1984.)

At first glance, John Proud seems like a typical sixteen-year-old kid. But he's not. John Proud has a problem, and the problem is a demon from the past who wants to take over John Proud's life. [Demons; Possession]

47. Avi. **Something Upstairs.** New York: Avon Flare, 1990. 116 pp. ISBN
B   0-380-70853-1. (First published by Franklin Watts, 1988.)

A note to the reader from the author says this is a true story of ghosts, one told to him by a teacher. True or not, Kenny's adventures in this strange house with a haunted room are spellbinding. [Ghosts; Haunted houses]

Bachman, Richard. *See* Stephen King.

48. Baker, Scott. **Webs.** New York: TOR, 1989. 310 pp. ISBN 0-812-51557-9.
C   Other works: *Drink the Fire from the Flames.*

Brian has used hypnotism, perhaps a psychic power, to tie his wife, Julie, to him. But now she is hospitalized, and Brian finds himself alone in a strange house with spiders that grow larger and larger, weaving webs of terror and fear. [Paranormal abilities]

49. Ballard, John G. **The Unlimited Dream Company.** New York: Washing-
C   ton Square, 1985. 254 pp. ISBN 0-671-60537-2. (First published by Holt,
     Rinehart and Winston, 1979.)

Life changes radically for Blake after his small plane crashes in the Thames.
He finds the town of Shepperton, whose citizens hail him as a sort of messiah,
and Blake obliges them by transforming their village into a pagan paradise. But
this is not enough, for Blake then performs an even greater miracle by teaching
the people of Shepperton to fly. [Dreams; Paranormal abilities]

50. Barber, Antonia. **The Ghosts.** New York: Archway, 1975. 244 pp. ISBN
A   0-671-52763-0. (First published by Jonathan Cape, 1969.)

Can the course of history be changed? Two modern youngsters have the
chance to find out when two ghosts appeal to them for aid. Even though the
terrible crime that killed the ghost children occurred a century ago, the ghosts
believe that history can be changed if Lucy and her brother have the courage to
help them. [Ghosts; Time travel]

51. Barbet, Pierre. **Baphomet's Meteor.** New York: DAW, 1972. 144 pp. (First
C   published as *L'Empire du Baphomet* by Editions Fleuve Noir, Paris, 1972).

The medieval Knights Templar were reputed to worship the devil in the form
of the demon Baphomet. In this alternative world, Baphomet is triumphant, and
the knights continue to do his bidding. [Cults; The devil; Knights Templar]

52. Barker, Clive. **Volume One of Clive Barker's Books of Blood.** New York:
C   Berkley, 1986. 210 pp. ISBN 0-425-08389-6. (First published by Sphere,
     1984.)
     Sequels: Volumes 2 and 3 of *Clive Barker's Books of Blood.* Other works:
     The Damnation Game; Weaveworld; Cabal; The Great and Secret Show.

Horrible and gruesome tales with a very original twist, including "The Book
of Blood," "The Midnight Meat Train," "The Yattering and Jack," "Pig Blood
Blues," "Sex, Death and Sunshine," "In the Hills, the Cities." [Horror; Short
stories]

53. Barnes, Megan. **Teen Witch: Lucky 13.** New York: Scholastic, 1988, 187
B   pp. ISBN 0-590-441296-5.
     Sequels: *Be Careful What You Wish For; Gone with the Witch; Witch
     Switch.*

Most kids are excited when they become thirteen, real teenagers at last. But
when Sarah Connell turns thirteen, she finds out something special; she's a witch
with very magical abilities. At first it seems great to have these powers, but things
don't always work out as neatly as Sarah thinks they will. [Witchcraft]

54. Barth, John. **Chimera.** New York: Fawcett, 1973. 320 pp. ISBN
C   0-449-21113-4. (First published by Random House, 1972.)

A wonderful retelling of old stories. The stories are related by
Scheherazade's younger sister and others of the tales of Perseus and Bellerophon.
Common themes tie the stories together. Like the three heads of the chimera, the
stories are different yet are bound together as a whole. [Legends, Arabian;
Legends, classical]

55. Barton, Dan. **Banshee.** Toronto, Ontario: Worldwide, 1988. 382 pp. ISBN
C   0-373-97075-7.

This banshee is the soul of a tormented young woman who was buried alive.
Now the banshee wants revenge, and nothing will stop her. [Legends, Irish]

56. Bauer, Stephen. **Steven Spielberg's Amazing Stories.** New York: Charter,
C   1986. 234 pp. ISBN 0-441-01906-4.
      Sequels: *Steven Spielberg's Amazing Stories, Volume II.*

Stories from the television series, including "The Mission," "Vanessa in the
Garden," "Guilt Trip," "Mr. Magic," "The Main Attraction," "Ghost Train,"
"The Sitter," "Santa '85," "One for the Road," "Hell Toupee," "No Day at the
Beach." [Horror; Short stories]

57. Baum. L. Frank. **The Life and Adventures of Santa Claus.** New York:
B   Signet, 1986. 151 pp. ISBN 0-451-52064-5. (First published by Bobbs-
      Merrill, 1902.)
      Other works: *The Wonderful Wizard of Oz.*

Santa Claus, probably the world's most beloved folk hero, is made almost
human through his life story, from childhood to his reign as the bearer of gifts at
Christmastime. [Legends, Christian; Santa Claus]

58. Bawden, Nina. **Devil by the Sea.** New York: Lancer, 1957. 255 pp. (First
C   published in the United States by Lippincott, 1957.)

Children and adults often see things—and people—in different ways. Hilary,
a young English girl, believes that the strange man she meets is the devil, and
nothing her mother says can make her think otherwise. [The devil]

59. Bawden, Nina. **The Witch's Daughter.** New York: Archway, 1973. 212 pp.
A   ISBN 0-671-29559-4. (First published by Lippincott, 1966.)

Perdita, a young Scottish girl, has been a lonely child. But some visitors
come to her remote island and she makes her first friends, friends who lead her
into an exciting—and dangerous—adventure. Best of all, her new friends don't
seem to mind the rumors about her, especially that she is supposed to be
bewitched. [Legends, Celtic]

60. Beagle, Peter S. **A Fine and Private Place.** New York: Del Rey, 1979. 256
C   pp. ISBN 0-345-30081-5. (First published by Viking, 1960.)
      Other works: *Lila the Werewolf; The Last Unicorn.*

A gentle, quiet man makes his home in a cemetery mausoleum and finds
more romance in the world of the dead than he ever had in the world of the living.
The only trouble is, the ghostly lovers must fight for their existence in this semi-
earthly astral plane in order to stay together. [Ghosts]

61. Bellairs, John. **The Curse of the Blue Figurine.** New York: Bantam Sky-
B   lark, 1984. 200 pp. ISBN 0-553-15429-X. (First published by Dial, 1983.)
      Sequels: *The Mummy, the Will and the Crypt; The Spell of the Sorcerer's
      Skull; The Revenge of the Wizard's Ghost; The Eyes of the Killer Robot;
      Trolley to Yesterday; The Chessmen of Doom; The Secret of the Under-
      ground Room.*

Johnny Dixon loves fascinating adventure stories about ancient Egypt and horrible curses. One day he discovers an old blue figurine and finds out that ancient curses aren't just stories; they can be real. [Legends, Egyptian]

62. Bellairs, John. **House with a Clock in Its Walls.** New York: Dell, 1974. 192
B   pp. ISBN 0-440-43742-3. (First published by Dial, 1973.)
     Sequels: *The Figure in the Shadows; The Letter, the Witch and the Ring.*

Only Lewis can save the world from the doomsday clock placed in his uncle's house by Isaac Izard, an evil warlock. Time, however, grows shorter and shorter and shorter. And as Lewis desperately looks for the solution to the puzzle the clock ticks on. [Black magic]

63. Bellairs, John. **The Treasure of Alpheus Winterborn.** New York: Bantam
B   Skylark, 1983. 180 pp. ISBN 0-553-15419-2. (First published by Harcourt
     Brace Jovanovich, 1978.)
     Sequels: *The Dark Secret of Weatherend.*

Young Anthony is delighted when Miss Eells offers him a job at the library so he can earn some desperately needed money. He doesn't expect, however, that he will stumble into a strange mystery within the library, one that could cost him his life as he battles the powers of darkness. [Black magic]

64. Benary-Isbert, Margot. **The Wicked Enchantment.** New York: Ace, 1986.
B   149 pp. ISBN 0-441-88669-8. (First published in the United States by
     Harcourt Brace Jovanovich, 1955.)

Annemone runs away from home with her dog because she hates her father's new housekeeper. While living with Aunt Gundala she learns of mysterious goings on and resolves to solve the secret of the statue missing from the town's cathedral. [Evil]

65. Benet, Stephen Vincent. **The Devil and Daniel Webster and Other Stories.**
D   New York: Archway, 1972. 128 pp. ISBN 0-671-42889-6. (First published
     by Countryman Press, 1937.)
     Movie versions: *The Devil and Daniel Webster* (sometimes titled *All That
     Money Can Buy*), 1941. Director: William Dieterle. Stars: Walter Houston,
     Edward Arnold, Jane Darwell, and Anne Shirley.

Farmer Jabez Stone sells his soul to the devil in a time of desperation. It will take the best lawyer in the country to get Jabez Stone out of the deal. Contents include the title story as well as "Johnny Pye and the Fool-Killer," and "By the Waters of Babylon." [The devil]

66. Benoit, Hendra. **Hendra's Book.** New York: Scholastic, 1985. 148 pp. ISBN
A   0-580-33202-3.
     Companions: *Max's Book* by Maxwell Hurley and *Sal's Book* by Sal
     Liquori.

Three dissimilar teens discover they have superpowers. They are forced to form the Psi Patrol and work together to learn about the wonders of their fantastic new skills. [Paranormal abilities]

67. Benson, Edward Frederic. **The Flint Knife: Further Spook Stories by E. F.**
D **Benson.** Wellingborough, England: Equation, 1988. 184 pp. ISBN
1-85336-029-5.

Classic English tales of fear, including "The Flint Knife," "The Chippendale Mirror," "The Witch-Ball," "The Ape," "Sir Roger de Coverley," "The China Bowl," "The Passenger," "The Friend in the Garden," "The Red House," "Through," "The Box at the Bank," "The Light in the Garden," "Dummy on a Dahabeah," "The Return of Frank Hampden," "The Shuttered Room." [Horror; Short stories]

68. Benson, Edward Frederic. **The Tale of the Empty House and Other Ghost**
C **Stories.** London: Black Swan, 1986. 232 pp. ISBN 0-552-99222-4.

Traditional English ghost stories, including "The Face," "Caterpillars," "Expiation," "The Tale of an Empty House," "The Bus-Conductor," "How Fear Departed from the Long Gallery," "The Other Bed," "The Room in the Tower," "Mrs. Amworth," "And No Birds Sing," "Mr. Tilly's Seance," "Home, Sweet Home," "The Sanctuary," "Pirates." [Horror; Short stories]

69. Benson, Robert Hugh. **The Necromancers.** London: Sphere, 1974. 235 pp.
C ISBN 0-7221-1615-2. (First published by Hutchinson, 1909.)
Other works: *The Light Invisible; The Mirror of Shallott.*

When Laurie Baxter's love dies, he feels as if his own life has become deadly and meaningless. He turns to necromancy to try to bring his beloved back but finds that when one dabbles in mysterious arts, one may arouse more spirits than intended. [Black magic]

70. Berger, Terry, David Berger, and Karen Coshof. **The Haunted Dollhouse.**
C New York: Workman, 1982. 92 pp. ISBN 0-89480-206-2.
Other works: *Black Fairy Tales.*

A photographic essay with spare text tells a mysterious tale about Sarah's thirteenth birthday. Fanciful children sometimes imagine themselves in strange situations, but what Sarah imagines may be for real ... and permanent. [Haunted houses; Transformation]

71. Berger, Thomas. **Arthur Rex: A Legendary Novel.** New York: Delta,
C 1978. 499 pp. ISBN 0-385-28005-X. (First published by Delacorte, 1978.)

A contemporary view of the story of Camelot. The familiar figures of Arthur's story are fleshed out with modern problems. [Legends, Arthurian]

72. Bergstrom, Elaine. **Shattered Glass.** New York: Jove, 1989. 372 pp. ISBN
C 0-515-10055-2.
Sequels: *Blood Alone.*

Vampires have been around for a long time, and the Austras have been around a long time, too. Those who know the family view them as aristocratic Europeans, but the Austras know their blue blood is a curse that makes them vampires. [Vampires]

73. Biederstadt, Lynn. **The Eye of the Mind.** New York: Signet, 1981. 313 pp.
C   ISBN 0-451-11736-0.

Six psychics have been gathered together to produce a collective power for good, the prediction of disasters. Then the psychics realize that their power can be used to control future events as well, and they seem to be invincible. [Paranormal abilities]

74. Bierce, Ambrose. **The Complete Short Stories of Ambrose Bierce.** Lincoln:
D   University of Nebraska Press, 1970. 496 pp. ISBN 0-8032-6071-7.

Mysterious stories by a mysterious man who disappeared in 1916. Contents of part 1 ("The World of Horror"): "Haita the Shepherd," "The Secret of Macarger's Gulch," "The Eyes of the Panther," "The Stranger," "An Inhabitant of Carcosa," "The Applicant," "The Death of Halpin Frayser," "A Watcher by the Dead," "The Man and the Snake," "John Mortonson's Funeral," "Moxon's Master," "The Damned Thing," "The Realm of the Unreal," "A Fruitless Assignment," "A Vine on a House," "The Haunted Valley," "One of Twins," "Present at a Hanging," "A Wireless Message," "The Moonlit Road," "An Arrest," "A Jug of Sirup," "The Isle of Pines," "At Old Man Eckert's," "The Spook House," "The Middle Toe of the Right Foot," "The Thing at Nolan," "The Difficulty of Crossing a Field," "An Unfinished Race," "Charles Ashmore's Trail," "Staley Fleming's Hallucination," "The Night-doings at 'Deadman's,'" "A Baby Tramp," "A Psychological Shipwreck," "A Cold Greeting," "Beyond the Wall," "John Bartine's Watch," "The Man out of the Nose," "An Adventure at Brownville," "The Suitable Surroundings," "The Boarded Window," "A Lady from Redhorse," "The Famous Gilson Bequest," "A Holy Terror," "A Diagnosis of Death." Part 2 ("The World of War") includes some stories such as "An Occurrence at Owl Creek Bridge" that have supernatural overtones. Part 3 consists of tall tales in the American folklore tradition. [Horror; Short stories]

75. Bill, Alfred H. **The Wolf in the Garden.** New York: Centaur, 1972. ISBN
C   0-87818-008-7. 144 pp. (First published by Longmans, 1931.)

A village in upstate New York about two hundred years ago is the setting for this classic werewolf tale. After the arrival of the Comte de Saint Loup and his hound in the village, terrible things begin to happen that make the local citizens aware that the count is not a normal human being; in fact, he may not be a human being at all. [Werewolves]

76. Billias, Stephen. **The American Book of the Dead.** New York: Popular
C   Library, 1987. 213 pp. ISBN 0-445-20335-8.

Bertie Rupp started life as a simple country lad, but as a computer whiz he finds success in the city — at first. Then disaster strikes, and Bertie finds himself destitute and obsessed with finding a book full of mysterious secrets that may help him survive the nuclear holocaust Bertie is sure will happen. [Magic]

77. Bingley, Margaret. **Devil's Child.** New York: Popular Library, 1987. 253
C   pp. ISBN 0-445-20472-9. (First published in England by Judy Piatkis, 1983.)

All Laura had ever wanted was to get married and have children. She has done this, and her child, Edward, seems perfect. But Laura knows he is too perfect to be human; he can read people's minds and he has an evil soul. [Paranormal abilities]

78. Birkin, Charles. **The Smell of Evil.** New York: Award, 1969. 187 pp. (First
A   published by Tandem, 1965.)
     Other works: *The Kiss of Death; Death Spawn; Devil's Spawn; My Name is
     Death; So Pale, So Cold, So Fair; Spawn of Satan; Where Terror Stalked;
     Dark Menace.*

A collection of short stories with horrific themes, mainly set in Europe
following World War II. A pervasive mood of evil is present in these modern tales
of the macabre sure to send shivers down the reader's spine. Included are "The
Smell of Evil," "Text for Today," "The Godmothers," "Green Fingers," "Ballet
Negre," "The Lesson," "Is There Anybody There?," "The Serum of Doctor
White," "Dance, Little Lady," "Little Boy Blue," "The Cornered Beast," "The
Interloper," "The Cross." [Evil; Short stories]

79. Bischoff, David. **The Blob.** New York: Dell, 1988. 210 pp. ISBN 0-440-
C   20214-0.
     Movie versions: *The Blob*, 1958. Director: Irvin S. Yeaworth, Jr. Stars:
     Steve McQueen, Aneta Corseaut, Earl Rowe, and Olin Howlin. *The Blob*,
     1988. Director: Chuck Russell. Stars: Shawnee Smith, Donovan Leitch,
     Ricky Paul Goldin, Kevin Dillon, and Candy Clark.

The Blob first made its appearance with a youthful Steve McQueen some
years ago. Now the Blob is back, slimier than ever, with its appetite unsatiated for
human flesh. (This novelization is based on the 1988 film version.) [Horror;
Monsters, slime-type]

80. Bischoff, David, Rich Brown, and Linda Richardson. **A Personal Demon.**
C   New York: Signet, 1985. 253 pp. ISBN 0-451-13814-7.

Willis Baxter, college professor, sometimes drinks too much according to his
colleagues. Willis has no choice but to agree with them after the night he conjures
up a fetching, aggravating female demon who will not go away the morning after.
[Demons]

81. Bishop, Michael. **Ancient of Days.** New York: TOR, 1986. 409 pp. ISBN
C   0-812-53197-3.
     Other works: *Close Encounters with the Diety; Who Made Stevie Crye?*

When RuthClaire Loyd first spots the strange, primeval man in a pecan
grove in Georgia, no one realizes that he is more than a missing link from the
past. His mysterious powers of communication seem to reach to the heavens, yet
his own yearnings are for something much more attainable, a modern American
woman. [Paranormal abilities]

82. Bisson, Terry. **Talking Man.** New York: Avon, 1987. 192 pp. ISBN
C   0-380-75141-0.

The talking man is a wizard, living on the Kentucky-Tennessee border with
his lovely, spirited sixteen-year-old daughter, Crystal. Life for a wizard's family is
never easy, even with magic to lean on in times of trouble, and Crystal ends up
with more adventures than most teens. [Magic]

83. Black, Campbell. **Raiders of the Lost Ark.** New York: Ballantine, 1981.
C   181 pp. ISBN 0-345-29490-4.
    Sequels: *Indiana Jones and the Temple of Doom* by James Kahn and *Indiana Jones and the Last Crusade* by Rob MacGregor. Find Your Fate series books by different authors (see series list for titles and authors) who use the character Indiana Jones. Rob MacGregor has also written a series using the Indiana Jones character. Movie versions: *Raiders of the Lost Ark*, 1981. Director: Steven Spielberg. Stars: Harrison Ford, Karen Allen, Denholm Elliott, and Wolf Kahler.

A fast-paced story in exotic settings. The dashing archaeologist Indiana Jones attempts to thwart the Nazi plan to harness the occult powers of the ancient and mysterious Ark of the Covenant. [Legends, Jewish; Nazi occultism]

84. Black, Campbell. **The Wanting.** New York: Jove, 1987. 307 pp. ISBN
C   0-515-09177-4. (First published by McGraw-Hill, 1986.)

Young Danny has come to the seemingly peaceful summer home with his parents, and at first everything is perfect. All is not as perfect as it appears to be, however, for Danny starts to change—and not for the better. [Evil]

85. Black, Robert. **Death Angel.** New York: Pageant, 1988. 236 pp. ISBN
C   0-517-00835-1.

Summer is a time of baking hot cornfields in the Midwest, a time when kids are out of school and there is lots of fun to be had. But this summer there isn't any fun, for each boy receives a letter with an ominous message from Exodus, and then the scary package comes. [Evil]

86. Blackstock, Charity. (pseud. of Paula Allardyce). **Witches' Sabbath.** New
C   York: Paperback Library, 1967. 174 pp. (First published in England, 1951.)

Tamar Brown, a lovely young woman living in an English village, knows that there are rumors of witchcraft in the neighborhood. Her neighbors cannot forget Abigail Parkes, who was burned at the stake three hundred years ago, and they believe that Tamar is Abigail, returned from the dead. [Witchcraft]

87. Blackwood, Algernon. **Best Ghost Stories of Algernon Blackwood.** New
D   York: Dover, 1973. 396 pp. ISBN 0-486-22977-7.

E. F. Bleiler, a noted, respected author of Victorian ghost stories and an authority on supernatural fiction, has edited this collection, which includes "Accessory Before the Fact," "Ancient Lights," "Ancient Sorceries," "The Empty House," "The Glamour of the Snow," "Keeping His Promise," "The Listener," "Max Hensig," "The Other Wing," "Secret Worship," "The Transfer," "The Wendigo," "The Willows." [Ghosts; Short stories]

88. Blake, Susan. **The Haunted Dollhouse.** New York: Dell, 1984. 153 pp.
A   ISBN 0-440-93643-8. (Twilight series).

When Jessica's mother inherits an old bed-and-breakfast inn, she impulsively decides to drag Jessica to a new home and a new life. From the beginning, Jessica is uneasy about the old inn, which seems permeated with evil. She feels she is the only one who can put the evil to rest. [Ghosts]

89. Blatty, William Peter. **The Exorcist.** New York: Bantam, 1972. 416 pp.
C ISBN 0-553-24569-7. (First published by Harper & Row, 1971.)
Sequels: *Legion.* Movie versions: *The Exorcist*, 1973. Director: William
Friedkin. Stars: Ellen Burstyn, Linda Blair, and Max von Sydow.

An actress on location in Washington, D.C., finds her daughter, eleven-
year-old Regan, possessed by a horrible demon. Her efforts to save Regan pit the
frantic mother, two Catholic priests, and a dubious police detective against the
evils and terror of hell itself. The graphic descriptions and details of possession
are not for the faint at heart. [Exorcism; Possession]

90. Blaylock, James P. **Homunculus.** New York: Ace, 1986. 247 pp. ISBN
C 0-441-34258-2.
Other works: *The Digging Leviathan.*

Grave robbers, mad scientists, and obsessed searchers into hidden secrets
populate this funny story of Victorian London. [Black magic; Science gone
wrong]

91. Blaylock, James P. **Land of Dreams.** New York: Ace, 1988. 224 pp. ISBN
C 0-414-50347-0. (First published by Arbor House, 1987.)

A fantasy tale of a boy's search for his father in a wacky world turned upside
down. Jack finds the land of dreams in his search, but he discovers that you don't
always get what you think you want in that place of mysteries. [Magic]

92. Blaylock, James P. **The Last Coin.** New York: Ace, 1989. 328 pp. ISBN
C 0-441-47075-0. (First published by Ace as a hardcover in 1988.)

According to legend, thirty pieces of silver were used to pay off Judas for
betraying Christ. A nasty man by the name of Pennyman has all but one of these
coins, and he would do just about anything to get the last, owned by Andrew
Vanbergen. When Pennyman descends upon Vanbergen's inn, all sorts of supernatural shenanigans upset the Pacific Coast town. [Black magic; Legends,
Christian]

93. Blish, James. **Black Easter.** New York: Dell, 1968. 160 pp.
C Sequels: *The Day After Judgment.*

A classic struggle between good and evil is portrayed. The cruel forces of the
powers of Satan seem to be unstoppable, but one brave man is determined to
succeed. If he fails, the consequences are unthinkable. [The devil; Satanism]

Blixen, Karen. *See* Isak Dinesen.

94. Bloch, Robert. **Bogey Men: Ten Tales.** New York: Pyramid, 1963.
C Other works include *Pleasant Dreams; The Skull of the Marquis de Sade
and Other Stories; Strange Eons; Such Stuff as Screams Are Made Of; Cold
Chills; Tales in a Jugular Vein; Ariel; Out of My Head; American Gothic.*

Famed horror writer and author of *Psycho* has produced many shivery tales
of horror, including "The Animal Fair," "The Double Whammy," "Ego Trip,"
"Forever and Amen," "The Gods Are Not Mocked," "How Like a God," "In the

Cards," "The Learning Maze," "The Model," "The Movie People," "The Oracle," "The Play's the Thing," "See How They Run," "Space-Barn." [Horror; Short stories]

95. Bloch, Robert. **Firebug**. New York: TOR, 1988. 215 pp. ISBN 0-812-
C   52578-1. (First published by Regency, 1961.)

Phil Cronin, a struggling young writer, decides to investigate some religious scams. Then something scary starts to happen; every "church" he attends goes up in flames after Phil's visit. Phil also finds himself dreaming a lot about fire, and slowly he realizes the awful truth. [Dreams; Paranormal abilities]

96. Bloch Robert. **Twilight Zone, the Movie**. New York: Warner, 1983. 205
C   pp. ISBN 0-446-30840-4.
    Movie versions: *Twilight Zone, the Movie*, 1983. Directors: John Landis, Steven Spielberg, Joe Dante, and George Miller. Stars: Vic Morrow, Scatman Crothers, Bill Quinn, Selma Diamond, Kathleen Quinlan, Jeremy Licht, Kevin McCarthy, William Schallert, John Lithgow, and Abbe Lane.

This novelization of the stories composing the film includes "Bill," "Valentine," "Helen," and "Bloom." [Monsters; Paranormal abilities; Short stories; Time travel]

97. Boothby Guy. **Enter Dr. Nikola!** Hollywood, Calif.: Newcastle, 1975. 256
C   pp. ISBN 0-87877-032-1. (First published as *A Bid for Fortune* by Lock & Bowden, 1895.)
    Sequels: *Dr. Nikola; The Lust of Hate; Dr. Nikola's Experiment; Farewell, Nikola*. Other works: *Pharos, the Egyptian; The Lady of the Island*.

An exciting international tale of intrigue, kidnapping, and supernatural activities. Will Nikola succeed in using the beautiful maiden for his nefarious purposes, or will he be foiled by dauntless Richard Hatteras? [Black magic]

98. Borton, Douglas. **Dreamhouse**. New York: Onyx, 1989. 285 pp. ISBN
C   0-451-40121-2.
    Other works: *Manstopper*.

A creator of horror films should be immune to nightmares, but in Matthew Wilde's rented house is a scene over which he has no control, a savage and brutal nightmarish hell. [Legends, Native American]

99. Boucher, Anthony. **The Compleat Werewolf**. New York: Carroll & Graf,
C   1990. 256 pp. ISBN 0-88184-557-4. (First published by Doubleday, 1942.)

Those human-wolves have fun biting in "The Compleat Werewolf," "The Pink Caterpillar," "Q. U. R.," "Robine," "Snulbug," "Mr. Lupescu," "They Bite," "Expedition," "We Print the Truth," "The Ghost of Me." [Short stories; Werewolves]

100. Boyll, Randall. **Shocker**. New York: Berkley, 1990. 220 pp. ISBN
C   0-425-12263-8.
     Other works: *Darkman*. Movie versions: *Shocker*, 1990. Director: Wes Craven. Stars: Michael Murphy, Peter Berg, Mitch Pileggi, and Cami Cooper.

Horace Pinker has no respect for human life, and he has killed to prove it. Now he has been captured and will die in the electric chair. But the electricity doesn't kill Horace, and he escapes. Now he really doesn't like people! [Monsters; Science gone wrong; Transformation]

101.   Bradbury, Ray. **The Halloween Tree.** New York: Bantam, 1974. 160
B   pp. ISBN 0-553-25823-0. (First published by Knopf, 1972.)
       Other works: *Dinosaur Tales; The Martian Chronicles; The Illustrated Man; Dark Carnival; Dandelion Wine.*

The true meaning and mystery of Halloween is discovered by some youngsters who travel through time in search of a missing friend and find out about this most-spooky holiday. [Halloween; Legends, Christian; Time travel]

102.   Bradbury, Ray. **The October Country.** New York: Ballantine, 1955.
C   276 pp. ISBN 0-345-24620-X.

Strange, macabre tales by a master storyteller, including "The Dwarf," "The Next in Line," "The Watchful Poker Chip of H. Matisse," "Skeleton," "The Jar," "The Lake," "The Emissary," "Touched with Fire," "The Small Assassin," "The Crowd," "Jack-in-the-Box," "The Scythe," "Uncle Einar," "The Wind," "The Man Upstairs," "There Was an Old Woman," "The Cistern," "Homecoming," "The Wonderful Death of Dudley Stone." [Horror; Short stories]

103.   Bradbury, Ray. **Something Wicked This Way Comes.** New York: Ban-
C   tam, 1962. 215 pp. ISBN 0-553-23620-2. (First published by Simon and
       Schuster, 1962.)
       Movie versions: *Something Wicked This Way Comes*, 1983. Director: Jack Clayton. Stars: Jason Robards, Jr., Jonathan Pryce, Diane Ladd, and Pam Grier.

Will Halloway and Jim Nightshade are almost-fourteen-year-olds in a mid-western town in the earlier days of this century. One night, about a week before Halloween, Cooger & Dark's Pandemonium Shadow Show comes to town full of fascinations and mysteries. When Will and Jim discover the secret of the carnival, they hide from the sinister Mr. Dark. Can Will's father, the library's janitor, save the boys? [Black magic; Transformation]

104.   Bradley, Marion Zimmer. **Dark Satanic.** New York: TOR, 1988. 218
C   pp. ISBN 0-812-51602-8. (First published in 1972.)
       Other works: *Night's Daughter; The Firebrand.*

Jamie Melford knows that the book he is about to publish is full of ancient occult secrets that will attract attention, but he hasn't counted on danger along with the attention. Jamie's wife, Barbara, is not about to lose her beloved husband and is ready to fight awesome powers to get him back. She doesn't know a lot about witchcraft, but she knows enough to realize that she possesses no special gifts and must rely chiefly on love. [Satanism; Witchcraft]

105.   Bradley, Marion Zimmer. **The Inheritor.** New York: TOR, 1984. 414
C   pp. ISBN 0-812-51600-1.
       Sequels: *Witch Hill.*

Leslie Barnes is wary of her psychic talent, but her life in a wonderful new house in San Francisco forces her to use her special abilities to protect herself from the forces of evil. [Paranormal abilities]

106. Bradley, Marion Zimmer. **The Mists of Avalon.** New York: Ballantine/
C   Del Rey, 1984. 892 pp. ISBN 1-345-31452-2. London: Sphere, 1984.
      1,009 pp. ISBN 0-7221-1957-7. (First published by Knopf, 1982.)

Morgan LeFay is the central character in this intriguing version of the Camelot story. [Legends, Arthurian]

107. Bradley, Marion Zimmer. **Web of Light.** New York: Pocket Books,
C   1984. 208 pp. ISBN 0-671-44875-7. (First published by Starblaze
      Editions of Donning, 1983.)
      Sequels: *Web of Darkness.*

Ancient Atlantis is a land of magic and wonder. Two sisters, Domaris and Deoris, choose different sides of a powerful conflict, one that will determine the fate of their world. [Atlantis; Lost lands]

108. Bradshaw, Gillian. **In Winter's Shadow.** New York: Signet, 1983. 304
C   pp. ISBN 0-451-12276-3.
      Other works: *Hawk of May; Kingdom of Summer.*

Guinevere tells her own version of the dramatic passion and evil, magical machinations that will lead to the destruction of wonderful Camelot and its world of chivalry. [Legends, Arthurian]

109. Brandel, Marc. **The Hand.** New York: Berkley, 1981. 245 pp. ISBN
C   0-425-04838-1. (First published as *The Lizard's Tale* by Simon and
      Schuster, 1979.)
      Movie versions: *The Hand*, 1981. Director: Oliver Stone. Stars: Michael
      Caine, Andrea Marcovicci, Annie McEnroe, and Bruce McGill.

A successful cartoonist loses his drawing hand in an accident and finds adjustment very difficult. At first his concern centers around continuation of his career, but later his concern turns to fear. His severed hand has developed a will of its own—and even worse, the ability to move on its own. [Transformation]

110. Brandel, Marc. **Survivor.** New York: Avon, 1977. 221 pp. ISBN
C   0-380-00953-6. (First published by Simon & Schuster, 1976.)

Jane Claire is mesmerized by the works of artist Tagliatti, who died at an early age. Bluffing her way into a private showing of Tagliatti's works, Jane meets Wexford Bone, a collector of Tagliatti's works, and a strange psychic bond develops between the three. [Paranormal abilities]

111. Brandner, Gary. **Cat People.** New York: Fawcett, 1982. 221 pp. ISBN
C   0-449-14470-4.
      Other works: *The Brain Eaters; Floater; Hellborn.* Movie versions: *Cat
      People*, 1942. Director: Jacques Tourneur. Stars: Simone Simon, Kent
      Smith, Tom Conway, and Jack Holt. *Cat People*, 1982. Director: Paul
      Schrader. Stars: Natassia Kinski, Malcolm McDowell, and John Heard.

Beautiful Irena is haunted by strange visions and unnatural desires. Her yearnings do not seem to be like those of normal people, and she is fearful of finding out the truth about herself. It surely cannot be true that people become animals, or is it? (This novelization is based on the 1982 film version.) [Manimals; Transformation]

112. Brandner, Gary. **The Howling.** New York: Fawcett, 1981. 223 pp. ISBN
C   0-449-13155-6.
       Sequels: *The Howling II; The Howling III.* Movie versions: *The Howling,*
       1981. Director: Joe Dante. Stars: Dee Wallace, Patrick Macnee, and
       Dennis Dugan.

A tired young man and woman decide to go to the country for a vacation but discover to their horror that the neighbors are a bit weird, and the nearby woods are inhabited by strange beasts from which there seems to be no escape. [Horror; Transformation]

113. Brandner, Gary. **Quintana Roo.** New York: Fawcett, 1984. 251 pp. ISBN
C   0-449-12385-5.

The steamy jungles of Yucatan hold many secret terrors. Connie Braithwaite's husband has disappeared in the region called Quintana Roo, and she hires John Hooker to find him. But the legendary Muerateros, the "Dead Ones," will stop at nothing to maintain control over what is theirs. [Legends, Mayan]

114. Brandner, Gary. **... Walkers.** New York: Fawcett, 1980. 222 pp. ISBN
C   0-449-14319-8.

When people die they're dead, right? Wrong. In California Joana discovers that people don't even slow down with death, they just keep on walking and walking and walking. [Zombies]

115. Brautigan, Richard. **The Hawkline Monster.** New York: Pocket Books,
C   1976. 188 pp. ISBN 0-671-43786-0. (First published by Simon and
       Schuster, 1974.)

The Old West hardly seems to be the place for gothic goings-on, but there is an old house in Oregon that is the site of mysterious happenings and puzzling events. [Monsters]

116. Brennan, Alice. **The Devil's Dreamer.** New York: Prestige, 1971. 253
C   pp.

Carsa Winters seems to be a typical working woman sharing an apartment with a friend and, in general, enjoying life. Then one night she has a dream, a frightening dream from which she finally awakens only to find herself trapped in yet another dream from which there seems to be no escape. [Dreams; Gothic romance]

117. Brennan, Alice. **Ghost at Stagmere.** New York: Warner, 1973. 222
C   pp. ISBN 0-446-75076-X.

Stagmire is Gabrielle Fountainbleu's childhood home, and it has long been Gabrielle's dream to restore the old mansion to its former glory. But there are strange things going on at Stagmere, and Gabrielle may never leave Stagmere again. [Gothic romance]

118. Brennert, Alan. **Kindred Spirits.** New York: TOR, 1984. 320 pp. ISBN
A 0-8125-8103-2.

Michael and Ginny, two depressed teens, attempt suicide and fail. As they lie comatose, their spirits communicate, enabling them to understand their problems and cope with life. [Paranormal abilities]

119. Bretonne, Anne-Marie. **Dark Talisman.** New York: Popular Library,
C 1975. 254 pp. ISBN 0-445-00240-2.

A sultry Caribbean island is the site of Selena Danley's newly inherited property, an old plantation with many secrets, including black magic and voodoo. [Gothic romance; Voodoo]

120. Bretonne, Anne-Marie. **A Gallows Stands in Salem.** New York: Popular
C Library, 1975. 256 pp. SBN 445-00276-125.

Lovely Sabrina Highgate is old enough to yearn for love, especially from the handsome stranger Matthew Collins. But Sabrina is different from other young women her age; from early childhood she has seen her dead father in visions. Now she is accused of the dreaded crime of witchcraft by the hysterical young girls of Salem. [Gothic romance; Witchcraft]

121. Bridges, Laurie. **The Ashton Horror.** New York: Bantam, 1984. 160 pp.
A ISBN 0-553-25104-X. (Dark Forces series).

Dennis, the new kid at Ashton High, joins a fantasy-game club in order to make new friends. Little does he realize, though, that the game is for real and his lovely new girlfriend has been marked as a human sacrifice. [Fantasy games]

122. Bridges, Laurie, and Paul Alexander. **Devil Wind.** New York: Bantam,
A 1983. 152 pp. ISBN 0-553-22834-X. (Dark Forces series).

Little does Peter know when he blows an old whistle that he will summon a dreadful power from the ocean depths, one that he and his girlfriend Mary must battle for their sanity and salvation. [Demons]

123. Bridges, Laurie, and Paul Alexander. **Magic Show.** New York: Bantam,
A 1983. 135 pp. ISBN 0-553-22833-1. (Dark Forces series).

What more could an aspiring high school magician ask for than an ancient book of secrets? What Chris doesn't realize, however, are the very real dangers as he delves deeper into the old sorcerer's grimoire of dreadful spells. [Black magic; Legerdemain]

124. Bridges, Laurie, and Paul Alexander. **Swamp Witch.** New York: Bantam,
A 1983. 153 pp. ISBN 0-553-23606-7. (Dark Forces series.)

It seems great at first when Linda goes to stay with her friend Heather Clark while her father is away. But the Clark's servant, Tubelle, is a voodoo priestess who wants the best for her darling Heather, including Linda's boyfriend. [Voodoo]

125. Brookes, Owen. **The Widow of Ratchets.** New York: Ace, 1980. 411 pp.
C   ISBN 0-441-88769-4. (First published by Holt, Rinehart and Winston, 1979).

Lyndsay Dolben arrives in England to join her new husband only to be greeted with the devastating news that he is dead. She travels to his home, Ratchets, where she discovers more than a mournful ancestral home; she finds belief in magic still in existence, a belief Lyndsay must come to trust. [Legends, Celtic]

126. Brooks-Janowiak, Jean. **Winter Lord.** New York: Signet, 1983. 184 pp.
C   ISBN 0-451-12002-7.

Jane O'Neill, a lovely young widow, has moved as part of her quest to create a new life for herself. She needs to forget the power another woman held over her now-dead husband. She finds herself attracted to another man, Finn Daoine, who may understand the key to the mysteries in Jane's life. [Legends, Celtic]

127. Brown, George Mackay. **Time in a Red Coat.** Harmondsworth, England:
A   Penguin, 1986. 249 pp. ISBN 0-14-007401-5. (First published by Chatto & Windus, 1984.)

The girl is given two gifts at birth, an ivory flute and a bag of coins. The flute is magic, and through it she moves through time. As she progresses through many periods, she sees the horror of war and comes to be clothed in a red stained coat, symbolic of the blood that has been spilled. [Mysticism; Time travel]

128. Bruce, Leo. **Death on Allhallowe'en.** Chicago: Academy Chicago, 1988.
C   176 pp. ISBN 0-89733-292-X. (First published in England by Allen, 1970.)

Carolus Deene, a mystery-solving schoolmaster, is asked to look into the death of a schoolboy in Kent. Deene discovers a coven of witches in Clibburn and finds his own life in peril as he continues his investigations. [Occult mystery/detective; Witchcraft]

129. Brunn, Robert. **The Initiation.** New York: Dell, 1982. 154 pp. ISBN
A   0-440-94047-8. (Twilight series).

Most kids in a new school think they're outsiders at first, but Adam realizes quickly that more is going on at Blair Prep than his casual first impression. There really are some strange and frightening happenings, and Adam's invitation to join an exclusive club brings him face-to-face with a dreadful secret. [Vampires]

130. Brust, Steven. **To Reign in Hell.** New York: Ace, 1985. 268 pp. ISBN
C   0-441-81496-4.
     Other works: *Taltos; Jhereg; Yendi; Teckla; Phoenix.*

A tale from the very beginnings of time in which the angels, led by God, battle with that clever devil Satan for supremacy of the universe. [The devil; Heaven and hell]

131. Bryan, Amanda. **The Warning.** New York: Dell, 1985. 156 pp. ISBN
A   0-440-99335-0. (Twilight series).

Lois thinks it's great that Ronnie Reed wants her to be his girlfriend and doesn't see through his selfishness. Then her happiness is shaken when her typewriter starts writing her threatening messages. Who is sending Lois these messages? It isn't Ronnie, famous for his practical jokes. But who—or what—is it? [Prophecy]

132. Buchan, John. **Witch Wood.** New York: Carroll & Graf, 1989. 289 pp.
C   ISBN 0-88184-496-9. (First published in England in 1927.)
       Other works: *Pilgrim's Way; John MacNab.*

In seventeenth-century Scotland a young minister struggles against an ancient belief in witchcraft and finds his love for the beautiful Katrine taking over his mind and soul. [Legends, Celtic]

133. Buchanan, Marie. **Anima.** New York: Fawcett, 1973. 223 pp. SBN 449-
C   01827-125. (First published by St. Martin's Press, 1972.)
       Other works: *The Dark Backward.*

The Mintons seem to be an average English family, but something happens when the Blanchards move next door. Olive Minton is attracted to Giles Blanchard, but then she feels another being taking over her body and soul, and Olive no longer knows who—or what—she is. [Possession]

134. Bulgakov, Mikhail. **The Master and Margarita.** New York: Signet, 1967.
C   384 pp. ISBN 0-451-51701-6. (First published in the United States by
       Grove Press, 1967.)

Russian Communist doctrine does not admit to the existence of God and heaven or to the devil and hell. When the devil turns up in Russia with his entourage, things begin to happen that just cannot be permitted in a totalitarian state. [The devil]

135. Bull, Emma. **War for the Oaks.** New York: Ace, 1987. 309 pp. ISBN
C   0-441-87073-2.

A modern bustling city like Minneapolis seems an incongruous place for an ongoing battle between ancient beings. Only Eddi McCandry seems to know what's going on, because she can see the ghoulish hobgoblins and others of the mythical fairy court. [Fairies]

136. Bunting, Eve. **The Ghost Behind Me.** New York: Archway, 1984. 169 pp.
A   ISBN 0-671-49865-7.
       Other works: *The Haunting of Safekeep; Strange Things Happen in the Woods; Ghost of Summer.*

Cinnamon finds herself fearful of the lovely old house in San Francisco that is to be her summer home. Who is the elusive young man in the vintage car whom only she can see, and what does he want with her? [Ghosts]

137. Bunting, Eve. **The Ghosts of Departure Point.** New York: Scholastic
A   Point, n.d. 113 pp. ISBN 0-590-33116-7. (First published by Lippincott,
       1982.)

Vicki, a vibrant seventeen-year-old cheerleader, finds herself living an odd existence after she is killed in a car crash on Departure Point. When she meets another ghost, handsome Ted, she realizes that she is meant to do something, but she cannot figure out easily what it is. [Ghosts]

138. Burgess, Mason. **Child of Demons.** New York: Leisure, 1985. 347 pp.
C   ISBN 0-8439-2206-0.
      Other works: *Blood Moon.*

Wendy Matheson is only seven, but she has a great secret power. Her power is a voice called Adamm that comes to her in dreams, but what Adamm tells her comes true during the hours she is awake. [Demons]

139. Burgess, Mason. **Graveyard.** New York: Leisure, 1987. 320 pp. ISBN
A   0-8439-2534-5.

The windswept prairies of Manitoba seem a long way from the lush jungles of Haiti, but the high-school kids in Carlyle are about to find out that voodoo and zombies aren't a joke and that it isn't very smart to use graveyards for playgrounds ... not smart at all. [Voodoo; Zombies]

140. Burke, John. **The Devil's Footsteps.** New York: Fawcett, 1978. 221 pp.
C   ISBN 0-445-44204-4. (First published by Coward, McCann & Geoghegan, 1976.)

Bronwen Powys is a thoroughly twentieth-century young woman with a career and an active life. When she comes to Hexney to take pictures, however, she discovers an old and brutal evil. The evil is worshiped by the villagers of Hexney, even to the point of horrible sacrifices. Bronwen hopes that a magician, Dr. Alexander Caspian, will be able to stand up to the ancient evil, but there turns out to be more involved than a simple conflict between good and evil. [Legends, Celtic; Paranormal abilities]

141. Burkholz, Herbert. **The Sensitives.** New York: Berkley, 1989. 278 pp.
C   ISBN 0-425-11581-X. (First published by Atheneum, 1987.)

Espionage is a dangerous profession, but Ben Slade has an edge—he can read minds. Ben is not the only mind reader, however, for the KGB have their own special expert in this area. [Occult mystery/detective; Paranormal abilities]

142. Burrage, A. M. **Warning Whispers.** Wellingborough, England: Equation,
C   1988. 190 pp. ISBN 1-85336-083-X.

Classic English ghost stories, including "The Acquittal," "Warning Whispers," "Crookback," "For the Local Rag," "The Little Blue Flames," "The Recurring Tragedy," "The Case of Thissler and Baxter," "The Green Bungalow," "The Attic," "The Ticking of the Clock," "The Imperturbable Tucker," "The Boy with Red Hair," "The Garden of Fancy," "The Mystery of the Sealed Garret," "For One Night Only," "Father of the Man," "The Fourth Wall." [Ghosts; Short stories]

143. Butler, Nathan. **Kaheesh.** New York: Fawcett, 1983. 217 pp. ISBN
C   0-449-12550-5.

Carefree California, vacation site for Greg and Nancy Howard, becomes an ominous place when they encounter an old holy man, Kaheesh, living in the ruins of an old mansion. Greg is intrigued, but Nancy is afraid, for somehow she knows the old man is evil. [Cults; Legends, Native American]

Butters, Dorothy Gilman. *See* Dorothy Gilman.

144. Buzzelli, Elizabeth Kane. **Gift of Evil.** New York: Bantam, 1983. 301 pp.
C   ISBN 0-553-23740-3.

Quiet, fearful Mattie finds she has a new power, the gift of reading minds; shocking revelations come to her in dreams. At first Mattie's gift provides her with a new sense of confidence, but then she learns of her ultimate power, the ability to manipulate life and death. [Paranormal abilities]

145. Byrne, John L. **Fear Book.** New York: Warner, 1988. 249 pp. ISBN
C   0-446-34814-7.

One day in the mail, Sam and Joanne receive the usual assortment of mail-order catalogs, with one difference. One catalog is like nothing Sam has ever seen before, one he won't ever let Joanne see. He burns the catalog but it keeps coming in the mail. It seems to have a life of its own, and its fascination is indescribable, for its pages are filled with unspeakable terrors. [Evil]

146. Caidin, Martin. **The Messiah Stone.** New York: Baen, 1986. 407 pp. ISBN
C   0-621-65562-0.
    Other works: *Cyborg; Aquarius Mission; Exit Earth.*

Doug Stavers, a he-man mercenary, has a new mission—to locate the powerful Messiah stone, once worn by Christ and possessed of great power. Hitler owned it and nearly succeeded in his efforts to rule the world. Now it is rumored that another man of evil is after the stone, and if Doug doesn't stop him, the world will be in big trouble. [Legends, Christian]

147. Calder, Robert. **The Dogs.** New York: Dell, 1977. 228 pp. ISBN 0-440-
C   02102-1. (First published by Delacorte, 1976.)

Dogs are often called man's best friend. But man is not necessarily dogs' best friend. These dogs have been used as experimental animals; they are now viciously savage, and they are loose. [Science gone wrong]

148. Caldwell, Taylor. **Dialogues with the Devil.** New York: Fawcett, 1967. 192
C   pp. ISBN 0-449-23714-1.

A series of letters between the devil (Lucifer) and his brother, the archangel Michael, form the structure of an ongoing debate on the nature of good and evil. [Angels; The devil; Legends, Christian]

149. Caldwell, Taylor. **Wicked Angel.** New York: Fawcett, 1965. 176 pp.
C

Angelo appears to be like his name, beautiful and angelic. But Angelo is not what he seems. Angelo is pure evil, which seems even more frightening in one so young. [Evil]

150. Callahan, Jay. **Footprints of the Dead.** New York: Dell, 1983. 160 pp.
A   ISBN 0-440-92531-2. (Twilight series).

Dani, shocked and stunned by her parents' deaths, returns to her childhood home in the Caribbean. She discovers not the peace she had hoped for but rather horror in the frightening world of zombies. [Voodoo; Zombies]

151.   Calvino, Italo. **The Castle of Crossed Destinies.** New York: Harvest, 1977.
C   129 pp. ISBN 0-15-6154555-2. (First published in Italy as *Il castello dei desini incrociati* by Franco Maria Ricci, 1969.)

Some travelers who have formed a group for companionship entertain themselves by using a pack of tarot cards to tell stories. The cards and their arcane symbolism become more than idle pleasure, however, and the characters on the cards become more than fictional characters. [Mysticism]

152.   Cameron, Eleanor. **Beyond Silence.** New York: Laurel-Leaf, 1985. 208 pp.
A   ISBN 0-440-90582-6. (First published by Elsevier-Dutton, 1980.)

The recent death of his brother has troubled Andy greatly, but he becomes involved with an older, more ghostly tragedy when visiting his father's ancestral home in Scotland. At first Andy is only vaguely interested in this vacation, but as he learns more about the old Scottish castle, he finds himself drawn into an old, sad love story [Ghosts]

153.   Cameron, Eleanor. **The Court of the Stone Children.** New York: Puffin,
B   1990. 191 pp. ISBN 0-14-034289-3. (First published in the United States by Dutton, 1973.)

Nina is lonely; it's hard making friends in a new city. At first she is grateful when Dominique approaches her, then intrigued, for Domi is different — Domi has come from 200 years ago to get Nina's help in clearing the memory of Domi's father. [Time travel]

154.   Cameron, Ian. **Island at the Top of the World.** New York: Avon, 1970.
C   190 pp. ISBN 0-680-20966-125. (First published as *The Lost Ones* by Hutchinson, 1961.)
       Movie versions: *Island at the Top of the World*, 1974. Director: Robert Stevenson. Stars: David Hartman, Mako, Donald Sinden, Jacques Marin, and David Dwillim.

This story based on a tale by H. G. Wells follows seekers as they undergo dangers to find a lost colony of ancient Vikings in the polar wastelands. [Lost lands]

155.   Cameron, Lou. **Behind the Scarlet Door.** New York: Fawcett, 1971. 192
C   pp. SBN 449-02493-075.

When a Welsh folksinger is killed, Sergeant Morgan Price is assigned to the case. In the beginning, he knows nothing about witchcraft, but before the murder is solved, Sergeant Price knows a great deal more than he would like about modern black magic. [Occult mystery/detective; Witchcraft]

156.   Camp, Joe. **Oh Heavenly Dog.** New York: Scholastic, 1980. 139 pp. ISBN
A   0-590-31400-9.
       Movie versions: *Oh Heavenly Dog*, 1980. Director: Joe Camp. Stars: Chevy Chase, Benji, Jane Seymour, and Omar Sharif.

Benjamin Browning has just taken on a unique case, solving his own murder. There's only one hitch: Browning is returned to the world of the living as a dog, not as a man. [Heaven and hell; Transformation]

157. Campbell, Ramsey. **Ancient Images.** New York: TOR, 1990. 311 pp. ISBN
C   0-812-50263-9. (First published by Macmillan, 1989.)
    Other works: *The Doll Who Ate His Mother; The Height of the Scream;
    The Influence; The Inhabitant of the Lake and Less Welcome Tenants;
    The Nameless; Cold Print; The Best of Ramsey Campbell; Superhorror;
    Scared Stiff.*

Sandy Allan is rather excited when she hears that a print of never-released
Karloff/Lugosi film has been discovered. Then the deaths start, and Sandy
discovers that the old horror film is symbolic of more than the horror depicted in
its story. [Legends, Celtic]

158. Campbell, Ramsey. **Dark Feasts.** London: Robinson, 1987. 339 pp. ISBN
C   0-948164-37-9.

This collection of stories by a British master of dark fantasy includes "The
Room in the Castle," "Cold Print," "The Scar," "The Interloper," "The Guy,"
"The End of a Summer's Day," "The Whining," "The Words that Count," "The
Man in the Underpass," "Horror House of Blood," "The Companion," "Call
First," "In the Bag," "The Chimney," "The Brood," "The Voice of the Beach,"
"Out of Copyright," "Above the World," "Mackintosh Willy," "The Ferries,"
"Midnight Hobo," "The Depths," "The Fit," "Hearing Is Believing," "The
Hands," "Again," "Just Waiting," "Seeing the World," "Apples," "Boiled Alive."
[Horror; Short stories]

159. Campbell, Ramsey. **Demons by Daylight.** New York: Carroll & Graf, 1990.
C   192 pp. ISBN 0-88184-610-4. (First published by Arkham House, 1973.)

These early stories in a Lovecraft style include "Potential," "The End of a
Summer's Day," "At First Sight," "The Frankly Paragraphs," "The Interloper,"
"The Sentinels," "The Guy," "The Old Horns," "The Lost," "The Stocking," "The
Second Staircase," "Concussion," "The Enchanted Fruit," "Made in
Goatswood." [Evil; Short stories]

160. Campbell, Ramsey. **The Hungry Moon.** New York: TOR, 1987. 360 pp.
C   ISBN 0-812-51662-1. (First published by Macmillan, 1986.)

In the lovely English countryside many simple customs dating back to the
ancient Druids are practiced. These customs seem harmless, but in Moonwell a
stranger comes to town and the gentle customs of past centuries change, becoming evil and terrifying. [Legends, Celtic]

161. Campbell, Ramsey. **Incarnate.** New York: TOR, 1985. 512 pp. ISBN
C   0-8125-1650-8. (First published by Macmillan, 1983.)

A frightening study of dreams, reality, and terror by a master of British
horror. In the aftermath of a scientific experiment on prophetic dreaming, the
participants find that their lives will never be the same again. [Altered states of
consciousness; Dreams]

162. Campbell, Ramsey. **The Parasite.** New York: Pocket Books, 1981. 372
C   pp. ISBN 0-671-41905-6. (First published by Macmillan, 1980.)

Rose has supernatural powers because of a terrible childhood experience. Now that Rose is grown, she discovers that the terror of her early experience is not over; in fact, it is just beginning. [Paranormal abilities]

163. Campton, David. **The Vampyre.** New York: Barron's, 1988. 139 pp. ISBN
B   0-8120-4070-8. (First published by Hutchinson, 1986.) (Fleshcreepers series).

This story based on John Polidori's earlier work by the same title tells the tale of Lord Ruthven, a ruthless vampire loose in historic London. [Vampires]

164. Cantrell, Lisa W. **The Manse.** New York: TOR, 1987. 341 pp. ISBN
C   0-812-51673-7.
     Sequels: *Torments.* Other works: *The Ridge.*

Once a year on Halloween, the old manse becomes a haunted house, full of human-inspired horrors for the fun of people in town. But the old house has a history of real horror, and the manse is waiting and feeding on the fright of the Halloween visitors. This Halloween is going to be different. [Halloween]

165. Carey, M. V. **The Mystery of the Magic Circle.** New York: Random
C   House, 1981. 143 pp. ISBN 0-394-86427-1. (First published by Random House, 1978.) (The Three Investigators series).

Three bright teenagers get involved in a mystery of disappearing films. When they discover that the aging film star who owns the films is a witch, they find they may be in for more serious matters than they had bargained for. [Witchcraft]

166. Carleton, Barbee Oliver. **Mystery of the Witches' Bridge.** New York:
B   Apple, 1975? 304 pp. ISBN 0-590-41398-8. (First published as *The Witches' Bridge* by Holt, Rinehart and Winston, 1967.)

Thirteen-year-old Dan Pride is curious about his new home and his ancestors. After he finds out more, however, Dan isn't sure about a lot of things he used to think were just superstition. He's especially concerned about the ghostly fiddler who plays near the bridge just before someone dies. What's really scary is that only Dan can hear the music. [Ghosts]

167. Carr, John Dickson (pseud. Carter Dickson). **Below Suspicion.** New York:
C   Bantam, 1960. 186 pp. (First published in the United States by Harper & Row, 1949.)
     Other works: *The Devil in Velvet; The Demoniacs; The Dead Sleep Lightly; He Who Whispers; The Three Coffins.*

Sometimes people turn to devil worship to obtain personal power and sometimes out of curiosity. There are some, however, who turn to the devil because they are evil. Dr. Gideon Fell discovers such a group of evil devil-worshippers, and this time he may have met his match. [Occult mystery/detective; Satanism]

168. Carr, John Dickson. **The Burning Court.** New York: Award, 1969.
C   215 pp. (First published by H. Hamilton, 1932.)

At first, Marie Stevens seems to be an ordinary, albeit very beautiful, homemaker. She does seem to have odd quirks, however, such as a hysterical fear of fire. Could she possibly be a notorious nineteenth-century murderess returned from the dead? [Reincarnation]

169.   Carr, John Dickson. **Fire, Burn!** New York: Bantam, 1959. 214 pp. (First
C   published by Hamish Hamilton, 1957.)

When Detective-Superintendent John Cheviot grabs a cab in 1950, he is amazed to find himself delivered to the police offices in that same city, but in 1829. Due to his superior detective skills based on modern methods, he is able to solve a puzzling murder, but he also finds himself falling in love with a fascinating woman. [Occult mystery/detective; Time travel]

170.   Carroll, Joy. **The Moth.** New York: Dell, 1974. 271 pp. ISBN 0-440-05837-
C   125.

When Regina and Kate were little girls, Regina made Kate her obedient servent. Now Kate is grown up and Regina is dead, but Kate discovers that Regina's spirit and her very strong will are still alive. Kate must fight for survival in a way she never imagined. [Possession]

171.   Carvic, Heron. **Witch Miss Seeton.** New York: Berkley, 1988. 188 pp.
C   ISBN 0-425-10713-2. (First published by Harper & Row, 1971.)

At first glance retired art teacher Miss Seeton would seem to be a typical inhabitant of a sleepy English village. Miss Seeton, however, has a particular skill that is appreciated in different ways by the police. Miss Seeton has a gift for solving mysteries, including those of an occult nature. [Occult mystery/detective; Witchcraft]

172.   Cassedy, Sylvia. **Behind the Attic Wall.** New York: Camelot, 1985. 315 pp.
B   ISBN 0-380-69843-9. (First published by Crowell, 1983.)

Cranky, disagreeable Maggie has been labeled nasty and disobedient as well as difficult to manage. Maggie's great-aunts decide to take her into their big old house, and Maggie arrives prepared not to like it at all. After her arrival, however, Maggie begins to hear whispers that lure her into a magic world, one that changes her life forever. [Ghosts]

173.   Cave, Hugh B. **The Evil.** New York: Ace Charter, 1981. 309 pp. ISBN
C   0-441-21850-4.
       Other works: *Legion of the Dead; Murgunstrumm, and Others; The Nebu-
       lous Horror; Disciples of Dread; The Lower Deep; Lucifer's Eye.*

Two idealistic Americans in Haiti discover the terror and mysteries of voodoo. Sam, an agricultural expert, and Kay, a nurse, become embroiled in horror when Kay tries to protect a young Haitian boy and Sam tries to help Mildred, an old friend, locate her father in the steaming jungles. [Voodoo]

174.   Cave, Hugh B. **Shades of Evil.** New York: Charter, 1982. 307 pp. ISBN
C   0-441-75986-6.

It seems like an idyllic Florida retirement for Jack and Ruby until the morning Ruby sees a frightening figure rise up out of the lake, a figure bent on revenge. [Voodoo]

175. Caveney, Philip. **The Sins of Rachel Ellis.** New York: Berkley, 1979. 240
C   pp. ISBN 0-425-04144-1. (First published by St. Martin's Press, 1978.)

Pandora's great-great-aunt, Rachel Ellis, had been a lovely young southern woman when she first arrived in the wild countryside of Wales to claim her inheritance. After her arrival she had made a marvelous discovery, a way to keep her youth and beauty forever. There was a heavy price for this discovery, however, and perhaps courageous young Pandora will have to be the one to pay. [Satanism]

176. Chalker, Jack L. **The Messiah Choice.** New York: TOR, 1986. 380 pp.
C   ISBN 0-812-53290-2. (First published by Bluejay, 1985.)

Sir Robert McKenzie has turned his Caribbean island into a technological wonder, but when occult powers are invoked, the devil appears and injects midnight horror into the modern world. Gentle Angelique is aware of the menace, but her frail paralyzed body may not be sufficiently strong to battle the ultimate powers of evil. [Science gone wrong]

177. Chambers, Jane. **Burning.** New York: Jove, 1978. 157 pp. ISBN 0-515-
C   04450-4.

Cynthia, in desperate need of some peace and quiet, hires Angela to help with her kids, and they all move to an old New England farmhouse for a long vacation. This peaceful time is not to be, however, for two women of the past draw Cynthia and Angela into a frightening world of terror. [Ghosts; Paranormal abilities]

178. Chant, Joy. **The High Kings.** New York: Bantam Spectra, 1985. 250 pp.
C   ISBN 0-553-24306-3. (First published as a Bantam hardcover, 1983.)
      Other works: *Red Moon and Black Mountain; The Gray Mane of Morning.*

Arthur was not the only glorious ruler in the ancient days of Celtic Britain. There were also Bladad the blemished prince, the two queens of Locrin, Leir and his daughters, and other legendary figures whose epic tales match those of the better-known heroes and heroines of Camelot. [Legends, Celtic]

179. Chapman, Vera. **The King's Damosel.** New. York: Avon, 1978. 143 pp.
A   ISBN 0-380-0196-7. (First published by Collins, 1976.)
      Sequels: *The Green Knight; King Arthur's Daughter.*

Lady Lynetta is destined to wed crude Gaharis, but she is rescued by King Arthur, who makes her his royal messenger. Now her adventures really begin as she travels the magical and sometimes dangerous highways of the kingdom. [Legends, Arthurian]

180. Chappell, Fred. **Dagon.** New York: St. Martin's Press, 1987. 181 pp.
C   ISBN 0-312-90676-5. (First published in 1967.)
      Other works: *The Fred Chappell Reader.*

Hailed by August Derleth as an outstanding book, *Dagon* has been considered by many critics to be the best of many tales about H. P. Lovecraft's Cthulhu mythos (see item 657). In this story, a young author and his wife move to an old family farm so he can write about an ancient god. Little does he realize, however, that his description does not even begin to approach the awfulness of the horrors that await him. [Evil]

181. Charnas, Suzy McKee. **The Bronze King.** New York: Bantam, 1987. 189
A   pp. ISBN 0-553-27104-0. (First published by Houghton Mifflin, 1985.)
     Sequels: *The Silver Glove; The Golden Thread.*

Valentine feels nervous. She knows something is wrong somehow, but she doesn't know what. She is sure only of the strong feeling of fear and impending doom. Then she learns from an old street musician and his young friend that something is indeed going to happen—the destruction of the city—unless Valentine is able to stop it with aid from the bronze statue of King Jagiello. [Monsters]

182. Charnas, Suzy McKee. **The Vampire Tapestry.** New York: TOR, 1986.
C   294 pp. ISBN 0-812-53293-7. (First published by Simon and Schuster,
     1980.)

Dr. Wayland is a famous and respected anthropologist, and he is also something of a heartthrob to the young women students in his classes. But there is a different, more sinister side to Dr. Wayland, a side of explosive evil, for Dr. Wayland is a vampire. [Vampires]

183. Chayefsky, Paddy. (pseud. of Sidney Aaron). **Altered States.** New York:
C   Bantam, 1979. 205 pp. ISBN 0-553-12472-2. (First published by Harper &
     Row, 1978.)
     Movie versions: *Altered States*, 1980. Director: Ken Russell. Stars:
     William Hurt and Blair Brown.

Eddie Jessings's in-depth experiments to discover his true self through hallucinatory drugs result in a dangerous near-loss of his innermost being. [Altered states of consciousness]

184. Cheetham, Ann. **Black Harvest.** London: Armada/Fontana, 1985. 143
A   pp. ISBN 0-00-692199-X.
     Sequels: *The Beggar's Curse; The Witch of Flagg; The Pit.*

The Blakemans' family holiday in Ireland becomes more than they had bargained for when Colin becomes aware of an unnatural odor in the earth. Prill begins to dream of a death figure and little Alison falls prey to a mysterious illness. Only cousin Oliver stays calm, and it may be that Oliver knows more about the frightening events than the Blakemans realize. [Evil]

185. Cherryh, C. J. **Legions of Hell.** New York: Baen, 1987. 407 pp. ISBN
C   0-571-65653-8.
     Other works (with Janet Morris): *The Gates of Hell.*

Hell is reputed not to be the place to go, but there is no question about the fascination it holds. It's particularly intriguing when you consider the people who must be there, not only Caesar and other ancient villains but all the wrong-doers from all ages, all interacting with each other. Even the devil can't control this bunch. [Heaven and hell; Legends, Christian]

186. Chesbro, George C. **An Affair of Sorcerers.** New York: Signet, 1979.
C   265 pp. ISBN 0-451-09243-0. (First published by Simon and Schuster,
     1979.)
     Other works: *City of Whispering Stone.*

Mongo, a brilliant criminologist and private detective (and a dwarf), finds himself in the middle of a frightening and occult evil that may defeat even the most shrewd of logical intellects. [Occult mystery/detective]

187. Chesbro, George. **The Golden Child.** New York: Pocket Books, 1986.
A   221 pp. ISBN 0-671-63039-3.
     Movie versions: *The Golden Child*, 1987. Director: Michael Ritchie. Stars: Eddie Murphy, Charles Dance, Charlotte Lewis, Victor Wong, and J. L. Reate.

Life as a social worker in Los Angeles isn't dull, but Chandler Jarrell doesn't begin to know what action is until he is coerced into helping rescue the golden child, a mystical young lama, from the powers of evil. [Demons; Legends, Tibetan]

188. Chetwynd-Hayes, R. **And Love Survived.** New York: Zebra, 1990. 288
C   pp. ISBN 0-8217-3051-7. (First published as *The Dark Man* by Sidgwick in England, 1964.)

Can love survive time and conquer death? Anthony Strickland discovers that his love can as he mysteriously travels back in time to find the love of his life, beautiful and destructive Mary. [Time travel]

189. Chetwynd-Hayes, R. **Dominique.** New York: Belmont Tower Books,
C   1979. 172 pp. ISBN 0-505-51345-5.
     Movie versions: *Dominique*, 1978. Director: Michael Anderson. Stars: Cliff Robertson, Jean Simmons, Jenny Agutter, Simon Ward, Ron Moody, Judy Geeson, and Jack Warner.

Dominique, a beautiful young woman, is going mad, and suicide seems to be the only way she can escape the crushing nightmares and fears that crowd her mind. Yet Dominique is vengeful, and she returns from the dead to haunt those who encouraged her madness. [Ghosts]

190. Chetwynd-Hayes, R. **The Grange.** New York: TOR, 1988. 249 pp. ISBN
A   0-812-51626-5. (First published in England, 1985.)

Miles Harrington, a poor but honest soldier, is looking for gainful employment after the defeat of the Spanish Armada. At first he thinks he is fortunate in locating employment at Clavering Grange, that is, until he finds out the grange is haunted. [Ghosts; Haunted houses]

191. Childer, Simon Ian. **Worm.** London: Grafton, 1987. 189 pp. ISBN
A   0-586-06945-3.
     Other works: *Tendrils.*

Worms, plain old fishing worms, for example, don't seem very scary, but then they get big and voracious, with a taste for human flesh. You'd better look out. [Monsters, slime-type]

192. Chilton, I. M. **Nightmare.** New York: Scholastic, 1968. 95 pp.
A

When Gillian foolishly accepts the dare to ride the motorbike, she crashes. Her crash is not one from which she can easily recover, although she is not badly hurt physically. Gillian's mind has gone into another place, an evil place from which she may never be able to escape. [Dreams]

193. Christian, Catherine. **The Pendragon.** New York: Warner, 1978. 607 pp.
C ISBN 0-446-32342-X.

The story of Camelot as told by Bedivere, boyhood friend and faithful companion to the king throughout his eventful life. [Legends, Arthurian]

194. Christopher, John. **The Little People.** London: Sphere, 1978. 237 pp.
C ISBN 0-7221-2305-1. (First published in London by Hodden & Stoughton, 1966.)

Turning the old Irish castle into a hotel seemed to be a good idea, but Daniel and Bridget let themselves into more than the hard work they expected. The evil emanations might be associated in some strange way with the evil experiments of a Nazi concentration camp doctor. [Nazi occultism]

195. Chronister, Alan B. **Cry Wolf.** New York: Zebra, 1987. 320 pp. ISBN
C 0-82147-2094-5.

The young couple chose Larksboro as their new home because it was so peaceful, so perfect for their new life. But the woods around Larksboro are ominous and full of fearsome things that howl mournfully in the night. [Monsters]

196. Citro, Joseph. **The Unseen.** New York: Warner, 1990. 274 pp. ISBN
C 0-446-35839-8.
Other works: *Shadow Child; Guardian Angel; Dark Twilight.*

You can still find places where nature seems to rule, places like the Northeast Kingdom of upstate Vermont where the brooding forests protect the land. But something else protects this area as well—the Watcher, who is the vicious guardian of this legendary region. [Monsters]

197. Clapp, Patricia. **Jane-Emily.** New York: Laurel-Leaf, 1973. 151 pp. ISBN
B 0-440-94185-7. (First published by Lothrop, 1969.)
Other works: *Witches' Children.*

In 1912, Louisa reluctantly goes to spend the summer with her niece, nine-year-old Jane, and her grandmother. Unhappy at leaving her boyfriend behind, Louisa arrives at the gloomy old house in Lynn only to discover to her horror that Jane is battling for possession of her soul with Emily, Jane's aunt who has been dead for many years. [Ghosts; Possession]

198. Clark, Douglas W. **Alchemy Unlimited.** New York: Avon, 1990. 310 pp.
C ISBN 0-380-75726-5.

In the middle ages, alchemy was a respected science. Sebastian, having come down in rank and privilege, is apprenticed to Corwyn, a specialist in aquatic alchemy. Sebastian has many adventures, including a traditional quest, before he comes to fully appreciate the skills of his master. [Alchemy; Magic]

199. Clark, Lydia Benson. **Seance for Susan.** New York: Zebra, 1977. 240 pp.
C   ISBN 0-89083-263-3. (First published as *Demon Cat* in 1965.)

Susan's cousin Tildy is dead. Tildy the beautiful, rich, and spoiled cousin who dominated Susan in life. Now that Tildy is dead Susan should be free, but Tildy refuses to leave the living and takes over Susan's body and mind. [Possession]

Clemens, Samuel. *See* Mark Twain.

200. Clement, Henry. **The Hearse.** New York: Pinnacle, 1980. 213 pp. ISBN
C   0-523-41056-5.
      Movie versions: *The Hearse*, 1980. Director: George Bowers. Stars: Trish Van Devere, Joseph Cotton, David Gautreaux, Donald Hutton, Med Flory, and Donald Petrie.

Jane hopes for a quiet, peaceful time in the country. The school year has ended and the summer stretches ahead, a time to heal the wounds caused by her mother's death and her own recent divorce. But Jane's summer is not going to be peaceful, for even before she reaches the mysterious house she has rented, the ominous black hearse appears, an omen of worse to come. [Horror]

201. Cline, C. Terry, Jr. **Death Knell.** New York: Fawcett, 1987. 286 pp. ISBN
C   0-449-23639-0. (First published by Putnam, 1977.)
      Other works: *Damon; Mind Reader; Missing Persons; Prey.*

Teenage Pamela is the host to the spirit of another — vengeful Erika who died in the Holocaust. Lovely Pamela's own father was once a German officer, and now Pamela has become Erika's tool for revenge and family loyalties no longer seem to matter [Possession]

202. Clegg, Douglas. **Breeder.** New York: Pocket Books, 1990. 310 pp. ISBN
C   0-671-31206-5.

Pregnant Rachel and her husband are gentrifying a house in a seedy section of Washington, D.C. There are strange and awful things going on in the house and the neighborhood, and Rachel's child is slated to be fodder for a terrible beast in the basement. [Monsters]

203. Clegg, Douglas. **Goat Dance.** New York: Pocket Books, 1989. 422 pp.
C   ISBN 0-671-66425-5.

Little Teddy Amory almost drowns, but her father saves her. Then he learns that his daughter died after all and that something took possession of her under the water, something that wants to create hell on earth. [Possession]

204. Cody, C. S. (pseud. of Leslie Waller). **The Witching Night.** New York:
C   Lancer, 1968. 286 pp. (First published by World, 1952.)

The Indiana dunes serve as the locale for this story of modern-day witchcraft. Dr. Joe Loomis, vacationing in this peaceful locale, starts to read his host's collection of strange books. Then he meets the fascinating Abbie, and his life begins to fall apart. [Witchcraft]

205. Coffey, Frank. **The Shaman.** Toronto, Ontario: Paperjacks, 1988. 240 pp.
C   ISBN 0-7701-0901-2.

Kate Whitworth's life seems to be fraught with just too many problems. Her twelve-year-old daughter is suicidal over her parents' divorce. Then Kate gets the message her stepfather is gone—mysteriously dead in Mexico. This is only the beginning, however, for Kate discovers that the ancient cult responsible for her stepfather's murder needs a virgin sacrifice. Kate's daughter is its intended victim. [Legends, Aztec]

206. Cohen, Barbara. **Roses.** New York: Scholastic, 1985. 256 pp. ISBN 0-590-
A   33602-9. (First published by Lothrop, Lee and Shepard, 1984.)

A modernized version of *Beauty and the Beast* in which Isabel must go to work for a mysterious, deformed florist from whom her father has stolen a rose. At first Isabel is repulsed by her boss, then she grows to like him, but she still cannot bring herself to kiss him when he asks. [Fairy tales]

207. Cohen, Daniel. **The Headless Roommate and Other Tales.** New York:
A   Bantam, 1982. 138 pp. ISBN 0-553-24628-3. (First published by Evans,
      1980.)

Tales with a strong folklore element, including "Introduction—Tales in the Night," "The Headless Roommate," "The Phantom Hitchhiker," "The Babysitter and the Telephone," "The Telltale Seaweed," "The Bordeaux Diligence," "Frat Man," "The Funny Collar," "The Moon in the Middle," "The Death Car," "Surprise!" "The Roommate's Death," "Gramma's Last Trip," "The Boyfriend's Death," "Just the Two of Us," "The Hook," "The Man in the Backseat," "Bugs, Ants, Baby Sneakers, and Spider Eggs," "The Joke," "The Moving Coffin." [Horror; Short stories]

208. Collins, Mabel. **The Idyll of the White Lotus.** Wheaton, Ill.: Re-quest
C   Books, 1974. 142 pp. ISBN 0-8356-0301-6.

Young Sensa of ancient Egypt has been received into priesthood at an early age; only he is able to see the Lady of the White Lotus, a mysterious power who wants Sensa's soul for her own. [Legends, Egyptian; Mysticism]

209. Collins, Nancy A. **Sunglasses after Dark.** New York: Onyx, 1990. 256
C   pp. ISBN 0-451-40147-6.
      Other works: *Tempter.*

In today's society there is an after-dark world of mystery, rock music, drugs, and sex. Many strange people inhabit this world, including some real blood suckers. [Vampires]

210. Collins, Wilkie. **Tales of Terror and the Supernatural.** New York: Dover,
C   1972. 294 pp. ISBN 0-486-20307-7.
      Other works: *The Moonstone; The Woman in White.*

Victorian gothic tales of horror, including "The Dream-Woman," "A Terribly Strange Bed," "The Dead Hand," "Blow Up with the Brig!" "Mr. Lepel and the Housekeeper," "Miss Bertha and the Yankee," "Mr. Policeman and the Cook," "Fauntleroy," "A Stolen Letter," "The Lady of Glenwith Grange," "Mad Monkton," "The Biter Bit." [Horror; Short stories]

211. Combes, Sharon. **Cherron.** New York: Zebra, 1987. 314 pp. ISBN
C   0-8217-2043-0. (First published in 1980.)

Sharon is not a sweet, loving girl at all. In fact, she hates everyone in her family. She hates them enough that she finds super strength within herself to wreak horrible vengeance on them. [Paranormal abilities]

212. Conaway, J. C. **The Magician's Sleeve.** New York: Fawcett, 1979. 221
C   pp. ISBN 0-449-14120-9.

Shy Susannah has been brought up by a strict autocratic aunt. When she goes to art school and meets Michael, a psychiatrist, Susannah believes she finally has a chance for a normal life. But she has terrifying nightmares and scary things keep happening. [Black magic; Legerdemain]

213. Conaway, J. C. **Quarrel with the Moon.** New York: TOR, 1982. 319 pp.
C   ISBN 0-523-48033-4.

Urban sophisticates Josh Holman from the New York Institute of Anthropology and his friend, glamorous model Cresta Farraday, discover a colony that practices strange rites in the Appalachian mountains of West Virginia. Can there really be werewolves roaming the hills? Terrible deaths and disappearances are happening, and there seems to be no possible rational explanation. [Werewolves]

214. Condé, Nicholas. **The Legend.** New York: Signet, 1984. 399 pp. ISBN
C   0-451-13266-1.
     Other works: *In the Deep Woods.*

An adventurous quest to seek gold becomes a nightmare when an ancient Indian god turns its wrath on those who dare to ferret out the secrets of Legend Mountain. [Legends, Native American; Shamanism]

215. Condé, Nicholas. **The Religion.** New York: Signet, 1982. 377 pp. ISBN
C   0-451-12119-8. (Hardcover edition published by New American Library,
     1982. Reissued as *The Believers*, 1987.)
     Movie versions: *The Believers*, 1987. Director: John Schlesinger. Stars:
     Martin Sheen, Helen Shaver, Robert Loggia, Richard Masur, and Elizabeth
     Wilson.

A fascinating story of santeria (modern-day voodoo) practices in urban America today. Anthropologist Cal Jamison is at first only academically interested in the cult's practices, but he discovers to his horror that his seven-year-old son Chris has been targeted as a sacrificial victim. [Voodoo]

216. Conford, Ellen. **And This Is Laura.** New York: Archway, 1977. 183 pp.
B   ISBN 0-671-55504-9. (First published by Little, Brown, 1976.)

Laura comes from a family of superachievers, and she thinks that even her good grades and modest successes aren't enough. Then she discovers her psychic powers, which make her a real hit at school. As her image of the future becomes sinister, however, Laura decides her "gift" may not be so wonderful after all. [Paranormal abilities]

217. Conford, Ellen. **Genie with the Light Blue Hair.** New York: Bantam Star-
A   fire, 1990. 150 pp. ISBN 0-553-28484-3. (First published as a Bantam
      hardcover, 1989.)

One of Jeannie's presents for her fifteenth birthday is a lamp from her aunt and uncle. The lamp turns out to be a magic one, complete with a genie — but this genie is more like Groucho Marx than Barbara Eden! [Magic]

218. Cook, Robin. **Sphinx.** New York: Signet, 1980. 313 pp. ISBN 0-451-09745-
C   9. (First published by Putnam's, 1979.)
      Movie versions: *Sphinx*, 1980. Director: Franklin Schaffner. Stars: Lesley-
      Anne Down, Frank Langella, and Sir John Gielgud.

Much has been said about the strange and awesome curse placed on the ancient tomb of King Tutankhamen. Beautiful Erica is skeptical of these occult tales when she first arrives in Egypt, but she soon learns that there are many supernatural elements that cannot always be understood, even by archaeologists trained in scientific logic. [Legends, Egyptian]

219. Coontz, Otto. **Isle of the Shapeshifters.** New York: Bantam, 1985. 209 pp.
A   ISBN 0-553-24801-4. (First published by Houghton Mifflin, 1983.)

Is it possible for people to change into animals? Theo's visit to Nantucket brings discoveries about this legendary talent as well as new knowledge about her own ancestry. [Manimals; Transformation]

220. Coontz, Otto. **The Night Walkers.** New York: Pocket Books, 1983. 164
A   pp. ISBN 0-671-47523-1. (First published by Houghton Mifflin, 1982.)

Scary things are happening in Covendale, especially to the people. Can one brave teenage girl save herself, or will she become one of *them*? [Science gone wrong]

221. Cooper, Jeffrey. **The Nightmares on Elm Street.** New York: St. Martin's
A   Press, 1987. 216 pp. ISBN 0-312-90517-3.
      Sequels: *The Nightmares on Elm Street: Parts 4 and 5* by Joseph Locke.
      Movie versions: *Nightmare on Elm Street*, 1984. Director: Wes Craven.
      Stars: Heather Langen Kamp, Ronee Blakely, and John Saxon. *Part 2:
      Freddy's Revenge*, 1985. Director: Jack Sholder. Stars: Mark Patton and
      Robert Englund. *Part 3: Dream Warriors*, 1987. Director: Chuck Russell.
      Stars: Chuck Russell, Patricia Arquette, and Robert Englund.

Freddy Krueger is supposed to be dead. But he keeps coming back ... and back ... and back ... and back to Elm Street. First he comes in dreams, then somehow he becomes real, flashing his razor-embellished fingers, intent on revenge for his own horrible death. If you want to stay alive, don't go to sleep! [Dreams]

222.   Cooper, Susan. **Over Sea, Under Stone.** Harmondsworth, England:
B   Puffin, 1968. 221 pp. ISBN 0-14-030362-2. (First published by Harcourt
       Brace, 1966.)
       Sequels: *The Dark Is Rising; Greenwitch; The Grey King; Silver on the
       Tree.*

When Simon, Jane, and Barney go to visit Great-Uncle Merry in Cornwall,
they learn of the magnificent legend of King Arthur and of the grail possessed
with great power. Before their visit is over, they find themselves involved in a
quest as important as any undertaken by King Arthur's knights. [Legends,
Arthurian]

223.   Corelli, Marie. (pseud. of Mary Mills MacKay). **The Mighty Atom.** Lon-
C   don: Sphere, 1975. 190 pp. ISBN 0-7221-2544-5. (First published by
       Hutchinson, 1896.)
       Other works: *A Romance of Two Worlds; Ardath, the Story of a Dead
       Self; The Soul of Lilith; The Sorrows of Satan; Cameos; Ziska.*

An old-fashioned work that deals with the idea of purely intellectual,
brilliant children who can be trained as superbeings. [Science gone wrong]

224.   Corman, Avery. **Oh, God!** New York: Bantam, 1971. 149 pp. ISBN
C   0-553-11422-0.
       Movie versions: *Oh, God!*, 1977. Director: Carl Reiner. Stars: George
       Burns, John Denver, and Teri Garr.

Some years back there was a rumor that God was dead. God decides to come
to earth to find out just what is going on. His arrival is not announced by angels
blowing trumpets but by junk mail flyers inviting the readers to come and talk to
God. This results in some humorous goings-on. [Heaven and hell]

225.   Cormier, Robert. **Fade.** New York: Dell, 1989. 293 pp. ISBN 0-440-
A   20487-9. (First published by Delacorte, 1988.)

Highly respected young adult (YA) author Cormier turns to a different
subject with *Fade*, one that deals with the strange ability of teenager Paul
Moreaux to become invisible. This gift does not bring Paul happiness, however.
A sorrowful and savage tale results. [Paranormal abilities]

226.   Costello, Matthew J. **Sleep Tight.** New York: Zebra, 1987. 302 pp. ISBN
C   0-8217-2121-6.
       Other works: *Child's Play 2; Midsummer; Beneath Still Waters.*

The world of childhood isn't as sweet and innocent as it appears. Children
have terrible fears and even more terrible dreams. Some kids dream about the
bogeyman, but Noah dreams about the Tall Man, and Noah knows the Tall Man
is after is very soul [Dreams]

227.   Coville, Bruce. **Amulet of Doom.** New York: Bantam, 1985. 156 pp.
A   ISBN 0-440-90110-7. (Twilight series).

When Marilyn's adventuresome aunt dies mysteriously, only Marilyn seems
to think that the old Egyptian amulet might have had something to do with it. She
knows for sure when the evil of the amulet turns on her and she finds herself in a
dark and dangerous situation. [Demons; Legends, Egyptian]

228. Coville, Bruce. **Eyes of the Tarot.** New York: Bantam, 1983. 152 pp.
A   ISBN 0-553-23895-7. (Dark Forces series).

Surely the beautiful, strange pack of cards Bonnie finds tucked away in the McBurnie family attic couldn't be harmful. She becomes obsessed with the magical power of the cards and finds herself being sucked into a morass of evil, one from which she may not be able to escape. [Black magic]

229. Coville, Bruce. **Spirits and Spells.** New York: Dell, 1983. 152 pp. ISBN
A   0-440-98151-4. (Twilight series).

Gerry is intrigued with the Spirits and Spells game he finds and decides the old deserted house is just the place in which to play the game. Little do the players realize, however, that the house is perhaps too perfect a place to play, for the game becomes frighteningly real. [Fantasy games]

230. Coville, Bruce. **Waiting Spirits.** New York: Bantam, 1984. 150 pp. ISBN
A   0-553-26004-9. (Dark Forces series).

Lisa and her kid sister Carrie are restless and bored on vacation until their grandmother shows them how to contact the spirit world by means of automatic writing. Suddenly, the game becomes serious business and it looks as if the spirit world has come to be a dangerous and permanent part of Lisa's life. [Spiritualism]

231. Cowan, Dale. **Deadly Sleep.** New York: Dell, 1982. 167 pp. ISBN 0-440-
A   91961-4. (Twilight series).

Jaynie had thought her trip to Scotland to stay with Evelyn and her family would be a pleasant change. Then the strange voices and shimmering glow from the nearby lake remind her constantly of the lake's tragic past, and perhaps of its frightening present. [Ghosts]

232. Coyne, John. **Hobgoblin.** New York: Berkley, 1985. 342 pp. ISBN
C   0-425-05380-6. (First published by G. P. Putnam's Sons, 1981.)
        Other works: *The Legacy; The Shroud; The Hunting Season.*

Scott Gardiner loves playing Hobgoblin, a game in which he always takes the role of Brian Boru. Scott, however, isn't truly playing, for he really believes in monsters. So it doesn't really surprise him very much when he discovers real monsters lurking in his high-school corridors—but then he becomes very scared when he realizes what they're up to. [Fantasy games]

233. Coyne, John. **The Piercing.** New York: Berkley, 1980. 261 pp. ISBN
C   0-425-04563-3. (First published by G. P. Putnam's Sons, 1979.)

Betty Sue has become a national sensation. Some see her weekly stigmata as a miracle and some believe them to be a sham. Father Kinsella decides to investigate, but is he motivated by religious belief or carnal lust? [Legends, Christian; Mysticism]

234. Coyne, John. **The Searing.** New York: Berkley, 1981. 264 pp. ISBN
C   0-425-04924-8. (First published by G. P. Putnam's Sons, 1980.)

Cindy, a beautiful, autistic young girl, attracts everyone's attention. Cindy is viewed with pity by most people, but they do not realize that she is the key to a strange, awesome ecstasy that every woman in town experiences at the same time every evening. [Paranormal abilities]

235.   Crane, Caroline. **The Foretelling.** New York: Signet, 1982. 221 pp. ISBN
C   0-451-12475-8.

Psychics do not always welcome their gifts. Angela Dawn doesn't want to see the future when she looks into other people's hands. But it is worse when she looks into her own palm and sees danger and terror traced in the delicate lines. [Prophecy]

236.   Creasy, John. **Stars for the Toff.** New York: Prestige, 1968. 158 pp.
C

The Toff, famed solver of mysteries, must apply his skills to mysteries of a different nature—those of the occult and astrology. He is determined to save the life of a lovely young fortune-teller, but it is very difficult to anticipate the actions of the supernatural. [Astrology; Occult mystery/detective; Prophecy]

237.   Crowley, Aleister. **Moonchild.** New York: Avon, 1971. 319 pp. (First pub-
A   lished in England, 1917.)

Beautiful Lisa becomes the student of an exciting man with amazing powers who leads her into the hidden world of arcane knowledge. Then a group of evil sorcerers decides to take control of Lisa, and her body and soul become a battleground for occult powers beyond her control. [Magic]

238.   Crume, Vic. **The Ghost That Came Alive.** New York: Scholastic, 1975.
A   126 pp. ISBN 0-590-09912-4.
        Other works: *Mystery in Dracula's Castle.*

When the Blair family leave on vacation, they little suspect they will be forced to seek shelter for the night in a gloomy old mansion. Mysterious noises and goings-on complete the scene of terror. [Ghosts]

239.   Cusick, Richie Tankersley. **Evil on the Bayou.** New York: Dell, 1984.
A   148 pp. ISBN 0-440-92431-6. (Twilight series).
        Other works: *Teacher's Pet.*

Young Meg has been volunteered by her mother to nurse an old aunt. When her aunt recovers mysteriously, Meg knows her amateur skills are not the reason, particularly when odd things, including a strange and sudden death, begin to happen. [Black magic]

240.   Cusick, Richie Tankersley. **Scarecrow.** New York: Pocket Books, 1990.
C   280 pp. ISBN 0-671-69020-5.

Pamela is slowly recovering from a car accident in the seemingly peaceful Ozark hills. But her hosts' daughter Girlie is odd, and soon Pamela learns some of the secrets of the region, including ones about the frightening scarecrows. [Legends, Ozark]

241. Cusick, Richie Tankersley. **Trick or Treat.** New York: Scholastic, 1989.
A 209 pp. ISBN 0-590-44235-X.

When Halloween is coming, people like to play ghoulish tricks. But Martha is sure that the nasty phone calls and other tricks being played on her aren't just for fun—they're real, and the spooky old house she lives in may be the reason. [Halloween; Haunted houses]

242. Cutliffe, Hyne, C. J. **The Lost Continent.** New York: Ballantine, 1972.
C

The lost world of Atlantis, jewel of the ancient world, is rumored to have hosted a fabulous civilization. Here is a re-creation of that strange and beautiful place, a story of another time and place. [Atlantis; Lost lands]

243. Dahl, Roald. **Tales of the Unexpected.** Harmondsworth, England: Pen-
C guin, 1979. 282 pp. ISBN 0-14-005131-7. New York: Vintage, 1979. 471
pp. ISBN 0-394-74081-5. (First published by Michael Joseph, 1979.)
Other works: *Kiss, Kiss; Someone Like You; Charlie and the Chocolate Factory; James and the Giant Peach.*

An anthology of strange and macabre stories, some first published in other collections by the author, was the basis for a television series. American and English editions have the same contents, including these scrumptious little morsels: "Taste," "Lamb to the Slaughter," "Man from the South," "My Lady Love, My Dove," "Dip in the Pool," "Galloping Foxley," "Skin," "Neck," "Nunc Dimittis," "The Landlady," "William and Mary," "The Way Up to Heaven," "Parson's Pleasure," "Mrs. Bixby and the Colonel's Coat," "Royal Jelly," "Edward the Conquerer." [Horror; Short stories]

244. D'Ammassa, Don. **Blood Beast.** New York: Pinnacle, 1988. 384 pp.
C ISBN 1-55817-096-0.

Most people think the ugly old carved gargoyle high over the Sheffield library door is just an old-fashioned architectural ornament. But the gargoyle is more than cold stone, it is a savage monster ready to do its master's bidding. [Monsters]

245. Daniel, Colin. **Demon Tree.** New York: Dell, 1983. 153 pp. ISBN 0-440-
A 92097-3. (Twilight series).

Maggie is the new girl in town, and she begins to think there are some very strange things going on in Wells. Even the fog seems oppressive and frightening. In the middle of Wells there is a big old oak tree that Maggie finds herself avoiding whenever she can. She also avoids the people, who are just plain peculiar. [Cults]

246. Daniels, Dorothy. **Dark Island.** New York: Warner, 1972. 206 pp. ISBN
C 0-446-65626-7.
Other works: *Castle Morvant; The House of Broken Dolls; Witch's Castle; Diablo Manor; The Dark Stage; Darkhaven; Lady of the Shadows; House of False Faces; Mystic Manor; The Ancient Evil.*

Janet's brother is missing in mysterious Haiti, and Janet stays on the island illegally after her cruise ship leaves in hope of finding him. What she finds, however, is the terrible power of voodoo and a great fascination for her reluctant host on the island. [Gothic romance; Voodoo]

247.　Daniels, Dorothy. **Image of a Ghost.** New York: Warner, 1973. 175 pp.
C　　ISBN 0-446-75400-5.

Karen Kingsley seems to have it all. She's rich and beautiful and free to lead her own life as she will. Then one day Karen sees pictures of her mother in a French magazine, but it's not really her mother, for these are pictures of a ghost. [Ghosts; Gothic romance]

248.　Daniels, Gail. **Cancer, the Moonchild.** New York: Pacer, 1985. 160 pp.
A　　ISBN 0-448-47741-6. (Zodiac Club series).

When Mara goes on a family vacation after breaking up with her boyfriend, she isn't sure whether she believes the Chinese fortune-teller who tells her that a new fellow will soon enter her life. Includes Chinese horoscope information. [Astrology]

249.　Daniels, Gail. **The Stars Unite.** New York: Pacer Berkley, 1984. 160 pp.
A　　ISBN 0-399-21106-3. (Zodiac Club series).

Abby becomes very enthusiastic about astrology and persuades her friends to form an astrology club. Their new interest leads them into some very interesting situations, not to mention some star-crossed relationships. Includes compatibility charts. [Astrology]

250.　Daniels, Les. **The Black Castle.** New York: Ace, 1983. 240 pp. ISBN
C　　0-44-06515-5. (First published by Charles Scribner's Sons, 1978.)
　　　Sequels: *The Silver Skull; Citizen Vampire; Yellow Fog; No Blood Spilled.*

Don Sebastian is a vampire, but his secret is guarded by his brother, a Grand Inquisitor who provides his cursed brother with blood from the victims in his dungeons. [Vampires]

251.　Daniels, Philip. **The Dracula Murders.** New York: Lorevan, 1986. 190 pp.
C　　ISBN 0-931773-81-4. (First published by Robert Hale, 1983.)

It all starts with a Festival of Horror Ball, but before it is over there is a ritualistic murder and the shocking evidence that a real vampire is loose on the golf course. [Vampires]

252.　Dantz, William R. **Pulse.** New York: Avon, 1990. 284 pp. ISBN 0-380-
C　　75714-1.

Dr. Susan Cullen, a medical pathologist and troubleshooter, is sent to winter-gripped Maine to investigate a frightening phenomenon, corpses that refuse to die. There she undercovers a plot that could change the world. [Science gone wrong]

253. Darby, Catherine. **Moon in Pisces.** New York: Popular Library, 1978.
C   221 pp. ISBN 0-445-041838-8.
     Other works: *Whisper Down the Moon; Frost on the Moon; The Flaunting Moon; Sing Me a Moon; Cobweb Across the Moon.*

Lucy Bostock was orphaned at an early age, but she was lucky. She was taken in by loving relatives who whisked her away from perilous nineteenth-century London to their country manor. But Lucy cannot leave all the peril behind, for she has been marked by an ancient power for a special existence. [Evil]

254. Darke, Marjorie. **Messages: A Collection of Shivery Tales.** Harmonds-
A   worth, England: Puffin, 1985. 140 pp. ISBN 0-14-031749-X. (First published by Viking Kestrel, 1984.)

A collection of mysterious and scary stories, including "Messages," "A New Way with Old Transport," "Truth, Dare or Promise?" "Christmas Spook," "Now You See Me, Now You Don't!" "Close Encounter of Another Kind," "Eggshell Saturday," "Peanut." [Ghosts; Short stories]

255. David, Peter. **Howling Mad.** New York: Ace, 1989. 201 pp. ISBN 0-441-
C   34663-4.

When werewolves bite people, the people turn into werewolves, too. But when a werewolf bites a wolf, the poor creature finds himself "raised" from his totally bestial state to the "more civilized" existence of partial humanness. The poor beast-man finds more than he ever dreamed of in the streets of New York City as he/it tries to adjust to a different kind of life-style. [Werewolves]

256. Davidson, Avram and Grania Davis. **Marco Polo and the Sleeping Beauty.**
C   New York: Baen, 1988. 300 pp. ISBN 0-671-65372-5.

Marco Polo, true-life adventurer, spent a number of years in the fabled ancient Cathay. In this tale, Marco and his father and uncle are sent by Kublai Khan to rescue a mysterious princess who sleeps forever in eternal beauty. [Fairy tales]

257. Davies, Robertson. **High Spirits: A Collection of Ghost Stories.** Har-
C   mondsworth, England: Penguin, 1982. 198 pp. ISBN 01400.65069.

A collection of original ghost stories in the English Christmas ghost-story tradition by a noted Canadian author and humorist. Contents include "How the High Spirits Came About (A Chapter of Autobiography)," "Revelation from a Smoky Fire," "The Ghost Who Vanished by Degrees," "The Great Queen Is Amused," "The Night of the Three Kings," "The Charlottetown Banquet," "When Satan Goes Home for Christmas," "Refuge of Insulted Saints," "Dickens Digested," "The Kiss of Khrushchev," "The Cat That Went to Trinity," "The Ugly Spectre of Sexism," "The Pit Whence Ye Are Digged," "The Perils of the Double Sign," "Conversations with the Little Table," "The King Enjoys His Own Again," "The Xerox in the Lost Room," "Einstein and the Little Lord," "Offer of Immortality." [Ghosts; Short stories]

258. Davis, Don, and Jay Davis. **Sins of the Flesh.** New York: TOR, 1989. 400
C pp. ISBN 0-812-51679-6.

Jesse Sikes was turned into a raving bestial monster, and his mother has kept him imprisoned in the farm's root cellar. Now she is dying, and Jesse knows he can finally escape to wreak havoc and evil once more. [Monsters]

259. Davis, Maggie. **Forbidden Objects.** New York: TOR, 1986. 276 pp. ISBN
C 0-812-51687-7.

There often seems to be a more leisured pace to life in the South, but Frankie finds that an idle game with her cousin Julian will turn their lives into a frightening experience with old, alien powers. [Voodoo]

260. Deaver, Jeffery Wilds. **Voodoo.** Toronto, Ont.: PaperJacks, 1988. 265
C pp. ISBN 0-7701-0772-9.

Eleanor Bowers is the victim of an attack on her visit to the Caribbean, but she thinks it's over when she returns to her usual life in New York. But voodoo has a long reach, not bound by geographic borders. Eleanor is far from safe. [Voodoo]

261. DeClements, Barthe, and Christopher Greimes. **Double Trouble.** New
B York: Scholastic, 1988. 168 pp. ISBN 0-590-41248-5. (First published by
Viking Penguin, 1987.)

Faith and Phillip are orphaned twins, separated physically but able to communicate through special psychic bonds. Their special abilities have a way of getting them into trouble yet may be able to save them. [Paranormal abilities]

262. Dee, Ron. **Blood Lust.** New York: Dell, 1990. 264 pp. ISBN 0-440-20567-0.
C

One doesn't expect to find vampires in a St. Louis suburb, but an exceptionally charming one is on the loose, even seducing a minister's wife into leaving her husband. It's really hard to say no to a vampire when he offers such sexual thrills. [Vampires]

263. DeFelitta, Frank. **Audrey Rose.** New York: Warner, 1975. 462 pp. ISBN
C 0-446-36380-4. (First published by Putnam, 1975.)
Sequels: *For Love of Audrey Rose.* Other works: *The Entity.* Movie
versions: *Audrey Rose,* 1977. Director: Robert Wise. Stars: Marsha
Mason, John Beck, and Anthony Hopkins.

Can Ivy Templeton really be Audrey Rose, a young girl who died in a tragic automobile accident? Her parents become more and more uncertain as strange, eerie events take place. [Reincarnation]

264. DeFelitta, Frank. **Golgotha Falls: An Assault on the Fourth Dimension.**
C New York: Pocket Books, 1984. 341 pp. ISBN 0-671-50776-1. (First published by Simon & Schuster, 1984.)

An unhappy town has shut itself off from the world, but evil still seems to stalk its streets. Can the town be rid of its pervasive horror, or will it remain forever a site of satanic power? Will the combined power of one priest and two scientists be enough to overpower Satan? [Evil; Exorcism]

265. Delap, Richard, and Walt Lee. **Shapes.** New York: Charter 1987. 324 pp.
C   ISBN 0-441-76103-8.

Their upcoming marriage is what's primarily on Duane's and Maria's minds. But Duane has become nervous, and it seems to be more than wedding jitters. There's a vague "thing" out there somewhere, and the "thing" wants a mate, too. [Monsters]

266. de Lint, Charles. **Moonheart.** New York: Ace, 1984. 485 pp. ISBN
C   0-441-53721-9.
     Other works: *Jack the Giant Killer; The Riddle of the Wren; Greenmantle; The Little Country.*

Sara Kendall loves old things, antiques and historic tales. She has a curiosity about fantasy and how it may touch the real world, but she is amazed when somehow she finds herself involved not only in ancient Celtic beliefs but in Canadian Indian lore as well. [Legends, Celtic; Legends, Native American]

267. de Lint, Charles. **Mulengro: A Romany Tale.** New York: Ace, 1985. 351
C   pp. ISBN 0-441-54484-3.

There are many different ethnic groups in Ottawa, Canada, and one of the groups is the gypsies. Their culture has long been shrouded in mystery. Yet their ways are not so different, for they too have fears and know the evils of strange beings. Now they know the new terror that walks the streets—Mulengro—He Who Walks with Ghosts. [Gypsy lore]

268. de Lint, Charles. **Wolf Moon.** New York: Signet, 1988. 252 pp. ISBN
C   0-451-15487-8.

He used to be a normal sort of fellow, but then he turned into a werewolf and his life seemed changed forever. Kern finds himself lonely and unable to make friends. He has a powerful enemy, too, the sorcerous harper Tuiloch, who may keep Kern from the woman he loves. [Werewolves]

269. de Lint, Charles. **Yarrow: An Autumn Tale.** New York: Ace, 1986. 244
C   pp. ISBN 0-441-94000-5.

Cat Midheir, a fantasy writer living in Ottawa, balances her world of reality and dreams very nicely, and her dreams serve as inspiration for her stories. Then Lysistratus, the thief of dreams, steals Cat's sleeping fantasies, and Cat must go on a quest to get them back. [Dreams]

270. De Maupassant, Guy. **The Dark Side.** New York: Carroll & Graf, 1990.
C   252 pp. ISBN 0-88184-596-5. (First published by Carroll & Graf as a hard-
     cover, 1989.)

Somber tales by the nineteenth-century French writer of inexplicable happenings and the evil humans are capable of, includes "The Horla," "The Devil," "Two Friends," "Fear," "The Hand," "Coco," "The Mannerism," "The Madwoman," "Mohammed-Fripouille," "The Blind Man," "At Sea," "Apparition,"

"Saint-Antoine," "The Wolf," "Terror," "The Diary of a Madman," "A Vendetta," "The Smile of Schopenhauer," "On the River," "He?" "Old Milon," "The Head of Hair," "The Inn," "Mother Savage," "Was He Mad?" "The Dead Girl," "Mademoiselle Cocotte," "A Night in Paris," "The Case of Louise Roque," "The Drowned Man," "Who Knows?" [Horror; Short stories]

271.   De Maupassant, Guy. **Tales of Supernatural Terror.** London: Pan, 1972.
C   160 pp. ISBN 0-330-23397-1.

Disquieting tales of happenings that cannot be easily explained includes "The Hand," "Fear," "He?" "On the River," "Apparition," "The Spastic Mannerism," "Terror," "The Inn," "The Smile of Schopenhauer," "Was He Mad?" "The Wolf," "The Horla," "The Drowned Man," "The Dead Girl," "A Night in Paris," "Who Knows?" [Horror; Short stories]

272.   Denham, Alice. **The Ghost and Mrs. Muir.** New York: Popular Library,
A   1968. 127 pp. (See also entry 624.)

Captain Gregg is not everyone's idea of a perfect object for romance. He's gruff, bad tempered, and, in addition, he's dead. But Carolyn Muir shares her seaside cottage with the crusty ghost and the two learn to respect and appreciate each other. (Novelization based on the television series.) [Ghosts]

273.   DeWeese, Gene. **The Wanting Factor.** Chicago: Playboy, 1980. 303 pp.
C   ISBN 0-872-16693-7.

It's sometimes scary being a psychic, and Evanne discovers that her strange ability leads her to a network of horror in the seemingly normal college town where people are "losing" their souls. [Paranormal abilities]

274.   DeWeese, Jean. **The Carnelian Cat.** New York: Ballantine, 1975. 184 pp.
C   ISBN 0-345-24566-0. (Birthstone Gothic series).

Sorina is staying at the old West House in order to write the Howard family history, a tragic family mysteriously murdered the year before. At first she is only puzzled by the strange and beautiful cat with a carnelian charm around its neck; then she realizes the cat is a guide to another world, a past world of death. [Gothic romance]

275.   DeWeese, Jean. **The Moonstone Spirit.** New York: Ballantine, 1975. 183
C   pp. SBN 345-244706-X-095. (Birthstone Gothic series).

Venora Arlen is shocked by the suicide of her friend Julie. After receiving Julie's moonstone pendant, Venora finds herself dreaming — and even worse, knowing — that she must live through Julie's final days and death. [Gothic romance; Possession]

276.   Dickens, Charles. **The Complete Ghost Stories of Charles Dickens.** New
C   York: Washington Square, 1982. 408 pp. ISBN 0-671-49752-9.
         Other works: *The Supernatural Short Stories of Charles Dickens.* Movie
         versions: *A Christmas Carol*, 1951. Director: Brian Desmond Hurst. Stars:
         Alistair Sim, Kathleen Harrison, Jack Warner, and Michael Hordern. *A
         Christmas Carol*, 1984. Director: Clive Donner. Stars: George C. Scott,
         Nigel Davenport, Frank Finlay, and Edward Woodward.

Ghost stories by a famous English Victorian author, including "Captain Murderer's and the Devil's Bargain," "The Lawyer and the Ghost," "The Queer Chair," "The Ghosts of the Mail," "A Madman's Manuscript," "The Story of the Goblins Who Stole a Sexton," "Baron Koeldwethout's Apparition," "A Christmas Carol," "The Haunted Man and the Ghost's Bargain," "A Child's Dream of a Star," "Christmas Ghosts," "To Be Read at Dusk," "The Ghost Chamber," "The Haunted House," "Mr. Testator's Visitation," "The Trial for Murder," "The Signal-Man," "Four Ghost Stories," "The Portrait-Painter's Story," "Well-Authenticated Rappings." [Ghosts; Short stories]

277. Dickens, Charles. **The Haunted Man and the Haunted House.** Gloucester,
C   England: Alan Sutton, 1985. 123 pp. ISBN 0-86299-2144-1.

Two stories by an English master of ghost stories, one about a man who is said to be haunted by nameless fears and the other about a mysterious house that is so ominous that no one will go near it. [Ghosts; Haunted houses]

278. Dickens, Charles. **The Signalman and Other Ghost Stories.** Chicago:
C   Academy Chicago, 1988. 138 pp. ISBN 0-89733-307-1.

Spooky stories by an English master craftsman, including "The Signalman," "A Madman's Manuscript," "The Bagman's Story," "The Story of the Goblins Who Stole a Sexton," "The Story of the Bagman's Uncle," "The Baron of Grogzwig," "A Confession Found in a Prison in the Time of Charles the Second," "To Be Read at Dusk," "The Trial for Murder," "A Child's Dream of a Star," "Christmas Ghosts," "The Hanged Man's Bride," "Mr. Testator's Visitation." [Ghosts; Short stories]

279. Dickens, Monica. **The Haunting of Bellamy 4.** London: Fontana, 1986.
B   123 pp. ISBN 0-00-692646-0. (First published by William Collins Sons, 1986.)
     Sequels: *The Messenger; Ballad of Favour.*

The author, a great-granddaughter of Charles Dickens, spins a tale of Rose, Messenger of the Great Grey Horse, who must confront many dangers in order to solve the mystery of the frightening hospital ward. [Time travel]

280. Dickinson, Peter. **The Gift.** Harmondsworth, England: Puffin, 1975.
A   172 pp. ISBN 0-14-030731-1. (First published by Victor Gollancz, 1973.)
     Other works: *Annerton Pit; The Blue Hawk.*

Davy Price is able to see what others are thinking, truly a gift. Davy is fearful of his gift but finds he cannot shirk his duty, and he must use it to help his father. [Paranormal abilities]

281. Dickinson, Peter. **Healer.** Harmondsworth, England: Puffin, 1985. 214
A   pp. ISBN 0-575-03314-2. (First published in the United States by Delacorte, 1985.)

Pinkie Blackfoot is a healer and has few friends other than Barry Evans, her protector. Barry struggles to free Pinkie from her stepfather, who is exploiting her talents for his own gains, but finds greater dangers than he anticipated. [Paranormal abilities]

282.   Dickinson, Peter. **Tulku.** New York: Tempo, 1984. 216 pp. ISBN 0-441-
C   82630-X. (First published in the United States by Dutton, 1979.)

When young Theodore's father orders him to leave their besieged Chinese mission during the Boxer Rebellion, Theodore little suspects that he will end up in distant Tibet where magic and demons are real. [Legends, Tibetan; Mysticism]

283.   Dicks, Terrance. **Cry Vampire!** London: Hippo, 1985. 105 pp. ISBN
B   0-590-70405-2. (First published by Blackie and Son, 1981.)

Simon was always leery of the dark old house and when new tenants arrive from Transylvania, Simon is sure something is not quite right. Then animals start to suffer from loss of blood and Anna Markos disappears. Simon is sure vampires are to blame, but only his friend Sally believes him. [Vampires]

284.   Dickson, Carter (pseud. of John Dickson Carr). **The Plague Court Mur-
C   ders.** New York: International Polygonics, 1990. 312 pp. ISBN
       1-55882-062-0. (First published by William Morrow, 1934.)

In the first Sir Henry Merrivale detective novel, the dauntless crime-solver becomes involved with the ghost of Plague Court and a murdered psychic. [Haunted houses; Occult mystery/detective]

285.   Dinesen, Isak (pseud. of Karen Blixen). **Last Tales.** New York: Vintage,
C   1975. 341 pp. ISBN 0-394-71552-X. (First published by Curtis Publishing,
       1955.)
       Other works include *Winter's Tales; Angelic Avengers.*

Mysterious unworldly atmosphere haunts these stories by the master Danish writer, including "The Cardinal's First Tale," "The Cloak," "Night Walk," "Of Secret Thoughts and of Heaven," "Tales of Two Old Gentlemen," "The Cardinal's Third Tale," "The Blank Page," "The Caryatids: An Unfinished Gothic Tale," "Echoes," "A Country Tale," "Copenhagen Season," "Converse at Night in Copenhagen." [Mysticism; Short stories.]

286.   Dinesen, Isak. **Seven Gothic Tales.** New York: Vintage, 1972. 420 pp.
C   ISBN 0-394-74291-5. (First published by Random House, 1934.)

More mysterious stories by a greatly admired writer, including "The Deluge at Norderney," "The Old Chevalier," "The Monkey," "The Roads Round Pisa," "The Supper at Elsinore," "The Dreamers," "The Poet." [Mysticism; Short stories]

287.   Dobson, Margaret. **Soothsayer.** New York: Dell, 1987. 187 pp. ISBN
C   0-440-18149-6.

Jane Bailey might be assumed by some people to lead a placid life since she works in her aunt's bookstore. But her boyfriend, Phillip, keeps her busy in other ways, particularly with his detective cases. When Jane agrees to assist Phillip in finding Howard Springer, she gets involved with not only a missing person but his psychic mother as well. [Paranormal abilities]

288. Doherty, P. C. **Satan in St. Mary's.** New York: St. Martin's Press, 1989.
C   186 pp. ISBN 0-312-91357-5. (First published by Robert Hale, 1986.)
       Other works: *The Crown in Darkness: The Death of a King.*

The reign of Edward the First in England is a troubled time. Hugh Corbett's work as a clerk is generally a bit dreary, but he is called in to help solve mysterious goings-on precipitated by the secret societies of Simon de Montfort, aristocratic rebel and devil-worshiper. [Cults; Satanism]

289. Dohrman, Richard. **The Gatehouse.** New York: Dell, 1973. 396 pp. SBN
C   440-02812-150. (First published by Delacorte, 1971.)

The old gatehouse was strangely appealing to Carla, but after she moves in she finds herself possessed by unnatural sexual cravings that compel her to encourage the advances of many. Could she be possessed by the spirit of the gatehouse's former owner, a depraved degenerate? [Gothic romances; Possession]

290. Donner, Florinda. **The Witch's Dream.** New York: **Pocket Books, 1986.**
C   306 pp. ISBN 0-671-55202-3. (First published by Simon & Schuster, 1985.)

The supposedly factual account of a young woman's apprenticeship to a witch in Venezuela who is steeped in the ancient lore of her people. [Shamanism]

291. Donoso, Jose. **A House in the Country.** Harmondsworth, England:
C   Penguin, 1985. 352 pp. ISBN 0-14-007142-3. (First published as *Casa de Campo* by Seix Barral, 1978.)

A large family has gathered in the country at Marulanda, a beautiful old family dwelling. The Venturas are a family of power, but even the powerful are not exempt from strange happenings. One lovely sunny day the adult members of the family leave on a picnic, leaving the younger generation behind with crazy Uncle Adriano. The children believe they may have been deserted forever, and the macabre adventures begin. [Mysticism]

292. Douglas, Gregory A. **The Nest.** New York: Zebra, 1980. 448 pp. ISBN
C   0-89083-662-0.

Idyllic Cape Cod is a favorite vacation spot for many, but when the huge mutant insects leave their breeding ground to feast on human flesh, this Massachusetts resort area becomes a place of horror. [Monsters]

293. Downie, Jill. **The Raven in the Glass.** Toronto, Ont.: PaperJacks, 1987.
C   471 pp. ISBN 0-7701-0699-4.

At the turn of the century, two of the most exciting cities in the world were New York and Vienna. Beth Holman lives in a life of pampered ease in New York, and Gisela Valeska resides in a Vienna populated by exciting people such as her guardian, the magician Arcanus. Arcanus has strange and wonderful powers, powers he must use in order to save both Gisela and Beth from the evil plans of the fascinating Austrian count who has seemingly bewitched both girls. [Magic]

294. Doyle, Arthur Conan. **The Best Horror Stories of Arthur Conan Doyle.**
C   Chicago: Academy Chicago, 1989. 294 pp. ISBN 0-89733-265-2.

Scary stories from a master craftsman, including "The Captain of the Polestar," "The Case of Lady Sannox," "The Bend of the Cooperage," "The Horror of the Heights," "J. Habakukk Jephson's Statement," "John Barrington Cowles," "The Leather Funnel," "The Lift," "Lot No. 249," "The New Catacomb," "The Silver Hatchet," "The Striped Chest," "The Terror of Blue John Gap." [Horror; Short stories]

295. Doyle, Arthur Conan. **The Best Supernatural Tales of Arthur Conan**
C **Doyle.** New York: Dover, 1979. 302 pp. ISBN 0-486-23725-7.

The creator of Sherlock Holmes was fascinated by the occult and wrote a number of short stories dealing with unusual happenings, including "The Bully of Brocas Court," "The Captain of the Polestar," "The Brown Hand," "The Leather Funnel," "Lot No. 249," "J. Habakukk Jephson's Statement," "The Great Keinplatz Experiment," "A Literary Mosaic," "Playing with Fire," "The Ring of Thoth," "The Los Amigos Fiasco," "The Silver Hatchet," "John Barrington Cowles," "Selecting a Ghost," "The American's Tale." [Horror; Short stories]

296. Draco, F. **The Devil's Church.** New York: Lancer, 1969. 176 pp. ISBN
C 0-447-75195-0. (First published by Holt, Rinehart and Winston, 1951.)

The Tintagel family is an old, respected English family, but one with a history of evil. The youngest baron has married a lively young American woman who seems to bring happiness and light to the old mansion, which looks rather like a church. As a matter of fact, the mansion was a church once, but a church devoted to the devil rather than to God. [Satanism]

297. Drake, David. **The Dragon Lord.** New York: TOR, 1979. 320 pp. ISBN
C 0-812-53605-3.

The legend of Arthur told as a sword-and-sorcery adventure tale, with witches, dragons, and magic galore. [Legends, Arthurian]

298. Drake, David. **From the Heart of Darkness.** New York: TOR, 1983. 320
C pp. ISBN 0-812-53607-X

Tales of weirdness by an experienced, respected short-story writer, including "Men Like Us," "Something Had to Be Done," "The Automatic Rifleman," "Than Curse the Darkness," "Firefight," "The Red Leer," "The Shortest Way," "Best of Luck," "Dragons' Teeth," "Out of Africa," "The Dancer in the Flames," "Smokie Joe," "Children of the Forest," "Blood Debt," "The Barrow Troll," "The Hunting Ground." [Horror; Short stories]

299. Dreadstone, Carl. **Dracula's Daughter.** New York: Berkley, 1977. (Noveli-
C zation based on Bram Stoker's novella *Dracula's Guest*.) 212 pp. ISBN
0-425-03463-1.
Other works: *The Bride of Frankenstein; The Creature from the Black Lagoon; The Werewolf of London: The Wolfman.* Movie versions: *Dracula's Daughter*, 1936. Director: Lambert Hillyer. Stars: Gloria Holden, Otto Kruger, Marguerite Churchill, Irving Pichel, and Edward Van Sloan.

Young women sometimes find their fathers, even dead ones, hard to take. Dracula's daughter thinks her life is intolerable even though she is a wealthy countess. Yet her heritage cannot be denied, and she must play out her part as the descendant of the world's most famous vampire. [Vampires]

300. Dreadstone, Carl. **The Mummy.** New York: Berkley, 1977. 166 pp. ISBN
C   0-425-03445-3.
     Movie versions: *The Mummy*, 1932. Director: Karl Freund. Stars: Boris Karloff, Zita Johann, and David Manners.

When Dr. Muller decides to unwrap the ancient mummy, he has no idea that the Grand Priest Imhotep still has power, a terrible power that will affect everyone who stands in his way. [Legends, Egyptian; Mummies]

301. Drew, Wayland. **Dragonslayer.** New York: Ballantine/Del Rey, 1981. 218
A   pp. ISBN 0-345-32306-8.
     Movie versions: *Dragonslayer*, 1981. Director: Matthew Robbins. Stars: Peter MacNicol, Catlin Clarke, and Ralph Richardson.

Long ago there were still dragons to be found, fearsome dragons that terrorized the countryside and demanded the flesh of fair young virgins. In desperation the frightened people turn to Ulrich the sorcerer for help, but in the end it is his young assistant Galen who becomes the dragonslayer. [Dragons]

302. Dubbs, Chris. **Ms. Faust.** New York: Popular Library, 1987. 296 pp.
C   ISBN 0-445-20416-8. (First published by Richardson & Steirman, 1985.)

Rita Brandt is an assertive and ambitious career woman, willing to do anything to get ahead. She is even willing to make the ultimate deal with you-know-who to attain her goals. [The devil]

303. Duigon, Lee. **Lifeblood.** New York: Pinnacle, 1988. 432 pp. ISBN
C   1-55817-110-X.

Winslow Emerson is delighted with his new home of Millboro, New Jersey, a town full of neglected children whose busy parents are too involved in their own career pursuits to realize that the new doctor in town is not quite human. [Vampires]

304. Duigon, Lee. **Precog.** New York: Pinnacle, 1990. 288 pp. ISBN 1-55817-
C   304-8.

At first glance you'd think Robin was an average teenager with more interest in his baseball games than schoolwork. Robin's parents, both brilliant success stories, decide this isn't good enough, so Robin is sent to Biotechnix Institute to stimulate his mental capacities. Nobody expects, however, that this process will result in new, awesome powers for Robin. [Paranormal abilities; Science gone wrong]

305. Du Maurier, Daphne. **Don't Look Now.** New York: Dell, 1985. 320 pp.
C   ISBN 0-440-12122-1. (First published in the United States by Doubleday, 1971.)
     Other works: *Echoes from the Macabre: Selected Stories; Rebecca.* Movie versions: *Don't Look Now*, 1973. Director: Nicholas Roeg. Stars: Julie Christie and Donald Sutherland.

Stories dealing with possibilities of the supernatural in the lives of ordinary people, such as "Don't Look Now," "A Borderline Case," "The Breakthrough," "Not after Midnight," "The Way of the Cross." [Horror; Short stories]

306. Dunbar, Robert. **The Pines.** New York: Leisure, 1989. 359 pp. ISBN
C   0-8439-2800-X.

The Pine Barrens of New Jersey have long been reputed to be the home of a mysterious being, the Jersey Devil. Athena Monroe, a young widow living in the barrens with her son, finds something spooky about the area, although she finds it impossible to believe that the devil is real. [Legends, New Jersey]

307. Duncan, Lois. **Down a Dark Hall.** New York: Laurel-Leaf, 1983. 181 pp.
A   ISBN 0-440-91805-7. (First published by Little, Brown, 1974.)
     Other works: *Killing Mr. Griffin; Daughters of Eve; Ransom; The Twisted Window; They Never Came Back; Don't Look Behind You.*

Kit is unhappy at being sent to Blackwood, an exclusive school for girls, while her mother goes to Europe on a honeymoon trip. Then she decides the school will be okay when she meets the handsome piano teacher. She discovers, however, that her initial fears were not idle fancies, for there is a horrible evil at work in the school as the students develop strange new and obsessive talents. [Possession]

308. Duncan, Lois. **A Gift of Magic.** New York: Archway, 1972. 201 pp. ISBN
A   0-671-60110-5. (First published by Little, Brown, 1971.)

Nancy has special powers, abilities that frighten her at first. She learns to conceal them but finds that she cannot always make them do what she wants. [Paranormal abilities]

309. Duncan, Lois. **Locked in Time.** New York: Dell, 1986. 210 pp. ISBN
A   0-440-94942-4. (First published by Little, Brown, 1985.)

Nore arrives in Baton Rouge to spend the summer with her father and his new family. The strange and different environment diverts Nore at first, but then the dreams she's been having ever since her mother died gain in intensity. She also becomes very uneasy about Shadow Grove, her new family's home, and about her new stepmother, Lisette. [Eternal youth]

310. Duncan, Lois. **Stranger with My Face.** New York: Laurel-Leaf, 1981.
A   235 pp. ISBN 0-440-98356-8. (First published by Little, Brown, 1981.)

Laurie thinks her life is nearly perfect as the wonderful summer starts. Then she starts to have strange feelings and realizes that she is never alone. Who, or what, is the evil presence trying to take over Laurie's body, and maybe even her soul? [Possession]

311. Duncan, Lois. **Summer of Fear.** New York: Laurel-Leaf, 1977. 219 pp.
A   ISBN 0-440-98324-X. (First published by Little, Brown, 1976.)
     Movie versions: *Stranger in Our House*, 1978. Director: Wes Craven. Stars: Linda Blair, Lee Purcell, Jeremy Slate, Carol Lawrence, Macdonald Carey, Jeff McCracken.

Rachel's cousin Julia has just lost her parents and arrives to stay with Rachel's family. Everybody seems to like Julia, but Rachel senses something very wrong about her. Only Rachel seems able to recognize that Julia is unnatural, and only Rachel will be able to save herself from this frightening menace. [Witchcraft]

312. Duncan, Lois. **The Third Eye.** New York: Laurel-Leaf, 1985. 220 pp.
A   ISBN 0-440-98720-2. (First published by Little, Brown, 1984.)

In her senior year of high school Karen discovers she has psychic powers that can be used to help the police find lost children. Karen finds, however, that her special power puts a damper on her love life until she discovers that romance doesn't always come only with high-school boys. [Paranormal abilities]

313. Dunlop, Eileen. **Robinsheugh.** New York: Ace, 1986. 201 pp. ISBN
C   0-441-73201-1. (First published as *Swallow* by Oxford University Press, 1975.)
     Other works: *A Flute in Mayferry Street.*

Elizabeth is furious at being shipped off to her aunt's while her parents visit America. She knows she'll hate Scotland and is miserable at the thought of the time she'll have to spend there. Then she discovers the silver mirror, which somehow allows her to escape into time. At first it's fun to have a secret place to hide in, but then Elizabeth discovers that she can no longer control the mirror; the mirror is controlling her. [Time travel]

314. Dunn, Pauline (pseud. of Daun Dunn and Suzy Hartzell). **Demonic Color.**
C   New York: Zebra, 1990. 351 pp. ISBN 0-8217-3143-2.

Town, Indiana, seems on the surface to be a typical peaceful small town. But then Jimmy Arnold is cruelly murdered, and it is obvious that something abnormal is loose in Town, something that will change the little community forever. [Demons]

315. Eco, Umberto. **Foucault's Pendulum.** New York: Ballantine, 1990. 533 pp.
C   ISBN 0-345-36875-4. (First published in the United States by Harcourt Brace Jovanovich, 1988.)

Three publishing-house editors have become bored with the constant stream of occult manuscripts passing through their hands, and together they conceive the ultimate occult plot based on historical hints and facts. To their horror, however, they find that their occult plot is not just a game but a real and frightening possibility. [Cults; Illuminati; Knights Templar]

316. Egan, Robert and Louise Egan. **Little Shop of Horrors.** New York: Peri-
A   gee, 1986. 79 pp. ISBN 0-399-51319-1.
     Movie versions: *Little Shop of Horrors*, 1960. Director: Roger Corman. Stars: Dick Miller, Jonathan Haze, Jackie Joseph, and Myrtle Vail. *Little Shop of Horrors*, 1986. Director: Frank Oz. Stars: Rick Moranis, Ellen Green, and Vincent Gardenia.

Mushnik's floral shop in Skid Row is not doing well, that is, until nebish employee Seymour develops Audrey II, a most unusual plant with a very unusual taste in plant food. (This novelization is based on the 1986 musical movie version.) [Monsters]

317. Ehly, Ehren M. **Obelisk.** New York: Leisure, 1988. 392 pp. ISBN 0-8439-
C   2612-0.

Steve Harrison is overcome by memories of a far distant past dominated by
ancient Egyptian customs. This domination is an evil power that is draining Steve
of his life and soul. It is a power he cannot escape, not even in modern-day New
York. [Legends, Egyptian]

318. Ehrlich, Max. **The Cult.** New York: Bantam, 1979. 306 pp. ISBN 0-553-
C   12399-8. (First published by Simon and Schuster, 1978.)
      Other works: *The Glass Web; Reincarnation in Venice.*

The parents of the neophytes are frantic. They'll do anything to get their kids
back from the charismatic leader who has them enthralled. But sometimes people
go too far, and death can be the only answer. [Cults]

319. Ehrlich, Max. **The Reincarnation of Peter Proud.** New York: Bantam,
C   1975. 276 pp. ISBN 0-563-06444-1. (First published by Bobbs-Merrill,
      1974.)
      Movie versions: *The Reincarnation of Peter Proud*, 1975. Director: J. Lee
      Thompson. Stars: Michael Sarrazin, Jennifer O'Neill, and Margot Kidder.

Peter Proud has a growing conviction that is starting to dominate his life.
Peter Proud is almost sure he has lived before, and he seems obsessed with the
need to find out about this earlier life. [Reincarnation]

320. Eliot, Marc. **How Dear the Dawn.** New York: Ballantine, 1987. 280 pp.
C   ISBN 0-345-34315-8.

There are old and sleepy towns all along the Carolina coast, but they are not
all necessarily peaceful. In one of them an ancient evil is present, a blood-craving
monster who must satisfy his needs in the dark of the night. [Vampires]

321. Elliott, Tom. **The Dwelling.** New York: St. Martin's Press, 1989. 243
C   pp. ISBN 0-312-91551-9.

The old southern mansion sits deserted at the edge of a bayou. Anyone who
approaches the house becomes uneasy; its brooding presence implies a history of
dark deeds committed inside its walls. [Haunted houses]

322. Ellison, Harlan. **Strange Wine.** New York: Warner, 1979. 316 pp. ISBN
C   0-446-30659-2. (First published by Harper & Row, 1978.)

Contents include "Introduction: Revealed at Last!," "What Killed the
Dinosaurs?," "And You Don't Look So Terrific Yourself," "Croatoan,"
"Working with the Little People," "Killing Bernstein," "Mom," "In Fear of K,"
"Hitler Painted Roses," "The Wine Has Been Left Open Too Long and the
Memory Has Gone Flat," "From A to Z in the Chocolate Alphabet," "Lonely
Women Are the Vessels of Time," "Emissary from Hamelin," "The New York
Review of Bird," "Seeing," "The Boulevard of Broken Dreams," "Strange Wine,"
"The Diagnosis of Dr. D'arqueangel." [Horror; Short stories]

323. Elrod, P. N. **The Vampire Files: Bloodlist.** New York: Ace, 1990. 200
C   pp. ISBN 0-44106795-6.
      Sequels: *Lifeblood; Bloodcircle; Art in the Blood.*

Vampires tend to have different life-styles, and Jack Fleming's search for an elusive woman is complicated by his sometimes uncontrollable desire for sucking human blood. [Vampires]

324. Elwood, Roger. **Fantasy Island.** Middletown, Conn.: Weekly Reader,
B   1981. 125 pp.

Novelizations of four stories from the popular magical television program about an island where dreams come true, including "Mandy's Journey," "Flight of Fantasy," "Little Girl Lost," "The Man from Yesterday." [Magic]

325. Emery, Clayton. **Tales of Robin Hood.** New York: Baen, 1988. 309 pp.
C   ISBN 0-671-65397-0.

The legend of Robin Hood is well known, but it is not so well known that when Robin lived in Sherwood Forest there was magic in England, along wth sorcerers and wizards. Some of these special people were good and some were bad, very bad indeed. [Hood, Robin; Legends, England; Magic]

326. Endore, Guy. **The Werewolf of Paris.** New York: Ace, 223 pp. (First pub-
C   lished by Farrar and Rinehart, 1933.)
      Other works: *The Man from Limbo; Methinks the Lady; The Sword of God.*
      Movie versions: *The Curse of the Werewolf,* 1961. Director: Terence Fisher. Stars: Clifford Evans, Oliver Reed, and Yvonne Romain.

Bertrand Caillet is the son of a young French servant girl and a strange, cursed wanderer. Bertrand learns of his fate early; he must live his life as his unknown father had before him, a life filled with craving for the blood of beautiful young women. [Werewolves]

Ensley, Evangeline. *See* Evangeline Walton.

327. Erwin, Alan. **Skeleton Dancer.** New York: Dell, 1989. 265 pp. ISBN
C   0-440-20326-0.

Beck and John Ridgley are twins, fifteen-year-old kids from a wealthy suburban Texan home. They're on the prowl for the right kind of girl to have fun with, but they find something they haven't bargained for, the spirit of an Apache warrior who belongs to a bloody brotherhood of horror. [Legends, Native American]

328. Esler, Anthony. **Hellbane.** New York: Fawcett, 1975. 284 pp. ISBN
C   0-449-23266-2. (First published by William Morrow, 1975.)

In seventeenth-century England witch hunters roam the countryside seeking out the followers of Satan. One of the most diligent of the witch hunters is Nicholas Hellbane, who dares to match his powers against the devil's own daughter, Alys. [Witchcraft]

329. Essex, William. **Slime.** New York: Leisure Books, 1988. 365 pp. ISBN
C   0-8439-2640-6.
      Other works: *The Pack.*

Humans have not been kind to the earth, so why should the earth continue to nurture humans? The abuse heaped upon the blameless soil has gone far enough, and now an evil, terrible ooze is out to feed upon the humans who are trying to destroy the land. [Monsters, slime-type]

330. Estleman, Loren D. **Dr. Jekyll and Mr. Holmes.** Harmondsworth,
C England: Penguin, 1980. 252 pp. ISBN 01400.56653. (First published by Doubleday, 1979.)
Other works: *Sherlock Holmes vs. Dracula.*

The enormously clever Sherlock Holmes is back with a new adventure and a new villain to combat. Here is the story of the complicated Dr. Jekyll and his other side, Mr. Hyde, as told from the standpoint of Dr. John Watson. [Science gone wrong; Transformation]

331. Etchison, Dennis (pseud. Jack Martin). **The Fog.** New York: Bantam,
C 1980. 180 pp. ISBN 0-553-13825-1.
Movie version: *The Fog*, 1980. Director: John Carpenter. Stars: Adrienne Barbeau, Jamie Lee Curtis, Hal Holbrook, Janet Leigh, John Houseman, Tommy Atkins, and Nancy Loomis.

The novelization of a horror flick about the ghosts of seafaring men who are determined to have their revenge on the citizens of the coastal town of Antonio Bay. [Ghosts]

332. Etchison, Dennis. **Red Dreams.** New York: Berkley, 1987. 223 pp. ISBN
C 0-425-10398-6. (First published by Scream Press, 1984.)

An acclaimed modern writer gives us "Talking in the Dark," "Wet Season," "I Can Hear the Dark," "The Graveyard Blues," "On the Pike," "Keeper of the Light," "Black Sun," "Whit Moon Rising," "The Chill," "The Smell of Death," "Drop City," "The Chair," "Not From Around Here." [Horror; Short stories]

333. Eulo, Ken. **The Brownstone.** New York: Pocket Books, 1982. 322 pp.
C ISBN 0-671-46090-0.
Sequels: *The Bloodstone; Deathstone.* Other works: *Nocturnal; The House of Caine.*

Chandal lives in a lovely old New York City brownstone. Her life seems perfect as she surveys her beautiful home and handsome husband, but something strange is happening on the upscale upper East Side, something that Chandal cannot control [Evil]

334. Eulo, Ken. **The Ghost of Veronica Gray.** New York: Pocket Books,
C 1985. 279 pp. ISBN 0-671-54303-2.

Dorothy thinks she is the most ordinary sort of girl imaginable, so she is happy when she makes a new friend, exciting Veronica. During the gloomy rainy summer days Veronica introduces Dorothy to wonderful new ideas and finally shows her how to go into the past, where she must do Veronica's bidding. [Ghosts]

335. Fairman, Paul W. **Rest in Agony.** New York: Lancer, 1967. 223 pp. (First
C   published in a shorter version by Monarch, 1965.)

Hal has always been proud of his beautiful sister, Lisa, and fascinated by his powerful Uncle Amby. Then Hal receives a desperate message from his uncle, a message asking for help, and in order to save Lisa from satanists Hal must battle the forces of hell. [Satanism]

336. Falk, Margaret. **Darkscope.** New York: Pinnacle, 1990. 382 pp. ISBN
C   1-55817-364-1.

A dusty old mining town in Arizona seems a good place to start a new life after a divorce, but Chelsea McCord finds things a bit odd. She discovers an old box camera and sees strange images through the viewfinder, images that open the door to secrets of horror. [Science gone wrong]

337. Falkner, John Meade. **The Lost Stradivarius.** Gloucester, England: Alan
D   Sutton, 1987. 130 pp. ISBN 0-86299-342-3. (First published in the United
      States by Appleton, 1895.)
      Other works: *Moonfleet.*

The best-known violins are those made by Stradivarius, but this particular Strad seems to be the voice of evil incarnate. When it is played it summons forth secrets and terrible dreams. [Horror]

338. Farber, James. **Blood Island.** New York: Pocket Books, 1981. 323 pp.
C   ISBN 0-671-83012-0.

A lot of people envision lush tropical beaches when they think of luxury vacations. A new resort, meant to answer just such visions, is being built on the island of Carrefour, but the things that are happening aren't being planned by a social director. [Voodoo]

339. Farris, John. **All Heads Turn When the Hunt Goes By.** New York: Popu-
C   lar Library, 1977. 350 pp. ISBN 0-445-04360-1.
      Other works: *Wildwood; Child of the Endless Night; Fiends.*

An ancient evil force has been unleashed from the brooding plains of Africa and is now loose in America. It would seem that even the most sophisticated military know-how is not enough to combat this evil force. There are terrible consequences for all concerned. [Legends, African]

340. Farris, John. **Catacombs.** New York: TOR, 1987. 522 pp. ISBN 0-812-
C   58272-1. (First published in 1982.)

The Old Masters, kept under control by bloodstones, have been imprisoned in ancient catacombs in Africa. Now they are unearthed by archaeologists, now they are free, and their reign of international terror begins. [Legends, African]

341. Farris, John. **The Fury.** New York: Pocket Books, 1978. 349 pp. ISBN
C   0-445-08620-3. (First published by Playboy, 1976.)
      Movie versions: *The Fury*, 1978. Director: Brian De Palma. Stars: Kirk
      Douglas, John Cassavetes, Carrie Snodgrass, Amy Irving, Fiona Lewis,
      Andrew Stevens, Charles Durning.

Robin and Gillian have terrifying powers, and their loving parents want to protect them from those who want to use their powers for immoral purposes. But in the end, only Robin and Gillian will be able to save themselves. Yet it may be too late for Robin. [Paranormal abilities]

342. Farris, John. **Son of the Endless Night.** New York: TOR, 1986. 503 pp.
C   ISBN 0-812-58266-7.

A dark and terrible evil is loose in New England, an evil that is beyond the courts and the laws of humanity. Death and horror seem to be unstoppable. [Horror]

343. Farris, John. **The Uninvited.** New York: Dell, 1983. 272 pp. ISBN
C   0-440-19712-0. (First published by Delacorte, 1982.)

Barry turns to mystical lovers after the death of her boyfriend in an accident. Then her spiritual lovers soon take on powers of their own, and Barry finds her family, as well as herself, in danger as a result of her supernatural activities. [Black magic]

344. Faulcon, Robert (pseud. of Robert Holdstock). **Night Hunter.** New York:
C   Charter House, 1987. 184 pp. ISBN 0-441-57469-6.
       Sequels: *The Talisman; The Ghost Dance; The Shrine; The Hexing; Night Hunter; The Labyrinth.*

Dan Brady's wife and children have disappeared after a horrible raid on his peaceful home on Christmas Eve. After Dan is released from the hospital he resolves to find them, even after he is sure that he is not dealing with mere mortal thugs. [Demons]

345. Feist, Raymond E. **Faerie Tale.** New York: Bantam, 1989. 435 pp. ISBN
C   0-553-27783-9. (First published by Doubleday, 1988.)

It's hard to believe that fairies are real, but Phil Hastings finds out that the ancient kingdom of the magical folk exists in upstate New York. He also discovers that not all fairies are fey and harmless, and he soon becomes involved in an ages-old struggle between good and evil. [Fairies; Magic]

346. Fields, Morgan. **Deadly Harvest.** New York: Zebra, 1989. 357 pp. ISBN
C   0-8217-2762-1.

The little Texas town bakes on the hot high prairies, but some of the people who live in Hobart find their hands turning chilly and their blood running cold in their veins when they discover the ancient horrors that are loose in their town. [Legends, Native American]

347. Fifield, William. **The Devil's Marchioness.** New York: Avon, 1971. 463 pp.
C   SBN 380-00304-125. (First published in 1957.)

Marie-Madeline d'Aubray lived in seventeenth-century France and achieved great notoriety for her devotion to the devil and his works. She really lived and practiced secret rites. Finally, she died, executed for her many unspeakable crimes, but her memory lives on as one of the truly evil women of history. [d'Aubray, Marie-Madeline; Satanism]

348. Finch, Phillip. **In a Place Dark and Secret.** New York: Jove, 1987. 311 pp.
C   ISBN 0-515-09251-7. (First published by Franklin Watts, 1985.)

Young Sarah Stannard is starting a new life in Annapolis with her mother. She is unaware, however, of the terrible danger and frightening horror that await her, for Joseph Sherk is trying to find his daughter, who he refuses to believe is dead. There is no need for Sarah to meet Sherk, but she begins to have dreams that she cannot control. [Dreams]

349. Finney, Charles G. **The Circus of Dr. Lao.** New York: Vintage, 1983.
C   119 pp. ISBN 0-394-71617-5. (First published by Viking, 1935.)
      Other works: *The Unholy City; The Magician out of Manchuria; The Ghosts of Manacle.* Movie versions: *The Seven Faces of Dr. Lao*, 1964. Director: George Pal. Stars: Tony Randall, Barbara Eden, Arthur O'Connell, John Ericson, and Kevin Tate.

One day a fabulous circus comes to a small, dusty Arizona town. The mysterious proprietor is Dr. Lao, who seems able to perform any feat of magic. He introduces the townspeople to his exciting menagerie of mythical beasts and legendary figures. [Magic; Mysticism]

350. Fitzgerald, Julia. **Beauty of the Devil.** London: Fontana, 1989. 383 pp.
C   ISBN 0-00-617497-3. (First published by Collins, 1988.)
      Other works: *Salamander; The Jewelled Serpent; Taboo; The Astromance Series.*

Lakshmi is viewed as someone apart, even by her mother's people, the Romanies. She has a great gift, the power to enslave men with her dancing, and she determines to capture the reincarnation of her ancient love once again. [Gypsy lore; Reincarnation]

351. Fleischer, Leonore. **Heaven Can Wait.** New York: Ballantine, 1978. 169
C   pp. ISBN 0-345-27665-5.
      Movie versions: *Heaven Can Wait*, 1978. Directors: Warren Beatty and Buck Henry. Stars: Warren Beatty, Julie Christie, Jack Warden, and Dyan Cannon. *Here Comes Mr. Jordan*, 1941. Director: Alexander Hall. Stars: Robert Montgomery, Evelyn Keyes, and Claude Raines. (See also entry 765.)

This novelization of an updated version of the 1941 film *Here Comes Mr. Jordan* tells the story of a heavenly switch. When a quarterback for the Los Angeles Rams dies by accident (and before his time), he is placed in the body of an eccentric millionaire who is himself in the middle of a real jam. [Heaven and hell; Transformation]

352. Flint, Kenneth C. **Challenge of the Clans.** New York: Bantam Spectra,
C   1986. 328 pp. ISBN 0-553-25553-3.
      Sequels: *Storm upon Ulster; Riders of the Sidhe; Champion of the Sidhe; Master of the Sidhe; The Gods of Ireland* (written under pseud. Casey Flynn).

From ancient Irish legends comes the story of the magnificent Finn, a mighty hunter called Finn the Fair, who knows no fear. His enemies include the cruel high king and the dark powers of the sidhe (fairies), but in spite of the odds, Finn pursues his dream of justice. [Legends, Celtic]

353. Flowers, A. R. **De MoJo Blues: De Quest of High John de Conqueror.**
C   New York: Ballantine, 1987. 242 pp. ISBN 0-345-33995-9. (First published by Dutton, 1985.)

A wonderful story of three Vietnam War vets. One of them turns to the magic of hoodoo to reclaim his life as a contemporary African-American in Memphis, Tennessee. [Voodoo]

Flynn, Casey. *See* Flint, Kenneth C.

354. Forbes, Esther. **A Mirror for Witches.** Chicago: Academy Chicago, 1985.
C   214 pp. ISBN 0-89733-154-0. (First published by Houghton Mifflin, 1928.)

This is a sympathetic portrayal of seventeenth-century witch Doll Bilby, who prefers a demon lover to those of mortal origins. [Witchcraft]

355. Forsythe, Richard. **Fangs.** New York: Leisure Books, 1985. 380 pp. ISBN
C   0-8439-2275-3.

There are strange stories in many cultures about human babies being adopted by wild animals, babies who then become like the beasts of the forest. After they grow bigger, first as children and even as adults, these "humans" hunt and kill like their surrogate families. Can such things really happen? [Legends, Manimals]

356. Foster, Alan Dean. **Clash of the Titans.** New York: Warner, 1981. 304 pp.
C   ISBN 0-446-93675-8.
     Movie versions: *Clash of the Titans*, 1981. Director: Desmond Davis. Stars: Laurence Olivier, Harry Hamlin, Judi Bowker, Burgess Meredith, Sian Phillips, Maggie Smith, Claire Bloom, and Ursula Andress.

Perseus, son of Zeus and Danae, is forced to be a plaything of the gods as he goes through life first cursed and then protected by the whims of the Olympic beings. When he meets his true love, Andromeda, however, he resolves to let nothing stand in the way of her rescue from the dreaded Kraken and the misshapen Calibos—not even the famed Medusa with her head of snakes. [Legends, classical; Monsters]

357. Frail, Edward J. **Cult.** New York: Onyx, 1990. 241 pp. ISBN 0-451-
C   40189-1.

At first the odd pair of crime-solvers, homicide detective Matt Senacal and ex-priest Matt Frank Lattimore, couldn't find the connection between the various violent deaths around the country. Then they arrive in Eden, Vermont, and discover a town devoted to vengeance and life according to very ancient laws and customs. [Cults; Legends, Jewish]

358. Francis, Dorothy Brenner. **Blink of the Mind.** New York: Dell, 1982.
A   154 pp. ISBN 0-440-90496-X. (Twilight series).

Kelly knows her parents are going to die in a terrifying car crash, yet when the news actually comes, she is shocked and frightened. Kelly is alone in her belief in psychic powers. She is afraid this power may destroy her. [Paranormal abilities]

359. Franklin, Max. **The Dark.** New York: Signet, 1987. 187 pp. ISBN 0-451-
C   08242-7.
   Movie versions: *The Dark*, 1979. Director: John (Bud) Cardos. Stars: William Devane, Cathy Lee Crosby, Richard Jaeckel, Keenan Wynn, Jacquelyn Hyde, Biff Elliott, Vivian Blaine.

Dave Mooney, a cop in Los Angeles, thinks he's seen just about everything that's perverse and depraved. But then he becomes involved in a series of terrible killings that don't seem to have been perpetrated by humans. His suspicions are correct, and the horror continues. [Horror]

360. Freeman, Mary Wilkins. **The Wind in the Rose-Bush and Other Stories**
C   **of the Supernatural.** Chicago: Academy Chicago, 1986. 258 pp. ISBN 0-89733-232-6.

Short stories by a famous writer of traditional ghost stories, including "The Wind in the Rose-Bush," "The Shadows on the Wall," "Luella Miller," "The Southwest Chamber," "The Vacant Lot," "The Lost Ghost." [Ghosts; Short stories]

361. Friesner, Esther. **Here Be Demons.** New York: Ace, 1988. 233 pp. ISBN
C   0-441-32797-4.

Atamar, now a demon, was a failure in life and seemingly is a failure in death as well. Atamar is just not a proper citizen of hell, so he is told to shape up, get back to the world of the living, and corrupt some souls. Atamar takes on a group of young American archaeological students on a dig only to find out that his notions of sin are badly out-of-date in today's society. [Heaven and hell]

362. Fulton, Liz. **The Palm Dome.** New York: Pocket Books, 1991. 266 pp.
C   ISBN 0-553-28884-9.

Faye Wolsey has been called back to the Connecticut mansion for a sad task, to empty the house of dead Emmeline's personal effects. The estate, including the lovely antiques in the house, belong to Emmeline's nephew Maurizio. Maurizio, his friend Jack, and Faye discover in their explorations and redecorations that the old house has a secret, a secret of terror. [Evil]

363. Furlong, Monica. **Wise Child.** New York: Borzoi, 1987. 228 pp. ISBN
A   0-394-82598-5.

The ancient ways die hard in the remote Scottish byways. Here the Wise Child is abandoned and then adopted by Juniper. The Wise Child's natural gifts are honed and her supernatural powers grow. But the old ways are used for evil as well as good, and the Wise Child must use her abilities to save herself and Juniper. [Legends, Scottish; Witchcraft]

364.   Gale, Adela. **Angel Among Witches.** New York: Prestige, 1969. 175 pp.
C

The grim old castle of Froelichsburg was once the scene of horrible, bizarre occult rites. Those people who died in anguish still haunt that old castle and its present inhabitants, including lovely young nurse Joyce Miller. [Black magic; Ghosts]

365.   Gallagher, Stephen. **Valley of Lights.** Sevenoaks, England: New English
C   Library, 1988. 191 pp. ISBN 0-450-42268-2. (First published by New
       English Library in hardcover, 1987.)
       Other works: *Chimera; Follower.*

Sometimes you just can't keep a bad guy down, even by killing him. Even tough cops can't kill this murderer, because he just moves to another body and keeps coming back ... and back ... and back. [Reincarnation]

366.   Gallico, Paul. **Too Many Ghosts.** New York: International Polygonics,
C   1988. 288 pp. ISBN 0-930330-80-3. (First published by Doubleday, 1959.)

Old English ancestral homes are supposed to have a colorful ghost or two. But Lord Paradine's home is overrun with them, and he wants to get rid of them. So he hires Alexander Hero, a psychic investigator, to come and exorcise the ghosts. Alexander has a number of adventures, romantic and ghostly, before his job is completed. [Ghosts; Haunted houses]

367.   Gallico, Paul. **Thomasina.** New York: International Polygonics, 1988.
A   288 pp. ISBN 0-930330-93-5. (First published by Doubleday, 1957.)
       Movie versions: *Nine Lives of Thomasina*, 1963. Director: Don Chaffey.
       Stars: Patrick McGoohan, Susan Hampshire, and Karen Dotrice.

Thomasina is a cat with adventures and nine lives as well. She lives two of them in the Edinburgh home of a veterinarian, MacDhui, and his motherless daughter, Mary Ruadhl. After a bad injury, Thomasina is put to sleep, but in her next life she is eventually reunited with her family. [Reincarnation]

368.   Garden, Nancy. **Prisoner of Vampires.** New York: Dell Yearling, 1986.
B   213 pp. ISBN 0-440-47194-X. London: Corgi, 1987. 191 pp. ISBN
       0-552-52368-2. (First published by Farrar Strauss & Giroux, 1984.)

Alexander Darlington always seems to be getting in trouble. So much so, in fact, that the last time he did the judge called him a delinquent. But the trouble Alexander finds himself in at the library is a whole lot worse than getting caught stealing hubcaps. Alexander finds real vampires. [Vampires]

369.   Gardner, Craig Shaw. **The Lost Boys.** New York: Berkley, 1987. 220 pp.
A   ISBN 0-425-10044-8.
       Movie versions: *The Lost Boys*, 1988. Director: Joel Schumacher. Stars:
       Jason Patric, Corey Haim, Dianne Wiest, Barnard Hughes, Ed Herrmann,
       Corey Feldman, and Kiefer Sutherland.

Michael Emerson, the new kid in town, wants to join the best gang around, a bunch of bikers who seem to have a very good time. Yet even though the initiation to join the Lost Boys seems really weird, Michael doesn't believe that drinking the blood can have such terrible consequences. [Vampires]

370. Gardner, John. **Grendel.** New York: Ballantine, 1972. 140 pp. ISBN
C   0-345-28865-3. (First published by Alfred Knopf, 1971.)
    Other works: *Gilgamesh.*

The Beowolf legend is retold by the beast. How does it feel to be Grendel, the villain? In this version, Beowolf becomes the villain and is no longer the brave hero of legend. [Legends, English; Monsters]

371. Garfield, Leon. **Mr Corbett's Ghost & Other Stories.** Harmondsworth,
C   England: Puffin, 1971. 139 pp. ISBN 0-14-030510-6. (First published by
    Longmans, 1969.)

Supernatural stories by an English writer, including "Mr. Corbett's Ghost," "Vaarlam and Tripp," "The Simpleton." [Ghosts; Short stories]

372. Garner, Alan. **Elidor.** New York: Ballantine, 1981. 145 pp. ISBN 0-345-
A   29042-9. (First published by William Collins Sons, 1965.)

The eerie strangeness of a bombed-out part of the city is an irresistible place to explore. Roland and his friends find more than shattered buildings, however; they discover the way to go to Elidor, a shadowy kingdom threatened by great evil. [Evil]

373. Garner, Alan. **The Owl Service.** New York: Ballantine Del Rey, 1981.
A   176 pp. ISBN 0-345-29044-5. (First published by William Collins Sons,
    1967.)

When Alison and Gwyn discover the beautiful dinner plates hidden in the attic they little realize that they are going to be drawn into an ancient Celtic legend of tragedy and magic. [Legends, Celtic; Magic]

374. Garner, Alan. **Red Shift.** New York: Ballantine Del Rey, 1981. 156 pp.
A   ISBN 0-345-30071-8. (First published by William Collins Sons, 1973.)

The ancient stone ax is the key to time travel. Tom from the twentieth century finds himself living other lives, those of an ancient Celt in Roman Britain and a sober roundhead during England's Civil War. [Time travel; Transformation]

375. Garner, Alan. **The Weirdstone of Brisingame.** New York: Ballantine,
A   1978. 198 pp. ISBN 0-345-29043-7. (First published by William Collins
    Sons, 1960.)
    Sequel: *The Moon of Gomrath.*

Susan and Colin have heard about the powerful weirdstone and decide to look for it in the woods. There they enter a world of sorcery and danger that may destroy them. [Fairies; Magic]

376. Garnett, Bill. **The Crone.** New York: St. Martin's Press, 1987. 215 pp.
C   ISBN 0-312-90747-8. (First published by St. Martin's Press, 1984.)

A horrible monster created by a human crone is loose. The monster transforms itself into the disgusting things it devours, such as beetles and rats. It was conceived in hatred for only one purpose, to gain revenge on a philandering, careless man who had trifled with and destroyed the crone's lovely daughter. [Monsters]

377. Garnett, Bill. **Hellstrain.** New York: St. Martin's Press, 1988. 186 pp.
C   ISBN 0-312-91077-0. (First published as *The Down-Bound Train*, 1973).

Five cruel people get on a train that takes them on a hellish journey. No one would think to look at the five—the child, the business woman, the priest, the killer, and the doctor—that there is any bond between them. Yet all have a more than usual dose of inhumanity that is all they need to take this trip into terror. [Evil]

378. Garton, Ray. **Crucifax.** New York: Pocket Books, 1988. 387 pp. ISBN
C   0-671-62629-9.
     Other works: *Live Girls; Methods of Madness.*

Mace is today's embodiment of the pied piper. He's a charismatic rock musician with supernational powers. Everyone who comes under his spell seems doomed, including teenager Nikki, but Jeff Carr is determined to escape the web of this charmed spider. [Evil]

379. Garton, Ray. **Darklings.** New York: Pinnacle, 1985. 309 pp. ISBN
C   0-523-42368-3.

A horrible evil is stalking a comfortable town, and no one knows who the next victim will be. Those marked for destruction become crazed servants of the devil, who plays with their lives as though they are pawns on a chessboard. [The devil; Evil]

380. Garton, Ray. **Seductions.** New York: TOR, 1984. 277 pp. ISBN 0-523-
C   43317-4.

Tantalizing, seductive beings haunt the consciousness of bedeviled men. Once the men succumb, the lose more than virtue; their very lives are sucked out of them by these evil demons of the night. [Horror; Monsters]

381. Garton, Ray. **Warlock.** New York: Avon, 1989. 228 pp. ISBN 0-380-
C   7512-5.
     Movie versions: *Warlock*, 1988. Director: Steve Miner. Stars: Julian Sands, Lori Singer, and Richard E. Grant.

A warlock is snatched from the burning stake in seventeenth-century Salem and is set loose in contemporary Los Angeles to bring Satan's reign of hell to earth. But Redferne, the witchfinder from that same earlier time pursues the warlock, determined not to let him win. [Satanism]

382. Gates, R. Patrick. **Grimm Memorials.** New York: Onyx, 1990. 367 pp.
C   ISBN 0-451-40199-9.
     Other works: *Fear.*

Old Eleanor Grimm lives in an old mortuary surrounded by a cemetery and dark, dark woods. Eleanor is a witch, and if she can get enough young boys together for a particular sacrificial spell, she can prolong her life. But little Jackie has special powers, and maybe, just maybe, little Jackie can escape. [Black magic; Paranormal abilities]

383. Geary, Patricia. **Living in Ether.** New York: Bantam Spectra, 1987. 214
C   pp. ISBN 0-553-26329-3. (First published by Harper & Row, 1982.)

Deidre Gage seems at first just to be your average California flake, but her life takes odd twists, leading her to a journey through self-discovery of a very personal nature. [Paranormal abilities]

384. Geary, Patricia. **Strange Toys.** New York: Bantam Spectra, 1987, 247
C   pp. ISBN 0-553-26872-4.

At the age of nine Pet "loses" her weird sister Deane. At sixteen Pet tries to find her, only to see Deane disappear in a voodoo ceremony. Fifteen years after that, Pet discovers that Deane may still be alive, still taking part in strange ceremonies. [Voodoo]

385. Gelb, Jeff. **Specters.** New York: Bart, 1988. 241 pp. ISBN 1-55785-015-1.
C

Young Paul Silver has psychic powers, but they are not powers that give him the ability to find treasures and happiness. Instead, young Paul's special sight provides visions of the world of the dead and the realms of hell itself. [Heaven and hell; Paranormal abilities]

386. Gentry, Christine. **When Spirits Walk.** n.p.: Guild, 1988. 279 pp. ISBN
C   1-55547-227-3.

The southwestern region of the United States is steeped in the lore of ancient civilizations. When unexplainable things start to happen, it seems reasonable to turn to supernatural reasons. Nothing rational could account for the terrible deaths that are occurring. [Legends, Native American]

387. Gilbert, Stephen. **Willard.** New York: Lancer, 1971. 191 pp. ISBN 0-447-
C   75189-0. (First published as *Ratman's Notebooks* by Viking, 1968.)
      Sequels: *Ben* by Gilbert A. Ralston. Movie versions: *Willard*, 1971.
      Director: Daniel Mann. Stars: Bruce Davison, Elsa Lancaster, Ernest
      Borgnine, Sondra Locke, and Michael Dante.

The luck of Willard's family has changed, and Willard must work in a subordinate position for a man who was once his father's employee. Then Willard discovers a colony of rats in the run-down family home's garden, and Willard begins to communicate with the rats, training them to do his bidding. [Monsters, rat-type]

388. Giles, Raymond. **Night of the Warlock.** New York: Paperback Library,
C   1968. 160 pp. SBN 610-53677-0.

Dana has been bribed by her uncle to live with him in order to collect a legacy. Dana doesn't know what she's getting into until it's too late, because her uncle is a dangerous warlock who wants her body and soul in order to increase his own power. [Black magic; Satanism]

389. Gilman, Charlotte Perkins. **The Yellow Wallpaper.** Old Westbury, New
D   York: The Feminist Press, 1973. 63 pp. ISBN 0-912670-09-6. (First
     published by Small, Maynard, 1899.)
     Movie versions: *The Yellow Wallpaper*, 1989. Director: John Clive. Stars:
     Stephen Dillon, Julia Watson, Carolyn Pickles, and James Faulkner.

A frail and sickly woman becomes obsessed with the patterned wallpaper in
her sickroom. The climax builds to incredible horror. [Horror]

390. Gilman, Dorothy. (pseud. of Dorothy Gilman Butters). **Clairvoyant**
C   **Countess.** New York: Fawcett/Crest, 1978. 224 pp. ISBN 0-449-23561-0.
     (First published by Doubleday, 1975.)

A psychic Russian noblewoman investigates various crimes and finds
solutions to mysteries that frustrate the baffled police. [Occult mystery/detective;
Paranormal abilities]

391. Gilmour, H. B. **Eyes of Laura Mars.** New York: Bantam, 1987. 213 pp.
C   ISBN 0-553-12125-1.
     Movie versions: *Eyes of Laura Mars*, 1978. Director: Irvin Kershner.
     Stars: Faye Dunaway, Tommy Lee Jones, Brad Dourif, Rene Auberjo-
     nois, Raul Julia, Frank Adonis, Michael Tucker.

Laura Mars appears to many to be more beautiful than the people she photographs. Her instincts, too, seem to be uncanny. In spite of wondering, few
suspect her full power, a deadly force that spells danger and maybe even death.
[Paranormal abilities]

392. Gipe, George. **Back to the Future.** New York: Berkley, 1985. 248 pp.
A   ISBN 0-425-08205-9.
     Sequels: *Back to the Future II; Back to the Future III* written by Craig
     Shaw Gardner. Movie version: *Back to the Future*, 1985. Director: Roger
     Zemeckis. Stars: Michael J. Fox, Christopher Lloyd, Lea Thompson, and
     Crispin Glover.

Marty McFly isn't a very good student and, like a lot of kids, he doesn't seem
to care about getting ahead. But one day he is transported back in time where he
meets his own parents as teenagers and realizes that his own future existence is in
peril if his parents don't fall in love. [Time travel]

393. Gipe, George. **Gremlins.** New York: Avon, 1984. 278 pp. ISBN 0-380-
A   86561-0.
     Movie versions: *Gremlins*, 1982. Director: Joe Dante. Stars: Zach
     Galligan, Phoebe Cates, Hoyt Axton, and Polly Holliday.

A cute, harmless beastie propagates a destructive, malicious pack of fellow
creatures who turn a pleasant small town into a nightmare during the joyous
season of Christmas. [Monsters]

394. Gipe, George. **Resurrection.** New York: Pocket Books, 1980. 283 pp. ISBN
C   0-671-83210-7.
     Movie versions: *Resurrection*, 1980. Director: Daniel Petrie. Stars: Ellen
     Berstyn, Sam Shepherd, Richard Farnsworth, Roberts Blossom.

Edna has experienced a near-death episode, and now she has a strange new healing power that gives her life new purpose. But she becomes filled with fear and doubt as to the source of her power, for it is possible that her ability comes from the devil rather than from God. [Paranormal abilities]

395. Giroux, Leo, Jr. **The Rishi.** New York: Ivy, 1987. 460 pp. ISBN 0-8041-
C   011-6. (First published by M. Evans, 1985.)

Santha Wrench, a thoroughly Americanized modern woman, finds that she is having visions, strange and terrible visions of her native India that seem far from the cold streets of Boston. Her visions are not just dreams, however, for the ancient cult of Thuggee is thriving again, and Santha must participate. [Cults; Legends, Indian]

396. Goddin, Jeffrey. **Blood of the Wolf.** New York: Leisure, 1989. 366 pp.
C   ISBN 0-8439-2558-2.

Legends of werewolves have long existed in Europe, and there are tales of supernatural beasts in America as well. What causes a werewolf to be? Is it hereditary? Is there any escape from the dreadful curse? [Werewolves]

397. Godfrey, Sarah. **Aries Rising.** New York: Pacer, 1984. 160 pp. ISBN
A   0-399-21107-1. (Zodiac Club series).

Abby, the founder of the Zodiac Club, is delighted to go on a bike trip with her science class. Much as she likes her Zodiac Club friends, she's ready for new adventures without her constant companions. Includes the names of famous people born under the different astrology signs. [Astrology]

398. Godwin, Parke. **FireLord.** New York: Bantam. 1982. 369 pp. ISBN
C   0-553-25269-0. (First published by Doubleday, 1980.)
     Sequels: *Beloved Exile; The Fire When It Comes.*

In this version of the beloved King Arthur tales, Britain is a land with the stamp of the Roman presence still to be seen, although the beginnings of a new age can be sensed throughout the land. [Legends, Arthurian]

399. Godwin, Parke. **The Last Rainbow.** New York: Bantam Spectra, 1986.
C   424 pp. ISBN 0-553-25686-6. (First published by Bantam Spectra Trade, 1985.)

The old Celtic world of magic and Druids meets the new age of Christianity in the person of an ardent young priest who will someday be known to history as St. Patrick. [Legends, Celtic; Legends, Christian]

400. Goldman, William. **Magic.** New York: Dell, 1978. 251 pp. ISBN 0-440-
C   15141-4. (First published by Delacorte, 1976.)
     Movie versions: *Magic*, 1978. Director: Richard Attenborough. Stars: Anthony Hopkins, Burgess Meredith, Ed Lauter, and Ann-Margaret.

Those who deal with magic deal with a shadowy world of illusions that sometimes make it difficult to know what is real and what is not. Corky is a brilliant magician and should be able to tell the difference, but magic is a tricky business—a business that may just do Corky in. [Legerdemain; Magic]

401.   Goldstein, Lisa. **Dream Years.** New York: Bantam Spectra, 1986. 195 pp.
C   ISBN 0-553-25693-9. (First published by Bantam Hardcover, 1985.)

Robert, a young aimless surrealist in the Paris of the 1920s, follows an intriguing young woman into the future and finds himself caught up in the Paris riots of 1968. [Time travel]

402.   Goldstein, Lisa. **The Red Magician.** New York: Pocket Books, 1983.
A   156 pp. ISBN 0-671-41161-6.

Young Kicsi has found life in her little Jewish village in prewar Poland peaceful. Then one day a magician arrives with terrible predictions about the Holocaust, but only Kicsi believes him. Yet there is little Kicsi can do, and fate rushes toward her, mixed with magic and fear. [Legends, Jewish; Magic.]

403.   Gonzalez, Gloria. **A Deadly Rhyme.** New York: Dell, 1986. 136 pp. ISBN
A   0-440-91866-9. (Twilight series).

Angela was scared at first about going to a ritzy prep school, but she soon makes friends with Chrissy and even has a new boyfriend. Then things start to go wrong at Glencora, things that seem to be leading to a ghost that may be a harbinger of doom. [Ghosts]

404.   Gordon, John. **The Ghost on the Hill.** Harmondsworth, England: Puffin
A   Plus, 1982. 171 pp. ISBN 0-14-03-1372-9. (First published by Kestrel,
       1976.)

Jenny knows that Ralph, the sophisticated young university student who is new to her village, is greatly attracted to her, although she loves another. There are other attractions in the village as well, and a strange mystery of the past. Finally, a climax comes one summer evening, a climax that releases the ghost on the hill and resolves restive feelings. [Ghosts]

405.   Gordon, John. **The Giant Under the Snow.** Harmondsworth, England:
B   Puffin, 1971. 188 pp. ISBN 0-14-030507-6. (First published by
       Hutchinson, 1968.)

During a field trip to an ancient mound, Jonquil Winters wanders away and discovers an intriguing old amulet. She views the amulet as a great find until terrible things begin to happen. [Legends, Norse]

406.   Gorey, Edward. **Amphigorey.** New York: Perigee, 1980. unpaged. ISBN
C   0-399-50433-8. (First published by Putnam, 1972.)
       Other works: *Amphigorey Too; Amphigorey Also.*

Strange stories composed by a master of the understated macabre and with elegantly drawn illustrations. Included are "The Unstrung Harp," "The Listing Attic," "The Doubtful Guest," "The Object Lesson," "The Bug Book," "The Fatal Lozenge," "The Hapless Child," "The Curious Sofa," "The Willowdale Handcar," "The Gashly-crumb Tinnies," "The Insect God," "The West Wing," "The Wuggly Ump," "The Sinking Spell," "The Remembered Visit." [Horror; Short stories]

407. Gorog, Judith. **When Flesh Begins to Creep.** London: Lions, 1986. 142 pp.
B   ISBN 0-00-672777-8. (First published in the United States as *A Taste for Quiet* by Philomel, 1982.)

A series of stories about strange happenings, including "A Story about Death," "Those Three Wishes," "A Taste for Quiet," "Queen Pig," "Odd Jobs," "Low Hurdles," "The Storytellers," "A Little Love Story," "Minnie," "'If I Had the Wings of an Angel,'" "About Abner the Tinker," "Critch." [Horror; Short stories]

408. Goudge, Elizabeth. **The White Witch.** New York: Popular Library, 1958.
C   352 pp. (First published in the United States by Coward-McCann, 1958.)
      Other works: *The Little White Horse.*

Beautiful gypsy girl Froniga fascinates people in Elizabethan England. Her talents are extraordinary, and frightening to some. She loves Robert, but will her exotic charms prevail over those of her rival, gentle Jenny? A fine love story with rich historical details. [Gypsy lore; Witchcraft]

409. Goulart, Ron. **Bloodstalk.** New York: Warner, 1975. 141 pp.
C   Sequels: *On Alien Wings; Deadwalk; Blood Wedding; Deathgame; Snakegod.*

Vampirella, heroine of a comic-book series, is doomed to stalk an alien world, Earth, in search of her necessary sustenance. [Vampires]

410. Goulart, Ron. **The Curse of the Obelisk.** New York: Avon, 1987. 136 pp.
C   ISBN 0-380-89858-6.

Harry Challenge wasn't finding turn-of-the-century Paris as desirable a place to be as most people did. If it wasn't one thing it was another — and there did seem to be a lot of anothers, like ancient Egyptian curses, a beautiful vampire, giant bats, and a hypnotist, not to mention a walking mummy. [Curses; Monsters]

411. Granbeck, Marilyn. **The Magician's Daughter.** New York: Manor, 1977.
C   200 pp. ISBN 0-532-15256-1.

Lovely young Magda Karadine is alone in the world, except for her memories of a happier time when her father toured vacation hotels as a popular magician. But mysterious things start to happen when Magda goes home to the old resort her father bought, mysterious things that seem to have no explanation, even in the illusive world of magic. [Legerdemain]

412. Grant, Charles L. **For Fear of the Night.** New York: TOR, 1988. 277 pp.
C   ISBN 0-812-51834-9.
      Other works: *The Orchard; The Ravens of the Moon.*

Amusement parks are eerie places when they are deserted, and this one burned down ten days ago making it even stranger. Young Julie had died in the fire. Julie had enjoyed life and looked forward to returning to college with her friends. Some people think that Julie is still at the amusement park, but Julie isn't seeking fun any more. [Ghosts]

413.   Grant, Charles L. **The Nestling.** New York: Pocket Books, 1982. 406 pp.
C   ISBN 0-671-41989-7.

> An old Indian prophecy has foretold the coming of an ancient
> predator to the isolated Wyoming valley, and when it happens, the towns-
> people know they are in the control of something so powerful, so evil, that
> they will never be free again. [Legends, Native American]

414.   Grant, Charles L. **The Pet.** New York: TOR, 1987. 343 pp. ISBN 0-812-
C   51848-9. (First published in 1986.)

Don Boyd seems to be like a lot of other seventeen-year-old kids — plenty of
problems with school, family, girls, you name it. There are times when all Don
wants is to get even with everyone in his hometown. Then he has a chance to do
just that, and Ashford, New Jersey, becomes of scene of unbelievable terror.
[Monsters]

415.   Grant, Charles L. **The Sound of Midnight.** New York: Popular Library,
C   1979. 221 pp. ISBN 0-445-04398-0. (First published by Doubleday, 1978.)
       Sequels: *Hour of the Oxrun Dead; Nightmare Seasons; The Bloodwind;*
       Dialing the Wind; The Grave; The Last Call of Mourning; The Orchard;
       The Dark Cry of the Moon.

In this Oxrun Station book, the children acquire secret powers and use toys
to make the adults of the town do what the children want. [Evil]

416.   Grant, Charles L. **The Tea Party.** New York: Pocket Books, 1985. 312 pp.
C   ISBN 0-671-50511-X

Like many other quaint old-fashioned villages, Deerfield has a big old house.
Its name is Winterrest, but those who go there do not rest, nor do they indulge in
genteel tea parties. Those who go to Winterrest find themselves in the clutches of
an evil, terrible dwelling — a house that truly lives. [Evil]

417.   Grant, Maxwell. **The Shadow: The Ghost Makers.** New York: Bantam,
C   1970. 120 pp. SBN 553-5329-060.

The Shadow, a famous radio character, employs his arcane knowledge to
appear invisibly to the perpetrators of evil. "The Shadow knows...." [Magic]

418.   Graversen, Pat. **Stones.** New York: Zebra, 1991. 288 pp. ISBN 0-8217-
C   3268-4.

Cami is shocked by the sudden death of her father in a plane crash and she
must now adjust to a whole new life in New Hope, Pennsylvania, where Cami's
mother is going to run a rare-book store. Cami's mother decorates the flowerbeds
of their new home with some odd stones gathered by Cami's father on his last trip
to Turkey, stones that are in a different position every morning. The stones
seemingly have a mind of their own, a collective mind that has an awful purpose.
[Evil]

419.   Gray, Linda Crockett. **Scryer.** New York: TOR, 1987. 346 pp. ISBN
C   0-812-51872-1.
       Other works: *Siren; Mama's Boy*

In exotic New Orleans there are mysterious, powerful people scheming to absorb all the psychic power they can. They are utterly unscrupulous in their methods, and they do not balk at torture and murder, for that is the only way they can gain their evil goal. A gentle psychic girl seems to be no match for them, but Renee is not going to let them win without a fight. [Paranormal abilities]

420. Greeley, Andrew M. **The Magic Cup: An Irish Legend.** New York:
C   Warner, 1985. 304 pp. ISBN 0-446-32438-8. (First published by McGraw-Hill, 1979.)

Early Christianity vies with ancient pagan beliefs in this love story of legendary King Cormac set in ancient Ireland. Central to the story is the quest for that most magical and powerful of talismans, the Holy Grail. [Legends, Irish; Legends, Christian]

421. Green, Edith Pinero. **The Mark of Lucifer.** New York: Dell, 1974. 221 pp.
C   ISBN 0-440-05391-1.

The only person feeling more horror and desperation than one possessed by demons is the exorcist, for only those who deal directly with the devil know the full range of his terrible power. Emily knows that something evil has taken over her will, and it seems that only Henry can save her. [Exorcism]

422. Green, Kate. **Night Angel.** New York: Dell, 1991. 281 pp. ISBN 0-440-
C   20494-1.
      Other works: *Shattered Moon*

Maggie receives the mysterious box in the mail. She knows it is a summons to return to Berkeley and her friends of twenty years ago with whom she spent a summer doing drugs and witchcraft. [Occult mystery/detective]

423. Green, Simon. **Robin Hood, Prince of Thieves.** New York: Berkley,
C   1991. 234 pp. ISBN 0-425-13089-4.
      Movie versions: *Robin Hood, Prince of Thieves*, 1991. Director: Kevin Reynolds. Stars: Kevin Costner, Morgan Freeman, Christian Slater, Alan Rickman, and Mary Elizabeth Mastrantonio.

Robin's story is one of fighting injustice, righting wrongs, and engaging in daring adventures in a land of unscrupulous and ambitious men, superstition, and magic. With his band of merry men, Robin is an admirable, courageous figure. [Legends, English; Hood, Robin]

424. Greenan, Russel H. **It Happened in Boston?** New York: Fawcett, 1970.
C   256 pp. SBN 449-01376-095. (First published by Random House, 1968.)

A critically acclaimed story of darkness and mystery that draws the reader into the odd and haunted world of unusual characters and happenings. [Dreams]

425. Greenburg, Dan. **The Guardian.** New York: Berkley, 1990. 231 pp. ISBN
C   0-425-12130-5. (First published as *The Nanny* by Macmillan, 1987.)
      Movie versions: *The Guardian*, 1990. Director: William Friedkin. Stars: Jenny Seagrove, Dwier Brown, Carey Lowell, Brad Hall, and Miguel Ferrer.

Working couple Phil and Julie are delighted to discover the perfect person to look after their new baby boy. Nanny is wonderful, they think, but then Nanny starts to take over everyone and everything. [Evil]

426. Greene, Liz. **Nostradamus: A Novel.** New York: Bantam, 1983. 256 pp.
C   ISBN 0-553-23596-6. (First published by Norton, 1982.)

A fictionalized account of the man who claims to have seen the future, a man whose own life follows fascinating twists and turns in the turbulent times of the early Renaissance. [Nostradamus; Prophecy]

427. Greenwood, Joan. **Mists over Mosley.** New York: Bantam, 1987. 183 pp.
C   ISBN 0-553-26897-X. (First published by Walker, 1986.)

Inspector Jack Mosley comes to the little village of Upper Marldale and discovers a great deal of mischief going on, mischief probably being done by a coven of local witches. Then the tricks turn to serious business with a corpse is discovered. The inspector finds himself faced with one of the most challenging cases of his career. [Occult mystery/detective; Witchcraft]

428. Gregory, Stephen. **The Woodwitch.** New York: St. Martin's Press, 1988.
C   231 pp. ISBN 0-312-91736-8.
      Other works: *Cormorant.*

Wales has long been considered a somewhat magical place, and by some it is thought to be a dark and haunted land. Andrew Pinkney has come to a deserted cottage in this mysterious country to get over a tragedy in his life, but he has not escaped care; he has entered the realm of horror. [Legends, Welsh]

429. Gresham, Stephen. **Dew Claws.** New York: Zebra, 1986. 335 pp. ISBN
C   0-8217-1808-8.
      Other works: *Blood Wings; The Shadow Man; Midnight Boy; Runaway.*

Johnny Ray is a troubled child, but his new home with concerned foster parents seems to help erase the memories of a frightening background in Night Horse Swamp. Yet he cannot totally forget what happened there, and he will never be able to escape from the terror responsible. [Horror]

430. Grubb, Davis. **Twelve Tales of Suspense and the Supernatural.** New York:
C   Fawcett, 1964. 144 pp. SBN 449-02534-060.

The author of *The Night of the Hunter* provides some horror stories, including "Busby's Rat," "The Rabbit Prince," "Radio," "One Foot in the Grave," "Moonshine," "The Man Who Stole the Moon," "Nobody's Watching!" "The Horsehair Trunk," "The Blue Glass Bottle," "Wynken, Blynken, and Nod," "Return of Verge Likens," "Where the Woodbine Twineth." [Horror; Short stories]

431. Gunn, James. **The Magicians.** New York: Signet, 1980. 168 pp. ISBN
C   0-451-09317-8. (First published by Charles Scribner's Sons, 1976).

In pursuit of a missing person on a case, Casey discovers a convention of witches at a hotel. He soon identifies Solomon the Magus, his missing person, as the head of this group. Before he knows it, Casey is embroiled in a timeless clash between good and evil. [Satanism]

432. Gurney, David. **The Demonists.** New York: Manor, 1971. 285 pp. ISBN
C   0-532-19146-3. (First published as *The Conjurers* by Whitakers, 1971.)

Madame Joseph, the clairvoyant, has a seemingly normal home life with husband and older children. Her first husband died in the sinking of the *Seamew* years ago, and renewed interest in the shipwreck forces Madame Joseph to call on the powers of evil. [Demons]

Guthrie, Thomas Anstey. *See* F. Anstey.

433. Haaf, Beverly T. **The Chanting.** New York: Popular Library, 1991. 263
C   pp. ISBN 0-445-21058-3.

The house next door to Janet seems to have a story to tell. Janet hears the chanting, the voices of children who cannot rest easy in death, children who must find something. [Ghosts; Haunted houses; Nazi occultism]

434. Hagan, Chet. **The Witching.** New York: Leisure, 1982. 331 pp. ISBN
C   0-8439-2289-3.

The Pennsylvania Dutch country is noted for its lovely pastoral beauty and quaint customs. Not as well known to tourists are some dwellers' practices of the ancient powwow. Even this can be viewed as harmless and picturesque, but evil is obviously at work when people start to die. [Powwow]

435. Hagberg, David. **Last Come the Children.** New York: TOR, 1982. 347 pp.
C   ISBN 0-812-53987-7.

Satan worship has been used for centuries to gain power and obtain riches. Yet it seems incongruous that this could be going on in Madison, Wisconsin, in an average middle-class home. [Satanism]

436. Hagen, Lorinda. **Amy Jean.** New York: Belmont Tower, 1977. 252 pp.
C   ISBN 0-505-51151-7.

Lovely Amy Jean was too young and pretty to die at so early an age, but die she did, leaving a heartbroken husband behind. But Amy Jean lets him know that although she is gone, she will be reincarnated and be his new bride again someday. [Paranormal abilities; Reincarnation]

437. Haggard, H. Rider. **She.** Harmondsworth, England: Penguin, 1982. 300
C   pp. (First published by McKinlay, Stone, & MacKenzie, 1886.)
      Sequels: *Ayesha: The Return of She; She and Allan; Wisdom's Daughter.*
      Also: *The Journey to the Flame* by Richard Monaco (see entry 738). Movie
      versions: *She*, 1935. Directors: Irving Pichel and Lansing C. Holden.
      Stars: Helen Gahagan, Randolph Scott, and Helen Mack. *She*, 1965.
      Director: Robert Day. Stars: Ursula Andress, John Richardson, Peter
      Cushing. (Later version, 1985, starring Sandahl Berger, was "inspired" by
      the book and is set in a futuristic world. It bears little resemblance to the
      original novel.)

Hidden deep in the heart of Africa there is a country ruled by a mysterious white queen, She, who must be obeyed. Her reign has been talked of for centuries, for she is ageless and has lived for thousands of years. [Eternal youth; Lost lands]

438. Hahn, Mary Downing. **The Time of the Witch.** London: Fontana Lions,
A   1983. 156 pp. ISBN 0-00-672177-X. (First published in the United States by
      Houghton Mifflin/Clarion, 1982.)

Laura and Jason, two English kids, are upset. First their parents decide to
get a divorce; then it is decided that they must spend the summer with an
unknown aunt in the backwoods of West Virginia. Then Laura meets Maude
Blackthorne, reputed to be a witch, and Maude promises Laura her greatest
desires if she will only follow the magic spells. [Magic]

439. Hale, Michael. **The Other Child.** New York: Avon, 1986. 297 pp. ISBN
C   0-380-89950-7.

Little Becky has been an abused child, and at first death comes to her as a
release and a relief. But her netherworld is not a heaven full of pure angels and
angelic souls. It is a scary place occupied by the souls of others who have died in
violence and by the grim stalking figure of the Scissors Murderer. [Paranormal
abilities]

440. Halkin, John. **Fangs of the Werewolf.** New York: Barron's, 1988. 140 pp.
B   ISBN 0-8120-4071-6. (Fleshcreepers series).

The dark hills and valleys of Wales hide many mysteries. The Welsh know
not to ask too many questions, yet the strange and savage "wild dog" that roams
the countryside is too odd even for this secretive part of the world. [Werewolves]

441. Halkin, John. **Slime.** New York: Lorevan, 1984. 252 pp. ISBN 0-931773-
C   74-1.

Most of us thought the worst terror in the sea is sharks, but that was before
the deadly jellyfish menace appeared. Their slimy trail soon extends to land as
small jellyfish invade water pipes and sewer systems. Can the human race be
saved? [Monsters, slime-type]

442. Halkin, John. **Slither.** New York: Lorevan, 1980. 215 pp. ISBN 0-931773-
C   63-6.

Most people don't like worms particularly, but then they're nothing to fear,
either. But a new breed of worms is developing in the sewers of London, vicious
man-attacking worms that have an insatiable appetite for human flesh and blood.
[Horror; Monsters, slime-type]

443. Halkin, John. **Squelch.** New York: Critic's Choice, 1986. 250 pp. ISBN
C   1-55547-135-8.

Moths are frequently beautiful and usually look very fragile. But there is a
new strain of moths that are huge, and like to eat human flesh. [Monsters, insect-
type]

444. Hallahan, William H. **Keeper of the Children.** New York: Avon, 1979.
A   189 pp. ISBN 0-380-45203-0. (First published by Morrow, 1978.)

The story of a father's attempt to rescue his teenage daughter and her friends
from a commune run by a Tibetan monk who has promised to teach them the
secrets of the universe. [Cults; Mysticism]

445. Hallahan, William H. **The Search for Joseph Tully.** New York: Avon,
C   1977. 283 pp. ISBN 0-380-01696-6. (First published by Bobbs-Merrill,
1974.)

Albert Clabber has been excommunicated, yet he refuses to give up his
search for a man who lived centuries ago. He thinks that maybe he has found this
man, who in this age is called Pete Richardson. Perhaps Richardson is the man
responsible for terrible deaths in an earlier time, perhaps not, but Clabber is
determined to find the truth. [Reincarnation]

446. Halliwell, Leslie. **The Ghost of Sherlock Holmes: Seventeen Supernatural**
C   **Stories.** London: Panther, 1984. 254 pp. ISBN 0-586-05995-4.

Mysterious tales of supernatural doings, mostly in England, such as "The
Late Mr. Llewellyn," "The Beckoning Clergyman," "House of the Future," "The
Centurion's Road," "Blood Relation," "The Temple of Music and the Temple of
Art," "Remembrance of Things Past," "Brain Scan," "The Blackamoor's Drum,"
"The Girl by the River," "Hands with Long Fingers," "The Viaduct," "Lady of
the Midnight Sun," "The Moving Rocks," "Demon," "The House on the Cliff,"
"The Ghost of Sherlock Holmes." [Horror; Short stories]

447. Hambly, Barbara. **Beauty and the Beast.** New York: Avon, 1989. 242 pp.
C   ISBN 0-380-75795-8.
Sequels: *Beauty and the Beast — Masques* by Ru Emerson.

In the novelization of the television series, Catherine, a beautiful career
woman of intelligence and wealth, is brutally attacked. She is rescued by Vincent,
the "Beast" who lives in a hidden world beneath the streets of New York. [Fairy
tales; Monsters]

448. Hamilton, Virginia. **The Magical Adventures of Pretty Pearl.** New York:
B   Harper Trophy, 1986. 309 pp. ISBN 0-06-440178-2. (First published by
Harper & Row, 1983.)

The child goddess Pretty Pearl lives with other gods on a mountaintop in
Africa, but then Pretty Pearl and her smart-aleck brother, John de Conquer,
decide to investigate the world of men. [Legends, African]

449. Hamilton, Virginia. **Sweet Whispers, Brother Rush.** New York: Avon,
A   1983. 215 pp. ISBN 0-380-65193-9. (First published by Philomel, 1982.)
Sequels: *Justice and Her Brothers; Dustland; The Gathering.*

Fourteen-year-old Tree must care for her older retarded brother. Through a
ghost, Brother Rush, Tree learns about her family and her black heritage and
grows in personal understanding. [Ghosts; Time travel]

450. Harbinson, W. A. **Otherworld.** New York: Dell, 1985. 399 pp. ISBN
C   0-440-16738-8. (First published by Corgi, 1984.)

The mysterious Amazon jungle sets the scene for this story of a youth, Alex
Poulson, who is torn between his exploitive father and the beauty of the simple
life led by the Indians. Alex reaches out to the Indians, who teach him the secrets
of their mystical beliefs. [Legends, primitive; Shamanism]

451. Hardie, Raymond. **Abyssos.** New York: TOR, 1987. 344 pp. ISBN 0-812-
C 51892-6.

An evil cult is at work in New York City, and the followers of Abyssos will not stop at anything, even murder, to gain the occult power they seek. Lieutenant Peter Doolan of the police department seems to be a very small hero to face such overwhelming odds. [Satanism]

452. Hardy, Robin, and Anthony Shaffer. **The Wicker Man.** New York:
C Pocket Books, 1979. 239 pp. ISBN 0-671-82671-9. (First published by Crown, 1978.)
Movie versions: *The Wicker Man*, 1973. Director: Robin Hardy. Stars: Edward Woodward, Christopher Lee, Britt Ekland, Diane Cilento, Ingrid Pitt, and Lindsay Kemp.

Neil Howie is a virtuous, some would say uptight, self-righteous policeman in Scotland who goes to an isolated island to investigate the mysterious loss of a child. The island is inhabited by the members of a commune who celebrate ancient Celtic rites, and Howie soon suspects that their rites include that of human sacrifice. [Cults; Legends, Celtic]

453. Harness, Charles L. **Lurid Dreams.** New York: Avon, 1990. 187 pp. ISBN
C 0-380-75761-3.
Other works: *Krono.*

William Reynolds is taking part in a bizarre experiment — he must travel back in time and change the course of history. His mission is to turn Edgar Allan Poe from a literary, drunken life to a calling as military hero, one who can help win the Civil War for the South. [Altered states of consciousness]

454. Harpur, Patrick. **The Serpent's Circle.** New York: Warner, 1986. 261 pp.
C ISBN 0-446-30026-8. (First published by St. Martin's Press, 1985.)

The Little Brothers of the Apostles has long been a secretive alternative monastic order with certain practices and rites not known to the outside world. The brothers of the order have long nursed a grudge against the Catholic church, which persecuted their pagan-based religion in past ages. At long last they plan to release their fury and power against their hated enemy. [Cults; Legends, Celtic]

455. Harris, Marilyn. **The Conjurers.** New York: Jove, 1985. 272 pp. ISBN
C 0-515-08362-3. (First published by Random House, 1974.)

The presence of hippie youths in a small peaceful English village results in abrasive conflict and strange occult occurrences. [Cults]

456. Harris, Marilyn. **The Diviner.** New York: Jove, 1984. 312 pp. ISBN
C 0-515-07877-8. (First published by Putnam, 1983.)

Young Mark Simpson doesn't understand at first why he is drawn to the abandoned naval base. Through ghostly visions he finds out about the tragic history of the base and the roles played by his own parents in a frightening tragedy. [Ghosts]

457. Harris, Marilyn. **The Portent.** New York: Jove, 1982. 424 pp. ISBN
C   0-515-06882-9. (First published by G. P. Putnam's Sons, 1980.)

The poor abused earth has had it, and Mother Nature is striking back by devouring people in Tomis as a revenge for pollution and waste. There seems to be no escape, but a few valiant people are determined to try. [Ecological horror]

458. Hautala, Rick. **Night Stone.** New York: Zebra, 1986. 592 pp. ISBN
C   0-8217-1843-6.
      Other works: *Moon Walker; Little Brothers; Moondeath; Moonbog.*

Little Beth doesn't like her family's new house in Maine. It's old, creepy, and full of shadows. Then Beth finds a strange hand-carved doll that becomes her new friend, her confidante, and, finally, her master. Beth is soon to be an agent of evil. [Possession]

459. Hawk, Douglas D. **Moonslasher.** New York: Critic's Choice, 1987. 352
C   pp. ISBN 1-55547-170-6.

An ancient order, the Brothers of the Obelisk, cannot be stopped from its purpose and rites. The bloody rituals the brothers must perform have but one end — the creation of a new Sekhet, the Slaughterer, and Annie will be its mother. [Cults]

460. Hawke, Simon. **Friday the 13th.** New York: Signet, 1987. 190 pp. ISBN
C   0-451-15089-9.
      Movie versions: *Friday the 13th*, 1980. Director: Sean S. Cunningham.
      Stars: Betsy Palmer, Adrienne King, Harry Crosby, Laurie Bartram, and
      Mark Nelson.

The story of Jason and the kids up at the lake has become a part of modern folklore. Jason seems to be indestructible, as the stream of movies about him continues to confirm. Is Jason real? Can he be killed? Or is he an inhuman beast, waiting in the lake for his next prey? [Eternal youth; Monsters]

461. Hawthorne, Nathaniel. **Great Short Works of Hawthorne.** New York:
D   Harper & Row, 1967. 372 pp. ISBN 0-06-083074-3. (First published in
      various places in the early nineteenth century.)

Hawthorne's work contains many mysterious and supernatural elements. This book includes "The Scarlet Letter," "My Kinsman, Major Molineux," "Roger Malvin's Burial," "Young Goodman Brown," "The Minister's Black Veil," "The Birthmark," "Rappaccini's Daughter," "Ethan Brand." [Horror; Short stories]

462. Haynes, Betsy. **The Power.** New York: Dell, 1982. 147 pp. ISBN 0-44-
A   97164-0. (Twilight series).

One day Meredith finds an ominous package in her locker at school — a curl of what appears to be her own hair and a message that brings her deeper and deeper into the terrors of knowing and even controlling her innermost self. [Possession]

463. Haynes, James. **Voices in the Dark.** New York: Dell, 1982. 153 pp. ISBN
A   0-440-99317-2. (Twilight series).

Christie's dreams seem very real to her, and she can't understand why she feels impelled to visit the barn night after night. She doesn't really feel frightened, yet deep down she senses a powerful evil she cannot control. [Dreams]

464. Heard, H. F. **A Taste for Honey.** New York: Lancer, 1967. 147 pp. (First
C   published by Vanguard, 1941.)
     Movie versions: *A Taste for Honey*, 1966. Director: Freddie Francis.
     Stars: Suzanna Leigh, Frank Finlay, Guy Dolman, and Catherine Finn.

Sydney Silchester prefers to live a quiet life and has chosen a pleasant spot in the country for that reason. A simple liking for honey, however, leads Sydney into a frightening situation from which only the mysterious Mr. Mycroft can rescue him. [[Monsters, insect-type]

465. Hearn, Lafcadio. **The Selected Writings of Lafcadio Hearn.** New York:
D   Citadel, 1979. 2d ed. 566 pp.
     Movie versions: *Kwaidan*, 1964. Director: Masaki Kobayashi. Stars:
     Rentaro Mikuni, Michiyo Aratama, Keiko Kishi, and Tatuya Nakadan.

An author with an exotic background writes mysterious tales with international settings, many Japanese, including "Kwaidan," "Some Chinese Ghosts," "Chita," "American Sketches," "Caribbean Sketches," "Japan." [Legends, Japanese; Short stories]

466. Heffernan, William. **Ritual.** New York: Signet, 1990. 350 pp. ISBN
C   0-451-16397-4. (First published by New American Library, hardcover,
     1988.)
     Other works: *The Corsican*

Some believe the ancient gods are as dead as their civilizations, but a follower of the ancient Toltec religion is stalking the streets of New York and sacrificing human victims as a tribute to his bloodthirsty god. [Legends, Toltec]

467. Heinlein, Robert A. **Waldo and Magic, Inc.** New York: Signet, 1970.
C   192 pp. ISBN 0-451-12365-4. (First published by Doubleday, 1940.)

A world and time in which magic is practiced as a commonplace craft is the setting for this charming tale of love and good versus evil. Archie Fraser is a hard-headed hardware and construction dealer. Not a magician himself, he avails himself of magical crafts. Then, demands for protection money and the evidence of demonic doings send him to Jemima and Dr. Worthington, practitioners for good. A classic battle between good an evil climaxes the tale. [Black magic; Demons]

468. Henrick, Richard. **Vampire in Moscow.** Lake Geneva, Wis.: TSR, 1988.
C   382 pp. ISBN 0-88038-552-9.

Even in godless Russia, supernatural incidents are scaring the bureaucrats. But how can you admit that a supernatural beast is responsible for bizarre killings when official policy states such things are not possible? [Vampires]

469. Henstell, Diane. **Deadly Friend.** New York: Bantam, 1985. 323 pp. ISBN
C   0-553-26380-3. (First published as *The Friend* by Bantam, 1985.)
     Other works: *New Morning Dragon.* Movie versions: *Deadly Friend*, 1986.
     Director: Wes Craven. Stars: Matthew Laborteaux, Kristy Swanson,
     Michael Sharrett, and Anne Twomey.

Paul, a brilliant scientist, has never been able to relate well to people, but
when he meets gentle Samantha he falls madly in love with her. When she is
tragically taken from him, he resolves to keep her with him somehow, whatever
the cost. [Science gone wrong]

470. Herbert, James. **Deadly Eyes.** New York: Signet, 1975. 205 pp. ISBN
C   0-451-12246-1. (First published as *The Rats* by New American Library,
     1974.)
     Other works include *Lair; The Survivor; The Dark; The Fog; Domain; The
     Jonah.* Movie versions: *Deadly Eyes*, 1983. Director: Robert Clouse.
     Stars: Sam Groom, Sara Botsford, and Scatman Crothers.

A story for those who love Lovecraft's "The Rats Behind the Wall." Human
revulsion has long been centered on rats, and this book will provide additional
reinforcement for this fear. Modern-day London is under attack by huge rats
who feed on live human flesh. Many gross details. [Monsters, rodent-type]

471. Herbert, James. **The Magic Cottage.** London: New English Library, 1987.
C   351 pp. ISBN 0-450-40937-6. (First published by Hodder & Stoughton,
     1986.)

At first it seems like a cottage in a fairy tale, complete with magic. But the
magic isn't only good, it is evil as well. The strange occurrences are bad enough,
but then the bats start coming, and Mike and Midge fear for their sanity and their
lives. [Black magic]

472. Herbert, James. **Shrine.** New York: Signet, 1984. 458 pp. ISBN 0-451-
C   12724-2.

Lovely young Alice can seemingly perform miracles, but reporter Fenn is not
so sure that her power comes from heavenly sources. Rather it seems to reek of
evil and doom, even as pilgrims seeking miraculous cures mob the little village.
[Legends, Christian; Possession]

473. Higham, Charles. **The Midnight Tree.** New York: Pocket Books, 1979.
C   239 pp. ISBN 0-671-82183-0.

The old religion practiced by the Druids has sometimes been a bloodthirsty
one. Their sacrifices fed the earth for centuries, and now the sinister Earth Spirits
demand more blood, that of young Mary Sullivan. [Legends, Celtic]

474. Hildick, E. W. **The Ghost Squad and the Halloween Conspiracy.** New
A   York: TOR, 1985. 170 pp. ISBN 0-812-56852-4.
     Sequels: *The Ghost Squad Breaks Through; The Ghost Squad and the Hal-
     loween Conspiracy; The Ghost Squad Flies Concorde*

Is there such a thing as good ghosts? Sure, if it's the ghost squad. Members
of the ghost squad team up with their human buddies to track down the malicious
mischief-makers who are putting some pretty nasty tricks in the treats for
Halloween. [Ghosts]

475. Hillerman, Tony. **The Blessing Way.** New York: Avon, 1978. 234 pp.
C   ISBN 0-380-39941-5. (First published by Harper & Row, 1970.)
     Other works/sequels: *Dance Hall of the Dead; The Dark Wind; The Fly on the Wall; The Ghostway; Listening Woman; People of Darkness.*

The southwestern desert seems spare and lonely, but there is a long tradition of mystery and old legends hidden in the deep sands and barren rocks. Anthropologist Bergen McKee becomes involved with Navajo traditions and legends as he searches with Lt. Joe Leaphorn for the murderous wolf-witch. [Legends, Native American; Occult mystery/detective; Shamanism]

476. Hillerman, Tony. **Skinwalkers.** New York: Perennial, 1987. 275 pp. ISBN
C   0-06-080893-4. (First published by Harper & Row, 1986.)

Navajo Tribal Police officer Jim Chee and Lieutenant Joe Leaphorn join forces in order to find a murderer hidden in the shrouds of Indian witchcraft. In the end there seems to be a logical explanation, but not everything can be explained by logic. [Legends, Native American; Occult mystery/detective; Shamanism]

477. Hilton, James. **Lost Horizon.** New York: Pocket Books, 1984. 275 pp.
C   ISBN 0-671-54148-X. (First published by Morrow, 1933.)
     Movie versions: *Lost Horizon*, 1937. Director: Frank Capra. Stars: Ronald Coleman, Edward Everett Horton, and Jane Wyatt. *Lost Horizon*, 1973. Director: Charles Jarrott. Stars: Peter Finch, Liv Ullmann, Sally Kellerman, and George Kennedy.

Escapees from a revolution find themselves in a hidden mysterious land, site of the legendary Shangri-La, where time seems to stand still. [Lost lands; Mysticism]

478. Hindle, Lee J. **Dragon Fall.** New York: Avon Flare, 1984. 139 pp. ISBN
A   0-380-88468-2.

Gabe Holden, a Canadian teenager, designs and constructs dragon-type monsters for a small toy factory. Gabe views his creations with affection until the night after a rock concert when they come to life and threaten Gabe and his family. The author wrote the book as a teen and won the first Avon Flare Competition. [Monsters]

479. Hinkemeyer, Michael T. **Summer Solstice.** New York: Berkley, 1977.
C   213 pp. ISBN 0-425-03329-5.

Katie's hometown, St. Alazara, is far north of Minneapolis, where Katie now lives with her husband. When her mother has a stroke, Katie returns to St. Alazara only to find that the shabby old town has changed. There is a new prosperity, but there is also a sense of evil, for the villagers have turned to an ancient religion that demands harsh payment. [Legends, Celtic]

480. Hintze, Naomi A. **Cry Witch.** New York: Bantam, 1976. 184 pp. ISBN
C   0-553-02489-2. (First published by Random House, 1975.)
     Other works: *Listen, Please Listen.*

Gigi Lang's mother died years ago, very mysteriously. Gigi herself has a confused memory of witches and a lovely old castle. Then Gigi's grandmother summons Gigi to that very same castle, and Gigi finds herself staying in the very same room her mother stayed in many years ago. [Witchcraft]

481. Hjortsberg, William. **Falling Angel.** New York: Warner, 1986. 242 pp.
C ISBN 0-446-31432-3. (First published by Harcourt Brace Jovanovich, 1978.)
Movie versions: *Angel Heart*, 1987. Director: Alan Parker. Stars: Mickey Rourke, Robert DeNiro, Lisa Bonet, and Charlotte Rampling.

Harry Angel is a seedy New York detective. He takes on the job of trying to locate Johnny Favorite, a crooner who has disappeared. Little does he know that the trail he follows will lead to voodoo rites, black magic, and the devil. [Satanism; Voodoo]

482. Hocherman, Henry W. **The Gilgul.** New York: Pinnacle, 1990. 350 pp.
C ISBN 1-55817-313-7.

Karen is a beautiful bride, but in the middle of the wedding ceremony she turns into an old hag screaming German curses. Karen has been possessed by the vengeful soul of a woman from the past, and Karen seems doomed. [Possession]

483. Hoffmann, E. T. A. **Tales of Hoffmann.** Harmondsworth, England:
D Penguin, 1982. 411 pp. ISBN 0-14-044392-4. (First published in nineteenth-century Germany.)

Grotesque and bizarre stories by an influential writer of the German romantic movement. There are sometimes rational explanations for his stories, sometimes not. Contents include "Mademoiselle de Sudery," "The Sandman," "The Artushof," "Councillor Krespel," "The Entail," "Doge and Dogaressa," "The Miners at Falun," "The Choosing of the Bride." [Mysticism; Short stories]

484. Holdstock, Robert (pseud. Robert Faulcon). **The Emerald Forest.** Har-
C mondsworth, England: Penguin, 1985. 252 pp. ISBN 0-14-00-7775-8.
Other works: *Necromancer*. Movie versions: *The Emerald Forest*, 1985. Director: John Borman. Stars: Charles Borman and Powers Boothe.

When little Tomme goes for a picnic with his parents he thinks the jungle is fascinating. Then he is stolen by Indians who rear him in their traditions, and it is only later that Tomme discovers that he must make a difficult choice between the mystical traditions of his adopted people and the culture of the white man. [Legends, primitive; Shamanism]

485. Holdstock, Robert. **Mythago Wood.** New York: Berkley, 1986. 274 pp.
C ISBN 0-425-08785-9. (First published by Arbor House, 1984.)

When Steven Huxley returns home after serving in World War II, he finds his brother working with their father in trying to make contact with mythic beings who live in Ryhope Wood. It soon becomes apparent that there is something very strange about the Wood. Perhaps it really is the home of another race of beings, one of them a fascinating woman. [Legends, Celtic]

486. Holzer, Hans. **The Clairvoyant.** New York: Belmont Tower, 1977. 251 pp.
C ISBN 0-505-51573-3.

Uschi Troll was born in sophisticated Vienna, but she possesses powers beyond those of worldly Europeans—the gift of seeing the future. In today's world this gift gives her the power to achieve personal goals, but her goal of happiness remains elusive. [Paranormal abilities]

487   Holzer, Hans. **Star of Destiny.** New York: Day, 1981. 192 pp. ISBN 0-8128-
C   7041-7. (First published by Stein and Day, 1974.)

A fictionalized account of the magical and alchemical tests of Rudolf von Habsurg, Holy Roman Emperor in the sixteenth century. Although such experimentations were not unusual in his day, Rudolf finds that he might be in deeper waters than he realizes. [Alchemy; Magic]

488. Hoppe, Joanne. **April Spell.** New York: Archway, 1982. 176 pp. ISBN
A   0-671-46527-9. (First published by Warne, 1979.)

While researching a paper for school, Jenny Littleton attends services at a spiritualist church and meets a man who will have great influence on her and her mother, an influence that may not be for the good. [Spiritualism]

489. Horlak, E. E. **Still Life.** New York: Bantam, 1988. 200 pp. ISBN 0-553-
C   27656-5.

Sarah, part Hopi, has an understanding of the ancient powers of her people, a power she will have to use to stop the evil purpose of Madelaine, an artist whose pictures create a spell of doom and death. [Legends, Native American; Shamanism]

490. Horowitz, Anthony. **The Devil's Door-bell.** New York: Pacer, 1983. 159
B   pp. ISBN 0-399-21140-3. (First published in the United States by Holt, 1984.)
      Sequels: *Night of the Scorpion.* Other works: *The Silver Citadel.*

Thirteen-year-old Martin is taken to live in a hostile new foster home after his parents are killed. Not only does his foster mother hint that he doesn't have long to live, he discovers a coven of witches in the neighborhood. [Witchcraft]

491. Horowitz, Lois. **She-Devil.** New York: Pageant, 1989. 334 pp. ISBN
C   0-517-01011-9.

A town called Happiness seems too good to be true, and those who suspect its name may be overly optimistic are right. There is evil lurking in Happiness, an evil that will take over the Freeman family and turn their lives into a living, never-ending hell. [Evil]

492. Houston, David, and Len Wein. **Swamp Thing.** New York: TOR, 1982.
A   223 pp. ISBN 0-523-48039-3.
      Sequels: *Return of the Swamp Thing* by Peter David. Movie versions:
      Swamp Thing, 1982. Director: Wes Craven. Stars: Louis Jourdan,
      Adrienne Barbeau, and Ray Wise.

Born in a comic, resurrected in a movie, and now living on in a novel, Swamp Thing is a victim of science run amok. Dr. Alec Holland battles the forces of demonic evil as well as tries to rescue his beloved Alice, but his body has been changed from that of a normal man to a half-vegetable creature. [Monsters; Science gone wrong]

493. Houston, James A. **Spirit Wrestler.** New York: Avon, 1981. 288 pp. ISBN
A   0-380-56911-6. (First published by Harcourt Brace Jovanovich, 1980.)

Young Shoona has been trained to be a shaman, a leader among his people. But he sometimes yearns for a more normal life, that of hunter, until he learns the meaning of his powers and the purpose of his life. [Legends, Inuit; Shamanism]

494. Howard, Elizabeth. **Mystery of the Metro.** New York: Random House
A   Byron Press, 1987. 140 pp. ISBN 0-394-87547-8.
    Sequels: *Mystery of the Magician; The Scent of Mystery.*

Paris, a lovely and courageous young Chicago teenager, travels to her namesake city at the turn of the century to visit the uncle she has never met. Upon her arrival, she discovers that her uncle has been murdered. It is up to her to struggle against the nefarious and supernatural powers of the mysterious Madame Meduse. [Magic]

495. Howard, Robert E. **Cthulhu.** New York: Baen, 1987. 245 pp. ISBN 0-671-
C   65641-4.

Robert Howard, author of the Conan stories and books, turns his story away from the world of Conan to the mysteries of H. P. Lovecraft's subterranean caverns. Here, ancient gods await their chance to overpower the earth. [Evil]

496. Howatch, Susan. **The Devil on Lammas Night.** New York: Fawcett, 1986.
C   246 pp. ISBN 0-449-21319-6.
    Other works: *The Waiting Sands.*

Nicola loves Evan and thinks that he loves her. Yet something must be wrong, for there seems to be no reason for Evan not to ask Nicola to marry him. Then Nicola becomes impatient and makes new friends, ones that practice unholy rites. [Satanism]

497. Howe, Imogen. **Fatal Attraction.** New York: Dell, 1982. 170 pp. ISBN
A   0-440-92496-0. (Twilight series).

Mirella is the new girl at school, and Janet knows there's something wrong with her. It's not just jealousy over Mirella's beauty and her attraction for Janet's boyfriend David. Mirella really seems to have an aura of evil. [Evil]

498. Howe, Imogen. **Vicious Circle.** New York: Dell, 1983. 147 pp. ISBN
A   0-440-99318-0. (Twilight series).

Jenny's life seemed terrific until the children of Dorset started disappearing. Everyone is frightened now, and Jenny is especially fearful for her lovely little sister Andrea. [Evil]

499. Howe, James. **What Eric Knew.** New York: Avon/Flare, 1986. 138 pp.
B   ISBN 0-380-70171-5.
    Sequels: *A Night without Stars; Stage Fright.* Other works: *Bunnicula; Howliday Inn; The Celery Stalks at Midnight; Morgan's Zoo.*

Young Sebastian Barth misses his lively friend Eric, who has moved away. Then Sebastian starts getting strange coded messages from Eric, messages that lead to the old cemetery and a ghostly figure standing amidst the tombstones. [Ghosts]

500. Huddy, Delia. **Time Piper.** New York: Tempo, 1984. 210 pp. ISBN 0-441-
A   81205-8. (First published by Greenwillow, 1979.)

When Luke goes to London to forget an odd young girl called Hare, he finds her there along with some other youngsters from an earlier age. Luke realizes then that his own scientific experiments are not the only way to travel through time, for the original pied piper has returned. [Time travel]

501. Hufford, Susan. **The Devil's Sonata.** New York: Popular Library, 1976.
C   255 pp. ISBN 0-445-00340-1.
      Other works: *Midnight Sailing.*

Hilda Hughes's young halfsister has become a strange and alien person, so Hilda decides to consult her psychiatrist, the mysterious Dr. Manning Whitlock. Dr. Whitlock resides in a brooding old mansion, and Hilda visits him there to find out about her sister. Then Hilda finds herself sinking into a pit of despondency and fear, a mood that may be orchestrated by Dr. Whitlock. [Satanism]

502. Hunt, Charlotte. **The Cup of Thanatos.** New York: Ace, 1968. 221 pp.
C   ISBN 0-441-12596-0.
      Other works: *Gemini Revenged; The Gilded Sarcophagus; The Lotus Vellum; The Thirteenth Treasure.*

Paul Holton is dismayed to discover that there are signs showing that the evil society of Thanatos is operating. When he discovers that lovely Sarah Wellington is their newest convert, he knows he must do something to stop the nefarious group from achieving its end. [Cults; Satanism]

503. Hunt, E. Howard (pseud. David St. John). **The Coven.** New York: Faw-
C   cett, 1972. 159 pp. ISBN 0-449-01989-0. (First published by Weybright & Talley, 1972.)
      Other works include: *The Sorcerers; Diabolus.*

Evil and witchcraft in Washington, D.C.? If anyone should know, it's the author, former Watergate conspirator and C.I.A. agent E. Howard Hunt. Jonathan Gault, the book's dauntless hero, is summoned to investigate the murder of a mysterious singer whose routines were said to resemble ritual tribal chants. [Voodoo; Witchcraft]

504   Hunter, Mollie. **The Haunted Mountain.** New York: Harper, 1973. 144
B   pp. ISBN 0-06-440041-7. (First published in the United States by Harper, 1972.)
      Other works include *The Wicked One: A Story of Suspense; A Stranger Came Ashore; The Walking Stones; The Kelpie's Pearls; The Thirteenth Member.*

Natives of Scotland know and respect the sidhe (fairies). MacAllister refuses to give them the corner of wasteland they want, and the sidhe are ready to avenge themselves on the stubborn crofter by taking away his freedom. [Fairies]

505. Hurley, Maxwell. **Max's Book.** New York: Scholastic, 1985. 151 pp. ISBN
A   0-590-33203-1. (Psi Patrol series).
     Companions: *Hendra's Book* by Hendra Benoit and *Sal's Book* by Sal
     Liquori.

Max is a member of the Psi Patrol, the biggest member at six-foot-seven.
Like Sal and Hendra, Max can do all sorts of fantastic things. [Paranormal
abilities]

506. Hurwood, Bernhardt J. **Ghosts, Ghouls & Other Horrors.** New York:
A   Scholastic, 1971. 144 pp.
     Other works: *The Invisibles.*

These very short stories make shivers run up and down, including "The
Haunted Cell," "The Ghost in the Radio Works," "The Skull of Burton Agnes
Hall," "Murder & Gold," "The Headless Woman," "The Ghost of Beauminster
School," "The Ghost of Berry Pomeroy Castle," "Little Sister," "The Return of
Lt. McConnel," "The Ghost of Lt. Schenck," "A Ghost Who Kept an Appoint-
ment," "The Old Man in Yellow," "The Spirit and the Scientist," "The Ghostly
Hunter," "The Dead Man Who Cleared His Name," "The Ghost and the Priest,"
"Captain Marryat and the Lady in Brown," "A Georgia House of Horror," "The
Artist with the Ghostly Master," "The Light at South Point," "The Case of the
Vampire Count," "The Treasure of Folly Island," "The Glowing Maggot of
Doom," "The Ghost Who Outsmarted His Relatives," "Evil on Canvas," "The
Ghost of the Werewolf," "The Little Ghost Who Cleared Her Name," "The
Haunted Vault," "The Ghost Who Demanded a Room," "The Spectral Hounds
of Kasli," "The Gorilla's Revenge," "The Dead Coach of Killeshandra," "The
Drunken Ghost of Tengilan," "The Ghostly Saxon at Tintern Abbey," "The
Bleeding Skeleton Hand," "The Face in the Sea," "The Vampire Cat of Montauk
Point," "The Phantom Murder," "The Ghostly Music Teacher," "The Toili of
Bryn Meherin," "The House That Was Not There," "The Curse of the Phantom
Wedding Guest," "The Doctor and the Corpse," "The Lucky Phantom Knocks,"
"The Terrible Omen of the Bumping Barrel," "The Dripping Letter," "The Ghost
of Gelston Castle," "The Phantom Gateman," "The Haunted Sports Car," "The
Vampire of Croglin Grange," "The Phantom Monk," "The Spectral Knockout,"
"The Wer-Jaguars of the Amazon." [Horror; Short stories]

507. Hurwood, Bernhardt J. **Kingdom of the Spiders.** New York: Ace, 1977.
C   180 pp. ISBN 0-4441-44512-8.
     Other works: *The Invisibles.* Movie versions: *Kingdom of the Spiders,*
     1977. Director: John (Bud) Cardos. Stars: William Shatner, Tiffany
     Bolling, and Woody Strode.

The peaceful little western town is the sort of place where nothing ever
happens. Then something does happen. The town is invaded, not by enemy
troops but by hordes of spiders determined to overturn human domination.
[Monsters, insect-type]

508. Hutson, Shaun. **Slugs.** London: Star, 1982. 208 pp. ISBN 0-352-31201-7.
C   Other works: *Breeding Ground; Erebus; Shadows; The Skull.*

A British "nasty" for readers who like their shivers in the repulsive vein. Here, the slugs are coming, millions and millions of them, and they ooze along endlessly in their search for their favorite food, human flesh. [Monsters, slime-type]

509.   Hutson, Shaun. **Spawn.** New York: Leisure, 1983. 365 pp. ISBN 0-8439-
C   2622-8.

Harold Pierce, a hospital orderly, has undertaken a mission to save the aborted fetuses consigned to the hospital's furnace. He tenderly buries the children in his personal cemetery. Then something happens and the children come to life, but not as innocent babes — as something very evil. [Horror; Monsters]

510.   Hyde, Christopher. **Styx.** New York: Playboy, 1982. 269 pp. ISBN
C   0-867-21173-3.

In a search for the missing link between Neanderthals and Cro-Magnon people, a group of scientists becomes trapped in a cave. There seems to be only one way out, the trail left by an ancient tribe that may still survive deep in the bowels of the earth. [Monsters]

511.   Ibbotson, Eva. **The Great Ghost Rescue.** London: Piccolo, 1976. 125 pp.
B   ISBN 0-330-24756-5. (First published by Macmillan, 1975.)

Humphrey the Horrible, along with the other ghosts in his family, has been quite contented in this nice old castle, but then the word gets out — the castle is going to be turned into a movie theater. At first Lord Bullhaven's offer seems like a good solution, sanctuary in another place, but Lord Bullhaven has a different idea in mind. He intends to get rid of the ghosts for good. [Ghosts]

512.   Ireland, Kenneth. **The Werewolf Mask.** London: Knight, 1985. 124 pp.
B   ISBN 0-340-35340-6. (First published by Hodder and Stoughton, 1983.)

Tales of terror for younger readers by an English writer, including "The Werewolf Mask," "The Haunted House," "The Empty Tomb," "The Girl Who Read Too Much," "The Creak on the Stairs," "The Eyes of Martin Franks," "Deadly Creature," "The Body Changer." [Horror; Short stories]

513.   Irving, Washington. **Rip van Winkle, or the Strange Men of the Moun-**
D   **tains: The Legend of Sleepy Hollow, or the Headless Horsemen.** New
         York: Scholastic, 1975. 80 pp. ISBN 0-590-40110-6.

Two tales of strange happenings in the still mountains of upstate New York. One is about a ne'er-do-well who falls in with some very odd bowling companions. The other is about a foolish schoolmaster who does not reckon on meeting the dreaded specter without a head. [Ghosts]

514.   Jaccoma, Richard. **The Werewolf's Tale.** New York: Fawcett, 1988. 283
C   pp. ISBN 0-449-13290-0.
         Other works: *Yellow Peril; The Adventures of Sir John Weymouth-Smythe.*

Disillusioned with life, Jimmy Underhill has turned to drink and accepting weird cases in his detective agency, cases from the world of the occult. In the course of his investigations he is bitten by a werewolf, becoming one himself. Now he becomes a secret agent, one who must battle Nazi followers in the secret world of New York. [Nazi occultism; Werewolves]

515. Jackson, Shirley. **The Haunting of Hill House.** Harmondsworth, England:
C Penguin, 1984. 246 pp. ISBN 0-1400-7108-3. (First published by Viking, 1959.)
Other works: *The Sundial; The Bird's Nest; The Road Through the Wall; We Have Always Lived in the Castle.* Movie versions: *The Haunting,* 1963. Director: Robert Wise. Stars: Julie Harris, Claire Bloom, Richard Johnson, and Russ Tamblyn.

Investigating a haunted house is never easy, but Dr. Montague takes on the task of Hill House with his assistant, Theodora Luke, who will someday own the house, and Eleanor, who is sensitive to poltergeists. During their stay, the house becomes more and more oppressive, and terror mounts as the investigators become terribly uncertain about what is really going on at Hill House. [Haunted houses]

516. James, David. **Croc'.** New York: Belmont, 1976. 211 pp. SBN 508-
C 50959-150.

Fascetti and Boggs are New York City sewer workers, a dirty but necessary job. They've never believed the urban folklore of alligators and crocodiles living in the sewers – until the day Fascetti finds one. [Monsters]

517. James, Henry. **The Turn of the Screw.** New York: Signet, 1962. 452 pp.
D ISBN 0-451-51669-9. (First published by William Heinemann, 1898.)
Movie versions: *The Innocents,* 1961. Director: Jack Clayton. Stars: Deborah Kerr, Michael Redgrave, Peter Wyngarde, Megs Jenkins, and Pamela Franklin.

The only possible salvation for two young children must come from their governess. Will she be able to protect them from the evil spirits who want them? Or is everything just in the governess's imagination? [Ghosts]

518. James, M. R. **The Penguin Complete Ghost Stories of M. R. James.**
D Harmondsworth, England: Penguin, 1985. 336 pp. ISBN 0-14-009017-7. (First published by Edward Arnold, 1931.)
Movie versions: *Casting the Runes,* 1957. Director: Jacques Tourneur. Stars: Dana Andrews, Peggy Cumming, Niall MacGinnes, and Althene Seyler.

Classic ghost tales by an English writer, including "Ash-tree," "Canon Alberic's Scrapbook," "Casting the Runes," "Count Magnus," "Lost Hearts," "Martin's Close," "The Mezzotint," "Mr. Humphreys and His Inheritance," "Number 13," "'Oh, Whistle, and I'll Come to You, My Lad,'" "Rose Garden," "School Story," "Stalls of Barchester Cathedral," "Treasure of Abbot Thomas." [Ghosts; Short stories]

519. James, Martin (pseud. of James Kisner). **Zombie House.** New York:
C Pinnacle, 1990. 352 pp. ISBN 1-55817-323-4.

Little Bobby is excited about his new home, even though it is old and smelly. But his mother sees spooky things in the house, and she turns out to be right. Now Bobby and his sister Nikki have to try to survive on their own, but it will be hard to escape from the evil of the house. [Ghosts]

520. James, Peter. **Possession.** New York: Dell, 1989. 305 pp. ISBN 0-440-
C   20463-1. (First published by Doubleday, 1988.)
      Other works: *Dead Letter Drop.*

Alex Hightower's son has been killed in an automobile accident in France, yet he keeps coming home to her in London. This is not a benign ghost, and Alex is terribly afraid of what he may want, for Alex isn't ready to enter the realm of the dead. [Ghosts; Possession]

521. James, Robert. **Blood Mist.** New York: Leisure, 1987. 365 pp. ISBN
C   0-8439-2523-X.

A savage beast is stalking the peaceful Carolinian countryside, a beast that cannot be stopped or killed, for it is already dead. [Monsters]

522. Jennings, Jan. **Vampyr.** New York: TOR, 1981. 304 pp. ISBN 0-523-
C   48010-5.

Dr. Theo James is devastated to learn he is dying. Then he meets fascinating Valan, a beautiful vampire who in spite of her long life and belief in immunity to love determines to save Theo. [Vampires]

523. Jensen, Ruby Jean. **Best Friends.** New York: Zebra, 1985. 318 pp. ISBN
C   0-8217-1691-3.
      Other works: *Home Sweet Home; Cat's Cradle; Such a Good Baby; Mama.*

Little Barry is only three. Surely, he must be the epitome of childhood innocence. Yet strange and not very nice things are happening. Is it possible that Barry's special friends, his pets, are responsible? [Horror]

524. Jensen, Ruby Jean. **Chainletter.** New York: Zebra, 1987. 382 pp. ISBN
C   0-8217-2162-3.

This chainletter is stronger than most. "Whosoever possesseth this letter and dares to break this chain shall suffer disaster and death to self, to fortune and to family" is written firmly. Would you dare to take a chance? [Horror]

525. Jensen, Ruby J[ean]. **The Lake.** New York: TOR, 1983. 320 pp. ISBN
C   0-812-51975-2.

The beautiful jewel-like lake seems a perfect place for the development of a vacation resort. But the developer hasn't planned for the unseen attraction, a monstrous evil thing that lives on the bottom of the lake and consumes human swimmers, leaving no traces behind. [Monsters]

526. Jensen, Ruby Jean. **Satan's Sister.** New York: Major, 1978. 160 pp. ISBN
C   0-89041-223-5.

Ellen is a cursed girl, for the deadly cat goddess, the nightmare girl, will not let Ellen alone. The nightmare girl wants everything Ellen has, including her very existence. [Possession]

527. Jeter, K. W. **Infernal Devices.** New York: Signet, 1987. 239 pp. ISBN
C   0-451-14934-3
     Other works: *Glass Hammer; Dark Seeker; Mantis.*

George Dower, a proper Victorian gentleman, lives in a proper Victorian life
in London. He doesn't like it when his life starts to go awry, seemingly precipitated by the mysterious Brown Leather Man, who is entirely too interested in the
odd inventions of George's father. [Science gone wrong]

528. Jeter, K. W. **Soul Eater.** New York: TOR, 1983. 314 pp. ISBN 0-812-
C   52011-4.

Dee is a frightened and very strange little girl. One night she feels a savage
need to fight back, and she strikes again ... and again ... and again. [Horror]

529. Johnson, Charles. **The Sorcerer's Apprentice.** Harmondsworth, England:
C   Penguin, 1987. 169 pp. ISBN 0-14-009865-8. (First published in the United
     States by Atheneum, 1986.)

Eight strange stories of wonderous magic and metamorphoses, each
presenting a brooding atmosphere and surreal happenings. Included are "The
Education of Mingo," "Exchange Value," "Menagerie, a Child's Fable," "China,"
"Alethia," "Moving Pictures," "Popper's Disease," "The Sorcerer's Apprentice."
[Short stories; Transformation]

530. Johnston, Mary. **The Witch.** New York: Popular Library, n.d. 256 pp.
C   (First published by Houghton Mifflin, 1914.)

Seventeenth-century England was the scene of great belief in and fear of
witches. This is the story of an accused witch, Joan Heron, whose beauty could
not save her from the fearful cries of a public terrified by the thought that Joan
has special, demonic powers. [Witchcraft]

531. Johnston, William. **Max Smart and the Ghastly Ghost Affair.** New York:
A   Tempo, 1969. 154 pp. SBN 448-05326-060.

Bumbling Max of the popular television series matches his wits against
KAOS one more time, but those dastardly villains have included some ghosts in
their evil plot. [Ghosts]

532. Johnston, William. **Miracle at San Tanco.** New York: Ace, 1968. 175 pp.

This book is based on the Flying Nun television series. Sister Bertrille faces
adventures in thwarting evil businessmen from upsetting her plans. [Paranormal
abilities]

533. Johnstone, William W. **The Devil's Kiss.** New York: Zebra, 1981. 449 pp.
C   ISBN 0-89083-717-1.
     Sequels: *The Devil's Heart; The Devil's Touch; The Devil's Cat.* Other
     works: *The Nursery.*

A terrible evil has come to the small town of Whitfield. Can it be that Satan
has come to earth from his underground kingdom? [The devil]

534. Johnstone, William W. **Rockinghorse.** New York: Zebra, 1986. 428 pp.
C   ISBN 0-8217-1743-X.

Little Jackie and Johnny think the old rockinghorse is the most beautiful thing they have ever seen. But the rockinghorse can take them to strange and terrible places—hardly a toy for good girls and boy. [Evil]

535. Johnstone, William W. **Sweet Dreams.** New York: Zebra, 1985. 397 pp.
C   ISBN 0-8217-1553-4.

A mysterious light, some sort of satanic fire, flickers over the peaceful town. Then pervasive horror invades the very fiber and soul of the community of Good Hope, and only ten-year-old Heather sees what is happening. [Evil]

536. Jones, Diana Wynne. **Fire and Hemlock.** New York: Berkley, 1985.
A   280 pp. ISBN 0-425-09504-5. (First published by Greenwillow, 1984.)
      Other works: *The Homeward Bounders, The Magicians of Caprona; Charmed Life; Power of Three; Eight Days of Luke.*

Polly, a casual young college student, finds herself with muddled memories and odd thoughts about the past. She's not sure what is real and what she may have read in her beloved fantasy books. She becomes very confused as she struggles with her dreams of the past. Her own actions somehow seem to be the key for learning what has truly happened. [Altered states of consciousness]

537. Jones, Diana Wynne. **Witch Week.** London: Magnet, 1985. 210 pp.
B   ISBN 0-416-52870-8. (First published by Macmillan, 1982.)

The second form is in an uproar. There's a witch, a real witch, in the class, but nobody knows for sure who it is. It takes a lot of deduction and education about witches before things settle down again, and it's doubtful that things will ever be the same again. [Witchcraft]

538. Jones, John G. **The Supernatural.** New York: Tudor, 1988. 375 pp.
C   ISBN 0-944276-17-2.
      Other works: *Amityville II.*

When you owe ruthless men money, you don't stop running. Lance Sullivan is trying to escape from his problems by running to Australia, but terrible dreams and forebodings warn him against collecting his seemingly miraculous inheritance. [Evil]

539. Kahn, James. **Poltergeist.** New York: Warner, 1982. 304 pp. ISBN
C   0-446-30222-8.
      Sequels: *Poltergeist II.* Movie versions: *Poltergeist*, 1982. Director: Tobe Hooper. Stars: Craig Nelson, JoBeth Williams, and Beatrice Straight.

Pretty little Carol Ann seems to sense the presence of beings other than her family in the house. Soon it becomes clear that something is causing odd things to happen, at first only irritating and strange, then frightening. Finally, little Carol Ann is taken away, and her mother must find her in another world. [Demons]

540. Kassem, Lou. **Dance of Death.** New York: Dell, 1984. 151 pp. ISBN
A   0-440-91659-3. (Twilight series).

Regan's life is ruined, and she has come to Ferncrest Manor to piece her life
together again. At first the old southern mansion seems the perfect place to get
her life back on track, but then Regan discovers there are two ghosts living there
with her, one seems to be good and the other very evil. [Ghosts; Haunted houses]

541. Katz, Shelley. **The Lucifer Child.** New York: Dell, 1980. 317 pp. ISBN
C   0-440-15076-6.
     Other works: *Alligator.*

Adam is a long-awaited child, born because of miraculous new technologies.
Adam is a wonderful child, but then doubt sets in, for although Adam looks
angelic it is obvious that his heart and soul are demonic. [Evil]

542. Katz, Welwyn Wilton. **Falseface.** New York: Laurel-Leaf, 1990. 196 pp.
A   ISBN 0-440-206766-6. (First published by Macmillan, 1987.)

Laney, like many teenagers, finds dealing with her parents' divorce hard, and
her mother seems to dislike Laney now because she looks like her father. Then
Laney makes a new friend, Tom Walsh, who has Iroquois blood and knows the
old Iroquois masks they find can be used for terrible evil. [Legends, Native
American]

543. Katz, Welwyn Wilton. **Witchery Hill.** New York: Laurel-Leaf, 1990.
A   244 pp. ISBN 0-440-20637-5. (First published by Macmillan, 1984.)

The Channel Islands are very isolated, but at first Mike Lewis is excited
about spending the summer on Guernsey with his father. Mike discovers that his
new friend Lisa believes there is an active coven of witches operating on the island
and that one of them is Lisa's own mother. [Satanism]

544. Katz, William. **Visions of Terror.** New York: Warner, 1981. 286 pp.
C   ISBN 0-446-91347-2.

Annie McKay has dreams, terrible dreams that appear to foretell the future.
When Annie dreams of her own murder, Annie's mother decides to take action
and save her daughter from seemingly certain destruction. [Dreams]

545. Kaufman, Robert, and Mark Gindes. **Love at First Bite.** Los Angeles:
C   Fotonovel, 1979. unpaged.
     Movie versions: *Love at First Bite,* 1979. Director: Stan Dragoti. Stars:
     George Hamilton, Susan St. James, Richard Benjamin, and Dick Shawn.

The Dracula story played for laughs in modern-day New York. Photos and
conversations from the film provide a comic-book approach to the story of a hero
with a fascinating, fatal appeal for beautiful women. [Vampires]

546. Kaye, Marvin, and Parke Godwin. **A Cold Blue Light.** New York:
C   Charter, 1983. 294 pp. ISBN 0-441-11503-9.
     Sequels: *Ghosts of Night and Morning* by Marvin Kaye.

Aubrey House is evil. Yet there are those who are willing to stay there overnight in order to discover the secret of its evilness. It will be a long night, perhaps an endless night for them. [Haunted houses; Paranormal abilities)

547. Keene, Carolyn. **Nancy Drew Ghost Stories.** New York: Wanderer, 1983.
C   160 pp. ISBN 0-671-46468-X.
      Sequels: *Nancy Drew Ghost Stories #2.*

Nancy Drew, girl detective, finds rational reasons for seemingly supernatural happenings. In spite of the promising titles, all the mysterious goings-on are discovered to be part of purely human schemes. The volume includes "The Campus Ghost," "The Ghost Dogs of Whispering Oaks," "Blackbear's Skull," "The Ghost Jogger," "The Curse of the Frog," "The Greenhouse Ghost." [Occult mystery/detective; Short stories]

548. Kelleher, Ed, and Harriette Vidal. **Prime Evil.** New York: Leisure Books,
C   1988. 293 pp. ISBN 0-8439-2669-4.
      Other works: *Madonna; The Breeder; The School.*

Satan likes the number thirteen. There are thirteen witches in a coven and a period of thirteen years is significant in devil worship. Thirteen years have passed since the last sacrifice was made, and the evil power is demanding a new victim. [Satanism]

549. Kemp, Sarah. **What Dread Hand.** Toronto, Ontario: Worldwide, 1988.
C   221 pp. ISBN 0-373-26005-9. (First published by Doubleday, 1987.)

Dr. Tina May is a skilled pathologist. Feeling in great need of a vacation, Tina heads for picturesque Cornwall only to discover a demonic cult at work in the neighborhood and a murder that must be solved. [Cults; Occult mystery/detective]

550. Key, Samuel M. **Angel of Darkness.** New York: Jove, 1990. 262 pp.
C   ISBN 0-515-10422-1.

He is a demented genius, a killer with an obsessive desire to create perfect music of evil and terror. To this end he tortures people to death, recording their agonized screams to incorporate into his most original music. Then a vision appears, an angel of beauty who is revealed as an angel of evil. [Evil]

551. Kilgore, Kathleen. **The Ghost-Maker.** New York: Avon/Flare, 1986.
B   162 pp. ISBN 0-380-70057-3. (First published by Houghton Mifflin, 1983.)

Lee is part of the psychics' activities in Cassadaga, Florida. He is not really a believer, however, until the seance, when he finds his world of reality slipping away. He no longer knows what to believe. [Paranormal abilities; Spiritualism]

552. Kilian, Crawford. **Lifter.** New York: Ace, 1986. 201 pp. ISBN 0-441-
A   48304-6.

When teenager Rick Stevenson wakes up one morning, he finds he is suspended six inches above his bed. With practice, Rick perfects his special skills only to discover that powerful men want to use him and his power for their own ends. [Paranormal abilities]

553. Killough, Lee. **Blood Hunt.** New York: TOR, 1987. 319 pp. ISBN
C   0-812-50594-8.

Garreth Mikaelian, a tough cop in San Francisco, is hot in pursuit of a
deadly killer who is leaving a trail of bizarre murders. Little does he suspect,
however, that the trail will lead him into a new life as a vampire with a personal
vengeance against the killer. [Vampires]

554. Kilworth, Garry. **The Rain Ghost.** New York: Scholastic, 1989. 121 pp.
A   ISBN 0-590-43415-2.

Steve is an average fourteen-year-old kid, except for one thing—he's being
followed. The thing that's following him isn't human, either; it's a ghost that
latched onto Steve on the moors. Now the ghost won't go away. [Ghosts]

555. King, Bruce. **Demon Shield.** New York: Lynx, 1989. 434 pp. ISBN
C   1-55802-293-7.

The old church has been desanctified, but it's not a neutral place—it is now a
place of evil and corruption, its foul atmosphere creeping throughout the entire
neighborhood. The people in the neighborhood know something is wrong, and
finally demonologist Merin Whitley takes on the struggle of cleansing the old
church once and for all. [Demons]

556. King, Frank. **Southpaw.** New York: Lynx, 1988. 229 pp. ISBN 1-55802-
C   000-4.
     Other works: *Raya; Night Vision.*

The Wolves had once had a winning season years ago, and now new owner
of the baseball team Bunny Bunsen is pushing the team toward another winning
streak. But there's something funny going on in the stadium, and ex-coach
Lombardi has a horrible feeling that there's a werewolf loose. [Werewolves]

557. King, Stephen (pseud. Richard Bachman). **Carrie.** New York: Signet,
C   1975. 245 pp. ISBN 0-451-13979-8. (First published by Doubleday, 1973.)
     Other works: *Salem's Lot; The Shining; The Stand; Skeleton Crew; The
     Dead Zone; Night Shift; Cycle of the Werewolf; Four by Bachman; Thin-
     ner; Misery; Tommyknockers; The Dark Half; Half past Midnight; Need-
     ful Things; Talisman* with Peter Straub. Movie versions: *Carrie*, 1976.
     Director: Brian De Palma. Stars: Sissy Spacek, Piper Laurie, William
     Katt, John Travolta, and Amy Irving.

A misfit teenager, awkward and shy, Carrie becomes the butt of a cruel
practical joke by her schoolmates. But they hadn't reckoned on Carrie's
telekinetic powers; nor did they realize that Carrie wouldn't take their jeers
quietly anymore. [Paranormal abilities]

558. King, Stephen. **Christine.** New York: Signet, 1983. 503 pp. ISBN 0-451-
C   12838-9. (First published by Viking, 1983.)
     Movie versions: *Christine*, 1983. Director: John Carpenter. Stars: Keith
     Gordon, John Stockwell, and Alexander Paul.

Teenage boys usually love cars, especially their own. But Arnie's car,
Christine, loves Arnie even more and will do anything to punish those who hurt

her or Arnie. Christine is a jealous protectress, and her love for Arnie becomes all-consuming as she destroys Arnie's enemies and then his friends. [Monsters]

559. King, Stephen. **Creepshow.** New York: Plume, 1982. unpaged. ISBN
A   0-452-25380-2.
     Movie versions: *Creepshow*, 1982. Director: George Romaro. Stars: Hal Holbrook, Adrienne Barbeau, Leslie Nielsen, E. G. Marshall, Ted Danson, and Viveca Lindfors.

A comic book styled on the E.C. Comics, beloved horror stories and graphics of the 1950s, with a series of short, gruesome tales told by a grim-reaper figure. The stories have the sardonic humor King's fans adore along with the violence and supernatural gore expected in this genre. [Monsters; Transformation; Zombies]

560. King, Stephen. **Fire-Starter.** New York: Signet, 1981. 401 pp. ISBN
C   0-451-09964-8. (First published by Viking, 1980.)
     Movie versions: *Fire-Starter*, 1984. Director: Mark Lester. Stars: David Keith, George C. Scott, Art Carney, and Drew Barrymore.

Charlie McGee has unusual powers; she can start fires just by thinking about them. Her strange gift is probably due to the fact that her parents took part in mind-drug tests for the Shop long before she was born. Now the Shop wants Charlie, and they'll stop at nothing to get her. [Paranormal abilities]

561. King, Stephen. **It.** New York: Signet, 1987. 1,093 pp. ISBN 0-451-14951-3.
C   (First published by Viking Penguin, 1986.)

Derry, Maine, has a terrible secret. Only seven people, who have escaped Derry, know this secret. They decide to return in order to save their old hometown. [Evil]

562. King, Stephen. **Pet Sematary.** New York: Signet, 1984. 411 pp. ISBN
C   0-451-13237-8. (First published by Doubleday, 1983.)
     Movie versions: *Pet Sematary*, 1989. Director: Mary Lambert. Stars: Dale Midkiff, Fred Gwynne, Denise Crosby, and Brad Greenquist.

At first it seems a charming idea for a small Maine town to have a burial ground for children to lay their dead pets to rest. But then it becomes obvious that the real cemetery which lies back in the woods, is not for pets. People buried there can come back from the dead, but they are no longer human. [Legends, Native American; Zombies]

563. King, Tabitha. **Small World.** New York: Signet, 1981. 311 pp. ISBN
C   0-451-11408-6. (First published by Macmillan, 1981.)
     Other works: *Caretakers; The Trap.*

Life in high places can do strange things to children, and Princess Dolly, whose father was once president of the United States, seems to be obsessed with her dollhouse. All it needs to make it perfect is a real live miniature person to live inside and make it truly a small world. [Transformation]

564. Kinsella, W. P. **Shoeless Joe.** New York: Ballantine, 1983. 224 pp. ISBN
C   0-345-34256-9. (First published by Houghton Mifflin, 1982.)
     Movie versions: *Field of Dreams*, 1989. Director: Phil Alden Robinson.
     Stars: Kevin Costner, Amy Madigan, Gaby Hoffman, Ray Liotta,
     Timothy Busfield, James Earl Jones, and Burt Lancaster.

An Iowa farmer is told, "If you build it, he will come." Ray decides this
means he must build a baseball diamond in the middle of his cornfield, and when
the field is complete, "he" comes—Shoeless Joe Jackson, legendary Chicago
Black Sox player. [Ghosts]

565. Kipling, Rudyard. **Puck of Pook's Hill.** New York: Signet, 1988. 271 pp.
A   ISBN 0-451-52168-4. (First published in 1906.)
     Sequels: *Rewards and Fairies.* Other works: *The Man Who Would Be
     King; The Jungle Books.*

There's a spot in England called Pook's Hill, and if the right people go there,
Puck—a famous fairy—will take them on adventures in England's past.
[Legends, English; Time travel]

566. Kisner, James (pseud. Martin James). **Poison Pen.** New York: Zebra,
C   1990. 317 pp. ISBN 0-8217-3096-7.

The new-age philosophy contains much from the old-age occult, as Roger
Kant discovers. Roger is a skeptic, a debunker of psychic phenomena, but he
finds out that not all he sees and feels can be explained away with rationality.
[Paranormal abilities]

567. Kittredge, Mary, and Kevin O'Donnell, Jr. **The Shelter.** New York: TOR,
C   1987. 376 pp. ISBN 0-812-52066-1.

Meadbury seems to be a perfect little jewel of a New England town. The
town is clean, its people friendly, and its streets without crime. Anyone who isn't
happy seems to be an outsider. Nicki Pialosta isn't happy, she doesn't fit in, and
she knows that something is very wrong in Meadbury. [Evil]

568. Klaveness, Jan O'Donnell. **The Griffin Legacy.** New York: Laurel-Leaf,
A   1985. 184 pp. ISBN 0-440-43165-4. (First published by Macmillan, 1983.)
     Other works: *Ghost Island.*

A stay with her grandmother and great-aunt in the family's old ancestral
home teaches Amy more than family history in a traditional way, for ghosts from
the past seek her help in untangling an old mystery. [Ghosts]

569. Klein, Robin. **Games.** London: Puffin, 1988. 150 pp. ISBN 0-14-032777-0.
A   (First published by Viking Kestrel, 1986.)

Kristy and Genevieve decide to hold a wild party in an old deserted house.
But the spoiled girls soon discover that the house on the edge of the Australian
bush has many secrets, some of them terrifying and dangerous. [Spiritualism]

570. Klein, T. E. **The Ceremonies.** New York: Bantam, 1985. 576 pp. ISBN
C   0-553-25055-8.

A summer as a renter on a quiet farm seems perfect for some research
writing. The young college teacher finds more than he bargains for, however, in

the seemingly peaceful countryside. An ancient ritual must be performed, and no one can stand in the way of the powerful evil that demands a human sacrifice. [Cults]

571.   Klein, T. E. **Dark Gods: Four Tales.** New York: Bantam, 1986. 261 pp.
C   ISBN 0-553-25801-X. (First published by Viking, 1985.)

Eerie tales in the H. P. Lovecraft tradition, such as "Children of the Kingdom," "Petey," "Black Man with a Horn," "Nadelman's God." [Evil; Short stories]

572.   Kline, Robert Y. **Campfire Story.** New York: Charter, 1990. 264 pp. ISBN
C   1-55773-424-0.

When a bunch of kids are sitting around a campfire making up ghoulish ways to die, imaginations can get out of hand. That's what happens when Lucius Cady comes up with a really gross and evil plan, but the group little suspects that the foul thing described by Lucius is really coming to get them. [Horror]

573.   Knight, Henry Adam. **The Fungus.** London: Star, 1985. 220 pp. ISBN
C   0 352 31546 6.
       Other works: *Carnosaur.*

It seems a quiet peril at first, then it grows—literally and figuratively—a body fungus that cannot be stopped. The lucky victims die quickly. [Monsters, slime-type]

574.   Knight, Harry Adam. **Slimer.** London: Star, 1983. 156 pp. ISBN 0-352-
C   31366-8.

There are many mysteries about the sea, and many mysteries in the sea itself. The horror of man-eating sharks is a mild peril when compared to the disgusting and terrible slimer. [Monsters, slime-type]

575.   Koch, C. J. **The Doubleman.** New York: Avon, 1987. 326 pp. ISBN 0-380-
C   70310-6. (First published by McGraw Hill, 1985.)

Pursuing a busy career as an Australian music producer should be satisfying, but Richard Miller wants more. In search of added meaning to existence, he turns to a fascinating group of people, the Rymers, but finds a terror he never expected. [Altered states of consciousness; Cults]

576.   Koltz, Tony. **Vampire Express.** New York: Bantam, 1984. 128 pp. ISBN
B   0-553-24099-4.

A game-style choice book in which the reader directs the action involving an expedition to prove the existence of vampires. [Vampires]

577.   Konvitz, Jeffrey. **Monster.** New York: Ballantine, 1982. 374 pp. ISBN
C   0-345-29447-5.
       Other works: *The Guardian; Loch Ness: A Tale of the Beast.*

Nessie, the Loch Ness monster, has been argued about for centuries. Is there really a great beast living in the isolated Scottish lake of Loch Ness? A small group of people find to their horror that the monster is there. Once aroused, the monster is a terrible foe. [Legends, Scottish; Monsters]

578.   Konvitz, Jeffrey. **The Sentinel.** New York: Ballantine, 1976. 315 pp. ISBN
C   0-345-30437-3. (First published by Simon & Schuster, 1974.)
       Movie versions: *The Sentinel*, 1977. Director: Michael Winner. Stars:
       Cristina Rains, Ava Gardner, Chris Sarandon, and Burgess Meredith.

A dedicated sentinel must guard the gateway to hell in order to protect the world from evil ... and the gateway is in Brooklyn. New sentinels must be selected at times for this awesome duty, and there is no escaping the charge once a choice has been made. [Evil]

579.   Koontz, Dean (pseuds. Richard Paige, Leigh Nichols, and Owen West).
C   **Darkfall.** New York: Berkley, 1984. 371 pp. ISBN 0-425-07187-1. (First
       published by W. M. Allen, 1984.)
       Other works: *Night Chills; Dreams; The Face of Fear; Shattered; The
       Vision; Whispers; Cold Fire; The Bad Place.*

Terrible, horrible rat-like things are attacking people. At first people think they are rats, but then it becomes increasingly clear that the attackers are worse than rats could possibly be. [Monsters, rodent-type]

580.   Koontz, Dean. **Phantoms.** New York: Berkley, 1983. 425 pp. ISBN 0-425-
C   06568-5. (First published by Putnam, 1983.)

Jenny Paige, a young doctor, arrives in lovely Snowfield with her kid sister. Instead of the expected wonderful new life, she finds death and unspeakable horror. [Horror]

581.   Koontz, Dean R. **Strangers.** New York: Berkley, 1986. 681 pp. ISBN
C   0-425-09217-8. (First published by G. P. Putnam's Sons, 1986.)

The strangers come from all over the country to compare notes in a motel in Utah because they can all vaguely remember something having happened there, but they're not sure what. [Paranormal abilities]

582.   Koontz, Dean R. **Twilight Eyes.** New York: Berkley, 1987. 405 pp. ISBN
C   0-425-10065-0. (First published in a shorter version as *The Land of
       Enchantment*, 1985.)

Carl Stanfeuss, now called Slim MacKenzie, has found a job in a carnival with a beautiful woman as boss. But the fearful goblins who inhabit the bodies of some humans are gathering and planning a terrible tragedy for the carnival. Only Slim can organize those with twilight eyes, the gift of seeing goblins, to try to stop them. [Demons; Paranormal abilities]

583.   Koontz, Dean R. **Watchers.** New York: Berkley, 1988. 483 pp. ISBN
C   0-425-10746-9. (First published by G. P. Putnam's Sons, 1987.)
       Movie versions: *Watchers*, 1988. Director: Jon Hess. Stars: Corey Heim,
       Barbara Williams, Michael Ironside, and Lala.

In its ceaseless experiments, science continues to develop new marvels, some good and some evil. From a single laboratory come two opposite beings, a marvelously intelligent dog and a brutal monster. Both escape. [Monsters; Science gone wrong]

584. Kotzwinkle, William. **Fata Morgana.** New York: Avon/Bard, 1983. 195
C   pp. ISBN 0-380-64691-9. (First published by Knopf, 1977.)
      Other works: *Doctor Rat; Elephant Bangs Tree; The Fan Man; Night-
      book; Swimmer in the Secret Sea.*

Police Inspector Paul Picard finds himself in a bewildering and mystical sub-
world of magic and legerdemain as he investigates a murder in nineteenth-century
Europe. [Legerdemain; Magic]

585. Koumaras, Terence J. **Eye of the Devil.** New York: Carroll & Graf, 1989.
C   318 pp. ISBN 1-55547-286-9.

There's long been a local legend about a demon, the Leedsville Devil, out
there in the bogs. Most people don't believe in the demon. Then someone or
something begins to brutally murder people. [Monsters]

586. Kressing, Harry. **The Cook.** New York: Ballantine, 1984. 244 pp. ISBN
C   0-345-31721-1. (First published by Random House, 1965.)

When the cook first arrives at the castle called Prominance, he seems perfect.
But gradually he seems less and less perfect, and soon the masters of the castle
become the servants of the cook. Then very strange and evil things start to
happen. [Evil]

587. Kroll, Joanna. **Sagittarius Serving.** New York: Bantam, 1985. 160 pp.
A   ISBN 0-399-21188-8. (Zodiac Club series).

Penny, a competitive tennis player, learns that winning isn't an end-all and
that in order to have friends she must learn to be sensitive to others' needs.
Includes sports for each zodiac sign. [Astrology]

588. Kunstler, James Howard. **The Hunt.** New York: TOR, 1987. 217 pp.
C   ISBN 0-812-52093-9.

R. J. Traveal thought the idea of hunting for Bigfoot in the California
mountains was a great one. Then it becomes plain that the beast he is seeking is
not a benign, gentle creature but a savage killer. Now who is the hunter?
[Abominable snowman]

589. Kurland, Michael. **Death by Gaslight.** New York: Signet, 1982. 279 pp.
C   ISBN 0-451-11915-0.
      Other works: *The Infernal Device.*

Sherlock Holmes's great nemesis, Professor Moriarty, must be extra smart to
thwart the brainy detective for so long. Could it be that Moriarty depends upon
satanic help to carry out his evil schemes? [Satanism]

590. Kurtz, Katherine. **Lammas Night.** New York: Ballantine, 1983. 438 pp.
C   ISBN 0-345-29516-1.

The witches of England are rumored to have called up the storms that
destroyed the Spanish Armada many years ago. Can more contemporary witches
stop the Nazi horror from invading England during World War II? [Witchcraft]

591. Lackey, Mercedes. **Children of the Night.** New York: TOR: 1990. 313 pp.
C   ISBN 0-812-52112-9.
    Other works: *Burning Water.*

Life in today's world isn't easy for a practicing witch, but Diana Tregarde does her best to use her power for good by thwarting the powers of occult evil. [Gypsy lore; Vampires]

592. Lagerkvist, Par. **The Sibyl.** New York: Vintage, 1963. 154 pp. ISBN
C   0-394-70240-9. (First published as *Sibyllan* by Bonnier in Sweden, 1956.
    First English version published by Chatto and Windus, 1958.)

The story of a priestess of the oracle of Delphi whose devotion to the pagan gods leads to heartbreak. A parable comparing pagan and Christian philosophies. [Mysticism]

593. Lakin, Rita. **Demon of the Night.** New York: Pyramid, 1976. 192 pp.
C   ISBN 0-515-03939-X.

Andy's loving wife, Elinor, has changed into a screaming, crude, hateful woman. Medical science calls it a nervous breakdown, but Andy is sure there's more involved, because he has seen Elinor change into the image of a dead woman and whisper strange words. [Possession]

594. Lansdale, Joe R. **The Magic Wagon.** New York: Bantam, 1988. 115 pp.
C   ISBN 0-553-27365-5. (First published by Doubleday, 1986.)
    Other works: *The Nightrunners; Dead in the West; The Drive In.*

Mud Creek, Texas, in 1909 is not the sort of place you'd expect great excitement, but not all things are predictable. One day the magic wagon comes to town, complete with the petrified body of Wild Bill Hickok. The forces of evil are also coming to town, and it's going to be up to Wild Bill to save the day. [Transformation]

595. Lara, Jan. **Limbo.** New York: Popular Library, 1988. 250 pp. ISBN
C   0-445-20826-0.

Not all evil things come from hell. Maribeth discovers that an evil force is threatening her daughter, but the evil is different from any Maribeth has ever heard of, for this evil comes from limbo and must feed on life in order to exist. [Evil]

596. Largent, R. Karl. **Pagoda.** New York: Leisure, 1989. 394 pp. ISBN
C   0-8439-2756-9.
    Other works: *Black Death; The Plague; The Prometheus Project.*

The exquisitely carved miniature pagoda that Carl Holton finds in a Burmese bazaar first enchants but later terrifies him, for whoever owns the pagoda is its guardian and must protect its awful secrets and power. [Legends, Burmese]

597. Largent, R. Karl. **The Witch of Sixkill.** New York: Leisure, 1990. 367 pp.
C   ISBN 0-8439-2984-7.

Revenge doesn't bring out the best in people, and when Charlie Frazier decides to get even with those who have done him wrong, he turns to a witch for help. But the witch's idea of getting even gets out of hand, and soon Charlie finds he can't stop the killings. [Black magic]

598. Laski, Morghanita. **The Victorian Chaise Lounge.** Chicago: Academy
C   Chicago, 1984. 119 pp. ISBN 0-890773-097-8. (First published by Houghton Mifflin, 1953.)

Attractive Melanie Langdon is ill, but not desperately so. When she falls asleep on her lovely antique Victorian chaise lounge she awakens to a world very different from the one she knows. She has gone back in time, and there appears to be no way to get back to her beloved husband and child. [Time travel]

599. Laubenthal, Sanders Anne. **Excalibur.** New York; Ballantine, 1973. 236
C   pp. ISBN 0-345-23416-2.

The Holy Grail and Excalibur on the Gulf Coast of the United States? Is it possible? Yes, if the legendary Madoc brought them in his twelfth-century voyage to the New World. [Legends, Celtic]

600. Lauria, Frank. **Baron Orgaz.** New York: Bantam, 1974. 343 pp. ISBN
C   0-553-08657-1.
     Other works: *Doctor Orient; The Priestess; Raga Six.*

Terrible things have started happening, some connected to the horror of human experimentation done by the Nazis. Others, which are even more mysterious, can only be linked to the frightening terrors of devil worship and secret powers. [Satanism]

601. Lawrence, Louise. **The Earth Witch.** New York: Ace, 1986. 183 pp. ISBN
A   0-441-18130-9. (First published by Harper & Row, 1981.)

At first Owen is attracted to Bronwen through pity, but as she grows more beautiful each day with the ripening of the summer crops, his sympathy turns to love and passion. Yet it would seem that their love cannot be, for Bronwen is not human. [Legends, Celtic]

602. Lawrence, Margery. **Bride of Darkness.** New York: Ace, 1967. 190 pp.
C   SBN 020-07300-050.

At first Keith Randolph is wildly infatuated with his new wife, Gilda, but his love gradually changes to horror, for he realizes that his bride and the mother of his son is a practicing witch who believes in the power of evil. [Satanism]

603. Lawrence, S. J. **Aquarius Ahoy!** New York: Pacer, 1985. 160 pp. ISBN
A   0-399-21222-1. (Zodiac Club series).

The Zodiac Club members are staunch friends for the most part, but when J. L., Jessica, and Penny all decide they like the same guy, the stars begin to clash. Includes best vacation locations for different signs of the zodiac. [Astrology]

604. Laws, Stephen. **Ghost Train.** New York: TOR, 1986. 314 pp. ISBN
C   0-812-52100-5. (First published by Beaufort, 1985.)

After Mark Davies's fall from a rushing train, every day is a waking hell of fear. Something is driving him back to the train station and the horrible train of terror. Mark knows he must get onto the ghost train once again, but he doesn't know why. [Horror]

605. Laws, Stephen. **Spectre.** New York: TOR, 1987. 275 pp. ISBN 0-812-
C   52102-1

Richard has had his photo of the Byker Chapter for ten years to remind him
of happy times and good friends. But the photograph is no longer the same as it
once was, any more than the people in the photo are the same. [Horror]

606. Laymon, Carl. **Nightmare Lake.** New York: Dell, 1983. 146 pp. ISBN
A   0-440-95945-4. (Twilight series).

An idyllic summer vacation with their family shouldn't have frightened Burt
and his sister Sammi. After they discover a skeleton and later another body,
however, they know their vacation is not going to be peaceful and restful at all.
[Evil]

607. Laymon, Richard. **Flesh.** New York: TOR, 1988. 407 pp. ISBN
C   0-812-52110-2.
     Other works: *The Woods Are Dark; The Cellar; Out Are the Lights;
     Beware; Allhallows Eve.*

Attractive Alison's life is like that of many college students. She studies,
shares an apartment with friends, and works at a job. She has love troubles, too.
But these troubles become very minor when she is faced with a horrible beast that
takes men's bodies and directs them to kill and eat humans. [Horror]

608. Lazuta, Gene. **Blood Flies.** New York: Charter, 1990. 265 pp. ISBN
C   1-55773-374-0.
     Other works: *Bleeder.*

Beneath Black Island a powerful evil is growing, an evil that has been
whispered about as an old Indian legend. The evil power is growing now, and
soon it will swim over the earth creating havoc and terror. [Legends, Native
American]

609. Leader, Mary. **Salem's Children.** New York: Leisure, 1979. 367 pp. ISBN
C   0-8439-0982-X.

Mitti thinks Peacehaven will be a great place to bring up her young daughters
and start a new life for herself. The little southwestern Wisconsin town was
Mitti's home once and was the home of her ancestors — ancestors descended from
the survivors of the Salem witchcraft trials. Mitti starts to have dreams, not the
peaceful dreams of her childhood, but forboding dreams of destruction.
[Witchcraft]

610. Leader, Mary. **Triad.** New York: Bantam, 1974. 213 pp. ISBN 0-553-
C   0787-150. (First published by Coward, McCann & Geoghegan, 1973.)

When Branwen Ericsson's baby dies, she is devastated. But the sorrow does
not end with Branwen's loss. She begins to fear for her own sanity, life, and soul.
[Possession]

611. Lee, Edward. **Ghouls.** New York: Pinnacle, 1988. 444 pp. ISBN 0-55817-
C   119-3.
     Other works: *Coven.*

Bodies do not lie quietly in their graves in Tylersville, Maryland. Graves have been opened, corpses are gone, and girls have been disappearing. The supernatural is suspected from the start, but it is hard to believe that the dead have come back to life, a strange and inhuman life. [Zombies]

612. Lee, Stan, and Larry Lieber. **The Incredible Hulk.** New York: Tempo,
A   1980. 223 pp. ISBN 0-448-17197-0.
       Movie versions: *The Incredible Hulk*, 1977. Director: Kenneth Johnson.
       Stars: Bill Bixby, Susan Sullivan, Jack Colvin, and Lou Ferrigno.

Straight from the pages of the comic strip come the adventures of Dr. David Banner, who cannot control his transformation into a powerful being who battles evil and corruption. [Transformation]

613. Lee, Tanith. **Lycanthia: Or, the Children of Wolves.** New York: NAL/
C   DAW, 1981. 220 pp. ISBN 0-87997-610-1.
       Other works include *Sabella: Or the Blood Stone; The Gorgon — and Other
       Beastly Tales; The Winter Players; Companions on the Road; Volkhavaar;
       East of Midnight; Dreams of Dark and Light.*

Christian Dorse finds that he is not the only claimant to his ancestral mansion; two werewolf relatives also declare their rights. [Exorcism; Werewolves]

614. Lee, Tanith. **Red as Blood: Or, Tales from the Sisters Grimmer.** New
C   York: DAW, 1983. 208 pp. ISBN 0-87997-790-6.

Macabre reworkings of familiar fairy-tale themes, such as "Paid Piper," "Red as Blood," "Thorns," "When the Clock Strikes," "The Golden Rope," "The Princess and Her Future," "Wolfland," "Black as Ink," "Beauty." [Fairy tales; Short stories]

615. Lee, Warner. **Into the Pit.** New York: Pocket Books, 1989. 278 pp. ISBN
C   0-671-66358-5.

Jason's first wife Glenda is hard to forget, but her memory is fading as Jason enjoys his life with his new family. But Glenda is not one to let go of what was once hers, and she returns from the grave to drag the family into her foul world. [Zombies]

616. LeFanue, J. Sheridan. **Carmilla and the Haunted Baronet.** New York:
D   Paperback Library, 1970. 221 pp. ISBN 0-486-20415-4.
       Movie versions of "Carmilla": *Blood and Roses*, 1961. Director: Roger
       Vadim. Stars: Mel Ferrer, Elsa Martinelli, and Annette Vadim. *The Vam-
       pire Lovers*, 1971. Director: Roy Baker. Stars: Ingrid Pitt, Pippa Steele,
       and Madeleine Smith.

Eerie works by a much-admired and imitated early gothic writer includes the two novellas of the title. [Ghosts; Vampires]

617. Lefebure, Charles. **Daughters of the Devil.** New York: Ace, 1972. 171
C   pp. SBN 441-13887-097.
       Other works: *The Blood Cults; Witness to Witchcraft.*

Fictionalized accounts of fourteen alleged witches from history. [Satanism]

618. Leiber, Fritz. **Conjure Wife**. New York: Ace, 1984. 224 pp. ISBN 0-441-
C   11749-X. New York: Award Books, 1968. 188 pp. (First published by
       Twayne, 1953.)
       Other works: *Gather, Darkness!; Night's Black Agents; Two Sought
       Adventure; Shadows with Eyes; Heroes and Horrors; Night Monsters; The
       Secret Songs; The Sinful Ones*. Movie versions: *Weird Woman*, 1944.
       Director: Reginald LeBorg. Stars: Lon Chaney, Jr., Anne Gwynne, and
       Evelyn Ankers. *Burn, Witch, Burn*, 1962. Director: Sidney Hayers. Stars:
       Janet Blair, Peter Wyngarde, Margaret Johnston. *Witches' Brew*, 1980.
       Director: Richard Schorr. Stars: Lana Turner, Richard Benjamin, and
       Teri Garr.

Sociology professor Norman Saylor is horrified to discover that his wife,
Tansy, is dabbling in witchcraft. She assures him she is using her skills only to
protect them from the evil doings of others at Hempnell College, but Norman
insists that she destroy her wares and give up occult arts. After she does, terrible
things begin to happen, proving that Tansy was right. When Tansy's very soul is
captured, Norman realizes he must fight witchcraft on its own ground. [Black
magic; Voodoo; Witchcraft]

619. Leiber, Fritz. **Our Lady of Darkness**. New York: Ace, 1984. 183 pp. ISBN
C   0-441-64417-1. (First published by Berkley-Putnam, 1977.)

Franz Westen's life has become disoriented and meaningless since the death
of his wife. Then he realizes that the solitude he yearns for is haunted by chilling
presences—paramental entities. The fragile relationships he has allowed into his
life now become his bastion against evil. [Evil]

620. Leigh, Veronica. **Voodoo Drums**. New York: Manor Books, 1976. 268
C   pp. ISBN 0-532-12443-1.
       Other works: *Dark Seed, Dark Flower; Cat O' Nine Tales*.

Claire Richardson has come home to her old family mansion in the
Louisiana bayou country and is looking forward to learning her family's heritage.
But that heritage includes something evil and frightening, and the sound of
voodoo drums begins to haunt her day and night. [Voodoo]

621. Leinster, Murray. **Time Tunnel**. New York: Pyramid, 1964. 140 pp.
C

This novel is based on the television series. The time tunnel provides a
gateway from the 1960s to any time in the past or future. In this tale, a greedy
antique dealer uses the tunnel to transport objects from Napoleon's time to the
present, oblivious to the more serious events around him. [Time travel]

622. Leroux, Gaston. **The Phantom of the Opera**. New York: Carroll & Graf,
D   1986. 357 pp. ISBN 0-88184-249-4. (First published in France, 1912.)
       Movie versions: *Phantom of the Opera*, 1925. Director: Rupert Julian.
       Stars: Lon Chaney, Mary Philbin, and Norman Kerry. *Phantom of the
       Opera*, 1943. Director: Arthur Lubin. Stars: Claude Rains, Susannah
       Foster, and Nelson Eddy. *Phantom of the Opera*, 1962. Director: Terence
       Fisher. Stars: Herbert Lom, Heather Sears, and Thorley Walters.
       Phantom of the Opera, 1983. Director: Robert Markowitz. Stars: Maxi-
       millian Schell, Jane Seymour, and Michael York. *Phantom of the Opera*,

1989. Director: Dwight A. Little. Stars: Robert Englund, Jill Schoelen, Alex Hyde-White, Billy Nighy, Stephanie Lawrence, and Terrance Harvey. *Phantom of the Opera*, 1990. Director: Tony Richardson. Stars: Burt Lancaster, Charles Dance, Teri Polo, Ian Richardson, Andrea Ferreol, Adam Storke, and Jean-Paul Cassel.

The huge and imposing opera house in Paris has many secret nooks and crannies. Lovely young Christine is anxious about her career and accepts the instruction of a mysterious hooded man who appears out of nowhere in order to help her. Little does she suspect, however, that the man is nursing a terrible grudge, as well as a great love for her. [Horror]

623.   Leslie, Josephine. **The Devil and Mrs. Devine.** New York: Pocket Books,
C   1974. 282 pp. ISBN 0-671-78382-3-1.

Danielle Devine was widowed young, and it would seem that she will never find another man to equal her dashing, handsome young husband. Some nights Danielle hears demanding whispers in her sleep, whispers that promise her eternal life and perpetual beauty in exchange for her soul. [The devil]

624.   Leslie, Josephine. **The Ghost and Mrs. Muir.** New York: Pocket Books,
A   1974. 143 pp. ISBN 0-671-77761-0. (First published in the United States by
       Ziff-Davis, 1945.)
       Movie versions: *The Ghost and Mrs. Muir*, 1947. Director: Joseph
       Mankiewicz. Stars: Gene Tierney, Rex Harrison, George Sanders, and
       Edna Best.

Newly widowed Mrs. Muir is finding it hard to make ends meet, so when she discovers it possible to rent Gull Cottage at a ridiculously low price, she moves in quickly. She discovers, however, that the cottage already has a resident, the ghost of a crusty sea captain who is at first determined to get rid of her. [Ghosts]

625.   Leslie, Peter. **The Seeds of Satan.** New York: Zebra, 1976. 236 pp. ISBN
C   0-89083-208-0.

Father Hayes is an exorcist, and when he arrives at the home of a Brazilian industrialist now living in Massachusetts, he senses that he is in for his greatest struggle, for he must deal with the powers of santeria, a form of voodooism. [Voodoo]

626.   Lester, Teri. **The Ouija Board.** New York: Signet, 1969. 157 pp.
C

On a Pacific cruise, lovely Lisa discovers that ouija is not just a parlor game. The board warns her not to go to Mooréa, for a terrible fate awaits her there. [Prophecy]

627.   Leven, Jeremy. **Satan: His Psychotherapy and Cure by the Unfortunate**
C   **Dr. Kassler, J.S.P.S.** New York: Ballantine, 1983. 512 pp. ISBN
       0-345-30265-6. (First published by Knopf, 1982.)

Satan returns to earth in the form of a computer and seeks the aid of a psychotherapist. His chosen therapist, Dr. Kassler, finds his new patient to be very different from his usual clients with some very funny results. [The devil]

628. Levin, Ira. **Rosemary's Baby.** New York: Dell, 1985. 218 pp. ISBN
C 0-440-17541-0. (First published by Random House, 1967.)
Other works: *Boys From Brazil; The Stepford Wives; Sliver.* Movie
versions: *Rosemary's Baby,* 1968. Director: Roman Polanski. Stars: Mia
Farrow, John Cassavetes, Ray Milland, and Ruth Gordon.

Pretty Rosemary, married to a struggling young actor, wants to have a baby,
but her husband Guy wants to wait until his career is better established. Then they
move to the apartment of their dreams, and things start to happen. Guy's career
takes off and Rosemary becomes pregnant. Other things, however, make
Rosemary think that all is not well, and her fears for her unborn baby become
paramount. [The devil; Satanism]

629. Levy, Edward. **Came a Spider.** New York: Berkley, 1980. 232 pp. ISBN
C 0-425-04481-5. (First published by Arbor House, 1978.)

Spiders are beasties that a lot of people don't like. When they get as big as the
spiders in this tale, nobody likes them. They have been sent by a vengeful earth to
punish humankind for its sorry treatment of the land and sea. [Monsters, insect-
type]

630. Lewis, Arthur H. **Hex.** New York: Pocket Books, 1970. 228 pp. (First
C published by Trident, 1969.)

An account of a true murder case in the 1920s in Pennsylvania, one that
plainly proved that witchcraft was still practiced in rural areas of that scenic state.
[Powwow; Witchcraft]

631. Lewis, Deborah. **Voices out of Time.** New York: Zebra, 1977. 224 pp.
C ISBN 0-89083-243-9.

The old ancestral home in Scotland, Cullcraig Castle, awes Alice
MacDonneaugh at first. Then she fears she is going mad, for she hears voices and
sees visions from the past that warn her of danger. [Witchcraft]

632. Lewis, Matthew G. **The Monk.** New York: Avon, 1975. 345 pp. ISBN
C 0-380-0046802.

During the Spanish Inquisition, a monk, Ambrosio, is one of the church's
greatest advocates. Then he meets the beautiful Matilda and follows her into the
enemy camp, which harbors the powerful force of the devil himself. [Satanism]

633. Lewis, Richard. **The Spiders.** New York: Signet, 1978. 170 pp. ISBN
C 0-451-09250-3.

The spiders are coming, and they will rule the earth. Nothing—not even
humans—can stop their inevitable domination. [Monsters, insect-type]

634. Lindsay, Joan. **Picnic at Hanging Rock.** Harmondsworth, England:
A Penguin, 1970. 213 pp. ISBN 0-1400-3119-9. (First published by Cheshire,
1967.)
Movie versions: *Picnic at Hanging Rock,* 1975. Director: Peter Weir.
Stars: Rachel Roberts, Dominic Guard, and Helen Morse.

A picnic at Hanging Rock on Valentine Day, 1900, seems like a festive idea for the Australian schoolgirls who set off for their day's outing in high spirits. Those who return, however, are badly frightened, and some never come back at all. What could have happened at this mysterious rocky site? [Vanishings]

635. Linzner, Gordon. **The Troupe.** New York: Pocket Books, 1988. 284 pp.
C   ISBN 0-671-66354-2.

Benny's life has been a mess with little purpose. But when his sister is killed, he joins forces with a new friend to find her killers, strange street performers who savage their victims. [Monsters]

636. Liquori, Sal. **Sal's Book.** New York: Scholastic, 1985. 148 pp. ISBN
A   0-590-33201-5. (Psi Patrol series).
      Companions: *Max's Book* by Maxwell Hurley and *Hendra's Book* by Hendra Benoit.

Sal likes being cool, but like it or not, his newly acquired psychic powers make him a member of the Psi Patrol along with two other teens he considers real creeps. [Paranormal abilities]

637. Littke, Lael. **Prom Dress.** New York: Scholastic, 1989. 167 pp. ISBN
A   0-590-44237-6.

The old lady Miss Catherine knows the dangers of the beautiful old antique dress, but one after another, the teenage girls find the frothy, creamy lace irresistible. It's as if the dress were calling to them, begging them to wear it one more time. [Evil]

638. Lively, Penelope. **Astercote.** London: Pan, 1973. 159 pp. ISBN 0-330-
A   23672-5. (First published by William Heinemann, 1970.)
      Other works: *Going Back; Uninvited Ghosts; The Voyage of QV 66.*

When Peter and Mair first find out about Astercote, they cannot see it at all. Then they are told that Astercote is all around them, a deserted village. The puzzlement grows as they learn more about the village and its mysterious past. [Magic]

639. Lively, Penelope. **The Driftway.** Harmondsworth, England: Puffin, 1985.
A   154 pp. ISBN 0-14-031497-0. (First published by William Heinemann, 1972.)

When Paul and his kid sister decide to run away from home, they ask for a ride with Old Bill, whose horse-drawn wagon on the old Driftway road is not likely to be suspected by the police. But Paul soon discovers that he is receiving other attentions, messages for people who have traveled the road before him, people who are—or should be—dead. [Ghosts]

640. Lively, Penelope. **The Ghost of Thomas Kempe.** Harmondsworth,
B   England: Puffin, 1984. 159 pp. ISBN 0-14-031496-2. (First published by William Heinemann, 1973.)

Young James thinks the family's new house is great, mostly because it's so old. Yet it isn't until later that he realizes the house is old enough to have a resident ghost, a socerer who causes all kinds of problems. [Ghosts; Haunted houses]

641. Lively, Penelope. **The House in Norham Gardens.** Harmondsworth,
B   England: Puffin, 1986. 174 pp. ISBN 0-14-031976-X. (First published by
     William Heinemann, 1974.)

Fourteen-year-old Clare lives in a wonderful old house in Oxford stuffed full
of anthropological treasures discovered years ago by her great-grandfather. One
item, though, a shield from New Guinea, seems to have special powers, and Clare
finds herself having strange and haunting dreams of another place far away.
[Altered states of consciousness; Legends, oceanic]

642. Lively, Penelope. **The Revenge of Samuel Stokes.** Harmondsworth,
B   England: Puffin, 1983. 138 pp. ISBN 0-14-031504-7. (First published by
     William Heinemann, 1981.)

The Thorntons move to a new housing development built on the grounds of
an old property now gone that was designed by Samuel Stokes two hundred years
before. They think little about the history of the place until strange things begin
to happen. They begin to wonder, particularly Tim, who is convinced that
Samuel Stokes is out for revenge for the destruction of his town. [Ghosts]

643. Lively, Penelope. **A Stitch in Time.** Harmondsworth, England: Puffin,
B   1986. 140 pp. ISBN 0-14-031975-1. (First published by William
     Heinemann, 1976.)

Maria is enjoying her vacation on the beach as she searches for shells, fossils,
and other treasures. Then she meets some other kids including a very odd girl
named Harriet who lived a hundred years ago. [Ghosts]

644. Lively, Penelope. **The Whispering Knights.** Harmondsworth, England:
B   Puffin, 1987. 155 pp. ISBN 0-14-031977-8. (First published by William
     Heinemann, 1971.)

The old barn seems a perfect place to play, even though a witch supposedly
once lived there. But when William, Susie, and Martha create a witch's spell,
strange things begin to happen, things that could only happen because of evil
spirits. [Black magic]

645. Lively, Penelope. **The Wild Hunt of the Ghost Hounds.** New York: Ace,
A   1986. 150 pp. ISBN 0-441-88810-0. (First published by William
     Heinemann, 1971.)

When thirteen-year-old Lucy arrives to spend her summer holiday with her
aunt, she hopes to renew some old friendships. Everyone is growing up and
changing, however. Caroline and Louise seem interested only in their ponies, and
Kester has become a loner. Then the villagers revive an ancient hunting dance,
and Kester's uncle predicts dire happenings. [Legends, Celtic]

646. Llewelyn, Morgan. **The Horse Goddess.** New York: Pocket Books, 1983.
C   464 pp. ISBN 0-671-46055-2. (First published by Houghton Mifflin, 1982.)

Epona, daughter of a Celtic chieftain in ancient Europe, is so anxious to flee
the responsibilities and life of a shaman that she runs away from her village with a
Scythian stranger. She becomes his woman and learns to love his way of life on
the Sea of Grass, but she finds she cannot escape her own unique destiny and her
special powers. [Legends, Celtic, Shamanism]

647.   Lloyd, Elizabeth. **Witch Child.** New York: Zebra, 1987. 352 pp. ISBN
C   0-8217-2230-1.

Witchcraft stalks the stark New England landscape in the late seventeenth century. For Rachel the story starts when Goody Glover is hanged as a witch. Rachel believes Goody has taken over her body and lives on, feeding on Rachel's terror. [Possession; Satanism]

648.   Lofts, Norah. **The Haunting of Gad's Hall.** New York: Fawcett, 1980.
C   320 pp. ISBN 0-449-24272-2. (First published by Doubleday, 1978.)
       Other works: *The Claw; The Witches.*

Gad's Hall is a famous old house in the neighborhood, perhaps more famous than need be. Gad's Hall is not a happy place, and evil emanates from a mysterious locked room in the attic. [Evil]

649.   Logan, Les. **The Game.** New York: Bantam, 1983. 149 pp. ISBN 0-553-
A   22835-8. (Dark Forces series).

Ouija becomes the means for a demon to take over the crippled Julie as she attempts to possess her twin sister, Terri. [Possession]

650.   Logan, Les. **Unnatural Talent.** New York: Bantam, 1983. 166 pp. ISBN
A   0-553-23607-5. (Dark Forces series).

Andrew desperately wants to please his father, the high-school coach, by becoming a super basketball player. He even performs a magical rite from an old book of spells and finds that he must pay an awful price for becoming a basketball whiz. [Black magic]

651.   Long, Frank Belknap. **Night Fear.** New York: Zebra, 1979. 318 pp. ISBN
C   0-89083-489-X.

Long was a contributor to the famous *Weird Tales* horror magazine of the 1930s. His stories are highly respected. This volume includes "Night-Fear," "Humpty Dumpty Had a Great Fall," "The Man from Nowhere," "The Unfinished," "Willie," "The Mississippi Saucer," "The Horizontals," "Two-Face," "Prison Bright, Prison Deep," "Johnny on the Spot," "It's a Tough Life," "And We Sailed the Mighty Dark," "The Were-Snake," "To Follow Knowledge," "Invasion," "The Horror from the Hills." [Horror; Short stories]

652.   Long, John Arthur. **The Sign of the Guardian.** New York: TOR, 1981. 253
C   pp. ISBN 0-812-52118-8.

There's a savage inhuman killer loose in Dune Beach. It's bestial rages are hard to imagine, so hard that it begins to seem that the beast is superstrong and, maybe, supernatural. [Monsters]

653.   Long, Lyda Belknap. **The Witch Tree.** New York: Lancer, 1971. 174 pp.
C   ISBN 0-447-74772-0.
       Other works: *Fire of the Witches; Legacy of Evil.*

Joan Rondon is trying to find her sister. In her search, she comes to a house of legend, an old house that whispers strangely in the night. The house seems to have memories, memories that materialize and endanger Joan beyond all belief. [Satanism]

654. Lord, J. Edward. **Elixir.** New York: Ballantine, 1987. 305 pp. ISBN
C   0-345-34070-1.
     Other Works: *Mandrake; Upright Man.*

A beautiful woman, Sondra Herran, has decided to commit murder. Her victim will be Rudolf Cavendar, a mysterious man with even more mysterious secrets who has destroyed Sondra's happiness. No law covers the crime committed, so Sondra must be responsible for her own revenge. [Science gone wrong]

655. Lord, J. Edward. **Incantation.** New York: Ballantine, 1987. 281 pp. ISBN
C   0-345-34072-8.

The ancient Scarab of Amon is a powerful amulet, and many seek it in order to make their dreams come true. But the venerable Egyptian charm is not easy to use, and its power cannot always be controlled. [Legends, Egyptian]

656. Loring, Ann. **The Mark of Satan.** New York: Award, 1969. 155 pp.
A

Julie is having terrible dreams of being sacrificed in gruesome rituals. Then Julie awakens and discovers that her dreams are real and that she is slated for a terrible death. [Satanism]

657. Lovecraft, H. P. **The Best of H. P. Lovecraft: Bloodcurdling Tales of**
C   **Horror and the Macabre.** New York: Ballantine Del Rey, 1983. 375 pp.
     ISBN 0-345-29468-8.
     Movies inspired by Lovecraft's work: *The Haunted Palace*, 1963. Director:
     Roger Corman. Stars: Vincent Price, Debra Paget, Lon Chaney, Jr., and
     John Derek. *The Curse of the Crimson Altar*, 1968. Director: Vernon
     Sewell. Stars: Boris Karloff, Christopher Lee, Barbara Steele, Mark Eden,
     and Virginia Wetherell. *The Dunwich Horror*, 1969. Director: Daniel
     Haller. Stars: Sandra Dee, Dean Stockwell, and Ed Begley. *Re-Animator*,
     1985. Director: Stuart Gordon. Stars: Jeffrey Combs and Barbara
     Crampton. *From Beyond*, 1986. Director: Stuart Gordon. Stars: Jeffrey
     Combs, Barbara Crampton, and Ken Foree.

A collection of some of Lovecraft's best-known tales, edited by Robert Bloch, the popular horror writer. Lovecraft is credited with creating the notion of the *Necronomicon*, a long-forgotten book of occult Arab lore, as well as the often-imitated theme of horrible monsters living in the bowels of the earth, often referred to as the Cthulhu mythos. Included are "The Rats in the Walls," "The Picture in the House," "The Outsider," "Pickman's Model," "In the Vault," "The Silver Key," "The Music of Erich Zann," "The Call of Cthulhu," "The Dunwich Horror," "The Whisperer in Darkness," "The Colour Out of Space," "The Haunter of the Dark," "The Thing on the Doorstep," "The Shadow Over Innsmouth," "The Dreams in the Witch-House," "The Shadow Out of Time." [Evil; Short stories]

658. Lovecraft, H. P. **The Case of Charles Dexter Ward.** New York: Ballan-
C   tine Del Rey, 1971. 127 pp. ISBN 0-345-33286-5. (First published in *Weird
     Tales*, 1941.)

Charles Dexter Ward is haunted by his family's past and he delves into hidden secrets. These secrets, however, include the raising of a terrible supernatural force, the dreaded Cthulhu. [Evil]

659. Lovelace, Delos W. **King Kong.** New York: Ace, 1976. 219 pp. ISBN
C   0-441-44470-1. (First published by Grosset & Dunlop, 1932.)
     Movie versions: *King Kong*, 1933. Directors: Merian C. Cooper and
     Ernest B. Schoedsack. Stars: Fay Wray, Robert Armstrong, Bruce Cabot,
     Frank Reicher, Sam Hardy, Noble Johnson, and James Flavin. *King
     Kong*, 1976. Director: John Guillermin. Stars: Jeff Bridges, Charles
     Grodin, Jessica Lange, John Randolph, Rene Auberjonois, Julius Harris,
     Jack O'Halloran, and Ed Lauter.

On a faraway island live strange huge beasts. The strangest and most awesome, however, is the giant gorilla King Kong, who should have been left on his native island and not transported to New York. (Novelization based on the 1933 film version.) [Monsters]

660. Lumley, Brian. **Demogorgon.** London: Grafton, 1987. 333 pp. ISBN
A   0-586-07031-1.
     Other works: *The Caller of the Black; Beneath the Moors; The Horror at
     Oakdene; The Burrows Beneath; The Transition of Titus Crow; The Clock
     of Dreams; Spawn of the Winds; The House of Cthulhu & Others; Ghoul
     Warning & Other Omens; The Return of the Deep Ones; Hero of Dreams;
     The Ship of Dreams; Psychomech; Psychosphere; Psychamok!*

The Demogorgon is thought to have existed only in very ancient times, but now it has come back, disturbed from its long sleep by archaeologists from the University of Chicago. [Monsters]

661. Lumley, Brian. **Necroscope.** New York: TOR, 1988. 505 pp. ISBN 0-812-
C   52166-8. (First published in hardcover by 1986.)
     Sequels: *Vamphyri!; The Source; Deadspeak.*

Those evil Russian spies will try anything to get the upper hand. Boris Dragosani is even willing to dabble in the secrets of vampires to learn the information he is after. Only Harry Keogh stands between Boris and his evil schemes, and Harry has a few arcane secrets of his own! [Vampires; Zombies]

662. Lurie, Alison. **Imaginary Friends.** New York: Avon, 1968. 288 pp. ISBN
C   0-380-70073-5.

Sociologist Dr. Roger Zimmern thinks it's a good idea to investigate a weird cult focused on Verena, a teenage psychic. He discovers that science doesn't answer all questions, particularly those of the heart. [Paranormal abilities]

Names beginning with "Mc" are alphabetized under "Mac."

663. MacAvoy, R. A. **Book of Kells.** New York: Bantam, 1985. 340 pp. ISBN
C   0-553-25260-7.

John Thornburn loves Ireland. One day he is transported back through time to an earlier, more-magical age. He falls in love with a fascinating young woman and goes on an important quest like the heroes of old. [Magic; Time travel]

664. MacAvoy, R. A. **Damiano.** New York: Bantam, 1985. 243 pp. ISBN
C   0-553-17154-2.
       Sequels: *Damiano's Lute; Raphael.*

Damiano is a wizard's son and alchemist, but his fever to learn makes him a
scholar and musician as well. His dreams of a peaceful life in Renaissance Italy
learning to play the lute from the angel Raphael are not to be, for he finds that he
alone can save his home city from the destruction of invading troops. [Alchemy;
Angels; Magic]

665. MacAvoy, R. A. **The Grey Horse.** New York: Bantam Spectra, 1987.
C   247 pp. ISBN 0-553-26557-1.

Ruairi MacEibhir is determined to win the woman he loves, even if it means
resorting to magic. [Legends, Celtic; Magic]

666. MacAvoy, R. A. **Tea with the Black Dragon.** New York: Bantam, 1983.
C   166 pp. ISBN 0-553-23205-3.
       Sequels: *Twisting the Rope.*

A modern-day woman seeks help from an oriental gentleman who claims
that magical powers are vested in his thousand-year-old black dragon. [Dragons;
Magic]

667. McBain, Ed (pseud. of Evan Hunter). **Ghosts.** New York: Bantam, 1981.
C   166 pp. ISBN 0-553-14518-5. (First published by Viking, 1980.)

The boys of the 87th Precinct are flummoxed by the latest crime they must
investigate. But the investigation goes slowly, and Steve Carella's best clues seem
to come from a medium, which does not conform with accepted New York City
police procedures. [Occult mystery/detective; Paranormal abilities]

668. McCammon, Robert R. **Blue World.** New York: Pocket Books, 1990.
C   435 pp. ISBN 0-671-69518-5. (First published in England by Grafton,
       1988.)
       Other works: *Baal; They Thirst; The Night Boat; Bethany's Sin; Swan
       Song; Stinger; Hour of the Wolf.*

A collection of McCammon's short stories, including "Yellowjacket
Summer," "Makeup," "Doom City," "Nightcrawlers," "Pin," "Yellachile's Cage,"
"I Scream Man!," "He'll Come Knocking at Your Door," "Chico," "Night Calls
the Green Falcon," "The Red House," "Something Passed By," "Blue World."
[Horror; Short stories]

669. McCammon, Robert R. **Mystery Walk.** New York: Ballantine, 1983. 419
C   pp. ISBN 00-345-31514-6. (First published by Holt, Rinehart & Winston,
       1983.)

Billy's Choctaw heritage may have given him strange and wonderful powers,
but they have also given him the ability to know he is being pursued by the
dreaded shape changer. [Paranormal abilities; Shamanism]

670. McCammon, Robert R. **Usher's Passing.** New York: Ballantine, 1985.
C   416 pp. ISBN 0-345-32407-2. (First published by Holt, Rinehart and Winston, 1984.)

Suppose that Poe's famous tale of the House of Usher is a true story, at least partially true. What if the Usher family still survives, possessed of great power but with the ancient curse still very much a part of all their lives? [Evil; Haunted houses]

671. McCullough, Colleen. **The Ladies of Missalonghi.** New York: Avon,
C   1988. 189 pp. ISBN 0-380-70458-7. (First published by Harper & Row, 1987.)

Women without men to protect and cherish them live a poor life in early twentieth-century Australia. There seems little hope that plain, practical Missy will be able to capture a man and save her mother and aunt from miserable poverty, but Missy has a powerful ally in the town's librarian. [Ghosts]

672. MacDonald, George. **Lilith.** London: Allison & Busby, 1987. 192 pp.
D   ISBN 0-85031-626-X.
      Other works: *The Princess and the Goblin; The Princess and Curdie; At the Back of the North Wind.*

The wealthy young hero of this tale returns to his ancient ancestral home in the country. But a peaceful, perhaps boring, life is not to be his lot, for a mysterious and enchanting spirit enters his world. She leads him into the strange and beautiful land of dreams. [Dreams]

673. McDowell, Michael. **Blackwater I: The Flood.** New York: Avon, 1983.
C   189 pp. ISBN 0-380-81489-7.
      Sequels: *Blackwater II; Blackwater III; Blackwater IV; Blackwater V; Blackwater VI.*

A devastating flood immobilizes a small Alabama town in the early twentieth century. Elinor, a fascinating woman with strange powers, is found in the middle of the destruction, and she decides to stay and become a member of the community. Her odd habits cause comment, however, and the townspeople don't even suspect all of her secret activities. [Transformation]

674. McEvoy, Marjorie. **The Wych Stone.** New York: Beagle, 1974. 188 pp.
C   ISBN 0-345-26605-6.

Perdita knew the life of companion to an elderly relative might be sad and dreary, but then she is swept off her feet by the fascinating Master of Wych-stones. Enchanted by her lover, Perdita eagerly marries him only to find that he serves a dark and evil master. [Satanism]

675. McGivern, William P. **The Seeing.** New York: Tower, 1980. 284 pp. ISBN
C   0-505-51493-1.

Little Jessica Mallory is having terrible dreams, or are they something more? Her mother finally realizes that Jessica is troubled by visions, not nightmares, and that her visions are being used for an evil purpose. [Paranormal abilities]

676. McGrath, Patrick. **Blood and Water and Other Tales.** New York: Ballan-
C   tine, 1989. 214 pp. ISBN 0-345-35585-7. (First published by Poseidon,
      1988.)

Eerie stories of wonder and horror, including "The Angel," "The Lost
Explorer," "The Black Hand of the Raj," "Lush Triumphant," "Ambrose Syme,"
"The Arnold Crombeck Story," "Blood Disease," "The Skewer," "Marmilion,"
"Hand of a Wanker," "The Boot's Tale," "The E(rot)ic Potato," "Blood and
Water." [Horror; Short stories]

677. McIntosh, J. T. **Transmigration.** New York: Avon, 1970. 176 pp. SBN
C   380-02375-075.
      Other works: *Six Gates from Limbo.*

Fletcher is an unusual man and one who would be envied by many if they
even suspected his supernatural strength. Fletcher cannot die. Instead, Fletcher is
able to move his consciousness from one body to another in a seemingly endless
chain. [Paranormal abilities]

678. McIntyre, Vonda N. **The Bride.** New York: Dell, 1985. 221 pp. ISBN
A   0-440-10801-2. (See also entry 703.)
      Other works: *Dreamsnake.* Movie versions: *The Bride*, 1985. Director:
      Franc Roddam. Stars: Sting, Jennifer Beals, Geraldine Page, and Clancy
      Brown.

After Frankenstein creates his famous monster, he decides to perfect his
skills and create a more delicate, beautiful model intended as the bride for his
original creation. But he is so successful that he falls in love with her himself.
[Monsters; Science gone wrong]

MacKay, Mary Mills. *See* Marie Corelli.

679. McKenney, Kenneth. **The Plants.** New York: Golden Apple, 1984. 243 pp.
C   ISBN 0-553-19828-9.
      Other works: *The Changeling* trilogy.

During an unusually wet summer in England, the plants emerge. At first they
make people think of lush tropical wonders, but then the wonder turns to terror
as the plants become menacing enemies that destroy and kill the human race.
[Ecological horror; Monsters]

680. McKillip, Patricia A. **The House on Parchment Street.** New York:
A   Aladdin, 1978. 192 pp. ISBN 0-689-70451-8.
      (First published by Atheneum, 1973.)

An American girl arrives to spend time with her English relatives in their
three-hundred-year-old house. Soon Carol and her English cousin, Bruce, realize
that only they can see the ghosts in the cellar, and there must be a reason the
ghosts are appearing only to them. [Ghosts]

681. McKinley, Robin. **Beauty.** New York: Pocket Books, 1985. 247 pp. ISBN
A   0-671-60434-1. (First published by Harper, 1978.)
      Other works: *Imaginary Lands; The Blue Sword; The Hero and the
      Crown.*

A retelling of *Beauty and the Beast* for today's teens, with a believable, matter-of-fact heroine who loves horses. [Fairy tales; Magic; Monsters]

682. McKinley, Robin. **The Door in the Hedge.** New York: Ace, 1982. 216 pp.
A   ISBN 0-441-15314-3. (First published by William Morrow, 1981.)

Four long fairy stories written in a commonsensical style, including "The Stolen Princess," "The Princess and the Frog," "The Hunting of the Hind," "The Twelve Dancing Princesses." [Fairy tales; Short stories]

683. MacLane, Jack. **Blood Dreams.** New York: Zebra, 1989. 350 pp. ISBN
C   0-8217-2680-3.
       Other works: *Keepers of the Beast.*

Hubert is just your average serial killer until the time comes when he starts to have problems with his head; it's as if his mind doesn't belong to him any more. [Paranormal abilities]

684. MacLeish, Roderick. **Prince Ombra.** New York: TOR, 1982. 379 pp. ISBN
C   0-812-54550-8.

Prince Ombra is the legendary master of human nightmares, and traces of his power can be found in many times and cultures. Now it is the modern age, and Prince Ombra is about to appear again and bring terror to the world. [Horror]

685. MacLeod, Charlotte. **The Curse of the Giant Hogweed.** New York: Avon,
C   1986. 168 pp. ISBN 0-380-70051-4. (First published by Doubleday, 1985.)

Professor Peter Shandy and his horticulture buddies from Balaclava College, U.S.A., find themselves whisked back to ancient Wales in the time when magic and legendary figures are real. Will Peter be able to cope in this new setting, and will he be stuck there forever? [Legends, Celtic; Magic]

686. McNally, Clare. **Ghost House.** New York: Bantam, 1979. 214 pp. ISBN
C   0-440-18244-8.
       Sequels: *Ghost House Revenge.*

When the VanBurens move to their new house, they little suspect the terror that awaits them in the home of a woman burned for witchcraft in an earlier time. [Ghosts; Haunted houses]

687. McNally, Clare. **Somebody Come and Play.** New York: TOR, 1987. 311
C   pp. ISBN 0-812-52164-1.

The Hollenbeck house is not a happy house, for it has been the scene of much sadness. Cassie's mother has told Cassie to stay away form the old place, but Cassie, Diane, and Lisa have found a fascinating room full of toys there. But toys are not all there is in the Hollenbeck house. There's also a very strange girl named Nicole, who thinks Cassie should have no other friends but her. [Ghosts]

688. McShane, Mark. **Seance on a Wet Afternoon.** New York: Fawcett, 1965.
C   128 pp. (First published by Doubleday, 1961.)
       Other works: *The Singular Case of the Multiple Dead.* Movie versions:
       Seance on a Wet Afternoon. Director: Bryan Forbes. Stars: Kim Stanley,
       Richard Attenborough, Patrick Mcgee, and Nanette Newman.

Myra has always had special gifts, but she is not satisfied to use them merely to help troubled people. Her specialness becomes an obsession that drives her to kidnapping in order to become famous and respected for her power. [Spiritualism]

689. Machen, Arthur. **Tales of Horror and the Supernatural.** New York:
C Pinnacle, 1971, 1973. 2 vol. SBN 523-00032-095; 523-00282-095.

Stories of terror by a reknowned British writer, including (volume 1) "The Great God Pan," "The White People," "The Inmost Light," "The Shining Pyramid," "The Great Return," (volume 2) "The Novel of the Black Seal," "The Novel of the White Powder," "The Bowmen," "The Happy Children," "The Bright Boy," "Out of the Earth," "N," "Children of the Pool," "The Terror." [Horror; Short stories]

690. Mahy, Margaret. **The Changeover: A Supernatural Romance.** New York:
A Scholastic, 1985. 224 pp. ISBN 0-590-33798-X. (First published in the
United States by Atheneum, 1984.)
Other works: *Alien in the Family; Dangerous Spaces; The Tricksters.*

Jacko, Laura's beloved younger brother, is being drained of his strength by a demon, and Laura turns to a teenage male witch to help save him. She learns, however, that she must pay a high price, that of becoming a witch herself. A story of courage and love set in modern-day New Zealand. [Witchcraft]

691. Mahy, Margaret. **The Haunting.** London: Magnet, 1984. 135 pp. ISBN
A 0-416-48420-4. (First published by Methuen, 1982.)
Barney is frightened when the ghostly spirit of a young boy appears to him. He learns that the spirit is that of his assumed-dead great-uncle, but then he discovers that Great-Uncle Cole is still alive. Barney must face some very strange truths about his mysterious family before the end of the story. [Paranormal abilities]

692. Malterre, Elona. **The Celts.** New York: Dell, 1988. 370 pp. ISBN 0-440-
C 20059-8.
Deirdre, a Celtic beauty of old Britain, is destined to marry the old king, but she loves handsome Naisha, a brave warrior who will let nothing stand in their way, not even the power of ancient sorcery and magic. [Legends, Celtic]

693. Manley, Mark. **Sorcerer.** New York: Popular Library, 1988. 309 pp. ISBN
C 0-445-20524-5.
Other works: *The Devil's Coin; Throwback.*

As a trained psychologist, Michael Dragon respects the power of the mind but also believes he understands the mind's limitations. That is before he meets the sorcerers, ancient magicians who can control minds for an ultimate purpose. [Magic]

694. Mannix, Daniel P. **The Wolves of Paris.** New York: Avon, 1979. ISBN
A 0-380-47553-3. (First published by E. P. Dutton, 1978.)
The great wolf Courtaud and his pack have become legendary as ruthless killers. Courtaud is feared and respected, thought by many to be more than

an animal because his uncanny skill and intelligence make him more than a match for the hunters who seek him. [Monsters]

695. March, Melisand. **The Mandrake Scream.** New York: Avon, 1977. 284 pp.
C   ISBN 0-380-00883-1. (First published by Mason/Charter, 1975.)
     Other works: *The Site.*

Bill wonders a lot about Vivian, a beautiful woman who seems so insistent about wanting him. Her advances are blatant, so blatant that Bill becomes uneasy. He even wonders whether Vivian is human; can she be some sort of succubus, an insatiable demon? [Demons; Horror]

696. Marley, Stephen. **Spirit Mirror.** Glasgow, Scotland: Fontana, 1988. 334
C   pp. ISBN 0-00-617521-X.

It is a time of ancient customs and rites in old China, and an evil is stirring in the land. Only Chia, the sorceress of Black Dragon Mountain, can battle the evil being, but the people hate and fear her almost as much as they do the evil itself. [Legends, Chinese]

697. Marlin, J. **Getting out the Ghost.** New York: Pacer, 1984. 128 pp. ISBN
B   0-399-21130-6.

Joyce is an insecure teenager until the spirit of Gretta Marie enters her body and Joyce suddenly becomes talented, smart, and popular. Then Gretta Marie starts doing things that Joyce doesn't like, but getting rid of Gretta Marie seems to be an impossible task. [Possession]

698. Marsh, Geoffrey. **The Tail of the Arabian Knight.** New York: TOR, 1988.
C   278 pp. ISBN 0-812-50652-9. (First published by Doubleday, 1986.)
     Other works: *The King of Satan's Eyes; The Fangs of the Hooded Demon; The Patch of the Odin Soldier.*

Farren Upshire needs the tail of the legendary horse Knight. The tail is a magical tail, and Farren thinks Lincoln Blackthorne can get it for him in spite of seemingly overwhelming odds. [Legends, Arabian]

699. Marsh, Ngaio. **Spinster in Jeopardy.** New York: Jove, 1980. 246 pp. ISBN
C   0-515-08718-1.

Inspector Roderick Alleyn, hero of a detective series, takes his lovely wife and young son with him to the picturesque mountains near the Riviera for a bit of vacation tacked onto a business trip. About the last thing he expects to find there is a coven of witches, not to mention murder. [Occult mystery/detective; Satanism]

700. Marten, Jacqueline. **Visions of the Damned.** New York: Playboy, 1979.
C   318 pp. ISBN 0-872-16529-9.

Michael Normand has a terrible gift; she can see the future. The future she sees is always of death, and the visions always come true. Michael turns to a psychiatrist for help, and what they discover together through hypnosis is the origins of the curse. [Paranormal abilities]

701. Martin, George R. R. **Fevre Dream.** New York: Pocket Books, 1983. 390
C   pp. ISBN 0-671-43185-4. (First published by Poseidon Press, 1982.)
      Other works: *Sandkings.*

A steamboat captain on the Mississippi finds that his mysterious backer, Joshua York, has embarked on a mission to save his fellow vampires from their blood-drinking habits and free them from the rapacious blood-master. [Vampires]

702. Martin, Jack (pseud. of Dennis Etchison). **Halloween III: The Season of**
C   **the Witch.** New York: Jove, 1982. 228 pp. ISBN 0-515-08594-4.
      Movie versions: *Halloween III: The Season of the Witch*, 1982. Director:
      Tommy Lee Wallace. Stars: Tom Atkins, Stacey Nelkin, and Dan
      O'Herlihy.

The hypnotic television and radio commercial is driving parents crazy, but little do they realize that the products being sold, halloween masks, have the power to destroy their children. [Evil]

703. Martin, Les. **The Bride.** New York: Random House, 1985. 93 pp. ISBN
A   0-394-87370-X. (See also entry 678.)
      Movie versions: See entry 678.

When Dr. Frankenstein produces a beautiful artificial woman as an intended bride for his famous monster, things don't work out as originally planned. She is such an improvement over the original model that the doctor falls in love with her himself. [Monsters; Science gone wrong]

704. Martin, Ralph. **The Man Who Haunted Himself.** New York: Award
C   Books, 1970. 139 pp.
      Movie versions: *The Man Who Haunted Himself*, 1970. Director: Basil
      Dearden. Stars: Roger Moore, Hildegard Neil, Alastair MacKenzie, and
      Hugh Mackenzie.

Harry Pelham is a respected ordinary businessman. Then something very weird and very frightening begins to happen. Harry keeps seeing himself, a double who will not let himself be identified. Somehow Harry knows this is more than a look-alike; it's his own ghost. [Ghosts]

705. Martin, Russ. **The Education of Jennifer Parrish.** New York: TOR, 1984.
C   319 pp. ISBN 0-812-52154-4.
      Other works: *The Desecration of Susan Browning; The Possession of
      Jessica Young; The Obsession of Sally Wing.*

Students at a coed military prep school become the potential new bodies for the corrupt old members of the Organization who seek to dominate the world through evil. [Satanism; Transformation]

706. Martin, Valerie. **Mary Reilly.** New York: Pocket Books, 1991. 183 pp.
C   ISBN 0-671-73150-5. (First published by Simon and Schuster, 1990.)

A story of scientific experimentation that results in a sad and sorry ending as related by the famous Dr. Jekyll's young maid, Mary Reilly. [Science gone wrong]

707. Martindale, T. Chris. **Nightblood.** New York: Warner, 1990. 322 pp.
C   ISBN 0-446-35530-5.
      Other works: *Where the Chill Waits.*

Chris Stiles is a trained killer, trained by the U.S. government to be a soldier in Viet Nam. But on the battlefield Chris discovers more than death; he learns of something more horrible, a fate as a vampire. [Vampires]

708. Marzollo, James. **Halfway Down Paddy Lane.** New York: Scholastic,
A   1984. 165 pp. ISBN 0-590-33296-1. (First published by Dial, 1981.)

When Kate goes to sleep one night in an old house, she doesn't expect to wake up in an earlier time. Yet she does. In nineteenth-century Massachusetts she learns what it's like to work in a textile mill and fall in love with a young man who believes he is her brother. [Time travel]

709. Masello, Robert. **The Spirit Wood.** New York: Pocket Books, 1987. 343
C   pp. ISBN 0-671-63572-7.

Peter and Meg Constantine can hardly believe their great good fortune. At last there is release from financial stress and worry. There is also a beautiful, mysterious new home — an estate that eventually pulls Peter into a new life and a new existence, an existence from which he may never escape. [Legends, Greek]

710. Mason, A. E. W. **The Prisoner in the Opal.** London: Sphere, 1974. 288
C   pp. ISBN 0-7221-5913-7. (First published in Great Britain by Hodder &
      Stoughton, 1928.) (The Dennis Wheatley Library of the Occult, vol. 10.)

Terrible things are happening that point to demonic rites and satanic worship. Can the powers of good overwhelm the powers of evil? [Satanism]

711. Mason, Anita. **The Illusionist.** London: Abacus, 1983. 283 pp. ISBN
C   0-349-12279-2. (First published by Hamish Hamilton, 1983.)

Here is the story of the legendary Simon Magus, who awes the ancient Roman emperors and populace with his magic. Can he be the promised Messiah? Or is he a charlatan, a force of evil? [Legends, Christian]

712. Masterton, Graham. **Death Trance.** New York, TOR, 1986. 409 pp.
C   ISBN 0-812-52187-0.
      Other works: *The Sphinx; The Devils of D-Day; Ikon; The Manitou; The
      Pariah; Revenge of the Manitou; Tengu; Mirror; Charnel House.*

Randolph Clare is devastated when his wife and children are murdered. In his efforts to salve his grief, he asks an Indonesian physician to help him enter the realm of the dead in order to say good-bye. The physician warns him of the terrible dangers of such a journey, but Randolph does not heed him until it is too late. [Legends, Indonesian]

713. Masterton, Graham. **The Djinn.** New York: TOR, 1982. 210 pp. ISBN
C   0-812-52178-1.

Harry Erskine doesn't look like a clairvoyant, but then what does a clairvoyant look like? At any rate, Harry gets involved in a very strange case centered around a mysterious jar in his relative's attic. The jar contains something so evil that a man has cut off his own face before his death. [Evil; Legends, Arabian; Paranormal abilities]

714. Masterton, Graham. **Night Warriors.** New York: TOR, 1987. 405 pp.
C   ISBN 0-812-52185-4.
     Sequels: *Death Dream.*

The nasty old devil is at it again, and only a team of night warriors can battle the evil power in the astral world of dreams. This world has other rules, and learning how to win may cost the dauntless band their lives ... and their souls. [Dreams]

715. Masterton, Graham. **Picture of Evil.** New York: TOR, 1985. 379 pp.
C   ISBN 0-812-52199-4.

An updated version of themes in *The Picture of Dorian Gray* by Wilde (see entry 1134). Jet-set brother and sister from the Connecticut Gray family must scout out fresh young living skins to preserve their rotting bodies as they seek an old family portrait. [Evil]

716. Masterton, Graham. **The Wells of Hell.** New York: TOR, 1982. 317 pp.
C   ISBN 0-523-48042-3. (First published by Pocket Books, 1980.)

Horrible evil in the Lovecraft tradition stalks a small New England town. Children start to disappear, but are they really gone, or hiding in terror because of what they have become—horrible, shell-encased monsters? [Evil; Monsters; Transformation]

717. Matheson, Richard. **Hell House.** New York: Bantam, 1972. 247 pp. SBN
C   553-07277-095. (First published by Viking, 1971.)
     Movie versions: *Legend of Hell House*, 1973. Director: John Hough.
     Stars: Roddy McDowell, Pamela Franklin, Clive Revill, Gayle Hunnicutt,
     Roland Culver, and Peter Bowles.

The old Belasco place in Maine is very famous in psychic circles; not only is it reputed to be haunted but it apparently fights viciously to protect its secrets. A brave band of investigators decides to tackle the evil old house, a deed for which they will pay a very high price indeed. [Haunted houses]

718. Matheson, Richard. **Shock!** New York: Dell, 1966. 191 pp. (First pub-
C   lished by Dell, 1961.)
     Other works: *Shock II; Shock III.*

Blood-curdling tales by a noted horror writer, including "The Children of Noah," "Lemmings," "The Splendid Source," "Long Distance Call," "Mantage," "One for the Books," "The Holiday Man," "Dance of the Dead," "Legion of Plotters," "The Edge," "The Creeping Terror," "Death Ship," "The Distributor." [Horror; Short stories]

719. Matheson, Richard. **Somewhere in Time.** New York: Ballantine, 1976.
C   278 pp. ISBN 0-345-33111-7. (First published as *Bid Time Return* by
      Viking, 1975.)
      Movie versions: *Somewhere in Time*, 1980. Director: Jeannot Szware.
      Stars: Christopher Reeves, Jane Seymour, Christopher Plummer, and
      Teresa Wright.

Richard Collier has just received a shock; his days are numbered and his life
wil soon end. He escapes to the nostalgic world of the old ocean liner *Queen
Mary*, where he meets a beautiful woman in a time that seems so much more
wonderful than his own. [Time travel]

720. Matheson, Richard Christian. **Scars.** New York, TOR, 1988. 262 pp.
C   ISBN 0-812-52254-0.

Collected stories by the son of Richard Matheson, including "Third Wind,"
"The Good Always Comes Back," "Sentences," "Unknown Drives," "Timed
Exposure," "Obsolete," "Red," "Beholder," "Dead End," "Commuters,"
"Graduation," "Conversation Piece," "Echoes," "Incorporation," "Hell," "Break-
Up," "Mr. Right," "Cancelled," "Mugger," "The Dark Ones," "Holiday,"
"Vampire," "Intruder," "Dust," "Goosebumps," "Mobius" (with Richard
Matheson), "Where There's a Will," "Magic Saturday." [Horror; Short stories]

721. Maxim, John R. **Platforms.** New York: TOR, 1987. 336 pp. ISBN 0-812-
C   52214-1. (First published by Putnam, 1980.)
      Other works: *Time out of Mind.*

The strange thing started happening in London at a suburban train station.
Then in Lake Forest, a suburb of Chicago. Now it's happening in Riverside, Connecticut, where an average commuter by the name of Halloran sees other
commuters who seem to be as average as he, but Halloran knows they're dead.
[Zombies]

722. Mayhar, Ardath. **The Wall.** New York: Space and Time, 1987. 121 pp.
C   ISBN 0-917053-06-0.
      Other works: *The World Ends in Hickory Hollow; Medicine Walk; Car-
      rots and Miggle.*

Alice Critten arrives in Louisiana to claim old Great-Aunt Eleanor's
property, a house surrounded by a massive wall. The wall is a considerable
barrier designed to keep out even death. [Ghosts]

Names beginning with "Mc" are alphabetized under "Mac."

723. Meaney, Dee Morrison. **Iseult.** New York: Ace Fantasy, 1985. 229 pp.
C   ISBN 0-441-373887-9.

Tristan, the virtuous knight, was honored in King Arthur's court, but when
he meets his uncle's beautiful wife, his honor seems a small price to pay for
ecstasy. [Legends, Arthurian]

724. Menegas, Peter. **The Nature of the Beast.** New York: Bantam, 1975. 240
C   pp. ISBN 0-553-08142-1.

Dee-Dee Burke is frightened by what's happening to her little boys. At first she thinks they are being initiated into the rites of ancient Celtic witchcraft, but then she discovers that they are involved with something far more horrifying, an ancient evil more savage than satanism. [Legends, Celtic; Satanism]

725. Merritt, Abraham. **Seven Footprints to Satan.** New York: Avon, 1942.
C   192 pp. (First published by Boni & Liveright, 1928.)
   Other works: *The Moon Pool; The Ship of Ishtar; The Face in the Abyss; Dwellers in the Mirage; Burn, Witch, Burn!; Thru the Dragon Glass; Creep, Shadow!; Three Lines of Old French; The Metal Monster; The Fox Woman and Other Stories.* Movie versions: *Seven Footprints to Satan*, 1929. Director: Benjamin Christensen. Stars: Robert Armstrong, Helen Mack, and Frank Reicher.

Dashing American heroes have long served as protagonists of pulp fiction. Here, James Kirkham, a daring explorer, takes on the ultimate foe — Satan himself. It is up to Kirkham to save the souls — and lives — of others as well as himself and the beautiful woman of his dreams. [Satanism]

726. Merritt, Abraham, and Hannes Bok. **The Black Wheel.** New York: Avon,
C   1981. 296 pp. ISBN 0-380-55822. (First published by New Collectors' Group, 1947.)

Composed from a fragment left at Merritt's death, the plot involves the plight of shipwrecked survivors à la "Gilligan's Island." This, however, is no comedy, for the mismatched survivors soon discover they are not alone on the island and an old wrong will come to terrorize them. The final climax is breathtaking as horrible ghouls pursue the hero through endless underground caves. [Curses; Zombies]

727. Meyrink, Gustav. **The Golem.** New York: Dover, 1976. 190 pp. ISBN
D   0-486-25025-3. (First published in the United States by Houghton Mifflin, 1928.)

A mysterious and obtuse story dwelling on the meaning of reality. [Legends, Jewish]

728. Michaels, Barbara. **Ammie, Come Home.** New York: Fawcett, 1979.
D   223 pp. ISBN 0-449-23926-8. (First published by Meredith, 1968.)
   Other works: *The Crying Child; The Dark on the Other Side; The Walker in Shadows; Be Buried in the Rain; Sons of the Wolf; Wait for What Will Come.* Movie versions: *The House That Would Not Die*, 1970. Director: John Llewellyn Moxey. Stars: Barbara Stanwyck, Michael Anderson, Jr., Doreen Lang, Richard Egan, Katherine Winn, and Mabel Albertson.

Ruth Bennett is a widow living a placid existence in her old Georgetown home until the presence of others revives an old tragedy. Ruth must then help lay some ghosts to rest. [Ghosts]

729. Michaels, Barbara. **Here I Stay.** New York: TOR, 1985. 317 pp. ISBN
C   0-812-52250-8. (First published by Congdon & Weed, 1983.)

Andrea is excited and exhausted as she and her Jim seem finally to have
realized their dream of running an old country inn in Maryland. The old family
house is full of quaint charm, but Andrea hadn't realized that there is an
unexpected extra—a ghost. [Ghosts; Haunted houses]

730. Michaels, Barbara. **Prince of Darkness.** New York: Fawcett, 1971. 224
C   pp. ISBN 0-449-02059-1. (First published by Meredith, 1969.)

When Peter Stewart first goes to the historic old town of Middleburg,
Maryland, the locals are unfriendly, but he thinks this is probably just the usual
wariness of strangers. Then he notices that the town is really very strange. He
finds threatening voodoo charms and realizes that there is a real effort to scare
him away from Middleburg; it is difficult to uncover the reason. [Witchcraft]

731. Michaels, Barbara. **The Wizard's Daughter.** New York: Fawcett, 1982.
C   256 pp. ISBN 0-449-20113-9. (First published by Dodd, Mead, 1980.)

Pretty Marianne Ransom becomes a companion to a wealthy old duchess
who encourages her to develop her second sight. It seems to be an easy way for a
penniless girl to earn a living, but Marianne soon becomes frightened of the
spirits she summons and even of her own power. [Paranormal abilities]

732. Michaels, Philip. **Come, Follow Me.** New York: Avon, 1983. 328 pp.
C   ISBN 0-380-83006-X.

Who is the evil musician who holds such power over children? Is he the Pied
Piper of Hamlin, returned to earth for a more sinister purpose? [Evil]

733. Miedaner, Terrel. **The Soul of Anna Klane.** New York: Ballantine, 1977.
C   227 pp. ISBN 0-345-27159-9. (First published by Coward, McCann &
        Geoghegan, 1976.)

Little Anna is dying of a brain tumor and her brilliant father is desperate
with grief and a feeling of helplessness. Then Anna is freed from her sentence of
death, but at the cost of losing her soul, and her father must now deal with the
aftermath. [Mysticism]

734. Millhiser, Marlys. **The Mirror.** New York: Fawcett, 1982. 352 pp. ISBN
C   0-449-20008-6.
        Other works: *Nightmare Country.*

When Shay Garrett looks in the strange antique mirror on her wedding eve,
she is horrified to discover that her reflection is not her own but that of her young
grandmother. Shay's life is no longer her own, and she is trapped in a life she
doesn't want. [Transformation]

735. Miller, J. P. **The Skook.** New York: Warner, 1984. 307 pp. ISBN 0-446-
C   32861-8.

The Skook is an imaginary beast, made up to entertain Span Barrman's kids
when they were young. When Span finds he desperately needs help after being
trapped in a huge underground cavern, the Skook turns up again, this time for
real, but Span isn't sure the Skook will be much help. [Monsters]

736. Minton, T. M. **Offerings.** New York: Leisure, 1986. 395 pp. ISBN 0-8439-
C   2370-9.

A group of dauntless scientists brave the primitive world of Oceania to investigate rumors of a living "missing link." Once there, however, they discover bestial beings who demand human sacrifices for their bloodthirsty god. [Legends, oceanic]

737. Mitchell, Kirk. **Never the Twain.** New York: Ace, 1987. 294 pp. ISBN
C   0-441-56973-0.

Rewriting history isn't easy to do, but Howard Hart is determined to make his ancestor, Bret Harte, rather than Mark Twain, the rich and honored author of his time. [Time travel]

738. Monaco, Richard. **Journey to the Flame.** New York: Bantam, 1985. 260
C   pp. ISBN 0-553-25373-5.
      Sequel to *She* by H. Rider Haggard (see entry 437). Other works: *Parsival;*
      The Grail War; Runes.

The author of *She* becomes a character in this new sequel to the famous tale of a fascinating magical kingdom in Africa ruled by a dynamic, powerful, and beautiful woman. [Eternal youth; Lost lands]

739. Monaco, Richard. **Unto the Beast.** New York: Bantam Spectra, 1987.
C   473 pp. ISBN 0-553-26144-4.

The power and evil of Nazism may not have come fully hatched from the twisted mind of Adolf Hitler. Its origin may well be seated in an ancient belief and power. [Nazi occultism]

740. Monahan, Brent. **Satan's Serenade.** New York: Pocket Books, 1989.
C   208 pp. ISBN 0-671-6728-8.

People driven by ambition will sometimes do anything to gain success. Jack Horn knows his career as an operatic tenor isn't going anywhere, but then he is taught to sing magnificently by Belinda Fausse. She dies tragically, and Jack is alone in her house. He finds that he is not alone and that Belinda's spirit will not let him go. [Ghosts]

741. Monette, Paul. **Nosferatu: The Vampyre.** New York: Avon, 1979. 172
C   pp. ISBN 0-380-44107-1.
      Movie versions: *Nosferatu, The Vampyre*, 1979. Director: Werner
      Herzog. Stars: Klaus Kinski, Isabelle Adjani, and Bruno Ganz.

A brooding version of the old classic about the immortal vampire. This vampire plainly shows his relationship to bats, and although he is fascinating, he is hardly sensual. [Vampires]

742. Monteleone, Thomas F. **The Magnificent Gallery.** New York: TOR, 1987.
A   248 pp. ISBN 0-812-52216-8.
      Other works: *Crooked House* (with John DeChancie); *Fantasma.*

Brampton, Iowa, seems to be a perfect peaceful Midwestern town. Then Mr. Magister arrives driving his long black carnival wagon with a shooting gallery unlike any other seen before by the people of Brampton. Soon, everyone in Brampton will be caught up in evil and terror ... and very great changes. [Horror]

743.   Monteleone, Thomas F. **Night-Train.** New York: Pocket Books, 1984.
C   337 pp. ISBN 0-671-44952-4.

Very far beneath New York City, is a fascinating maze of tunnels that must be searched one by one for a missing train. The tunnels are not deserted but inhabited by a frightening terror. [Evil]

744.   Mordane, Thomas. **Bloodroot.** New York: Dell, 1982. 285 pp. ISBN
C   0-440-10411-4.

Quaint New England villages often have gnarled old oak trees as well as odd customs practiced by the locals, so Laura and Mark Avery do not think anything is amiss. They learn to their horror, however, that their dream of a peaceful and productive life with a growing family is not to be. [Evil]

745.   Morrell, David. **The Totem.** New York: Fawcett, 1979. 255 pp. ISBN
C   0-449-20856-7.

Potter's Field, Wyoming, is a poky little Western town until the strange deaths and the growing terror overcome the people in the community. [Evil]

746.   Moses, Ryan O. **Evilway.** New York: Zebra, 1990. 288 pp. ISBN 0-8217-
C   3042-8.

Young Rebecca is excited by her family's vacation on a houseboat on a lake in Utah. She can't understand why people seem edgy about the deaths that occurred earlier on the boat. But the old Navajo, Joe Redhill, knows the legends of his people, and he knows that the deaths are not over. [Legends, Native American]

747.   Mueller, Richard. **Ghostbusters: The Supernatural Spectacular.** New
A   York: TOR, 1985. 250 pp. ISBN 0-812-58598-4.
       Sequels: *Ghostbusters II* by Ed Naha. Movie versions: *Ghostbusters*, 1984.
       Director: Ivan Reitman. Stars: Bill Murray, Dan Ackroyd, Harold Rains,
       Sigourny Weaver, and Rick Moranis.

When a bunch of ne'er-do-well scientists band together to eliminate ghosts, they never dream they'll run into some evil entities so powerful they may even be beyond the skills of the ghostbusters. [Ghosts]

748.   Mullen, Victor. **Tree House.** New York: Zebra, 1989. 304 pp. ISBN
C   0-8217-2706-0.

Most kids think they're different, but Joshua is really different, for Joshua likes to kill. Joshua has a special place, a tree house, and it's there that Joshua nurtures his secrets and encourages his evil "friends" to come into his very being. [Demons]

749. Mundy, Talbot. **OM, the Secret of Ahbor Valley.** New York: Carroll &
C   Graf, 1984. 392 pp. ISBN 0-88184-045-9. (First published by Crown,
     1924.)
     Other works: *King of the Khyber Rifles.*

It is rumored that hidden deep in the Indian Hills there is a holy lama who
can reveal the secrets of the universe. It is also rumored that somewhere is a piece
of jade with great supernatural powers. In the 1920s, a reckless young
Englishman sets out to find the jade and discovers many other incredible things
on his journey. [Legends, Tibetan; Mysticism]

750. Munn, H. Warner. **Merlin's Ring.** New York: Ballantine Del Rey, 1981.
C   366 pp. ISBN 0-345-24010-3.
     Other works: *Merlin's Godson.*

A sweeping fantasy from Atlantis to the discovery of America in which
Merlin's godson is involved in many mythological and historical adventures.
Gwalchmai meets Corenice in ancient Atlantis, and their love endures through
all. [Legends, Arthurian; Atlantis; Eternal youth]

Munro, Hector Hugh. *See* Saki.

751. Murphy, Pat. **The Falling Woman.** New York: TOR, 1986. 287 pp. ISBN
C   0-812-54620-2.

Elizabeth Butler, an archaeologist working in the ruins of an old Mayan city,
finds herself slipping into the world and life of the ancient Mayan culture, a
world very different from the one she knows. [Legends, Mayan]

752. Myers, Robert J. **The Virgin and the Vampire.** New York: Pocket Books,
C   1977. 207 pp. ISBN 0-671-81016-2.
     Other works: *The Cross of Frankenstein; The Slave of Frankenstein.*

It is known that vampires have lived in many times and many places,
including nineteenth-century Georgetown. It is also thought, erroneously, that
vampires instinctively recognize their own kind. Beautiful Letitia thought that
Georgetown was her territory, and now it is invaded by another like herself. She
must find out who the stranger is. [Vampires]

753. Nathan, Robert. **Portrait of Jennie.** New York: Dell, 1977. 124 pp. (First
C   published by Knopf, 1940.)
     Movie versions: *Portrait of Jennie*, 1948. Director: William Dieterle.
     Stars: **Jennifer** Jones, Joseph Cotten, and Ethel Barrymore.

A poor struggling artist meets and paints the portrait of an enchanting girl
named Jennie. Every time he meets Jennie, however, she has become much older,
for, as she tells him, she has to catch up with him. [Time travel]

754. Naylor, Phyllis R. **The Witch's Sister.** New York: Aladdin, 1980. 160
A   pp. ISBN 0-689-70471-2. (First published by Atheneum, 1975.)
     Sequels: *Witch Water; The Witch Herself; The Witch's Eye; Witch Weed.*

Mrs. Tuggle is a most peculiar neighbor, young Lynn and her friend Mouse
agree. In fact, they think she's a witch. Lynn is frightened for her sister Judith,

who seems to find Mrs. Tuggle fascinating and is taking lessons from her. Judith says they're dancing lessons, but Lynn thinks they may be lessons in something else, something much more dangerous. [Witchcraft]

755.   Nazel, Joe. **Satan's Master.** Los Angeles: Holloway House, 1974. 224 pp.
C   ISBN 0-87067-259-2.
       Other works: *The Black Exorcist;* The Iceman series.

Barbados Sam is an evil voodoo priest, and it seems unlikely that young Roger Lee will be able to combat and defeat this powerful villain. [Voodoo]

756.   Neiderman, Andrew. **Night Howl.** New York: Pocket Books, 1986. 277
C   pp. ISBN 0-671-60634-4.
       Other works: *Someone's Watching; Imp; Brainchild; Love Child; Blood Child.* Rumored to be the author of V. C. Andrews' posthumously published books.

Little Bobby and his dog are faithful friends and companions until the day King turns vicious and has to be destroyed. But Bobby doesn't forget his old friend and sees him everywhere, first in his dreams. Then everyone in town is aware of King, for the dog has been turned into a monster of revenge. [Horror; Science gone wrong]

757.   Neiderman, Andrew. **Perfect Little Angels.** New York: Berkley, 1989.
C   262 pp. ISBN 0-425-11775-8.

Elysian Fields might as well be Stepford, for the teenagers of this town must conform and be wonderful kids or be turned into the children their parents would really like them to be. [Science gone wrong]

758.   Neill, Robert. **Witch Bane.** London: Arrow, 1968. 224 pp. (First pub-
C   lished by Hutchinson, 1967.)
       Other works include: *The Devil's Door.*

England's civil war is full of brutality and hardship as neighbors fight each other and the religious fervour of the Cromwellian forces becomes a harsh cleanser of evil in the land. Young Mary Standen is accused of being a witch but is rescued by Major Dick Rowley. Yet she may not survive the turmoil of her times, for once accused of witchcraft, the stigma is nearly impossible to remove. [Witchcraft]

759.   Nesbit, E. **The Book of Dragons.** Mahwah, N.J.: Watermill Press, 1987.
B   153 pp. ISBN 0-8167-0852-5.
       Other works: *The Phoenix and the Carpet; Five Children and It; The Enchanted Castle.*

The many kinds of dragons are shown in these stories: "The Book of Beasts," "Uncle James, or the Purple Stranger," "The Deliverers of Their Country," "The Ice Dragon, or Do as You Are Told," "The Island of the Nine Whirlpools," "The Dragon Tamers," "The Fiery Dragon, or the Heart of Stone and the Heart of Gold," "Kind Little Edmund, or the Caves and the Cockatrice." [Dragons; Short stories]

760. Nesbit, E. **In the Dark.** Wellingborough, England: Equation, 1988. 173
C   pp. ISBN 1-85336-080-5.

Scary stories, including "Man-Size in Marble," "Uncle Abraham's Romance," "From the Dead," "The Three Drugs," "The Violet Car," "John Charrington's Wedding," "The Pavilion," "Hurst of Hurstcote," "In the Dark," "The Head," "The Mystery of the Semi-Detached," "The Ebony Frame," "The Five Senses," "The Shadow." [Horror; Short stories]

761. Nesbit, E. **Tales of Terror.** London: Magnet, 1985. 126 pp. ISBN 0-416-
B   51830-3. (First published by Methuen, 1983.)

A famous English children's author from the turn of the century writes stories meant to do a bit of scaring, including "In the Dark," "Man-Size in Marble," "The Violet Car," "John Charrington's Wedding," "The Shadow," "The Five Senses," "The Three Drugs." [Horror; Short stories]

762. Netter, Susan. **Storm Child.** New York: Dell, 1983. 150 pp. ISBN 0-440-
A   98289-8. (Twilight series).

When Cindy first gets the job as a mother's helper, she is pleased and excited. She'll get to spend the summer at a posh resort, and her charge, Ian, seems easy to deal with at first. As the summer progresses, however, Cindy finds that Ian has an amazing power that becomes related somehow to the violent thunderstorms of the area. [Paranormal abilities]

763. Neville, Katherine. **The Eight.** New York: Berkley, 1990. 598 pp. ISBN
C   0-345-36623-9. (First published by Random House, 1987.)

An old and strangely beautiful chess set is the interweaving theme of this tale of mysteries through the centuries. If the pieces of the chess set are scattered, they cannot be used for unlimited power, but Catherine Velis is on a quest to bring the pieces back together again. [Legends, Christian]

764. Neville, Robert. **Deathday.** New York: Leisure, 1986. 400 pp. ISBN
C   0-8439-2378-4.

The amulet seems a little thing, but a woman accused of witchcraft has died to protect its secret. A workman finds the amulet in the cemetery, and great evil is awakened, evil that will bring about great sorrow in the little village of Medford. [Satanism]

765. Newman, Michael. **Heaven Can Wait.** Los Angeles: Fotonovel, 1978.
C   unpaged. ISBN 0-8-9752-001-7.

A pictorial account based on the 1978 movie remake of a football player who goes to heaven before he's ready (see entry 351). He is returned to earth but in the person of another man, a man with lots of problems. [Heaven and hell; Transformation]

766. Newman, Sharan. **Guinevere.** New York: St. Martin's Press, 1981. 257
C   pp. ISBN 0-312-35321-9.
     Sequels: *Guinevere Evermore; The Chessboard Queen.*

Young Guinevere is a cherished young lady who even has her own unicorn. When she reluctantly grows up, however, she must face reality in the person of smitten young Arthur who wants to make her his queen. [Legends, Arthurian]

767. Nichols, Beverley. **The Tree That Sat Down.** London: Fontana, 1975.
B   192 pp. ISBN 0-00-670993-1. (First published by Johnathan Cape, 1945.)
Other works: *The Stream that Stood Still; The Mountain of Magic.*

There really are enchanted forests ... somewhere. In one such magical place, there are witches, wizards, and rivalries. And when beings of such awesome power have conflicts, terrible things are sure to happen. [Magic]

768. Nichols, John. **The Milagro Beanfield War.** New York: Ballantine,
C   1987. 312 pp. ISBN 0-345-3446-4.
Movie versions: *The Milagro Beanfield War*, 1988. Director: Robert Redford. Stars: Ruben Blades, Richard Bradford, Sonia Braga, and Julie Carmen.

A local quarrel is escalating over the cultivation rights of a bean field. An old man in the village can talk to angels, and his wisdom is pivotal to the outcome of the story. [Angels]

769. Nichols, Leigh (pseud. of Dean Koontz). **The Eyes of Darkness.** New
C   York: Pocket Books, 1981. 312 pp. ISBN 0-671-82784-7.
Other works: *The House of Thunder; The Key to Midnight.*

Tina Evans's young son Danny is dead, the result of a tragic accident. The sad young mother has been trying to adjust to this loss, but then she discovers frightening messages that seem to come from beyond the grave. Now Tina must find the truth, although she little suspects how terrible that truth will be. [Science gone wrong]

770. Nichols, Leigh (pseud. of Dean Koontz). **Shadowfires.** New York: Avon,
C   1987. 436 pp. ISBN 0-380-75216-6. (First published by Nkui, 1987.)

Rachael has mixed feelings when her violent ex-husband is killed, but the feelings coalesce into fear when the body disappears from the morgue and she becomes sure someone is watching her. But who will believe that the dead can walk again? [Zombies]

771. Nichols, Lynn J. **Taurus Trouble.** New York: Pacer, 1984. 160 pp. ISBN
A   0-399-21109-8. (Zodiac Club series).

Cathy is pleased by her chance to work at the local newspaper but realizes that her Leo sign and that of her nemesis, Danny Burns—a Taurus—mean a lot of conflict. [Astrology]

772. Nimmo, Jenny. **The Snow Spider.** London: Magnet, 1987. 142 pp. ISBN
B   0-416-06492-2. (First published by Methuen, 1986.)
Sequels: *Orchard of the Crescent Moon; The Chestnut Soldier.*

Wales is a country long steeped in magical traditions, and when Gwyn's grandmother gives him odd gifts for his birthday, gifts that will test his own magical abilities, Gwyn is not surprised. Gwyn does not expect, however, that he **will need to battle the actual powers of evil, helped only by the elegant snow** spider. [Legends, Welsh]

773. Niven, Larry, and Jerry Pournelle. **Inferno.** New York: Pocket Books,
C   1976. 237 pp. ISBN 0-671-67055-7.

Allen Carpentier finds that death does not end with oblivion. For him, at least, death is merely the portal to another existence, this time in hell. [Heaven and hell]

774. Nixon, Joan Lowery. **A Deadly Game of Magic.** New York: Laurel-
C   Leaf, 1985. 148 pp. ISBN 0-440-92102-3. (First published by Harcourt,
     Brace, Jovanovich, 1983.)
     Other works include *The Seance; The Specter.*

When four youngsters take refuge in a mysterious house, they soon realize that the dangers of the storm outside are nothing compared to the bizarre happenings inside. [Legerdemain; Magic]

775. Nolan, Madonna Spray. **The Burning Ground.** New York: Pocket Books,
C   1987. 277 pp. ISBN 0-671-62664-7.

Brett, on her first trip to England, decides to provide some focus for her trip and tries to find out more about Elizabeth Will, a beautiful young poet who has committed suicide. Brett's search leads her to Yorkshire and Elizabeth's bereaved husband, who sees in Brett a reincarnation of Elizabeth. At first Brett is flattered, then she becomes frightened. She finds her own self slipping away, and a strange person seems to be taking over her body and mind. [Possession; Reincarnation]

776. Norton, Andrew, and Phyllis Miller. **House of Shadows.** New York: TOR,
A   1985. 250 pp. ISBN 0-812-54743-8. (First published by Atheneum, 1984.)

The old house seems full of secrets. Susan finds herself having dreams of the children who once lived in the house many years ago, children who met a savage fate at the hands of vengeful Indians. Those things happened in the past, but Susan discovers that magic can make past events repeat themselves, and she finds herself in great danger. [Legends, Native American; Magic]

777. Nuelle, Helen. **The Haunting of Bally Moran.** New York: Manor, 1976.
C   231 pp.

The old castle in Ireland is rumored to be haunted, but sensible Peggy is doubtful. Then Peggy begins to walk in her sleep, and dreams of events that happened centuries ago haunt her restless nights. What is the secret of strange Bally Moran? [Haunted houses]

778. Nunez-Harrell, Elizabeth. **When Rocks Dance.** New York: Ballantine,
C   1988. 309 pp. ISBN 0-345-34771-4. (First published by G. P. Putnam's
     Sons, 1986.)

Three women of the Caribbean, Emilia, Marina, and Virginia, must work together to preserve their obeah religion in the face of white cultural impact. [Shamanism; Voodoo]

779. Nye, Robert. **Beowulf: a New Telling.** New York: Laurel-Leaf, 1982.
C   96 pp. ISBN 0-686-85864-6. (First published by Hill & Wang, 1968.)
     Other works: *Merlin.*

A modernized version of the Beowulf legend, which describes the adventures of a hero opposing the monster Grendel and his mother. [Legends, English; Monsters]

780   Oates, Joyce Carol. **Mysteries of Winterthurn.** New York: Berkley, 1985.
C   516 pp. ISBN 0-425-08022-6. (First published by E. P. Dutton, 1984.)
       Other works: *Bellefleur; A Bloodsmore Romance.*

Winterthurn is a brooding old house, full of family secrets and unspeakable deeds. It is up to Xavier Kilgarvan to try to bring it all to an end, but Xavier is so lovesick for Perdita, he may not be equal to the task. [Horror]

781.   Oates, Joyce Carol. **Night-Side.** New York: Fawcett Crest, 1977. 318 pp.
C   ISBN 0-449-24206-4.
       Other works: *Bellefleur.*

Intricate, mysterious stories by a highly respected American writer, including "Night-Side," "The Windows," "Lover," "The Snowstorm," "The Translation," "The Dungeon," "Famine Country," "Bloodstains," "Exile," "The Giant Woman," "Daisy," "The Murder," "Fatal Woman," "The Sacrifice," "The Thaw," "Further Confessions," "The Blessing," "A Theory of Knowledge." [Horror; Short stories]

782.   O'Branagan, Devin. **Spirit Warriors.** New York: Pocket Books, 1988. 360
C   pp. ISBN 0-671-66774-2.

Three different people from three widely different cultural backgrounds come together to combat evil. Fay, the gypsy girl, Neva, a southwestern Native American, and Eric, tortured survivor of Viet Nam, must do battle to preserve goodness. [Gypsy lore; Legends, Native American]

783.   O'Branagan, Devin. **Witch Hunt.** New York: Pocket Books, 1990. 338
C   pp. ISBN 0-671-68455-8.

From seventeenth-century Massachusetts to nineteenth-century Nebraska and now to contemporary Colorado, the evil curse of the Hawthornes will not be put to rest. Leigh has married into this family and is determined to save her loved ones from the inevitable doom of the Hawthornes. [Satanism]

784.   O'Brien, Fitz-James. **The Fantastic Tales of Fitz-James O'Brien.** London:
D   Calder, 1977. 149 pp. ISBN 0-7145-3617-2.

Supernatural stories by a nineteenth-century author and edited by Michael Hayes. Included are "The Diamond Lens," "The Lost Room," "What Was It?," "The Wondersmith," "Seeing the World," "The Pot of Tulips," "The Dragon Fang Possessed by the Conjurer Piou-Lu." [Horror; Short stories]

785.   O'Brien, Richard. **Evil.** New York: Dell, 1989. 214 pp. ISBN 0-440-20226-4.
C

Fifteen years ago the best and the brightest of Everton High celebrated their graduation. Now they decide to return for a reunion; they gather at the grave of the class nerd, Raymond. [Ghosts]

786. Obstfeld, Raymond. **The Reincarnation of Reece Erikson.** New York:
C   TOR, 1988. 312 pp. ISBN 0-812-58658-1.

Training for the Olympics is hard, consuming work, and Reece Erikson has
become so intent on his goal to win the decathlon that he doesn't notice how he's
changing. But his Cory does; she knows that the changes are extreme and that her
husband is literally becoming another person. [Possession; Reincarnation]

787. O'Callaghan, Maxine. **Dark Visions.** New York: TOR, 1988. 346 pp. ISBN
C   0-812-52352-0.
     Other works: *The Bogeyman*

Dreams can bring sweet release, but Mitch's dreams are nightmares in which
she sees death and murder and horror. Mitch believes her dreams, or visions, can
help the police solve crimes, but she doesn't realize that the murderer has now
marked her for death. [Paranormal abilities]

788. O'Har, George M. **Psychic Fair.** New York: Pocket Books, 1989. 324 pp.
C   ISBN 0-671-67601-6.

A teenage boy and a ouija board arouse the spirit of Andrew St. Loup, a
Confederate colonel from the Civil War. This spirit cannot rest until his affairs
are set in order. [Ghosts]

789. O'Hara, Gerald John. **Malsum.** New York: Avon, 1981. 307 pp. ISBN
C   0-380-77289-2.

Malsum has already paid a heavy price for his devil worship; his two sons are
dead. Yet Malsum will not cease from his course, a path that will lead the old man
into terror. [Legends, Native American]

790. Oleck, Jack. **The Vault of Horror.** New York: Bantam, 1973. 122 pp.
C   SBN 553-08010-095.
     Movie versions: *The Vault of Horror* (also known as *Tales from the Crypt
     II*), 1973. Director: Ward Baker. Stars: Ward Baker, Daniel Massey,
     Anbna Massey, Terry Thomas, Glynis Johns, and Curt Jurgens.

Tales from the Crypt and *The Vault of Horror* were swell comic books some
years ago. Here are some stories that first appeared in them and still have the
power to scare. [Horror; Short stories]

791. Olesker, J. Bradford. **Beyond Forever.** New York: Signet, 1981. 182 pp.
C   ISBN 0-451-09565-0.

Keith, a skillful surgeon, is accidentally killed, and his loving wife, Joanna,
is devastated. But even as Joanna struggles to build a new life for herself, she
cannot forget Keith, who seems to be determined not to be forgotten. [Ghosts]

792. Olson, Paul F. **Night Prophets.** New York: Onyx, 1989. 350 pp. ISBN
C   0-451-40175-1.

The life of a vampire is thought by most to be a life of anguish, but some
people choose to live an eternal life in spite of all the warnings. [Vampires]

793. O'Neill, Timothy R. **Shades of Gray.** New York: Ballantine, 1988. 337 pp.
C ISBN 0-345-35425-7. (First published by Viking, 1987.)

West Point Military Academy does not encourage fanciful thinking and dreaming. Yet one cadet's obsessive dreams become infectious, and eventually all at the academy learn more than they ever thought about life after death. [Ghosts]

794. Orgill, Douglas, and John Gribbin. **Brother Esau.** New York: TOR, 1984.
C 288 pp. ISBN 0-8125-8680-8. (First published by Harper & Row, 1983.)

Suppose somebody really finds an abominable snowman? Dr. Liliane Erckmann and her team of scientists find there are great problems in making such a great discovery. [Abominable snowman]

795. Osborn, Nancy. **The Demon Syndrome.** New York: Bantam, 1983. 166
C pp. ISBN 0-553-22616-9.

Ann Haywood and her family are happy when they finally are able to afford the house of their dreams. Then Ann finds her happiness shattered by the presence of a demon spirit in the house, a spirit that is determined to take over Anne's body and corrupt her soul. [Demons; Possession]

796. Osborne, Louise. **The Satan Stone.** New York: Popular Library, 1977.
C 287 pp. ISBN 0-445-03179-4.
Other works: *Keys of Hell.*

Carolyn Porter has come to Penetralia, a huge desolate mansion, on an aimless holiday. She can't help but wonder if she has somehow been called there by dark and evil forces that want her — body and soul. [Gothic romance]

797. Osier, John. **Covenant at Coldwater.** New York: Ballantine, 1983. 228 pp.
C ISBN 0-345-32987-2.

Southern swamps hide many secrets, and Coldwater swamp is no exception. The swamp becomes a hiding place for inhuman beasts who have left their graves and seek the flesh of living persons. The swamp is not a good place to be, day or night. [Zombies]

798. Owen, Dean. **Konga.** Derby, Conn.: Monarch, 1960. 144 pp.
C Movie versions: *Konga*, 1961. Director: John Lemont. Stars: Michael Gough, Margo Johns, Jess Conrad, and Claire Gordon.

Professor Decker is not the antiseptic scientist he appears to be to most people. Also, his experiments with little monkeys are hardly orthodox. When Professor Decker turns tiny Konga into a huge beast, he knows he has a way to get rid of his enemies. [Monsters; Science gone wrong]

799. Page, Thomas. **The Hephaestus Plague.** New York: Bantam, 1975. 217 pp.
C ISBN 0-553-04943-1. (First published by Putnam's, 1973.)
Movie versions: *Bug*, 1975. Director: Jeannot Szwarc. Stars: Bradford Dillman, Joanna Miles, Richard Gilliland, and Jaimie Smith Jackson.

There are a lot of creepy-crawly insects out there, but there have never been any quite like this before. They're large, carbon-eating, and capable of setting fires. They are also intelligent, very intelligent, and they're out to take over the world. [Monsters, insect-type]

800. Paige, Richard (pseud. of Dean R. Koontz). **The Door to December.** New
C York: Signet, 1985. 405 pp. ISBN 0-451-13605-5.

An exciting tale of pursuit and mystery, throughout which Dr. Laura
McCaffrey tries to bring her daughter Melanie back from the catatonic state
induced by behavior modification experiments. [Altered states of consciousness]

801. Paine, Michael. **Cities of the Dead.** New York: Charter, 1988. 246 pp.
C ISBN 1-55773-009-1.
Other works: *The Colors of Hell; Owl Light.*

There have long been stories and rumors about the curse of King Tut's tomb.
Here is the fictionalized account, told by Howard Carter, of what really
happened. [Legends, Egyptian]

802. Palatini, Margie. **Capricorn & Co.** New York: Pacer, 1984. 160 pp.
A ISBN 0-399-21186-1. (Zodiac Club series).

The members of the Zodiac Club are very close friends, as Gail finds out
when she starts to experiment with a new business with her boyfriend. Her plans
don't include her Zodiac buddies, and that means trouble. Includes appropriate
gift ideas for every zodiac sign. [Astrology]

803. Palatini, Margie. **Scorpio's Class Act.** New York: Pacer, 1985. 160 pp.
A ISBN 0-425-08406-X. (Zodiac Club series).

Not one of the Zodiac Club members is from a really exclusive family, and
when J. L. gets a chance to date Chad she considers leaving her old friends behind
and joining a high-society set. Includes gem stones for every zodiac sign.
[Astrology]

804. Pape, Sharon. **The Godchildren.** New York: Charter, 1986. 260 pp. ISBN
C 0-441-29450-2.

Aria and Thera are twin sisters, separated at birth. Aria has the power to call
on the heavenly forces of good, and Thera possesses an equally strong power to
bring forth the rages of hell. With the reunion of the sisters the immortal struggle
begins again. [Evil]

805. Parry, Michel. **Countess Dracula.** New York: Beagle, 1971. 140 pp. SBN
C 8441-94081-075.
Movie versions: *Countess Dracula*, 1972. Director: Peter Sasdy. Stars:
Ingrid Pitt, Nigel Green, Peter Jeffrey, and Lesley-Anne Down.

The countess seems to have everything; her hated husband has died and she
has power, money, and a beautiful daughter. But the countess wants
more—beauty for herself—and she will stop at nothing to obtain her desire.
[Bathody, Countess Elizabeth; Vampires]

806. Pascal, Francine. **Hangin' Out with Cici.** New York: Archway, 1978. 231
A pp. ISBN 0-671-43879-4. New York: Laurel-Leaf, 1985. 160 pp. ISBN
0-440-93364-1. (First published by Viking, 1977.)

Thirteen-year-old Victoria thinks her mother, Cici, doesn't understand her. When Victoria travels back in time, she finds herself best friends with her own mother as they engage in adventures together. And Cici seems to get into worse trouble than Victoria ever dreamed possible! [Time travel]

807. Patterson, James. **Virgin.** New York: Golden Apple, 1984. 229 pp. ISBN
C   0-553-19824-6. (First published by McGraw Hill, 1980.)

There is a prophecy about a newborn baby who will be the salvation of all. But the same prophecy foretells the birth of another child, one who will be all that is foul and bestial. [Evil]

808. Paul, Barbara. **Liars & Tyrants & People Who Turn Blue.** New York:
C   Pinnacle, 1982. 183 pp. ISBN 0-523-41607-5. (First published by
     Doubleday, 1980.)

Some people like Shelby Kent have the gift of seeing auras. Shelby's particular gift is very sure, especially when people tell lies. This ability makes her valuable to some and a threat to others who are willing to kill to put her gift to rest forever. [Paranormal abilities]

809. Payne, Bernal C., Jr. **Trapped in Time.** New York: Archway, 1986. 151
A   pp. ISBN 0-671-54360-1. (First published as *It's About Time* by
     Macmillan, 1984.)

You have to be careful about traveling in time. You must never disturb the past, for it may change the future. Gail and Chris find this out the hard way when they travel back in time to meet their own parents as teenagers. [Time travel]

810. Pearce, Philippa. **The Shadow-cage: And Other Tales of the Supernatural.**
A   Harmondsworth, England: Puffin, 1978. 151 pp. ISBN 0-14-03-1073-8.
     (First published by Kestrel, 1977.)

An English author describes strange goings-on with these stories: "The Shadow-Cage," "Miss Mountain," "Guess," "At the River-Gates," "Her Father's Attic," "The Running-Companion," "Beckoned," "The Dear Little Man with His Hands in His Pockets," "The Dog Got Them," "The Strange Illness of Mr. Arthur Cook." [Horror; Short stories]

811. Pearlman, Gilbert. **Young Frankenstein.** New York: Ballantine, 1974. 152
A   pp. ISBN 345-24268-8.
     Movie versions: *Young Frankenstein*, 1974. Director: Mel Brooks. Stars:
     Gene Wilder, Peter Boyle, Marty Feldman, Teri Garr, and Madeline
     Kahn.

Freddy Frankenstein has just received word that he is the "lucky" heir to the Frankenstein estate, a great disappointment to his various weird relatives who lust after the family fortune. All Freddy has to do is take possession, which turns out to be quite an arduous task. [Monsters; Science gone wrong]

812. Peck, Richard. **Dreamland Lake.** New York: Laurel-Leaf, 1982. 153 pp.
A   ISBN 0-440-92079-5. (First published by Holt, Rhinehart and Winston,
     1973.)
     Other works: *Secrets of the Shopping Mall.*

Brian and Flip are horrified when they discover a body in the woods near Dreamland Lake. Curious about the dead man, they investigate and find the answers to frightening secrets. [Satanism]

813. Peck, Richard. **The Ghost Belonged to Me.** New York: Laurel-Leaf,
A   1983. 253 pp. ISBN 0-440-93075-8. (First published by Viking, 1977.)
     Sequels: *Ghosts I Have Been; The Dreadful Future of Blossom Culp; Blossom Culp and the Sleep of Death.*

Blossom Culp is a delightful, irrepressible youngster living (and trying to survive in school) just prior to World War I. Her tales of her amazing family (her mother is a gypsy with the sight) and her own abilities to see more than others make her a notorious character with her classmates. Blossom doesn't care, except about Alexander, because she really wants to be his friend. [Paranormal abilities]

814. Perl, Linda. **Annabelle Starr, E.S.P.** New York: Archway, 1984. 134 pp.
A   ISBN 0-671-50350-2. (First published by Clarion, 1983.)
     Other works: *Marleen, the Horror Queen.*

Annabelle discovers she has secret, psychic abilities, but she is uncertain whether this power will be enough to protect her brother Scott from being taken away from her. [Paranormal abilities]

815. Peters, David. **Psi-Man: Mind-Force Warrior.** New York: Charter/
C   Diamond, 1990. 202 pp. ISBN 1-55773-399-6. First in a numbered series.

Chuck Simon has special powers discovered only when he becomes the target of Complex, a supersecret government agency that wants to turn Chuck into a psychic killing machine. [Paranormal abilities]

816. Pevsner, Stella. **Footsteps on the Stairs.** New York: Archway, 1984. 150
B   pp. ISBN 0-671-52411-9. (First published by Simon & Schuster, 1970.)

Experimenting with ESP is fun, but Chip and his friends discover that there aren't always scientific explanations for all that happens. In fact, it seems as if there may be some real ghosts involved. [Ghosts]

817. Pfefferle, Seth. **Stickman.** New York: TOR, 1987. 279 pp. ISBN 0-812-
C   52417-9.

Africa is an ancient place full of ancient beliefs. A camera crew photographing endangered species comes in contact with a frightening image of the past, a stickman who is not just a primitive painting but very real. [Legends, African]

818. Picano, Felice. **The Mesmerist.** New York: Dell, 1978. 394 pp. ISBN
C   0-440-15213-5. (First published by Delacorte, 1977.)
     Other works: *Smart as the Devil; Eyes.*

Center City, Nebraska, is only a few years removed from being a raw frontier town. The people who live there are used to combating the powers of nature, and they remember the tales of horror about Indian raids. They figure they can handle just about anything, but then the strange young man with hypnotic eyes arrives in Center City, and the citizens will have to fight their greatest battle, one they may not win. [Evil]

819.   Piccirilli, Tom. **Dark Father.** New York: Pocket Books, 1990. 280 pp.
C   ISBN 0-671-67401-3.

Old family homes often hold many secrets. In Samuel and Daniel's home they wonder about their parents, the father they have never known and their mother, who is only a vague memory. Then the brothers learn that their father is coming back, and they learn that he is not Ward Cleaver. [Evil]

820.   Pike, Christopher. **Spellbound.** New York: Archway, 1988. 211 pp. ISBN
A   0-671-64979-5.
       Other works: *Last Act; Gimme a Kiss; Slumber Party; Chain Letter; Final Friend I, II, III; The Tachyon Web; Sati; Die Softly.*

Jason's former girlfriend, Karen Holly, is dead, and Jason says a grizzly bear killed her. Now Jason has a new girlfriend, and Cindy's brother Alex is worried about her. Alex and his friends, Joni and Bala from Africa, decide to solve the mystery of Karen's death. [Shamanism]

821.   Pike, Christopher. **Witch.** New York: Archway, 1990. 225 pp. ISBN
A   0-671-69055-8.

Julia is a witch by heritage, a good witch who practices her power for helping people. Her mother had warned Julia never to look in her watch with moonlight reflected in it, but Julia does. She sees a vision of a future with a fascinating young man who dies in her arms, and Julia decides to change the future. She will not let this young man die. [Paranormal abilities; Witchcraft]

822.   Plante, Edmund. **Transformation.** New York: Leisure, 1987. 351 pp.
C   ISBN 0-8439-2490-X.
       Other works: *Garden of Evil; Seed of Evil.*

Sally Martin's pregnancy seems worse than any she's ever heard of. It's almost as if there's something inhuman growing inside her. Sally knows what has happened, knows about the being in her closet. But she doesn't know what will happen next. [Monsters]

823.   Poe, Edgar Allan. **The Tell-Tale Heart and Other Writings.** New York:
C   Bantam, 1982. 432 pp. ISBN 0-553-21575-2.
       Some movies based on Poe's works: *House of Usher*, 1960. Director: Roger Corman. Stars: Vincent Price, Mark Damon, and Myrna Fahey. *The Fall of the House of Usher*, 1982. Director: James L. Conway. Stars: Martin Landau, Robert Hays, and Charlene Tilton. *The Mask of the Red Death*, 1964. Director: Roger Corman. Stars: Vincent Price, Hazel Court, and Jane Asher. *The Pit and the Pendulum*, 1961. Director: Roger Corman. Stars: Vincent Price, John Kerr, and Barbara Steele. *The Tomb of Ligeia*, 1964. Director: Roger Corman. Stars: Vincent Price, Elizabeth Shepherd, and John Westbrook.

This assortment of tales by an American master includes "The Tell-Tale Heart," "The Black Cat," "The Cask of Amontillado," "The Fall of the House of Usher," "The Masque of the Red Death," "The Facts in the Case of M. Valdemar," "Ligeia," "The Murders in the Rue Morgue," "The Purloined Letter," "A Descent into the Maelstrom," "The Pit and the Pendulum," "Ms. Found in a Bottle," "The Premature Burial," "William Wilson," "Eleonora," "Silence—A Fable," "The Narrative of Arthur Gordon Pym." [Horror; Short stories]

Polidari, John. *See* entry 163.

824. Pope, Elizabeth Marie. **The Perilous Gard.** New York: Tempo, 1984. 211
A   pp. ISBN 0-441-65956-X. (First published by Houghton Mifflin, 1974.)

Kate is a spirited young damsel who is banished from the royal court by an angry Queen Mary. She is sent to a mysterious castle in the windswept North, where she discovers the secret kingdom of faerie. Not only does she discover the elusive legendary beings, she becomes their prisoner. [Fairies]

825. Pope, Elizabeth Marie. **The Sherwood Ring.** New York: Tempo, 1985.
A   180 pp. ISBN 0-441-76111-9. (First published by Houghton Mifflin, 1958.)

When Peggy first visits her family's ancestral home in upstate New York, she thinks she'll find interesting old antiques, not the ghostly secrets of the past. [Ghosts]

826. Popescue, Petru. **In Hot Blood.** New York: Fawcett, 1989. 328 pp. ISBN
C   0-449-14554-9.

Laura Walker visits New Orleans hoping to heal a bruised heart but meets a strange new man, Alan Emory, in the romantic old city. He wants more than her heart—he wants her blood. [Vampires]

827. Porter, Barry. **Junkyard.** New York: Zebra, 1989. 284 pp. ISBN 0-8217-
C   2816-4.

Everyone knows that scavengers like rats and wild dogs live in dumps and junkyards; this junkyard holds something more than usual vermin. [Monsters]

828. Potocki, Jan. **The Saragossa Manuscript.** New York: Avon, 1961. 224 pp.
C   (First published in Paris, 1804.)

Gothic tales of mystery and adventure. Includes a series of tales in the tradition of Chaucer and Boccaccio, all with a supernatural twist. [Horror; Short stories]

829. Prantera, Amanda. **The Cabalist.** London: Abacus, 1985. 184 pp. ISBN
C   0-349-12800-6.
        Other works: *Strange Loop.*

Venice is a fabled city of beauty, but there are mysteries to be found there. Dying old Joseph Kestler tries to preserve the secrets of his craft, numerology. But this age is not kind to wizards, and the old man has problems, problems compounded by the nasty child demon, the Catcher. [Legends, Jewish; Magic]

830. Price, E. Hoffman. **The Devil Wives of Li Fong.** New York: Del Rey,
C   1979. 217 pp. ISBN 0-345-28448-8.

In ancient China, magic is an everyday part of life. Li Fong, a student apothecary, is delighted with his beautiful wives until he discovers they are really spirit-demons. Then the evil Chang Lu turns his venom on Li Fong, who decides in the end it may be a good thing to have wives with special talents. [Legends, Chinese]

831. Prince, Alison. **The Ghost Within.** London: Magnet, 1986. 119 pp. ISBN
A   0-416-52140-1. (First published by Methuen, 1984.)

Stories of odd happenings, most with English settings, including "The Lilies," "Herb," "The Fire Escape," "Photographs," "The Fen Tiger," "Dundee Cake," "The Pin," "The Glass Game." [Short stories]

832. Pronzoni, Bill. **Masques.** New York: Berkley, 1983. 213 pp. ISBN 0-4255-
C   05936-7. (First published by Arbor House, 1981.)

Exotic New Orleans is full of narrow old streets and dark old houses. Mysteries abound there and include the dangerous secrets of ancient voodoo, still practiced on those who dare to offend people with the special power. [Voodoo]

833. Prose, Francine. **Marie Laveau.** New York: Berkley, 1977. 374 pp. SBN
C   425-03727-4.

Living outside the fringes of respectable New Orleans society, beautiful and powerful Marie Laveau is able to exert her will on everyone she pleases with her voodoo spells and power. [Laveau, Marie; Voodoo]

834. Ptacek, Kathryn. **In Silence Sealed.** New York: TOR, 1988. 306 pp. ISBN
C   0-812-52449-7.
     Other works: *Blood Autumn.*

Athina and August Kristonosos are beautiful Greek sisters living in turbulent times. They are admired by the great Romantic poets of their day, Keats, Byron, and Shelley, but the admiration of these brilliant young men will not stop the sisters from destroying the poets. [Evil]

835. Ptacek, Kathryn. **Kachina.** New York: TOR, 1986. 306 pp. ISBN 0-812-
C   52445-4.

A properly reared young lady starts to have strange dreams on a trip to the New Mexico Territory. Her anthropologist husband seems unconcerned about Elizabeth, but she finds her dreams becoming more and more real and finds herself turning into the vengeful leader of the Konochine tribe. [Legends, Native American; Shamanism]

836. Ptacek, Kathryn. **Shadoweyes.** New York: TOR, 1984. 314 pp. ISBN
C   0-812-51858-6.

Terrible, rapacious evil beings called shadoweyes are on a rampage, eating animal and human flesh. Can Chato Del-Klinne, the Apache hero, save the world from this horrible menace? [Monsters]

837. Quinn, Daniel. **Dreamer.** New York: TOR, 1988. 345 pp. ISBN 0-812-
C   52475-6.

Greg Donner has become the frightened victim of dreams. He no longer knows what is reality and what takes place in other worlds. His whole existence has become a jumbled mess as he struggles to retain his sanity. [Dreams]

838. Quinn, Simon. **The Devil in Kansas.** New York: Dell, 1974. 188 pp. ISBN
C   0-440-02170-0.

This novel is the first in The Inquisitor series. Our hero, Francis Xavier Killy, modern soldier of the church, takes on the powers of Satan in the complex modern world. [Satanism]

839. Ramie, Florence. **Toyland.** New York: Leisure, 1986. 395 pp. ISBN
C   0-8439-2391-1.

You'd think the MacKenzie family one of the most ordinary American families around until you found out some of the things going on in their house—things that promise knowledge of dark secrets from the past. [Ghosts]

840. Ramsay, Jay. **Night of the Claw.** New York: TOR, 1985. 367 pp. ISBN
C   0-812-52500-0.

A gruesome tale of child murder and cannibalism. Not for the squeamish; only for those who really like violence. [Cults; Legends, primitive]

841. Randall, Florence Engel. **The Watcher in the Woods.** New York:
A   Scholastic, 1980. 202 pp. ISBN 0-590-31334-7. (First published by
      Atheneum, 1980.)
      Movie versions: *The Watcher in the Woods*, 1980. Director: John Hough.
      Stars: Bette Davis, Carol Baker, David McCallum, Lynn-Holly Johnson,
      Kyle Richards, Ian Bannen.

Jan hates the idea of moving, and she hates it worse after it is accomplished fact. It's no fun being the new girl in a strange high school. Then things start to happen at home, creepy things. Younger Ellie hears strange songs, and the television is doing its own programming. Worst of all, Jan knows that someone is watching them, for there is a presence nearby, the watcher in the woods. [Ghosts]

842. Randisi, Robert J., and Kevin D. Randle. **Once upon a Murder.** Lake
C   Geneva, Wis.: Windwalker, 1987. 219 pp. ISBN 0-46363-00295-4.

Miles Paladon, a gumshoe in 1939 Chicago, stops a bullet in a seedy alley. When he opens his eyes, he finds himself in a medieval society with an arrow in his shoulder and another mystery on his hands. [Time travel]

843. Ransom, Daniel. **The Forsaken.** New York: St. Martin's Press, 1988.
C   305 pp. ISBN 0-312-90947-0.
      Other works: *The Babysitter; Daddy's Little Girl.*

Young Patrick is at camp, and something frightening is happening to him. He seems to be turning into another person. It's not a matter of approaching manhood but something evil that he can't control. [Possession]

844. Read, Cameron. **The Forsaken.** New York: Pinnacle, 1982. 343 pp. ISBN
C   0-523-41595-8.

The Hamilton family lives in a beautiful old North Carolina house, but there is something strange about the noises in the evening when people try to go to sleep. A gentle story reportedly based on a true ghost experience. [Ghosts; Haunted houses]

845. Rechy, John. **The Vampires.** New York: Dell, 1971. 276 pp. ISBN 0-440-
C   09532-1.

It's no wonder that people who dabble in the occult get a bad reputation. Criminals are not above using any power available to gain their ends, even the powers of Satan. [Satanism]

846. Reed, Dana (pseud. of Edwina Berkman). **The Gatekeeper.** New York:
C   Leisure, 1987. 399 pp. ISBN 0-8439-2500-0.
     Other works: *Deathbringer.*

Erica Walsh is delighted with the old empty house she has found. Now she'll be able to settle down and raise her kids, bringing all of them a much-needed stability. But the old house is not a haven after all, for at night there are strange noises and voices, rough hands awaken her, and there is a sense of doom waiting for them all. [Horror]

847. Reed, Dana. **Sister Satan.** New York: Leisure, 1984. 400 pp. ISBN
C   0-8439-2472-1

Lauren's homelife is miserable. Her chief reason for living seems to be baby-sitting for her younger brothers and being the target of her father's fury. She longs for a sister to share her problems with, but when her greatest wish is answered, Lauren realizes that sisters aren't always sweet and sympathetic. [Evil]

848. Reed, Ishmael. **Mumbo Jumbo.** New York: Avon Bard, 1978. 256 pp.
C   ISBN 0-380-01860-8. (First published by Doubleday, 1972.)
     Other works: *A Secretary to the Spirits; The Freelance Paulbearers.*

An outrageous and original work dealing with hoodoo (voodoo). Whether or not it is real or fantasy is left to the reader to decide. [Voodoo]

849. Rees, E. M. **Gemini Solo.** New York: Pacer, 1985. 160 pp. ISBN 0-448-
A   47727-0. (Zodiac Club series).

Ann Crawford finds her new friends are great after the family moves to Connecticut, but she miscalculates when she fixes her twin brother up with Abby, the founder of the Zodiac Club. Includes the perfect places to live for each zodiac sign. [Astrology]

850. Rees, E. M. **Libra's Dilemma.** New York: Pacer, 1984. 160 pp. ISBN
A   0-399-21108-X. (Zodiac Club series).

Librans have a strong sense of fair play, and Mara's is sorely tested when she discovers her boyfriend is involved in a cheating scandal. Includes food ideas for the zodiac signs. [Astrology]

851. Rees, E. M. **Pisces Times Two.** New York: Pacer, 1985. 160 pp. ISBN
A   0-448-47731-9. (Zodiac Club series).

When her father presents her with a new stepmother, Elizabeth decides their house just isn't big enough for two temperamental Pisces people. Includes the right dog for every zodiac sign. [Astrology]

852. Reeves-Stevens, Garfield. **Children of the Shroud.** New York: Popular
C   Library, 1990. 323 pp. ISBN 0-445-21014-1.
    Other works: *Bloodshift; Brighteyes; Dark Matter.*

The relic of the shroud of Turin, rumored to hold the actual mirror image of the face and body of Jesus, is considered to be a powerful talisman. It has power, all right, a power that has been transmitted to a race of superior children who may be able to save the world if they choose. [Legends, Christian; Science gone wrong]

853. Regan, Dian Curtis. **Jilly's Ghost.** New York: Avon Flare, 1990. 137 pp.
A   ISBN 0-380-75831-8.

Jilly isn't afraid of Mr. MacGregor, the ghost who haunts the grounds of her family's home. He seems to be a benevolent presence, almost comforting at times, but when the ghostbuster moves in next door, Jilly is afraid that Mr. MacGregor's ghostly existence is in peril. [Ghosts]

854. Relling, William, Jr. **Brujo.** New York: TOR, 1986. 338 pp. ISBN 0-812-
C   5210-8.

Santa Catalina has long been a favorite spot for outings, but the day Mark Baldwin visits, there is no peace and quiet. The old shaman has aroused his allies, the birds and beasts of the island, to strike back at those who have brought "civilization" to the island, and no one is supposed to escape from their fearful revenge. [Shamanism]

855. Relling, William, Jr. **New Moon.** New York: TOR, 1987. 280 pp. ISBN
C   0-812-52512-4.

A crazed murderer is loose in New York, one who takes human organs from his victims for use in unspeakable rituals. Detective-Sergeant Len Malecke is hot on the trail of the killer, but he has not reckoned on dealing with a magician of eternal, evil power. [Black magic; Satanism]

856. Renault, Mary. **The King Must Die.** New York: Bantam, 1974. 416 pp.
C   ISBN 0-553-26065-0. (First published by Pantheon, 1958.)
    Sequels: *The Bull from the Sea.* Other works: *Last of the Wine.*

An exciting, detailed portrayal of life in ancient Greece based on the legend of Theseus. [Legends, classical]

857. Rhodes, Daniel. **Next, After Lucifer.** New York: TOR, 1988. 258 pp.
C   ISBN 0-812-52505-1.
    Sequels: *Adversary*

John McTell is trained as an observant lawyer as well as highly educated as a historian. He is fascinated by the ruins of a stronghold of one of the Knights Templar, burned at the stake centuries ago for black sorcery. But those who have met such deaths do not lie easy, and the spirit of the old Knight Templar comes forth to capture the soul of John McTell. [Cults; Knights Templar; Satanism]

858.   Rice, Anne. **Interview with the Vampire.** New York: Ballantine, 1977.
C   346 pp. ISBN 0-345-25608-5. (First published by Knopf, 1977.)
        Sequels: *The Vampire Lestat; Queen of the Damned.* Other works: *The Witching Hour.*

The journey and adventures of a sympathetic vampire are recounted as he wanders from New Orleans to Europe in his search for happiness. [Vampires]

859.   Rice, Anne. **The Mummy.** New York: Ballantine, 1989. 436 pp. ISBN
C   0-345-36000-1.

Ramses, the ancient ruler of a bygone era, is resurrected in Edwardian England as a handsome, debonair gentleman who enchants all the women he meets, including Julie, daughter of the archaeologist who dug him up and Cleo, his love from an ancient time. [Legends, Egyptian; Mummies]

860.   Rice, Jeff. **The Night Stalker.** New York: Pocket Books, 1973. 192 pp.
C   ISBN 0-671-78343-2.
        Sequels: *The Night Strangler.* Movie versions: *The Night Stalker,* 1971.
        Director: John Llewellyn Moxey. Stars: Darren McGavin and Carol Lynley. Later spin-off television series.

Las Vegas, that town of glitz and bright lights, seems an odd place to find a vampire. But a newspaper reporter down on his luck does find one and discovers that getting others to believe in this occult murderer is very hard work indeed. [Vampires]

861.   Richards, Tony. **The Harvest Bride.** New York: TOR, 1987. 279 pp. ISBN
C   0-812-52520-5.

Tom Auden keeps remembering terrible things that happened fifteen years ago in Viet Nam, but it seems long ago and far away. Then something weird and awful happens. Sam Loong's puppet theater starts to perform in Tom's neighborhood, and Tom starts to remember more than he would like. [Horror]

862.   Riefe, Alan. **Viper.** New York: Charter, 1990. 271 pp. ISBN 1-55773-430-5.
C

Felicity Jane now lives in India with her Aunt Helen; exotic snakes are her only friends. But she remembers her mother's murder and discovers that she has a special power over snakes, a power she can use to avenge her mother's death. [Monsters]

863.   Rimmer, Steven William. **Coven.** New York: Ballantine, 1989. 295 pp.
C   ISBN 0-345-35750-7.

In the seventeenth century, fear of witchcraft was rampant in Europe, and those suspected of practicing the craft were burned at the stake. Yet the lives of contemporary witches is no less perilous, as Mark discovers to his astonishment and horror. [Satanism; Witchcraft]

864.   Ringel, Harry. **The Tender Seed.** New York: Popular Library, 1986.
C   278 pp. ISBN 0-445-20249-1.

Mimi has inherited her grandmother's blessing, some would say a curse. Like many children, Mimi believes she is different, and indeed she is, for Mimi is psychic. But Mimi has not learned how to, or decided whether to, use her gift for good or for evil. It's hard for kids to know what to do. [Paranormal abilities]

865. Robbins, David. **The Wrath.** New York: Leisure, 1988. 368 pp. ISBN
C   0-8439-2629-5.
Other works: *Blood Cult; The Wereling.*

When people think of ancient Egyptian tombs, they generally visualize golden treasures. But there are other things to be found in the tombs, including a disease so terrible that it threatens to change the world forever. [Legends, Egyptian; Transformation]

866. Roberts, Nadine. **Evil Threads.** New York: Fawcett Juniper, 1988. 152
A   pp. ISBN 0-449-70303-7.

Jenny Fox always thought she was a pretty average teenager. Then she starts communicating with a new friend, a spirit who wants revenge. [Spiritualism]

867. Robinson, Kim Stanley. **Escape from Kathmandu.** New York: TOR, 1989.
C   313 pp. ISBN 0-812-50059-8.

Expatriot Americans living in the Himalayas discover that many of the fabled magical legends of ancient Tibet are true. Yet everything is not as they had thought. [Legends, Tibetan]

868. Rodgers, Alan. **Blood of the Children.** New York: Bantam, 1990. 299
C   pp. ISBN 0-553-28335-9.
Other works: *Fire.*

The children of Green Hill are special, and they know it. Before reaching puberty, all the children belong to a special deadly cult of evil. Upon reaching adolescence, however, they lose all memory of the cult. But there are always new children to swell the ranks of the sinister band. [Cults]

869. Rodgers, Mary. **Freaky Friday.** New York: Perennial, 1977. 145 pp. ISBN
B   0-06-080392-4. (First published by Harper & Row, 1972.)
Movie versions: *Freaky Friday*, 1977. Director: Gary Nelson. Stars: Barbara Harris, Jodie Foster, John Astin, Patsy Kelly, Dick Van Patten.

When Annabel and her mother both feel equally frustrated over a lack of understanding, something happens. Annabel finds herself in her mother's body, and her mother finds herself in Annabel's. When it's all over, both are glad to be back in the right bodies, and both appreciate each other more. [Transformation]

870. Rodgers, Mary. **Summer Switch.** Harmondsworth, England: Puffin, 1984.
B   173 pp. ISBN 0-14-031631-0. (First published by Harper & Row, 1982.)
Movie versions: *Summer Switch*, 1984. Director: Ken Kuapis. Star: Robert Klein.

When Benjamin Andrews wishes he is his father, he is momentarily stunned to find that it has really happened. There he is in his father's body, and his father is in Ben's. Ben has to go to work, and Ben's father has to go to summer camp. Coping in such a situation is not easy, and both Ben and his father have many problems. [Transformation]

871. Roessner, Michaela. **Walkabout Woman.** New York: Bantam Spectra,
C   1988. 275 pp. ISBN 0-553-27545-3.

Raba is a young aborigine girl living in the Australian outback. Raba experiences wonderful dreams that take her to a magical place. Then trouble enters Raba's world, and she must use ancient secrets to save herself and her whole tribe. [Dreams; Legends, Aboriginal]

872. Rohmer, Sax (pseud. of Arthur Henry Ward). **The Insidious Dr. Fu**
C   **Manchu.** New York: Zebra Kensington, 1985. 331 pp. ISBN
      0-821-71668-9. (First published by Doubleday, 1939.)
      Other works: *The Drums of Fu Manchu; The Trail of Fu Manchu; The
      Dreams of Fu Manchu; The Fire Goddess; Sinister Madonna; The Dream
      Detective.* Some movies based on the Fu Manchu books: *The Mask of Fu
      Manchu*, 1921. Director: Charles Brabin. Stars: Boris Karloff, Lewis
      Stone, Kane Morley, and Jean Hersholt. *Face of Fu Manchu*, 1965.
      Director: Don Sharp. Stars: Christopher Lee, Nigel Green, and Tsai Chinn.
      The Brides of Fu Manchu, 1966. Director: Don Sharp. Stars: Christopher
      Lee, Douglas Wilner, and Marie Versini. *Vengeance of Fu Manchu*, 1968.
      Director: Jeremy Summers. Stars: Christopher Lee, Douglas Wilmer, and
      Tsai Chinn.

The evil villain makes full use of black magic and nasty scientific practices to prolong his life and gain power. Only Nyland Grant of Scotland Yard is able to occasionally thwart the nefarious doctor as Grant doggedly pursues him through a tangled web of horror and danger. [Black magic]

873. Rohmer, Sax. **Sumuru.** New York: Fawcett, 1951. 159 pp.
C

Many have thought that Rohmer's villain, Dr. Fu Manchu, is the most evil creation of fiction, but they may not know about Sumuru, sometimes called a female Bluebeard. She uses her ill-gotten secrets of terror to gain power and wealth, cutting a swath of mystery and horror. [Science gone wrong]

874. Romkey, Michael. **I, Vampire.** New York: Fawcett, 1990. 360 pp. ISBN
C   0-449-14638-3.

A confessional-style story of a vampire that portrays the breed as neither good nor bad but rather as having the frailties and virtues of humankind. [Vampires]

875. Ronson, Mark. **Ghoul.** New York: Critic's Choice, 1987. 202 pp. ISBN
C   1-55547-153-6. (First published by Hamlyn, 1980.)
      Other works: *Bloodthirst; Ogre.*

There are many ancient and dangerous burial grounds in the Middle East, the cradle of civilization. As well as treasures and artifacts that tell us about the past, there are terrible secrets and fearsome powers. One is the ghoul, a foul creature with a horrible hunger. [Legends, Arabian; Monsters]

876. Ronson, Mark. **Plague Pit.** New York: Critic's Choice, 1987. 191 pp. ISBN
C   1-55547-169-2. (First published by Hamlyn, 1981.)

In excavating in old London, workers accidentally break into an old burial crypt from the time of the great plague. Then, a few days later, a new plague is visited upon the land, one every bit as powerful as the earlier one and one that cannot be stopped. [Horror]

877.   Ross, Clarissa (pseud. of W. E. D. [Dan] Ross). **Satan Whispers.** 1981.
C   Other works: *The Ghost and the Garnet; Phantom of the Swamp; Gemini in Darkness*; novelizations of "Dark Shadows" stories on television.

Sarah is a delightful child except for her violent tantrums. At first her family hopes Sarah will outgrow her unreasonable temper scenes, but they seem to get worse. Then, terrible things start to happen, and it seems as if Sarah is some embodiment of an ancient evil. [Possession]

Ross, W. E. D. (Dan). *See* Clarissa Ross and Marilyn Ross.

878.   Ross, Leona C. **Resurrexit.** New York: Leisure, 1986. 384 pp. ISBN
C   0-8439-2331-8.

All small towns have queer old ladies living in them, and Newtown, Maine, is no exception. What people don't realize, however, is that Florence Willowby is more than a little odd. She is obsessed with the memories of her past, which will drive her to anything, even human sacrifice. [Horror]

879.   Ross, Marilyn (pseud. of W. E. D. [Dan] Ross). **Barnabas Collins.** New
C   York: Paperback Library, 1968. 157 pp.
       Sequels: Twenty-six additional titles, all based on the ABC television series "Dark Shadows." (See Books in Series appendix.) Other works: *Dark Stars over Seacrest; Message from a Ghost; Phantom of Fog Island; Witches' Cove; The Aquarius Curse; Shorecliff; Satan's Rock; Phantom Manor; Mistress of Ravenswood; Memory of Evil; A Gathering of Evil; Desperate Heiress; Beware My Love.* Movie versions: *House of Dark Shadows*, 1970. Director: Dan Curtis. Stars: Jonathan Fried, Grayson Hall, and Kathryn Leigh Scott. Television series revived in 1991 starring Ben Cross.

Barnabas Collins, an old (175 years old, in fact) but still handsome and fascinating vampire, comes to live in the old Collins House. His tragic eyes attract women, but the women do not realize the terrible secret he holds within himself. [Vampires]

880.   Ross, Marilyn. **Phantom of the 13th Floor.** New York: Popular Library,
C   1975. 252 pp. ISBN 0-445-08363-1.

You'd think with all the hotels in New York, Joan wouldn't have to go to the Brant, a place she has always avoided because of her grandmother's mysterious and tragic death there. But Joan decides to go to the Brant and there finds herself embroiled in a sinister world where the dead have come back to the world of the living. [Ghosts]

881.   Roszak, Theodore. **Bugs.** New York: Pocket Books, 1983. 313 pp. ISBN
C   0-671-45408-0. (First published by Doubleday, 1981.)

Computer-literate people often talk of bugs in their programs, but the bugs in the Brain, a new supercomputer, are very real creepy-crawly bugs with a killing instinct. [Monsters; Science gone wrong]

882. Rothberg, Abraham. **The Sword of the Golem.** New York: Bantam, 1973.
C   247 pp. ISBN 0-553-06967-1. (First published by McCall, 1971.)

Rabbi Judah Low Ben Bezalel creates a superbeing out of clay and gives it life as the legendary golem to be a champion for the Jewish people. But the golem cannot always be controlled, and it becomes a destructive killing machine. [Legends, Jewish; Science gone wrong]

883. Roueche, Berton. **Feral.** New York: Avon, 1983. 128 pp. ISBN 0-380-
C   65508-X. (First published by Harper & Row, 1974.)

A perfect resort house becomes a far-from-perfect residence of terror when countless wild creatures surround it making the Bishops prisoners in their own home. [Monsters]

884. Rovin, Jeff. **Re-Animator.** New York: Pocket Books, 1987. 223 pp. ISBN
C   0-671-63723-1.
      Movie versions: *Re-Animator*, 1985. Director: Stuart Gordon. Stars:
      Jeffrey Combs, Bruce Abbott, Barbara Crampton, Robert Sampson, and
      David Gale.

Herbert West is brilliant, and a man with a mission. He knows he has the skill to bring the dead back to life. But is it really life? The corpses move, but they're not human, and they're not happy with Herbert for what he's done. Based on work by H. P. Lovecraft. [Science gone wrong]

885. Ruddy, Jon. **The Bargain.** New York: Knightsbridge, 1990. 293 pp. ISBN
C   1-877961-52-3.

Count Dracula lives a pretty secluded life in Romania these days, but when Hitler sends his troops into Transylvania, the count finds it necessary to take firm action against the intruders. [Vampires]

886. Rudorff, Raymond. **The Dracula Archives.** New York: Pocket Books,
C   1972. 208 pp. ISBN 0-899-19436-2. (First published by Arbor House,
      1971.)
      Other works: *The House of the Brandersons*.

A collection of documents, letters, diaries, and other memorabilia provides firm "proof" of Count Dracula's existence. [Vampires]

887. Rush, Allison. **The Last of Danu's Children.** New York: TOR, 1984.
C   315 pp. ISBN 0-8125-5250-4. (First published by Houghton Mifflin, 1982.)

Ancient Celtic gods appear in modern England and affect the lives of three teenagers. Anna Marchant is especially affected, for she is stolen by Cernunnos. Anna's sister Kate and Matt Cooper must try to save her, but even with the help of Danu's children, born of Light, they may not be able to succeed. [Legends, Celtic]

888. Russell, Ray. **Sagittarius.** Chicago: Playboy, 1971. 184. pp.
C   Other works: *The Case Against Satan; Sardonicus and Other Stories;
      Unholy Trinity*.

Short fiction in a gothic style. Included are "Sagittarius," "Ripples," "Sardonicus," "The Room," "Comet Wine," "Ounce of Prevention," "Naked in Xanadu," and "A Night in the Byzantine Palace." [Horror; Short stories]

889. Russo, John. **The Awakening.** New York: Pocket Books, 1983. 311 pp.
C   ISBN 0-671-45259-2.
    Other works: *Black Cat; Bloodsister; Limb to Limb; Midnight; Inhuman; Majorettes; Voodoo Dawn; Children of the Dead.*

Benjamin Latham on the outside is young and handsome, but on the inside he's got some real problems, including animalistic needs. [Vampires]

890. Russo, John. **Living Things.** New York: Popular Library, 1988. 274 pp.
C   ISBN 0-445-20666-7.

Unscrupulous lords of the underworld will often do anything to gain power, and this one has turned to the very powers of hell itself to be master of his world. [Voodoo]

891. Russo, John, and George Romero. **Night of the Living Dead.** New York:
C   Pocket Books, 1981. 176 pp. ISBN 0-671-43768-2.
    Sequels: *Midnight of the Living Dead; Return of the Living Dead.* Movie versions: *Night of the Living Dead*, 1968. Director: George Romero. Stars: Duane Jones, Judith O'Dean, Russell Streiner, Karl Harmand, Keith Wayne.

Based on a horror film, this is the story of frightened people holed up in a deserted farmhouse while inhuman cannibalistic zombies do their best to get them. [Zombies]

892. Ryan, Alan. **The Kill.** New York: TOR, 1982. 312 pp. ISBN 0-523-48055-5.
C   Other works: *Dead White; Cast a Cold Eye; Panther!; Halloween Horrors.*

The private dream of many New Yorkers is to throw it all away and run to the idyllic beauties of the wooded Catskill Mountains. Jack and Megan, however, discover terror in the wooded darkness, an unbelievable horror that will destroy their happiness forever. [Horror]

893. Saberhagen, Fred. **Frankenstein Papers.** New York: Baen, 1986. 308 pp.
C   ISBN 0-671-65550-7.

The story of Frankenstein's creation from the monster's point of view. Who says that such a creation cannot have a soul? This "creation," alas, turns out to be an alien from outer space rather than the product of the laboratory. [Monsters; Science gone wrong]

894. Saberhagen, Fred. **An Old Friend of the Family.** New York: TOR, 1987.
C   247 pp. ISBN 0-812-52550-7. (First published by Ace, 1979.)
    Sequels: *The Holmes/Dracula File; The Dracula Tapes; Thorn.*

Teenager Judy Southerland has just been hit with a double whammy, her sister Kate has been murdered and her brother Johnny kidnapped. Judy's grandmother asks Judy to help her summon an old friend who will be able to help them. But her grandmother doesn't tell Judy that the old friend is a vampire. [Vampires]

895. Sackett, Jeffrey. **Stolen Souls.** New York: Bantam, 1987. 341 pp. ISBN
C   0-553-26937-2.
     Other works: *Candlemas Eve; Blood of the Impaler; The Demon.*

When the old Earl of Selwyn lies dying, he forces his nephew and heir to swear he will never open the seven boxes of Egyptian mummies. His nephew promises but then sells the mummies to a college in the United States. The boxes are opened, and soon the college town of Greenfield becomes the scene of death and terror. [Legends, Egyptian; Mummies]

896. Sage, Alison. **The Devil Rides Out.** London: Beaver, 1987. 155 pp. ISBN
B   0-09-949750-6. (A retelling of the story by Dennis Wheatley, see entry
     1124.)

Simon Aaron's behavior has been very strange, and he is keeping secrets from his loyal friends who are determined to battle even the forces of darkest hell for Simon's soul. [Satanism]

897. Saint Alcorn, Lloyd. **Dreamquest: Halberd, Dream Warrior.** New York:
C   Signet, 1987. 253 pp. ISBN 0-451-15016-3.

Halberd, the might Viking swordsman and shaman, determines to find and kill the murderer of his brother Valdane. The search for the murderer covers many miles and many wonderful adventures, for Halberd's world is lived in by people of strange and secret powers. [Dreams; Legends, Norse]

898. Saint George, Judith. **Haunted.** New York: Bantam, 1982. 158 pp. ISBN
B   0-553-20868-3. (First published by Putnam, 1980.)

Alex Phillip's summer of house-sitting seems easy at first. Then weird things start to happen, and Alex is afraid that there are forces at work with which he won't be able to deal — forces that are not human. [Ghosts]

Saint John, David. *See* E. Howard Hunt.

899. St. John, Wylly Folk. **The Ghost Next Door.** New York: Archway, 1972.
B   152 pp. ISBN 0-671-55390-9. (First published by Simon & Schuster, 1971.)

When Sherry goes to visit her aunt in a quiet little Georgia town, people are not puzzled at first when she talks about her playmate whom no one else can see. Then other clues make the puzzlement turn to fear as people realize Sherry's friend may be long-dead Miranda, drowned in a desolate pond. [Ghosts]

900. Saki (pseud. of Hector Hugh Munro). **Humor, Horror, and the Super-**
C   **natural: 22 Stories by Saki.** New York: Scholastic, n.d. 158 pp.

Clever and scary stories by a master teller of tales. This collection includes "Gabriel-Ernest," "The Bag," "Tobermory," "Mrs. Packletide's Tiger," "Sredni Vashtar," "The Easter Egg," "Filboid Studge," "Laura," "The Open Window," "The Schartz-Matterklume Method," "A Holiday Task," "The Storyteller," "The Name Day," "The Lumber Room," "The Disappearance of Crispina Umberleigh," "The Wolves of Cernograntz," "The Guests," "The Penance," "The Interlopers," "The Mappined Life," "The Seven Cream Jugs," "The Gala Programme." [Horror; Short stories]

901. Samuels, Victor. **The Vampire Women.** New York: Popular Library,
C   1973. 190 pp. ISBN 0-445-00503-0.

John and Victoria Hamilton are on a quest to find Count Dracula's castle. Victoria's sister Carolyn has come along for fun. Fun is not what they find, however, for Count Dracula is still in his castle, and terrible things happen, especially at night in the dark. [Vampires; Werewolves]

902. Sanders, Joan. **Baneful Sorceries.** London: Corgi, 1971. 284 pp. ISBN
C   0-552-08794-7. (First published by Macdonald, 1970.)

France in the Renaissance was a time of luxury for the wealthy and of misery for the poor. For all it was a time of superstition, and some dared to practice the ancient black arts. Lovely young Margot Renard is first fascinated by her new life as the bride of a Parisian nobleman, but she discovers the horror and awfulness of the corrupt court, a corruptness that will ultimately bring her great misery. [Satanism]

903. Saralegui, Jorge. **Last Rites.** New York: Charter, 1985. 279 pp. ISBN
C   0-441-47185-4.
    Other works: *Shadow Stalker.*

An evil beast is loose in charming San Francisco, and its power has insinuated itself into unsuspecting innocent victims who turn to vile practices. [Vampires]

904. Sarrantonio, Al. **The Boy with Penny Eyes.** New York: TOR, 1987.
A   278 pp. ISBN 0-812-52560-4.
    Other works: *Totentanz; The Worms.*

Billy Potter, an eleven-year-old drifter, has special powers, but he seems to bring terrible death with him when he comes into a new town. Those who befriend Billy had better be careful, for they may not live long. [Paranormal abilities]

905. Sauer, Julia L. **Fog Magic.** New York: Archway, 1977. 125 pp. ISBN
B   0-671-29817-8. (First published by Viking, 1943.)

Young Greta likes the mysterious fog that sometimes shrouds her village. One day, though, Greta discovers that the fog can change things and take her into another world. [Time travel]

906. Saul, John. **Comes the Blind Fury.** New York: Dell, 1980. 384 pp. ISBN
C   0-440-11475-6.
    Other works: *Brainchild; The God Project; Cry for the Strangers; Punish the Sinners; When the Wind Blows; Hell Fire; Second Child; The Unloved; The Unwanted.*

A nineteenth-century blind child is taunted and hounded to her death by the other village children. The anger of the child lives on as an avenging spirit bound on seeking retribution. [Ghosts]

907. Saul, John. **Creature.** New York: Bantam, 1990. 377 pp. ISBN 0-553-
C   28411-8. (First published by Bantam Hardcover, 1989.)

Mark is a frail kid until his family moves to a new town where a sports clinic
makes him into a fantastic football hero. But the drugs go awry, and Mark is
doomed to a life as an inhuman beast living apart from those he loves. [Science
gone wrong]

908. Saul, John. **Nathaniel.** New York: Bantam, 1984. 343 pp. ISBN 0-553-
C   24172-9.

When young Michael's father dies, Michael and his pregnant mother return
to his father's desolate family home. Michael soon discovers that someone — or
something — is invading his mind. Can it be the spirit of Nathaniel, a long-dead
child? Terror mounts as Michael's mother struggles to save her son. [Ghosts]

909. Saul, John. **Sleepwalk.** New York: Bantam, 1991. 449 pp. ISBN 0-553-
C   28834-2.

A lot of adults find teenagers irritating, but not irritating enough to kill
them. Yet in Borrego, New Mexico, someone is doing just that, and the
murderer's powers seem to be omnificent. [Legends, Native American]

910. Saul, John. **Suffer the Children.** New York: Dell, 1977. 378 pp. ISBN
C   0-440-18293-X.

The Congers are very grateful for their lovely daughter Elizabeth, who is so
helpful with her younger, autistic sister, Sarah. But Sarah's disability was caused
by a traumatic experience, and Elizabeth is not as good as she seems. Old
atrocities lurk in the Congers' house, and new atrocities seem to happen only too
often. [Evil]

911. Sauter, Eric. **Predators.** New York: Pocket Books, 1987. 360 pp. ISBN
C   0-671-61719-2.

Wolves have long been considered powerful mystical animals by the natives
of northern Canada. When a hunting party is savaged by wolves, only two remain
alive, a man and a wolf. They start to hunt each other, and a string of tragedies
leads to a final showdown with unusual consequences. [Transformation]

912. Savage, Adrian. **Blake House.** New York: Pocket Books, 1990. 254 pp.
C   ISBN 0-671-67250-9.
       Other works: *Unholy Communion.*

New York City is full of interesting sights. One that most sightseers don't
bother to visit is Blake House, a run-down building on the lower East Side, where
a definite aura of evil prevails. [Black magic]

913. Saxon, Peter. **The Killing Bone.** New York: Berkley, 1968. 159 pp.
C
       Sequels: *The Curse of Rathlaw; Through the Dark Curtain; The Haunting
       of Alan Mais; Dark Ways to Death.* Other works: *Brother Blood; The
       Vampires of Finistere; Vampire Moon; Satan's Child.*

A classic tale of good against evil. Can the Guardians, only five in all, summon enough superhuman strength to combat the powers of a dangerous witchdoctor in the outback? [Legends, Aboriginal]

914. Scanlon, Noel. **Apparitions.** New York: Lorevan, 1986. 208 pp. ISBN
C   0-931773-57-1. (First published by Robert Hale, 1984.)

A desolate Irish island is turned into a commune by the followers of Guru Pradavana. One of the followers dies, and she is cremated on a funeral pyre. Then it is discovered that she really isn't dead at all, merely in a trance, and that she was arbitrarily sacrificed to a greedy god. [Legends, Indian]

915. Scanlon, Noel. **Black Ashes.** New York: St. Martin's Press, 1987. 222
C   pp. ISBN 0-312-90270-0. (First published by St. Martin's Press, 1985.)

At first Bob Roberts thinks his assignment to India, where he is to take over for a recent suicide, sounds like fun, a great adventure. But the man who committed suicide doesn't seem to be really dead; his malevolent spirit seems very present in the house. Deirdre, Bob's teenage daughter, especially feels the ominous presence, for it seems to want her particularly. [Legends, Indian]

916. Scarborough, Elizabeth. **The Drastic Dragon of Draco, Texas.** New York:
C   Bantam Spectra, 1986. 247 pp. ISBN 0-553-25887-7.
     Other works: *Browyn's Bane; The Unicorn Creed; Nothing Sacred.*

Dragons are supposed to be long dead or legendary, but a dragon is terrorizing the countryside surrounding a little western town. No one seems able to do anything about it, however, until Delores, a brave young woman decides to tackle the beast. [Dragons]

917. Scarborough, Elizabeth. **The Goldcamp Vampire: or the Sanguinary Sour-**
C   **dough.** New York: Bantam Spectra, 1987. 247 pp. ISBN 0-553-26717-5.

When the Klondike gold rush starts at the turn of the century, many disparate people head for the goldfields. Usually people don't ask too many questions about strangers, but there is one that everyone is wondering about—Vasily Bladovitch Bledinoff, who turns out to be a charming, sophisticated vampire. [Vampires]

918. Scarm, Arthur N. **The Werewolf vs. Vampire Woman.** Beverly Hills,
C   Calif.: Guild-Hartford, 1972. 190 pp.
     Movie versions: *The Werewolf vs. Vampire Woman*, 1970. Director:
     Anthony Dawson. Stars: Anthony Franciosa, Michele Mercier, Peter
     Carsten, and Silvano Tranquilli.

A wonderful spoof on all those great horror movies still shown on the television screen. The werewolf man and the vampire woman make a terrific team as they cut a swath of blood through their neighborhood. [Vampires; Werewolves]

919. Schoell, William. **Bride of Satan.** New York: Leisure, 1986. 396 pp. ISBN
C   0-8439-2423-3.
     Other works: *Spawn of Hell; The Pact.*

Reporter Dorothy Hunter believes herself to be a typical contemporary New Yorker. But her city is no longer the place she thinks she knows so well. A terrible evil is stalking its streets, leaving violence in its wake. [Demons]

920.   Schoell, William. **Late at Night.** New York: Leisure, 1986. 382 pp. ISBN
C   0-8439-2319-9.

A group of young people foolishly gather for a weekend on Lammerty Island, long reputed to be haunted by terror and violence. One of the campers discovers an ancient book that describes their very own group perfectly and their deaths by terrible means. Now the daring investigators realize their mistake in underestimating the powers of evil, for their lives may well be the price they pay. [Evil]

921.   Schoell, William. **Shivers.** New York: Leisure, 1985. 398 pp. ISBN
C   0-8439-2235-4.

A horrible being is slowly taking over the city, picking as its first victims the weak and powerless. But its ultimate aim is to touch everyone, for it is Prime Evil. [Evil]

922.   Schow, David J. **Lost Angels.** New York: Onyx, 1990. 252 pp. ISBN
C   0-451-40186-7.
        Other works: *Kill Riff; Seeing Red.*

A leading splatterpunk writer tells about a downside of life in "Red Light," "Brass," "Pamela's Get," "The Falling Man," and "Monster Movies." [Horror; Short stories]

923.   Scot, Michael. **Burial Rites.** New York: Berkley, 1987. 248 pp. ISBN
C   0-425-10109-6. (First published as *The Ice King* by New English Library, 1986.)

It seems at first to be a usual sort of archaeological excavation of a ruined Viking ship. But the dead do not like to be disturbed, and they have the power to unleash a long-forgotten god — or is it a devil? [Legends, Nordic]

924.   Scott, Melissa, and Lisa A. Barnett. **The Armor of Light.** New York:
C   Baen, 1988. 504 pp. ISBN 0-671-69783-8.

The England of Elizabeth I is a time of glorious renaissance. There is a flowering of the arts and investigative sciences, including the work of the infamous Dr. John Dee, an infamous investigator of the supernatural. [Magic]

925.   Scott, R. C. **Blood Sport.** New York: Bantam, 1984. 144 pp. ISBN 0-553-
A   23866-3. (Dark Forces series).

Bob Lindquist finds to his sorrow and horror that his infatuation with a beautiful girl has led him into a night world he cannot escape. [Evil]

926.   Scott, Sir Walter. **The Supernatural Short Stories of Sir Walter Scott.**
C   London: Calder, 1977. 217 pp. ISBN 0-7145-4086-2.

Strange tales, mostly with Scottish settings, including "The Tapestried Chamber," "My Aunt Margaret's Mirror," "Wandering Willie's Tale," "The Two Drovers," "The Highland Widow." [Horror; Short stories]

927. Sefton, Catherine. **Emer's Ghost.** London: Magnet, 1983. 137 pp. ISBN
B   0-416-26510-3. (First published by Hamish Hamilton, 1981.)
       Other works: *The Ghost Girl; Island of the Strangers.*

Emer cannot believe that the battered old doll is trouble. How could it be?
But not only is the doll trouble, it has power and cries real tears. [Ghosts]

928. Seltzer, David. **The Omen.** New York: Signet, 1976. 208 pp. ISBN 0-451-
C   11989-4.
       Sequels: *Damien: The Omen, Part II* by Joseph Howard; *The Final
       Conflict: Omen III* by Gordon McGill; *Omen IV: Armageddon 2000* by
       Gordon McGill; *Omen V: The Abomination* by Jack Mason. Other works:
       One Is a Lonely Number; The Other Side of the Mountain; Prophecy.
       Movie versions: *The Omen*, 1976. Director: Richard Donner. Stars:
       Gregory Peck, Lee Remick, and David Warner.

The devil's son has been born again, and his evil cannot be comprehended at
first by his wealthy, loving parents. Eventually they come to see this child for
what he is, yet will they be able to stop him and save the world? [Satanism]

929. Serling, Rod. **Stories from the Twilight Zone.** New York: Bantam, 1986.
C   418 pp. ISBN 0-553-34329-7.
       Movie versions: *Twilight Zone: The Movie*, 1983. Directors: John Landis,
       Steven Spielberg, Joe Dante, and George Miller. Stars: Vic Morrow,
       Scatman Crothers, Kathleen Quinlin, Kevin McCarthy, and John
       Lithgow.

Stories from the successful television series, including "The Mighty Casey,"
"Escape Clause," "Walking Distance," "The Fever," "Where is Everybody?" "The
Monsters Are Due on Maple Street," "The Lonely," "Mr. Dingle, the Strong," "A
Thing About Machines," "The Big, Tall Wish," "A Stop at Willoughby," "The
Odyssey of Flight," "Dust," "The Whole Truth," "The Shelter," "Showdown with
Rance McGrew," "The Night of the Meek," "The Midnight Sun," "The Rip Van
Winkle Caper." [Horror; Short stories]

930. Serling, Rod. **Rod Serling's Night Gallery 2.** New York: Bantam, 1972.
C   152 pp. ISBN 0-553-07203-0.
       Earlier collection: *Rod Serling's Night Gallery.*

Spooky stories from Rod Serling's successful television series, including
"Collector's Items," "The Messiah on Mott Street," "The Different Ones,"
"Lindemann's Catch," "Suggestion." [Horror; Short stories]

931. Serling, Rod. **The Twilight Zone.** New York: Tempo, 1965. 190 pp.
A

Stories selected and adapted by Walter B. Gibson for young adults,
including "The Ghost of Ticonderoga," "Back There," "Judgment Night," "The
Curse of Seven Towers," "The Avenging Ghost," "Return from Oblivion," "The
House on the Square," "Death's Masquerade," "The Riddle of the Crypt," "Dead
Man's Chest." [Horror; Short stories]

932. Service, Pamela F. **The Reluctant God.** New York: Fawcett Juniper, 1990.
B   182 pp. ISBN 0-449-70339-8. (First published by Atheneum, 1988.)
      Other works: *Winter of Magic's Return; A Question of Destiny; Tomor-row's Magic.*

As an archaeologist's daughter, Lorna Padgett would rather go on digs with her father than study in school. On one dig Lorna finds the unexpected when an ancient Egyptian prince becomes her friend. [Ghosts; Legends, Egyptian]

933. Service, Pamela F. **When the Night Wind Howls.** New York: Fawcett
A   Juniper, 1987. 120 pp. ISBN 0-449-70279-0.

Sidonie's folks have just gotten a divorce. Sidonie moves with her mother to a small town in Indiana where they become involved in a local theater group. It seems like a good way to make some new friends, but neither counted on meeting some ghosts in the haunted theater. [Ghosts]

934. Setlowe, Richard. **The Haunting of Suzanna Blackwell.** New York: Signet,
C   1985. 298 pp. ISBN 0-451-13556-3.

For years Suzanna has been comforted by the presence of her mother's ghost. Now, however, there are other ghosts in her life, and they threaten to destroy those relationships that are most important to her, as well as her own personality. [Ghosts; Possession]

935. Sharman, Nick. **The Cats.** New York: Signet, 1979. 154 pp. ISBN 0-451-
C   08654-6. (First published by New English Library, 1977.)

Cat lovers might change their minds if they run up against these cats infected with a virus that turns them into killers. [Science gone wrong]

936. Sharman, Nick. **The Switch.** New York: Signet, 1984. 287 pp. ISBN
C   0-451-13102-9.

Trudy Lawrence is totally charmed by Mark Anderson. But after meeting Mark her old boyfriend is killed and horrifying specters appear. Trudy finds her life haunted and hideous, and she may never be able to escape. [Ghosts]

937. Shea, Robert, and Robert Anton Wilson. **The Illuminatus! Trilogy: The**
C   **Eye in the Pyramid; The Golden Apple; Leviathan.** New York: Dell, 1988.
      805 pp. ISBN 0-440-53981-1. (First published as separate volumes by Dell,
      1975.)
      Sequels (by Robert Anton Wilson): *Historical Illuminatus Chronicles; The Widow's Son; Nature's God*

An epic journey into the world of ancient lore, which has survived into the modern age by means of a secret society. [Cults; Illuminati; Knights Templar]

938. Shecter, Ben. **Game for Demons.** New York: Trophy, 1972. 193 pp. SBN
C   06-440054-9. (First published by Harper & Row, 1972.)
      Other works: *The River Witches; Conrad's Castle.*

Can Gordie Cassman handle the problems that seem worse than usual? Not only does his mother seem all screwed up, his own mind seems to be going, too. [Demons]

939. Sheldon, Walter J. **The Beast.** New York: Fawcett, 1980. 288 pp. ISBN
C   0-449-14327-9.

Anthropologist Zia Marlowe is determined to find proof that the legendary Bigfoot lives, but she doesn't realize that her discovery of the beast will be decided upon by Bigfoot himself. [Abominable snowman]

940. Shelley, Mary. **Frankenstein.** New York: Bantam, 1981. 240 pp. ISBN
D   0-553-21172-2. (First published by Lackington, Hughes, Hardin, Mayor & Jones, 1818.)
      Movie versions: *Frankenstein*, 1931. Director: James Whale. Stars: Colin Clive, Mae Clarke, and Boris Karloff. *Frankenstein: The True Story*, 1973. Director: Jack Smight. Stars: James Mason, Leonard Whiting, Michael Sarrazin, and David McCallum. Another movie, *Gothic*, deals with the circumstances of the writing of *Frankenstein* in Switzerland, as does *Frankenstein Unbound*.

The legendary tale of a scientist whose creation becomes more powerful—and more human—than his creator had intended. [Science gone wrong; Transformation]

941. Sherman, Jory. **Vegas Vampire.** Los Angeles: Pinnacle, 1980. 176 pp.
C   ISBN 0-523-40223-6. (Chill series).
      Sequels: *Satan's Seed; Chill; Bamboo Demons; The Phoenix Man; House of Scorpions; Shadows.*

Beautiful showgirls from the Gold Dust Queen in Las Vegas are being murdered, and Dr. Russell (Chill) Chillders is called in for consultation. Chill is not a usual consultant, however; he's a psychic investigator who specializes in the occult, and these murders do not appear to be normal homicides. [Paranormal abilities; Vampires]

942. Shirley, John. **Dracula in Love.** New York: Zebra, 1990. 283 pp. ISBN
C   0-8217-3001-0. (First published by Kensington, 1979.)

Getting to know who and what your parents are can be tough, and when your father is Dracula, you don't look forward to his visits with pleasure. [Vampires]

943. Shryack, Dennis, and Michael Butler. **The Car.** New York: Dell, 1977.
C   235 pp. ISBN 0-440-11032-7.
      Movie versions: *The Car*, 1977. Director: Elliott Silverstein. Stars: James Brolin, Kathleen Lloyd, John Marley, Ronny Cox, R. G. Armstrong, John Rubinstein.

A sleek, powerful black car has appeared in a sleepy southwestern town. The car seems to have no driver, and yet it prowls the town seeking victims. No one can stop the car, and no one knows what—or who—it is. [Evil]

944. Siciliano, Sam. **Blood Farm.** New York: Pageant, 1988. 336 pp. ISBN
C   0-517-00660-X.

People are generally more concerned with the weather than anything else in the middle of a harsh Iowa winter, but Angela quickly discovers that weather isn't all that can kill. She accepts a ride with a guy driving a hearse, and their journey becomes a journey of terror to Blut Farm. [Ghosts]

945. Siddons, Anne Rivers. **The House Next Door.** New York: Ballantine, 1980.
C   279 pp. ISBN 0-345-29330-2. (First published by Simon & Schuster, 1979.)
      Other works: *Fox's Earth.*

It is bad enough just having the brooding presence of the evil house in the neighborhood, but its evil seems to grow. Soon the frightened people who live near the house know they must destroy it before the house destroys them. [Haunted houses]

946. Siegel, Scott. **The Companion.** New York: Bantam, 1983. 134 pp. ISBN
C   0-553-23676-8. (Dark Forces series).

Lots of kids have secret pretend friends, but Jeff's pal Kim has somehow materialized into a possessive evil demon. [Demons]

947. Silverberg, Robert. **The Book of Skulls.** New York: Bantam, 1983. 196 pp.
C   ISBN 0-553-23057-3. (First published by Scribners, 1972.)
      Other works: *Lord Valentine's Castle.*

Four college students go on a pilgrimage to the House of Skulls, a place in the southwestern desert where an ancient brotherhood guards a powerful secret, the gift of eternal life. But there is a heavy price to be paid for the gift; all of the four will not be permitted to live out their lives. [Eternal youth]

948. Silverberg, Robert. **Gilgamesh the King.** New York: Bantam Spectra, 1985.
A   306 pp. ISBN 0-553-25250-X. (First published by Arbor House, 1984.)

A hero of ancient Sumeria, Gilgamesh is part god, part man, and a slayer of demons. This modernized version of a fascinating legend includes all the elements of our favorite epics: intrigue, quests, romance, and betrayal. [Legends, Sumerian]

949. Silverstein, Herma. **Mad, Mad Monday.** New York: Archway, 1989. 149
B   pp. ISBN 0-671-67403-X. (First published by Dutton, 1988.)

Miranda decides to use magic spells to get the boy of her dreams interested in her, but her spell in the graveyard doesn't turn out as she expects, for she gets the ghost of a long-dead teen, Monday, who has a mission all his own. [Ghosts]

950. Silverstone, Lou. **The Mad Book of Horror Stories, Yecchy Creatures,**
A   **and Other Neat Stuff.** New York: Warner, 1986. 192 pp. ISBN
      0-446-32286-5.

Horror comics in the zany style familiar to *Mad* readers, including "Gefilta — The Killer Carp," "The Horror Movie Hate Book," "The Curse of the Werewolf," "The Creatures That Come from the Headlines," "A Mad Look at Dracula," "That House in Vomityville," "The Fall of the House of Gusher," "Dr. Hackyl & Mr. High," "A Mad Look at Igor," "Camp Sleep-Away." [Horror; Short stories]

951. Simmons, Dan. **Song of Kali.** New York: TOR, 1986. 311 pp. ISBN
C   0-812-52566-3. (First published by Bluejay, 1985.)
     Other works: *Carrion Comfort; Prayer to Broken Stones; Obsessions;
     Summer of Night.*

At first Bobby thinks his assignment to go to Calcutta to write a story, all
expenses paid, sounds great, that is before he gets to Calcutta. What happens to
Bobby in Calcutta is so terrible that he will never go there again. [Legends,
Indian]

952. Simon, Jean. **Darksong.** New York: Zebra, 1990. 347 pp. ISBN 0-8217-
C   2893-8.

The old radio isn't really an antique yet, but it seems special to Dallas
Munroe, who buys it. To her horror and surprise, however, the radio doesn't play
the Top 40; it has a deadlier message. [Science gone wrong]

953. Simon, Jean. **Wild Card.** New York: Zebra, 1991. 288 pp. ISBN 0-8217-
C   3270-6.

Mick McGee is puzzled at first by the fascinating tarot cards her mother
keeps in a beautiful box. But then she discovers that the cards have great power;
not only do they foretell the future, they control the future as well. Mick finds
herself obsessed with her new power and develops a new life-style, one that will
lead her into an atmosphere of evil and deceit. [Prophecy]

954. Simpson, George E., and Neal R. Burger. **Ghostboat.** New York: Dell,
C   1985. 412 pp. ISBN 0-440-15421-9. (First published by Dell, 1976.)

Navy Commander Ed Frank is determined to find out why the submarine
Candlefish, lost in 1944, has mysteriously returned. He embarks on a dangerous
voyage to find the unspeakable truth and finds an incredible answer hidden deep
in the ocean. [Vanishings]

955. Sinclair, Quinn. **The Boy Who Could Draw Tomorrow.** New York: Dell
C   Emerald, 1984. 221 pp. ISBN 0-440-00745-3.

Hal and Peggy Cooper have just decided their lives and careers are paying
off. Both are doing well in their high-pressure jobs, well enough that they can
afford to move to a better apartment in the affluent upper East Side of New
York. Their darling boy Sam is enrolled in the best private school around and his
future seems boundless, but the pictures Sam draws become more and more dis-
turbing, and what's worse, the scenes in his pictures come true. [Paranormal
abilities]

956. Singer, Isaac Bashevis. **The Magician of Lublin.** New York: Fawcett Crest,
C   1980. 288 pp. ISBN 0-449-20966-0. (First published by Farrar, Straus &
     Giroux, 1960.)
     Other works: *Satan in Goray.* Movie versions: *The Magician of Lublin*,
     1979. Director: Menachen Golan. Stars: Alan Arkins, Louise Fletcher,
     Valerie Perrine, and Shelley Winters.

Yasha Mazur, the magician of Lublin, is a man of extraordinary talents
although not a hero in his own hometown. He is more than a stage magician, for
he can read minds and communicate with spirits. All in all, he is not a man
destined to lead a common life. [Magic; Paranormal abilities]

957. Singer, Isaac Bashevis. **The Seance.** New York: Fawcett, 1981. 255 pp.
C   ISBN 0-449-24364-8. (First published by Farrar, Straus & Giroux, 1968.)

Tales of mystery by a master storyteller, including "The Seance," "The Slaughterer," "The Dead Fiddler," "The Lecturer," "Cockadoodledoo," "The Plagiarist," "Zeitl and Rickel," "The Warehouse," "Henne Fine," "Getzel the Monkey," "Yanda," "The Needle," "Two Corpses Go Dancing," "The Parrot," "The Brooch," "The Letter Writer." [Mysticism; Short stories]

958. Singer, Marilyn. **Ghost Host.** New York: Scholastic, 1988. 199 pp. ISBN
A   0-590-41547-6. (First published by Harper & Row, 1987.)

A high-school football player has enough to deal with what with sports, school, family, and friends to take up time. But Bart Hawkins has extra problems; he lives in a haunted house and one of the ghosts is a real meanie. [Ghosts]

959. Sirota, Michael B. **Demon Shadows.** New York: Bantam, 1990. 233 pp.
C   ISBN 0-553-28366-9.

There are some old stories about people caught in the wintery clasp of no escape in the California mountains, and some of these stories, including those of cannibalism, are true. Those who were eaten have restless spirits, as a band of contemporary people discover on what they think is a quiet artists' retreat. [Ghosts]

960. Skipp, John, and Craig Spector. **Fright Night.** New York: TOR, 1985.
C   250 pp. ISBN 0-812-52564-7.
     Other works: *Dead Lines; The Cleanup; The Scream.* Movie versions:
     Fright Night, 1985. Director: Tom Holland. Stars: Chris Sarandon,
     William Ragsdale, Amanda Bearse, Stephen Geoffreys, Roddy McDowall.

Like a lot of other kids his age, Charley Brewster likes horror movies, but he doesn't really believe them until he gets a look at his new next-door neighbor, obviously a clever vampire. [Vampires]

961. Skipp, John and Craig Spector. **The Light at the End.** New York: Bantam,
C   1986. 385 pp. ISBN 0-553-25451-0.

The Ancient One has come to New York to enlarge his evil clan. Rudy is his first victim, but Rudy decides to become all-powerful himself. Rudy's friends are among his victims as he roams the subway tunnels and bizarre night-world of Greenwich Village. A small force, however, gathers to stop Rudy before it is too late. Or is it too late already? [Vampires]

962. Slaughter, Frank G. **Devil's Gamble.** New York: Pocket Books, 1978.
C   408 pp. ISBN 0-671-82215-2. (First published by Doubleday, 1977.)

The self-proclaimed satanist Lynne Talman has been killed in a plane accident, but her message of evil and power seems to survive. Janet Burke is also a victim of the plane crash, but she is saved by Mike Kerns, a brilliant surgeon who discovers too late that Janet is no longer the person she once was. [Possession; Satanism]

963. Sleator, William. **Blackbriar.** New York: Scholastic Point, 1982. 217 pp.
A   ISBN 0-590-40308-7. (First published by Dutton, 1972.)
Other works: *House of Stairs; Singularity; Among the Dolls; The Boy Who Reversed Himself.*

Young Danny Chilton finds Blackbriar fascinating, even if it is a bit scary. His new friend Lark helps Danny discover the meaning behind the mystery, and it is far scarier than Danny had originally thought. It is bad enough when they find out that Blackbriar had once been a pesthouse, a place where plague victims were brought to die in earlier times, but the mysterious lights on a nearby hill hint at even worse secrets. [Witchcraft]

964. Sleator, William. **Fingers.** New York: Bantam Starfire, 1985. 197 pp.
A   ISBN 0-553-25004-3. (First published by Atheneum, 1983.)

Sam's mother is hungry to have her two sons succeed, and when Humphrey, the younger, burns out as a child-prodigy pianist, she decides to make Sam into another famous pianist. He is to play the compositions that he has written himself, but they will be publicized as newly discovered works by a dead genius. The scheme works until Sam finds his hands are no longer his own as he plays. [Possession]

965. Sleator, William. **Into the Dream.** New York: Scholastic Apple, n.d. 154
B   pp. ISBN 0-590-33982-6. (First published by Dutton, 1979.)

Francine Gill and Paul Rhodes are having the same dream every night. The dream shows a mysterious glowing object, a run-down motel, and a small boy in danger. Somehow Francine and Paul must stop a terrible horror from happening even though they are in terrible danger themselves. [Dreams]

966. Sloane, Robert C. **A Nice Place to Live.** New York: Crown, 1981. 278
C   pp. ISBN 0-517-545152.
Other works: *The Vengeance.*

The Marinos think their new house is perfect. Then odd things start to happen, and Mr. Marino starts to behave very strangely. Can he be becoming someone else, or even some*thing* else? [Evil]

967. Smith, A. C. H. **Labyrinth.** New York: Holt Owl, 1986. 183 pp. ISBN
A   0-03-007322-4.
Movie versions: *Labyrinth*, 1986. Director: Jim Henson. Stars: David Bowie, Mia Sara, and the Jim Henson puppets.

Courageous Sarah has wished the pest away, and now she must go into the goblin world to try to save her little brother Toby. If she is not in time, the fascinating goblin king, Jareth, will keep him forever. [Fairies]

968. Smith, David C. **The Fair Rules of Evil.** New York: Avon, 1989. 180 pp.
C   ISBN 0-380-75684-6.

David and Ginny are devastated by their parents' deaths. David turns to religion, becoming a priest, but Ginny turns to consolation through the spirit world. She is sucked into more than harmless seances, and David must face the powers of evil in order to save her. [Satanism]

969.   Smith, Lady Eleanor. **A Dark and Splendid Passion.** New York: Ace,
C   n.d. (First published in England by Hutchinson, 1941.)

World War II is a very grim and frightening time in England. Mary, bride of
Lord Rohan, must wait in his ancestral home for news of her husband, who is in
the war. As she explores her new home, Mary is fascinated at first with the old
diary and an odd portrait in a hidden room. But history becomes frightening
reality when Mary realizes that an evil possessive spirit is determined to always be
the current Lady Rohan. [Possession]

970.   Smith, Gregory Blake. **The Devil in the Dooryard.** New York: Ballantine,
C   1987. 308 pp. ISBN 0-345-34706-4. (First published by William Morrow,
       1986.)

John Wheelwright, descendant of a Mayflower settler and a member of
Boston society, loves history, particularly the history of the early colonial days
and the story of Samuel Mavericke. His love of the past becomes so intense,
however, that he finds the past replacing the reality of present times and places.
[Ghosts]

971.   Smith, Guy N. **Bloodshow.** London: Arrow, 1987. 207 pp. ISBN 0-09-
C   952270-5.
       Other works: *Son of the Werewolf; Wolfcurse; The Slime Beast; Thirst;
       Bats out of Hell; Caracal; Warhead; Blood Circuit; The Undead;
       Accursed; The Walking Dead; Throwback; The Graveyard Vultures; The
       Blood Merchants; Cannibal Cult; The Druid Connection; The Sucking Pit.*

The Laird of Benahee has turned his old ruined castle in the Scottish high-
lands into a haunted mansion to attract tourists and money to the area. But
playing with evil is a dangerous business, for the demons of hell can be easily
roused. [Evil]

972.   Smith, Guy N. **Entombed.** New York: Dell, 1987. 189 pp. ISBN 0-440-
C   12280-5. (First published by Arrow, 1982.)

There are still memories in the Welsh hills of the terrible lives led by children
of the past who were forced to work in the dark, dangerous mines. But there was
one mine that was even worse than the others, for some of those children became
ritual sacrifices for satanic worshippers. The souls of these children do not rest
easy. These children have not been laid to rest. [Ghosts]

973.   Smith, Guy N. **The Neophyte.** London: New English Library, 1986.
C   312 pp. ISBN 0-450-05858-1.

Joby is a witch-boy. Except for his loyal friend Ally and the mysterious,
alluring, and fascinating Sally Ann, the villagers all hate the teenager. Sally Ann
wants Joby because she is a witch, too, but Joby wants no part of his heritage and
fights desperately to gain his freedom. [Horror; Witchcraft]

974.   Smith, Guy N. **The Origin of the Crabs.** New York: Dell, 1988. 186 pp.
C   ISBN 0-440-20021-0. (First published by New English Library, 1979.)
       Sequels: *Crabs' Moon; Killer Crabs; Crabs on the Rampage; Night of the
       Crabs.*

Giant voracious crabs are threatening England. They'll eat anything that lives and breathes, including people. Yum, yum, here they come. [Monsters, slime-type]

975. Smith, Guy N. **The Wood.** New York: Dell, 1987. 191 pp. ISBN 0-440-
C   19753-8. (First published by the New English Library, 1985.)

At first the woods seem like a sanctuary to pretty Carol Embleton, who is escaping from a crazy rapist. Naked, she runs into the woods only to find that others have been there before. They are now dead but still present. [Ghosts]

976. Smith, James V. **Beastmaker.** New York: Dell, 1988. 382 pp. ISBN
C   0-440-20042-3.
      Sequels: *Beaststalker.*

There are some monsters on the loose, uncontrollable monsters that kill savagely and brutally. Science has created them, but will science have the skill to destroy them? [Monsters; Science gone wrong]

977. Smith, Janet Patton. **The Twisted Room.** New York: Dell, 1983. 154 pp.
A   ISBN 0-440-98690-7. (Twilight series).

When Lisa first spots the girl in the window next door, she wonders about her. She seems lonely, almost as if she is in trouble. Then she finds out the truth about Marie Worthington and realizes that Marie isn't really alive any more. Lisa becomes very afraid. [Ghosts]

978. Smith, Martin Cruz. **Nightwing.** New York: Jove, 1977. 255 pp. ISBN
C   0-515-06124-7. (First published by Norton, 1977.)
      Movie versions: *Nightwing*, 1979. Director: Arthur Hiller. Stars: Nick
      Mancuso, David Warner, and Kathryn Harrold.

The beauty of the southwestern desert becomes more and more fearsome as the power of rapacious superbats becomes more apparent to the leaders of the tribes in the area. [Legends, Native American; Monsters]

979. Smith, Susan. **Samantha Slade: Monster-Sitter.** New York: Archway,
B   1987. 129 pp. ISBN 0-671-63713-4.
      Sequels: *Confessions of a Teenage Frog; Our Friend; Public Nuisance No.
      1; The Terrors of Rock and Roll.*

Twelve-year-old Samantha earns money the same way a lot of kids her age do, by babysitting. But Samantha's charges are a bit weird—Lupi is much hairier than usual and Drake eats really strange stuff. And their home is really something, full of dead things and pet bats. [Monsters]

980. Smith, Thorne. **Topper.** New York: Ballantine/Del Rey, 1980. 208 pp.
C   ISBN 0-345-28722-3. (First published by Grosset & Dunlap, 1933.)
      Sequels: *Topper Returns; Topper Takes a Trip.* Other works: *I Married a
      Witch; Twilight of the Gods.* Movie versions: *Topper*, 1937. Director:
      Norman McLeod. Stars: Cary Grant, Constance Bennett, and Roland
      Young. *Topper*, 1979. Director: Charles Dubin. Stars: Kate Jackson,
      Norman Stevens, and Jack Warden.

George and Marian Kirby, wealthy sophisticates, are surprised to find themselves in a ghostly state. They decide that in order to free themselves from this limbo-like existence they must do a good deed. They fix upon their mild henpecked banker, Topper, as a worthy recipient of their attentions, and then the fun begins. [Ghosts]

981. Snow, Bradley. **Andy.** Bramalea, Ont.: Downhome Productions, 1990.
C   203 pp. ISBN 1-895109-00-0.

A lot of kids have imaginary friends, and Jamie needs his, Andy, badly. Jamie's widowed mother has shifting moods, and only Andy can give Jamie the comfort and stability he craves. But Andy isn't a kid like Jamie, and he's not really imaginary. And Andy isn't really the friendly type. [Monsters]

982. Snyder, Gene. **Tomb Seven.** New York: Charter, 1985. 279 pp. ISBN
C   0-441-81643-6.

Most archaeological work involves tedious, painstaking searches in out-of-the-way places. Sometimes, however, the lucky scientists find great treasures, making it all seem worthwhile. Tomb Seven, hidden in the mountains of Mexico, seems to be such a find, but its discoverers have not reckoned with the fury of disturbed ancient gods. [Legends, Aztec]

983. Soesbe, Douglas. **Scream Play.** New York: Charter, 1990. 268 pp. ISBN
C   1-55773-387-2.

The spectacular old movie palaces of the past have no place in today's world of multiplex theaters, so the old Odeon is going to be torn down. But the old theater is not going without a fight, and on the final night it's open to the public, there is a horror show like none ever seen before. [Evil]

984. Somers, Suzanne. **Romany Curse.** New York: Unisystem, 1971. 140 pp.
A

A century ago, lovely Adela Barron and her mother travel to Florida to sell an old family mansion. When they arrive, they find the place is full of squatters, gypsies from a nearby camp. Adela is fascinated by their customs and even more fascinated by the dashing Django, but she finds it is not safe to dabble in ancient secrets. [Gothic romance; Gypsy lore]

985. Somtow, S. P. (pseud. of Somtow Sucharitkul). **Vampire Junction.** New
B   York: Berkley, 1985. 362 pp. ISBN 0-425-09091-4. (First published by
      Donning, 1984.)

A horrifying and gruesome tale of vampires and rock music, an impressionistic series of images that could shatter quiet sleep for some nights to come. [Vampires]

986. Sorrels, Roy. **The Eyes of Torie Webster.** New York: Pinnacle, 1990. 288
C   pp. ISBN 1-55817-388-9.

Torie Webster is a rising young media star, a newscaster with an unerring sense for a good story. One day Torie finds the old diary of a woman burned for witchcraft in 1693, and Torie begins to wonder if she is the reincarnation of old Lizzie Dedalus. [Satanism]

987. Sparger, Rex. **The Bargain.** New York: Bantam, 1983. 152 pp. ISBN
A   0-553-22823-4. (Dark Forces series).

The Coastals, a high-school rock group, want success. Little do they realize, though, when they make an agreement with Chort, that the deal includes more than fame and fortune. Their very souls are the price they must pay. [The devil]

988. Sparger, Rex. **The Doll.** New York: Bantam, 1983. 135 pp. ISBN 0-553-
A   22824-2. (Dark Forces series).

Cassie collects dolls, and when she sees a special, lifelike doll at the state fair, she knows she must have it. But special powers come with the doll, and it has evil designs on Cassie's soul. [Evil]

989. Spark, Muriel. **The Bachelors.** Harmondsworth, England: Penguin, 1963.
C   215 pp. ISBN 0-14-001910-3. (First published by Macmillan, 1960.)

Patrick Sefton is a medium, a conduit to the other world. He knows the secrets of many people, and his upcoming trial for forgery has those he knows secrets about in a state of panic. [Spiritualism]

990. Speare, Elizabeth, George. **The Witch of Blackbird Pond.** New York:
A   Laurel-Leaf, 1972. 249 pp. ISBN 0-440-49596-2. (First published by
      Houghton Mifflin, 1958.)

Kit Tyler knew her life in cold, Colonial Connecticut would be very different from her luxurious home in the Caribbean. She did not realize how very different and dangerous it would be, however, until she is accused of witchcraft. [Witchcraft]

991. Spearing, Judith. **Ghosts Who Went to School.** London: Hippo, 1987.
B   139 pp. ISBN 0-590-40452-0.

Even young ghosts get bored, so Wilbur and Mortimer Temple are sent to school with some very hilarious results. It seems there are no schools for ghosts, so the Temple boys join human classmates, who are not thrilled with them. [Ghosts]

992. Spicer, Dorothy. **The Witch's Web.** New York: Ballantine, 1975. 184 pp.
C   ISBN 0-345-24707-8.
      Other works: *The Crystal Ball.*

Shelley Chase can't resist taking the job she found out about so mysteriously. The job is at Black Turrets, her dead father's home and a place she has never been. Only after she enters Black Turrets, however, does she realize she has made a mistake, for Black Turrets has been waiting for her. [Gothic romance; Witchcraft]

993. Stahl, Ben. **Blackbeard's Ghost.** New York: Scholastic, 1976. 174 pp.
B   ISBN 0-590-03056-6. (First published by Houghton Mifflin, 1965.)
      Movie versions: *Blackbeard's Ghost*, 1968. Director: Robert Stevenson.
      Stars: Peter Ustinov, Dean Jones, Suzanne Pleshette, and Elsa Lancaster.

At first J.D. thinks it'll be fun to conjure up a ghost, particularly the ghost of the famous pirate Blackbeard. He's delighted with his success when the ghost appears, but then he realizes that having a ghost around is not making life easy! [Ghosts]

994. Stamper, J. B. **Tales for the Midnight Hour.** New York: Apple, 1977.
B 124 pp. ISBN 0-590-40323-0.

Some stories that it's better not to think about too long, for they are stories about the world of horror, including "The Furry," "The Black Velvet Ribbon," "The Boarder," "The Ten Claws," "The Jigsaw Puzzle," "The Face," "The Mirror," "The Egyptian Coffin," "The Old Plantation," "Phobia," "The Train Through Transylvania," "The Attic Door," "The Tunnel of Terror," "The Fortune Teller," "The Stuffed Dog," "A Free Place to Sleep," "The Gooney Bird." [Horror; Short stories]

995. Stanwood, Brooks. **The Seventh Child.** New York: Dell, 1982. 315 pp.
C ISBN 0-440-19122-X.
Other works: *The Glow.*

Is it possible for a terrible past to live again? Seven children find out they are merely pawns used by a terrible evil to reenact a horrible deed from the past. [Witchcraft]

996. Starks, Christopher. **Possession.** New York: Fawcett, 1983. 182 pp. ISBN
C 0-449-12547-5. (First published by Random House, 1982.)

Ginny has been an abused wife, and she isn't sorry when Brink is no longer around to bully her. Then Brink's spirit comes back from the land of the dead and is determined to take over Ginny's mind. [Possession]

997. Steiger, Brad. **The Hypnotist.** New York: Dell, 1979. 346 pp. ISBN
C 0-440-13771-3.

Noted occult authority Steiger turns his talents to telling a story of terror about a man of irresistible charm and ability. He can cure most ills and has great power, and he believes that he was once a satanist who lived centuries before in France, for his power to heal does not seem to come from God. [Reincarnation; Satanism]

998. Stein, Duffy. **The Owlsfane Horror.** New York: Dell, 1981. 474 pp. ISBN
C 0-440-16781-7.

Sandy Horne thinks picturesque Vermont will be the perfect place for a week of fun. And Owlsfane seems the perfect old house. But Owlsfane's atmosphere is not one of peace and quiet. Owlsfane has a bloody history and is not a place to rest easy. [Haunted houses]

999. Steinbeck, John. **The Acts of King Arthur and His Noble Knights.** New
C York: Ballantine/Del Rey, 1981. 464 pp. ISBN 0-345-28955-2. (First published by Farrar, Straus & Giroux, 1976.)
Movie versions: *Excalibur*, 1981. Director: John Borman. Stars: Nicol Williamson, Nigel Terry, and Helen Mirren.

A noted American author's version of eight tales from Malory's manuscript about King Arthur and his knights. [Legends, Arthurian]

1000.   Stern, Steven. **Hex.** New York: Pocket Books, 1989. 362 pp. ISBN
C   0-671-66325-9.

A peaceful small town seems the perfect place for Kris Merrill to concentrate on finishing a writing job and get over a bitter divorce. Then Kris starts to hear about goings-on in the town and countryside that are unusual, weird, and evil. [Powwow]

1001.   Stevenson, Anne. **A Game of Statues.** New York: Fawcett, 1974. 223
C   pp. SBN 449-02088-125. (First published by G. P. Putnam's Sons, 1972.)

Lovely young widow Ginny and her young son Ben come to live with Mrs. Sendall. At first things seem idyllic, a perfect place to heal old wounds and prepare for a new life. But then odd things start to happen, including ghosts in the garden and even death. [Ghosts]

1002.   Stevenson, E. **The Avenging Spirit.** New York: Dell, 1983. 148 pp. ISBN
A   0-440-90001-8. (Twilight series).

Christina is fascinated by the beauty, power, and mystery of the mountain that hovers over Thunder Rock. But her fascination involving the mountain does not bring Christina peace; instead she finds unrest and an increasing sense of approaching doom. [Evil]

1003.   Stevenson, Florence. **Moonlight Variations.** New York: Jove, 1981. 213
C   pp. ISBN 0-515-05655-3.
       Other works: *A Feast of Eggshells.*

Lorrie MacIvor has fallen in love with fascinating Dario Paull. But Dario is not an ordinary man, for Dario was once the lover of Lorrie's ancestor, Barbary Clinton, over a century ago. [Ghosts]

1004.   Stevenson, Robert Louis. **The Body Snatcher and Other Stories.** New
C   York: Signet, 1988. 350 pp. ISBN 0-451-52153-6.
       Other works: *The Master of Ballantrae; The Supernatural Short Stories of Robert Louis Stevenson.* Movie versions: *The Body Snatcher,* 1945. Director: Robert Wise. Stars: Boris Karloff, Henry Daniell, Edith Atwater, Russell Wade, Rita Corday, and Bela Lugosi.

A collection of mysterious tales by a master, including "The Body Snatcher," "The Sire de Maletroit's Door," "The Pavilion on the Links," "Markheim," "Olalla," "The Bottle Imp," "The Beach at Falesa," "Weird of Hermiston." [Horror; Short stories]

1005.   Stevenson, Robert Louis. **Dr. Jekyll and Mr. Hyde.** New York: Bantam,
D   1981. 128 pp. ISBN 0-553-21200-1. (First published by Longmans, Green, 1888.) (See also entry 706.)
       Movie versions: *Dr. Jekyll and Mr. Hyde,* 1932. Director: Rouben Mamoulian. Stars: Frederic March and Miriam Hopkins. *Dr. Jekyll and Mr. Hyde,* 1941. Director: Victor Fleming. Stars: Spencer Tracy and Ingrid Bergman.

A respected doctor by day, Dr. Jekyll experiments in his lab and finds a way to alter his appearance and personality to that of dissipated Mr. Hyde, who roams the dark streets of London in search of depraved pleasures. [Science gone wrong]

1006.   Stevermer, C. J. **The Alchemist: Death of a Borgia.** New York: Ace
C   Charter, 1981. 200 pp. ISBN 0-441-01426-7.
      Sequels: *The Duke and the Veil.*

Nicholas Coffin, an English alchemist, is in Renaissance Rome, a Rome controlled by the powerful Borgias. His skill in detection using arcane arts is known to the Borgias, who give him a mystery to solve. The only hitch is, if Nicholas can't find a murderer in two days' time, Nicholas will pay with his life. [Alchemy; Magic]

1007.   Steward, Fred Mustard. **The Mephisto Waltz.** New York: Berkley, 1982.
C   212 pp. ISBN 0-425-05343-1. (First published by Coward, McCann &
      Geoghegan, 1969.)
      Other works: *Star Child; A Rage Against Heaven.* Movie versions: *The*
      Mephisto Waltz, 1971. Director: Paul Wendkos. Stars: Alan Alda,
      Jacqueline Bisset, Barbara Parkins, and Curt Jurgens.

Myles Clarkson, once an aspiring concert pianist, is fascinated by the attention of Duncan Ely, an aging renowned pianist. Only Myles's wife seems to sense impending doom as Myles becomes more and more manipulated by the sinister Duncan. [Evil]

1008.   Stewart, Kerry. **Ruby.** New York: Berkley, 1978. 195 pp. ISBN 0-425-
C   03640-5.
      Movie versions: *Ruby*, 1977. Director: Curtis Harrington. Stars: Piper
      Laurie, Stuart Whitman, Roger Davis, Janit Baldwin, Crystin Sinclaire,
      Paul Kent.

Ruby's daughter Leslie is haunted by a past she didn't create. At the moment of Leslie's conception her father was exterminated by a gangland boss in cahoots with Ruby. In that moment between life and death, the souls of Leslie and her father agree that Leslie will stop at nothing to avenge her father's death. [Evil]

1009.   Stewart, Mary. **The Crystal Cave.** New York: Fawcett Crest, 1984. 384
C   pp. ISBN 0-449-20644-0. (First published by Morrow, 1970.)
      Sequels: *The Hollow Hills; The Last Enchantment; The Wicked Day.*

The magical story of Camelot and an early Britain full of magic as seen through the eyes of Merlin. [Legends, Arthurian]

1010.   Stewart, Mary. **Touch Not the Cat.** New York: Ballantine, 1984. 302
C   pp. ISBN 0-449-20608-4. (First published by Morrow, 1976.)

Bryony Ashley must use all of her special powers to solve the mysteries of her family and bring peace to her own life. [Paranormal abilities]

1011.   Stewart, Mary. **A Walk in Wolf Wood.** New York: Fawcett/Crest, 1980.
B   188 pp. ISBN 0-449-20111-2. (First published by Morrow, 1980.)

John and Margaret follow a strange man into the forest and find themselves in another time. They decide to help Lord Mardian but quickly discover that evil men do not want Lord Mardian cured of his werewolf curse. [Time travel; Werewolves]

1012.   Stewart, Michael. **Monkey Shines.** New York: Vintage, 1988. 323 pp.
C   ISBN 0-394-75926-5. (First published by Random House, 1983.)
        Movie versions: *Monkey Shines*, 1985. Director: George Romaro. Stars:
        Jason Beghe, John Pankow, Melanie Parker, and Joyce Van Patten.

Allan Mann seems to have everything going for him with a handsome face, a
healthy body, and bright future, but then comes the day of the accident and he is
sentenced to live the rest of his life in a wheelchair. He is provided with a
helpmate, Ella, a trained monkey who will be his companion and helper. But Ella
seems to possess special intelligence and a mind that is attuned to evil. [Science
gone wrong]

1013.   Stewart, Ramona. **The Possession of Joel Delaney.** New York: Dell,
A   1980. 215 pp. ISBN 0-440-17643-3. (First published by Little, Brown,
        1970.)
        Movie versions: *The Possession of Joel Delaney*, 1972. Director: Waris
        Hussein. Stars: Shirley MacLaine, Perry King, Lisa Kohane, David
        Elliott, Michael Hordern, Miriam Colon, and Lovelady Powell.

Norah is troubled about her younger brother Joel. She cannot believe that he
was responsible for the horrible murders and mutilations of beautiful women, yet
there are times when Joel behaves so strangely that Norah has doubts. At last she
starts to investigate, for she must know the truth and try to save her brother.
[Possession]

1014.   Stewart, Ramona. **Sixth Sense.** New York: Dell, 1980. 211 pp. ISBN
A   0-440-18015-5. (First published by Delacorte, 1979.)

Nancy Parsons discovers that she has powers of ESP that enable her to
"join" the mind of a vicious killer. Soon, however, the killer finds out about
Nancy, and he decides to make her his next victim. [Paranormal abilities]

1015.   Stine, R. L. **Fear Street: The New Girl.** New York: Archway, 1989. 168
A   pp. ISBN 0-671-67685-7.
        Sequels: *The Surprise Party; The Overnight; Missing; The Wrong
        Number; The Sleepwalker; Haunted; Halloween Party; The Stepsister;
        Ski Weekend.*

The kids who live on Fear Street don't have it quite as tough as the kids who
live on Elm Street, but it's a scary place all the same. Most of the mysteries can be
explained rationally in the end ... sort of ... but it's always exciting here, and
teens have to be alert all the time to stay alive. [Horror]

1016.   Stoker, Bram. **Dracula.** New York: Bantam, 1981. 402 pp. ISBN 0-553-
D   22148-X. (First published by Constable, 1897.)
        Other works: *Jewel of the Seven Stars* (see entry 23); *The Lady of the
        Shroud.* Movie versions: *Dracula*, 1931. Director: Tod Browning. Stars:
        Bela Lugosi, David Manners, and Helen Chandler. *Count Dracula*, 1970.
        Director: Jess Frances. Stars: Christopher Lee, Herbert Lom, and Klaus
        Kinski. *Dracula*, 1973. Director: Dan Curtis. Stars: Jack Palance, Simon
        Ward, Nigel Davenport, and Pamela Brown. *Dracula*, 1979. Director:
        John Badham. Stars: Frank Langella, Laurence Olivier, Donald
        Pleasance, and Kate Nelligan.

The classic tale that has spawned so many movies, plays, and books. That suave count has a fascination for many that will not die. [Vampires]

1017. Stoker, Bram. **The Lair of the White Worm.** London: Target, 1986.
C   156 pp. ISBN 0-426-20226-0. (First published in London by Rider, 1911.) Movie versions: *The Lair of the White Worm*, 1988. Director: Ken Russell. Stars: Amanda Donohoe, Hugh Grant, Catherine Oxenberg, Peter Capaldi, Sammi Davis, Stratford Johns, and Paul Brooke.

There is an ancient terror lurking in the dark hills. The English countryside is not peaceful and gentle, for a terrible beast is loose on the land, a beast that must be fed. [Monsters]

1018. Storr, Catherine. **Marianne Dreams.** Harmondsworth, England: Puffin,
B   1964. 204 pp. ISBN 0-14-030209-3. (First published Faber and Faber, 1958.)

Marianne is a thoughtful child. She enjoys drawing pictures. One night she dreams about the picture she drew that day, and the boy in the picture becomes a strange friend who is in danger. [Dreams]

1019. Straub, Peter. **Ghost Story.** New York: Pocket Books, 1979. 567 pp.
C   ISBN 0-671-44198-1. (First published by Coward, McCann & Geoghegan, New York, 1978.)
       Other works: *Floating Dragon; Under Venus; Mystery;* and with Stephen King, *Talisman.* Movie versions: *Ghost Story*, 1981. Director: John Irving. Stars: Fred Astaire, Melvyn Douglas, Douglas Fairbanks, Jr., John Houseman, Craig Wasson, and Alice Krige.

Four old men share a terrible secret from the days of their youth. They think they are safe from repercussions, but they don't reckon on the vengeful spirit of the long-dead girl they once wronged. [Ghosts]

1020. Straub, Peter. **Julia.** New York: Pocket Books, 1976. 294 pp. ISBN
C   0-671-49564-X. (First published by Coward, McCann & Geoghegan, 1975.)

Julia has a lot of problems. She seems to be going crazy, but what's causing her condition is very problematical. Her husband seems to be interested in driving her mad, her child's death was most unsettling, and there seems to be a ghost roaming the house. Poor Julia. [Ghosts]

1021. Straub, Peter. **Shadowland.** New York: Berkley, 1981. 468 pp. ISBN
C   0-425-05056-4. (First published by Coward, McCann & Geoghegan, 1980.)

Two prep-school teenagers arrive at Shadowland for a summer vacation. Their vacation turns into a dizzying and mysterious voyage of magic and terror, a vacation from which there may be no escape. [Magic]

1022. Strickland, Brad. **Children of the Knife.** New York: Onyx, 1990. 317
C   pp. ISBN 0-451-40208-1.
       Other works: *ShadowShow.*

There's plenty in today's world to make children different and fearful, but Peter Collins thinks something is very wrong and is determined to find out its cause, even through the perils of terror. [Science gone wrong]

1023. Strieber, Whitley. **Cat Magic.** New York: TOR, 1987. 441 pp. ISBN
A   0-812-51550-1.
        Other works: *Black Magic; Satan's Church; Communion.*

When Amanda Walker comes home, she believes she has a great commission
as an illustrator, the kind of work she has always wanted to do. Granted, her new
patron is a witch, but that doesn't bother Amanda at first. But there are other
powers at work as well in Maywell, New Jersey, and Amanda finds her dream job
turning into a horrible nightmare. [Cults; Science gone wrong]

1024. Strieber, Whitley. **The Hunger.** New York: Pocket Books, 1982. 307 pp.
C   ISBN 0-671-42737-7. (First published by William Morrow, 1981.)
        Movie versions: *The Hunger*, 1983. Director: Tony Scott. Stars:
        Catherine Deneuve, David Bowie, and Susan Sarandon.

Miriam is a true vampire from an ancient race and is forced to outlive all her
lovers. Although her lovers never fully die, they are unable to continue forever as
her companions. John has been Miriam's lover for 200 years, but his time is drawing to an end, and Miriam must find someone new to take his place. [Vampires]

1025. Strieber, Whitley. **The Wolfen.** New York: Bantam, 1979. 275 pp. ISBN
C   0-553-20268-5. (First published by William Morrow, 1978.)
        Movie versions: *The Wolfen*, 1981. Director: Michael Wadleigh. Stars:
        Albert Finney, Diane Venora, Geoffrey Hines, and Edward James Olmos.

New York has been becoming more and more like a savage jungle every day
in the view of a hardened police detective, and now a new breed of creatures are
apparently doing their "work" in the city, causing havoc and death wherever they
strike. The beasts are strange, vicious killers, not the creatures usually seen in
urban environments. [Monsters]

1026. Sudak, Eunice. **X.** New York: Lancer, 1963. 126 pp.
C   Movie versions: *X*, 1963. Director: Roger Corman. Stars: Ray Milland,
        Diana Van Der Vlis, Harold J. Stone, John Hoyt, and Don Rickles.

Dr. Xavier is a scientist obsessed with vision. He wants to see everything,
even more than one can see with normal sight. Dr. Xavier has been trained to
solve problems, and he solves this one by developing X-ray vision. At first he
thinks his discovery is wonderful; but he later realizes that it may not be so great
after all. [Science gone wrong]

1027. Sullivan, Faith. **Mrs. Demming and the Mythical Beast.** New York: TOR,
C   1988. 407 pp. ISBN 0-812-52598-1.

In the middle of a deteriorating marriage, Larissa Demming finds a fascinating creature in her private woodsy escape place. He is a satyr, a Greek pan
who satisfies Larissa's need for a new sexuality in her life and convinces her to
take him home. [Legends, Greek]

1028. Suskind, Patrick. **Perfume.** New York: Pocket Books, 1987. 310 pp.
A   ISBN 0-671-64370-3.

Vampires don't always seek blood. In eighteenth-century France there once
lived a monster so strange and vile that he could satisfy his perverted lust only by
absorbing scent, as well as life, from his hapless victims ... young and innocent
virgins. [Monsters; Vampires]

1029.   Suster, Gerald. **The Devil's Maze.** New York: Dell, 1983. 254 pp. ISBN
C   0-440-01854-4.

Worship of Satan has been an alternative practice in many times and places, including fin-de-siècle London. Charles Renshawe is determined to eradicate this blasphemous religion and dares to confront the evil Dr. Lipsius. [Satanism]

1030.   Sutcliff, Rosemary. **The Light Beyond the Forest.** London: Knight,
A   1980. 148 pp. ISBN 0-340-25821-7. (First published by Bodley Head,
        1979.)
        Sequels: *The Sword and the Circle; The Road to Camlann.*

This version of the King Arthur legend centers on the quest for the Holy Grail and the efforts of the knights of the Round Table to find this most holy relic. [Legends, Arthurian]

1031.   Swain, E. G. **Bone to His Bone: The Stoneground Ghost Tales of E. G.**
D   **Swain.** Wellingborough, England: Equation, 1989. 192 pp. ISBN
        1-85336-097-X.

Classic English ghost stories, including "The Man with the Roller," "Bone to His Bone," "The Richpins," "The Eastern Window," "Lubrietta," "The Rockery," "The Indian Lampshade," "The Place of Safety," "The Kirk Spook," "From the Diggings," "One Man Went to Mow," "One Good Turn ...," "The Marsh Lights," "Providing a Footnote," "Off the Record (Or, the Recording Angel)." [Horror; Short stories]

1032.   Swazee, Ruth. **A Time of Night.** New York: Manor, 1978. 208 pp. ISBN
C   0-532-15387-1.

Astral projection seems to be one of the most compelling psychic arts. How attractive it sounds to be able to project one's consciousness anywhere in the world! Three novices practice astral projection until they can make themselves appear physically in the new location as well. It all seems harmless until they realize that one of them is a murderer, now able to commit crimes while his physical body remains in view, a perfect alibi. [Paranormal abilities]

1033.   Sykes, Pamela. **Mirror of Danger.** New York: Archway, 1976. 215 pp.
A   ISBN 0-671-49518-6. (First published by Thomas Nelson, 1973.)

At first it seems like an exciting new game when Lucy meets an old-fashioned girl in the old mirror's reflection. When Alice takes her back in time, however, Lucy realizes that Alice has a frightening purpose to her friendship, one that will keep Lucy trapped in the past forever. [Ghosts]

1034.   Syvertsen, Ryder, and Adrian Fletcher. **Psychic Spawn.** New York: Pop-
C   ular Library, 1987. 376 pp. ISBN 0-445-20420-6.

Those rotten Nazis just never give up. This time they plan to live on through superchildren who will ultimately overpower the world and bring about the dreamed-of Third Reich. [Science gone wrong]

1035.   Talbot, Michael. **The Bog.** New York: Jove, 1987. 314 pp. ISBN 0-515-
C   09049-2. (First published by William Morrow, 1986.)

Bogs are smelly, dangerous, and mysterious. Those who live near bogs stay away, but young archaeologist David Macauley has no better sense than to enter the bog. Those who go into the bog never know what they may find there, and some will never get out. [Monsters]

1036.   Tallant, Robert. **The Voodoo Queen.** Gretna, La.: Pelican, 1983. 314 pp.
C   ISBN 0-88289-332-7. (First published by Putnam, 1956.)

Marie Laveau is today still revered in New Orleans, a city she once ruled unofficially with her voodoo powers. [Marie Laveau; Voodoo]

1037.   Tannen, Mary. **Second Sight.** New York: Ivy, 1988. 227 pp. ISBN
C   0-8041-0389-5. (First published by Knopf, 1987.)
         Other works: *Hutley Nutley and the Missing Link.*

There's a psychic in New Jersey by the name of Destiny Ortega. At first glance she seems to be a run-of-the-mill fortune-teller, but Destiny is a talented and accurate prophesier, and her pronouncements are amazingly precise. [Prophecy]

1038.   Tannen, Mary. **The Wizard Children of Finn.** New York: Avon Camelot,
A   1982. 214 pp. ISBN 0-380-57661-9.
         Sequels: *The Lost Legend of Finn.*

When Fiona and her brother, Bran, wander into the wood, they meet a mysterious enchanted boy named Finn who takes them to his home — the Ireland of two thousand years ago. [Time travel]

1039.   Tarr, Judith. **The Isle of Glass.** New York: TOR, 1986. 276 pp. ISBN
A   0-812-55600-3. (First published by Bluejay, 1985.)
         Sequels: *The Hound and the Falcon; The Hounds of God.*

Elf-born Brother Alfred has many trials in the world of humans. His quest to help bring peace to his world seems doomed to failure as he tries to understand the strange ways of mankind. [Fairies; Paranormal abilities]

1040.   Taylor, Bernard. **Moorstone.** New York: St. Martin's Press, 1988. 161
C   pp. ISBN 0-312-91238-2. (First published as *The Moorstone Sickness* by
         St. Martin's Press, 1982.)
         Other works: *The Kindness of Strangers.*

Hal and Rowan decide to escape from the city to the English countryside, There, living on the moors, they find life in the quaint village of Moorstone almost too perfect until they discover that the villagers are not simple rustics; they know more than most people could imagine. [Cults]

1041.   Taylor, Domini. **Gemini.** New York: Fawcett Crest, 1986. 267 pp. ISBN
C   0-449-21077-4. (First published by Atheneum, 1984.)

Peter and Pandora are very close, even for twins. Alone they have strange powers, but together they possess incredible strength that enables them to do anything they want to do. [Horror]

1042.   Tem, Steve Rasnic. **Excavation.** New York: Avon, 1987. 280 pp. ISBN
C   0-380-75173-9.

Reed Taylor, an archaeologist, is working on the old Taylor house not only for the purposes of scientific discovery but to find out something about his own family's past. The further he goes with his investigation, however, the more he realizes that the past is not dead. [Evil]

1043.   Tennant, Emma. **Hotel de Dream.** London: Faber and Faber, 1986. 190
C   pp. ISBN 0-571-13867-5. (First published by Victor Gollancz, 1976.)

Mrs. Routledge runs a boarding house in London where an odd group of misfits live. These people have vivid dreams, and their dreams start to merge with reality. [Dreams]

1044.   Tepper, Sheri S. **Blood Heritage.** New York: TOR, 1986. 287 pp. ISBN
C   0-812-52623-6.
        Sequels: *Bones.* Other works: *Jinian Footseer; Marianne, the Magus and the Manticore; The Revenants.*

Badger Ettison misses his wife terribly but soon discovers that there are worse things than death. He finds out that demons are real, and the only way Badger can see to work his way out of this horrible situation is to resort to magic. [Demons]

1045.   Tessier, Thomas. **Phantom.** New York: Berkley, 1985. 228 pp. ISBN
C   0-425-08027-7. (First published by Atheneum, 1982.)
        Other works: *The Talisman; The Nightwalker; The Fates; Shockwaves.*

Little Ned Covington is like a lot of little kids; he's scared of monsters that he knows are hiding in his room. And Ned is right—there really are monsters in his room, monsters that will not go away. [Ghosts]

1046.   Teweles, Claude. **The Wilds.** New York: Dell, 1989. 213 pp. ISBN
C   0-440-20393-7.

As the old television commercial used to say, "Don't try to fool Mother Nature!" Fourteen campers are ready to spend a weekend where the Donner Party perished in the nineteenth century. They find that nature is not only cruel but can be evil as well. [Evil]

1047.   Thompson, Donald. **The Ancient Enemy.** New York: Fawcett, 1979.
C   220 pp. ISBN 0-449-14216-7.

Bugs are durable, and roaches are particularly so. In a peaceful desert area roaches have taken over so completely that a young couple may not be able to escape with their lives. [Monsters, insect-type]

1048.   Thompson, Gene. **Lupe.** New York: Ballantine, 1978. 305 pp. ISBN
C   0-345-27561-6. (First published by Random House, 1977.)

Emily is frightened. Strange and terrible things she cannot understand are happening in her life, and it seems the only person who can help is a mysterious, malicious child by the name of Lupe. [Satanism]

1049. Thompson, Joyce. **Harry and the Hendersons.** New York: Berkley,
A   1987. 233 pp. ISBN 0-425-10155-X.
       Movie versions: *Harry and the Hendersons*, 1987. Director: William
       Dear. Stars: John Lithgow, Melinda Dillon, Margaret Langrick, Joshua
       Rudoy, Kevin Peter Hall, David Suchet, Lainie Kazan, Don Ameche, and
       M. Emmet Walsh. Later spin-off television series.

When the Hendersons go away for a family camping trip, they little suspect
that they will return home with a fantastic acquisition. Harry is a wonderful
person (or thing), but he is a little large to keep around the house, and other
people seem interested in him for less than friendly reasons. [Abominable
snowman]

1050. Thornton, Lawren. **Imagining Argentina.** Garden City, N.Y.: Double-
C   day, 1987. 214 pp. ISBN 0-385-24027-9.

The horrors of life in recent Argentina, where people have disappeared never
to be heard of again, seem almost too awful to be real. Here we have the story of
a talented man who can help the friends and relatives of the missing people by
telling them what has—and is—happening to them. [Paranormal abilities]

1051. Tigges, John. **Evil Dreams.** New York: Leisure, 1986. 397 pp. ISBN
C   0-8439-2309-1.
       Other works: *The Legend of Jean Marie Cardinal; The Hands of Lucifer;
       As Evil Does; The Immortal; Comes the Wraith.*

Dreams should not have the power to control a person's life. Jon Ward's
dreams of terror are so intense he is desperate to find relief. Then his dreams
become even more lifelike, and Jon finds himself overpowered by a vengeful
spirit who plans to use Jon for evil purposes. [Demons; Dreams]

1052. Tigges, John. **Garden of the Incubus.** New York: Leisure, 1982. 319
C   pp. ISBN 0-8439-2371-7.
       Sequels: *Unto the Altar; Kiss Not the Child.*

When Bobbe Moore declares her intention to become a nun rather than
marry her handsome suitor, she is almost as surprised as her friends and family.
But Bobbe's will does not seem to be her own anymore, and she finds that the
convent is not a safe place for her or her soul. [Possession]

1053. Tolstoy, Alexis. **Vampires: Stories of the Supernatural.** Harmondsworth,
C   England: Penguin, 1946. 183 pp.

Scary stories by the cousin of Russian Leo Tolstoy. Contents include
"Amena," "The Family of a Vourdalak," "The Reunion after Three Hundred
Years," "The Vampire." [Short stories; Vampires]

1054. Town, Mary. **Paul's Game.** New York: Laurel-Leaf, 1983. 192 pp. ISBN
A   0-440-96633-7. (First published by Delacorte, 1983.)

Andrea and her friend, gentle Julie, have ESP powers. Fascinating Paul
starts to date Julie and it soon becomes plain to Andrea that he is able to
influence Julie's behavior and thoughts. It seems that only Andrea will be able to
save Julie from Paul's unhealthy influence. [Paranormal abilities]

1055.   Townsend, Tom. **Panzer Spirit.** New York: Pageant, 1988. 274 pp. ISBN
C   0-517-00819-X.

Life on an army base in preglasnost Germany has its tensions, but tank
expert Jim Fafner doesn't expect to deal with the supernatural Nazi Jagdpanther
tank that refuses to "die." [Ghosts]

1056.   Trainor, Joseph. **Watery Grave.** New York: Dell, 1983. 168 pp. ISBN
A   0-440-99419-5. (Twilight series).
        Other works: *Family Crypt.*

Something—or someone—seems to be calling to Julie. Is it Lavinia, whose
name appears mysteriously in her schoolbook, or is it the strange man she
encounters in the fog while she is trying to find her way home? Whoever it is,
there seems to be no escape for Julie. [Ghosts]

1057.   Tremayne, Peter. **Bloodmist.** New York: Baen, 1988. 310 pp. ISBN
C   0-671-65425-X.
        Other works: *Kiss of the Cobra; The Ants; The Morgow Rises!;
        Snowbeast!*

The beautiful ancient land of Ireland is the home of many legends and
stories. Aonghus, son of Orba Mac Doelta, has been enjoined never to touch a
spear else his people will be driven from the homeland. Yet he cannot remember
this constraint when his sense of justice is aroused, and a story of magic and
daring adventures begins. [Legends, Irish]

1058.   Tremayne, Peter. **Bloodright: A Memoir of Mircea, Son of Vlad Tepes,**
C   **Prince of Wallachia, Also Known as Dracula ... Born on This Earth in**
        the Year of Christ 1431, Who Died in 1476 But Remained Undead. New
        York: Dell, 1980. 251 pp. ISBN 0-440-10509-9. (First published as
        Dracula Unborn by Corgi, 1977.)
        Sequels: *The Revenge of Dracula; Dracula My Love.*

Mircea lives a swashbuckling life, saving beautiful damsels and defeating evil
villains. [Vampires]

1059.   Tremayne, Peter. **Nicor!** London: Sphere, 1987. 211 pp. ISBN 0-7221-
C   8609-6.

In our relentless search for oil beneath the earth, something is bound to be
aroused. It is the Nicor, vicious water demon, who once ruled the world and who
may rule again. [Monsters]

1060.   Tremayne, Peter. **Raven of Destiny.** New York: Signet, 1986. 284 pp.
C   ISBN 0-451-14620-4. (First published by Methuen, 1984.)

Bran Mac Morgor, brave hero of the ancient Celts, finds himself in the
Greece of Alexander the Great where his enemies are the ancient gods themselves.
Will Bran's love for Merope of Zaforas be strong enough to overcome such great
odds? [Legends, Celtic; Legends, Greek]

1061. Tremayne, Peter. **Zombie!** New York: St. Martin's Press, 1987. 183 pp.
C   ISBN 0-312-90923-3. (First published by St. Martin's Press, 1981.)

June and Steve Lambert, both English born and bred, are amazed when they first hear that June has a grandmother in the Caribbean. When they arrive to visit her, however, they find they are too late, for the old lady is dead. June is heir to more than the moldering old estate; she is now the new Mama Mamba, mistress of an undead clan. [Zombies]

1062. Tryon, Thomas. **Harvest Home.** New York: Fawcett, 1978. 415 pp.
C   ISBN 0-449-23496-7. (First published by Knopf, 1973.)
        Other works: *The Night of the Moonbow.* Movie versions: *Secret Dark Harvest Home*, 1978. Director: Leo Penn. Stars: Bette Davis, David Ackroyd, Rosanna Arquette, Rene Auberjonois, and Norman Lloyd.

A peaceful New England town changes from a pleasant home to a haunted, frightening setting for terror and mystery. [Cults; demons]

1063. Tryon, Thomas. **The Other.** New York: Fawcett Crest, 1978. 288 pp.
C   ISBN 0-449-24088-6. (First published by Knopf, 1971.)
        Movie versions: *The Other*, 1972. Director: Robert Mulligan. Stars: Uta Hagen, Diana Muldaur, Chris and Martin Udvarnoky.

How could twins be so different, one so good and one so bad? Only their Russian-born grandmother seems to be aware of what is happening to Niles and Holland, and nobody believes her. [Possession]

1064. Turton, Godfrey. **The Devil's Churchyard.** New York: Pocket Books,
C   1971. 232 pp. ISBN 0-671-77339-9. (First published by Doubleday, 1970.)

Out in the country, on a hillside overlooking a river, there is a circle of stones surrounding an ancient, evil altar. Reverend Mr. Brink has decided that Kate Evans will be the altar's next victim, for an evil god must be served. [Satanism]

1065. Tuttle, Lisa. **Familiar Spirit.** New York: TOR, 1989. 279 pp. ISBN
C   0-812-52644-9. (First published in 1983.)
        Other works: *Gabriel.*

Sarah was happy until Brian fell in love with someone else. Devastated by the loss of her lover, Sarah is at first grateful for her strange dreams, dreams in which she is promised Brian's return in exchange for a little thing ... her soul. [Possession]

1066. Twain, Mark (pseud. of Samuel Clemens). **A Connecticut Yankee in**
D   **King Arthur's Court.** New York: Bantam 1981. 274 pp. ISBN
        0-553-21143-9. Harmondsworth, England: Penguin, 1972. ISBN
        0-14-043064-4. (First published by Harper, 1889.)
        Movie versions: *A Connecticut Yankee in King Arthur's Court*, 1949.
        Director: Tay Garnett. Stars: Bing Crosby and Rhonda Fleming.

A practical, hard-headed Yankee goes back in time and discovers himself in King Arthur's court. Unimpressed with magical doings, our hero unveils Merlin as a charlatan and triumphs over evil with plain old American ingenuity. [Legends, Arthurian; Time travel]

1067. Twain, Mark. **The Mysterious Stranger and Other Stories.** New York:
D   Signet, 1980. 256 pp. ISBN 0-451-52458-66. (First published by Harper &
      Row, 1916.)
      Movie versions: *The Mysterious Stranger*, 1982. Director: Peter Hunt.
      Stars: Lance Kerwin, Chris Makepeace, and Fred Gwynn.

A novella (packaged with other nonsupernatural stories) in which a contemporary youth travels to Renaissance Austria. [Time travel]

1068. Updike, John. **The Witches of Eastwick.** New York: Fawcett Crest,
C   1985. 343 pp. ISBN 0-449-20647-5. (First published by Knopf, 1984.)
      Movie versions: *The Witches of Eastwick*, 1987. Director: George Miller.
      Stars: Jack Nicholson, Cher, Susan Sarandon, Michelle Pfeiffer,
      Veronica Cartwright, Richard Jenkins, Keithe Jochim, and Carol
      Struycken.

Suburban women looking for new meaning in life turn to the attractions offered by a fascinating new man in town who turns out to be the devil himself. [The devil; Witchcraft]

1069. Uttley, Alison. **A Traveller in Time.** New York: Ace, 1986. 197 pp.
C   ISBN 0-441-82213-4. (First published by Faber and Faber, 1939.)

Penelope visits relatives who live in an ancient house. There she discovers that she can live in two worlds, the past and the present. In the past world she becomes involved in a dangerous plot to liberate Mary Queen of Scots. [Time travel]

1070. Van Ash, Cay. **Ten Years Beyond Baker Street.** New York: Perennial,
C   1988. 435 pp. ISBN 0-06-080947-7. (First published by Harper & Row,
      1984.)
      Other works: *The Fires of Fu Manchu.*

Sherlock Holmes is generally a match for any criminal, but will he be able to thwart the nefarious Dr. Fu Manchu? The diabolical villain has captured Nayland Smith, and only Holmes, now in retirement, can possibly save Smith. [Magic; Occult mystery/detective]

1071. Vance, Steve. **The Hyde Effect.** New York: Leisure, 1986. 399 pp. ISBN
C   0-8439-2360-1.

Southern California has become notorious for bizarre murders, but a series of gruesome deaths make even the natives pause. There appears to be a savage supernatural beast at work. [Werewolves]

1072. Vardeman, Robert E. **The Screaming Knife.** New York: Avon, 1990.
C   217 pp. ISBN 0-380-75856-3.
      Other works: *Ancient Heavens.*

Sometimes, usually in desperation, the police turn to psychics to help them solve crimes. This time Peter Thorne may have met his match in an unknown killer who stabs his female victims with a mysterious crystal knife. [Paranormal abilities]

1073. Veley, Charles. **Play to Live.** New York: Dell, 1982. 151 pp. ISBN
A   0-440-96950-6. (Twilight series).

Joey's great desire is to be on the football team, but when he finally achieves his goal, he realizes that it may not have been such a great idea. The other guys on the team are sort of strange, and he suspects that Mr. Wynn is more than just a kindly supporter of the team. [Evil]

1074. Verne, Jules. **Carpathian Castle.** New York: Ace, 1963. 190 pp. (First
C   published in France, 1895.)
       Other works: *Mysterious Island; 20,000 Leagues under the Sea.*

The brooding old castle in Transylvania is said to be haunted. An investigation builds to an exciting climax as the stories about the castle are literally and figuratively exploded. Not everyone can be convinced, however, that there is a rational explanation for the ghostly occurrences, and even today the castle ruins are the scene of strange and mysterious happenings. [Haunted houses]

1075. Vigliante, Mary. **Worship the Night.** New York: Leisure Books, 1982.
C   280 pp. ISBN 0-8439-2302-4.

Lea is strangely childlike, although she's over thirty years old. Her mother has kept her under tight rein for many years, a tight rein of repressed religion and strict house rules. Now Lea's mother is dead, and Lea finds herself on vacation by herself in a desolate cabin. Her feelings are strange and passionate, and soon she finds herself yearning for that which only the devil can provide. [Satanism]

1076. Vinge, Joan D. **Ladyhawke.** New York: Signet, 1985. 252 pp. ISBN
A   0-451-13321-8.
       Movie versions: *Ladyhawke*, 1985. Director: Richard Donner. Stars:
       Matthew Broderick, Rutger Hauer, and Michelle Pfeiffer.

The sinister bishop of Aquila has placed a spell on the woman he wants, beautiful Lady Isabeau, and on her lover, Etienne Navarre. By day she is a hawk and by night he is a wolf, together forever, forever apart. Brash Philippe, a young street urchin, is determined to help the doomed and desperate lovers but finds himself caught up in the bishop's evil schemes and in grave peril. [Black magic; Transformation]

1077. Vinge, Joan D. **Santa Claus: The Movie.** New York: Berkley, 1985. 244 pp.
A   ISBN 0-425-08385-3.
       Movie versions: *Santa Claus*, 1985. Director: Jeannot Szwarc. Stars:
       Dudley Moore, John Lithgow, David Huddleston, and Burgess Meredith.

Most kids stop believing in Santa Claus when they're very young, but suppose Santa is for real? And what happens if one of his elves decides to desert Santa's workshop and get involved in the contemporary American business world? [Legends, Christian]

1078. Voigt, Cynthia. **Building Blocks.** New York: Fawcett, 1985. 121 pp. ISBN
A   0-449-70130-1. (First published by Atheneum, 1984.)

Like a lot of kids, Brann hates it when his parents fight. To escape their wrangling, he goes to the basement and falls asleep in an old play fortress his father once built. When he wakes up, he finds he has traveled into his own father's childhood. [Time travel]

1079. Vonnegut, Kurt. **Slaughterhouse-Five: Or, The Children's Crusade.** New
C   York: Dell, 1974. 224 pp. ISBN 0-440-18029-5. (First published by Dela-
      corte, 1969.)
      Movie versions: *Slaughterhouse Five*, 1972. Director: George Roy Hill.
      Stars: Michael Sachs, Ron Leibman, and Valerie Perrine.

Billy Pilgrim finds himself stuck in time and is bounced from one time to
another without logic or will. One moment he may be a student, the next a
military prisoner of war in Dresden, and the next even an exhibit in a zoo on a
faraway planet. [Time travel]

1080. Wagner, Karl Edward. **Why Not You and I?** New York: TOR, 1987.
C   306 pp. ISBN 0-812-52708-9.

Terrifying tales from an acknowledged master, including "Into Whose
Hands," "Old Loves," "More Sinned Against," "Shrapnel," "The Last Wolf,"
"Neither Brute Nor Human," "Sign of the Salamander" (by Curtiss Strykker),
"Blue Lady, Come Back," "Silted In." [Horror; Short stories]

1081. Wagner, Sharon. **Echoes of an Ancient Love.** New York: Ballantine,
C   1976. 236 pp. ISBN 0-345-24859-7.

Zita decides to go to Greece to throw herself into the work of an archaeological dig. She's trying to forget her canceled wedding plans, but she doesn't count
on becoming involved in another love affair, one that is as old as the ancient
country she is in. [Legends, Greek]

1082. Wagner, Sharon. **Haitian Legacy.** New York: Avon, 1974. 224 pp. ISBN
C   0-380-20289-0.

Jinnell DuMortaine is very pleased with her quiet, lovely life in New Orleans
until the day her cat brings home a dead bird that has obviously been used in a
voodoo rite. Then Jinnell inherits a plantation in Haiti, but after she arrives to see
her new property, frightening things begin to happen. [Gothic romance; Voodoo]

1083. Wakefield, H. Russell. **The Best Ghost Stories of H. Russell Wakefield.**
C   Chicago: Academy Chicago, 1982. 232 pp. ISBN 0-89733-066-8.

Good supernatural stories by an English author, including "The Red Lodge,"
"'He Cometh and He Passeth By,'" "Professor Pownall's Oversight," "The
Seventeenth Hole at Duncaster," "'Look Up There,'" "Blind Man's Bluff," "Day-
Dream in Macedon," "Damp Sheets; A Black Solitude," "The Triumph of
Death," "A Kink in Space-Time," "The Gorge of the Chirels," "'Immortal Bird,'"
"Death of a Bumble Bee." [Ghosts; Short stories]

1084. Walker, Paul. **The Altar.** New York: Pocket Books, 1983. 224 pp. ISBN
C   0-671-4296-3.

Culmar Lakes is not your average peaceful small town, for in Culmar Lakes
savage sacrifices are made of young girls to a pagan god that will not be
appeased. [Cults]

1085. Walker, Robert W. **Disembodied.** New York: St. Martin's Press, 1988.
C   263 pp. ISBN 0-312-91110-6.
      Other works: *Aftershock.*

Jacob Koslor is a psychic, and he's not afraid of danger and adventure. One adventure kills him, but his assistant, Cathrina Vaughan, knows he is still alive on the astral plane. Cathrina knows that now his soul is in danger and only she can save him. [Paranormal abilities]

1086. Wallace, Patricia. **Water Baby.** New York: Zebra, 1987. 301 pp. ISBN
C   0-8217-2188-7.

Kelly is only seven and loves the water. She swims beautifully and views the sea as her friend until her family is killed in a boating accident. She still finds the sea fascinating, but now she sees it differently and knows the sea can be horrible as well as delightful. Kelly is a friend of the sea, and she can make the sea do her bidding. [Evil]

1087. Walpole, Horace. **The Castle of Otranto.** Oxford, England: Oxford
D   University Press Paperback, 1982. 115 pp. ISBN 0-19-281606-3. (First
      published in London by Lownds, 1764.)

The first gothic novel, complete with ruins, ghosts, terror, and adventure. Young lovers must surmount many obstacles before their dreams of romance can be realized. [Gothic romance]

1088. Walsh, Jill Paton. **A Chance Child.** New York: Avon, 1978. 139 pp.
C   ISBN 0-380-48561-1. (First published in the United States by Farrar,
      Straus & Giroux, 1978.)

Creep, a desperate abused child, finds himself transported back in time to a harsh age of child labor. In spite of the hardships, he finds happiness by means of faith and hard work, leaving a message to be found in the future by those who search for him. [Time travel]

1089. Walter, Elizabeth. **Snowfall and Other Chilling Events.** New York: Stein
C   and Day, 1966. 278 pp. ISBN 0-8128-8208-3.

Icily scary stories, including "Snowfall," "The New House," "The Tibetan Box," "The Island of Regrets," "The Drum." [Horror; Short stories]

1090. Walters, R. R. **Ladies in Waiting.** New York: TOR, 1986. 411 pp. ISBN
C   0-812-52700-3.
      Other works: *The Ritual.*

The old house seems evil to Adrienne as soon as she enters it. There are eerie spirits all over the house, even in the garden, and their whispers follow her wherever she goes. Then her husband discovers some portraits of women hidden from sight, and these women, too, seem to be alive. [Possession]

1091. Walters, R. R. **Lily.** New York: TOR, 1988. 408 pp. ISBN 0-812-52703-8.
C

First he sees a strange, ominous black bird on the beach; then the mysterious, sensuous Lily appears and moves into his life. Lily is evil, but who—or what—is Lily? [Demons]

1092.   Walton, Evangeline (pseud. of Evangeline Ensley). **Prince of Annwyn.**
C   New York: Ballantine Del Rey, 1974. 178 pp. ISBN 0-345-27737-6. (First
        published by Random House, 1971.)
        Sequels: *The Children of Llyr; The Song of Rhiannon; The Island of the
        Mighty.*

The ancient Mabinogian legend of Wales has served as an inspiration to
many writers. Here, the author retells these wonderful stories, including that of
Prince Pwyll who is set to a task by the King of Death. Pwyll finds his task
complicated by temptation in the form of a beautiful woman, and he fears he
may succumb to her charms. [Legends, Celtic; Magic]

1093.   Walton, Evangeline. **Witch House.** New York: Ballantine Del Rey,
C   1979. 196 pp. ISBN 0-345-28020-2. (First published by Arkham House,
        1945.)

Dr. Gaylord Carew, an investigator of supernatural phenomena, has been
called to Witch House by the desperate mother of a child who is overcome by the
power and rage of an ancient evil that permeates the old house in New England.
[Haunted houses]

Ward, Arthur Henry. *See* Sax Rohmer.

1094.   Warner, Mignon. **The Tarot Murders.** New York: Dell, 1981. 222 pp.
C   ISBN 0-440-16162-2. (First published by David McKay, 1978.)

Mrs. Charles, a well-known clairvoyant, is called upon to solve the mysterious murders that have been tied to the occult tarot cards left at the scene of the
crime. [Occult mystery/detective; Paranormal abilities]

1095.   Warner, Sylvia Townsend. **Kingdoms of Elfin.** Harmondsworth,
C   England: Penguin, 1979. 222 pp. ISBN 0-1400-4813-8. (First published in
        the United States by Viking, 1977.)

Stories about the complex elfin world and how elves manage to coexist with
humans. The intricacies of the fairy world are explored through the lives and
loves of these magical beings who sometimes come to the earth's surface to
surprise any human who happens to encounter them. [Fairies]

1096.   Warner, Sylvia Townsend. **Lolly Willowes: Or, The Loving Huntsman.**
C   Chicago: Academy Chicago, 1978. 252 pp. ISBN 0-915864-92-4. (First
        published in the United States by Viking, 1926.)

A quiet, gentle maiden lady revolts when she is forty-seven and makes a new
life for herself, one in which she makes a pact with the devil in order to stop her
family from making demands upon her. [The devil; Witchcraft]

1097.   Watson, Ian. **The Power.** New York and London: Headline, 1987. 232
C   pp. ISBN 0-7472-3041-2.

There is power that feeds on good, and there is power that feeds on evil and
corruption. It is the latter power that is growing in Melfort, and when the power
is strong enough, the dead will rise from their graves. [Zombies]

1098.   Weaver, Lydia. **Splashman.** New York: Signet, 1985. 190 pp. ISBN
A   0-451-14020-6.

Jane and her family find their usual summer fun on the beach destroyed by crummy weather and peculiar strangling seaweed. Then Jane rescues a strange boy, Peter Joyce, who claims his mother was a mermaid. Certainly there does seem to be something very unusual about Peter, but then she finds her feelings for him changing from disbelief to sympathy and finally to love. [Mermaids]

1099.   Webster, Josh. **The Doll.** New York: Zebra, 1986. 348 pp. ISBN 0-8217-
C   1788-X.

Gretchen is devoted to her doll, maybe more than to her own twin, Mary. Actually, Gretchen hates her sister, and somehow she knows that the doll hates Mary too. [Evil]

1100.   Weinberg, Robert. **The Devil's Auction.** New York: Leisure, 1990. 310
C   pp. ISBN 0-8439-2997-9. (First published by Weird Tales Library, 1988.)
        Sequels: *The Armageddon Box.*

Once a century there's a private auction for those "in the know." Every witch and warlock who's anybody will be there, and Valerie Lancaster decides to go to find out more about her father's death. [Black magic; Satanism]

1101.   Wellman, Manly Wade. **John the Balladeer.** New York: Baen, 1988.
C   306 pp. ISBN 0-671-65418-7.
        Other works: *What Dreams May Come; The School of Darkness; Who Fears the Devil?*

John, the mysterious balladeer who fights occult evil in the southern hills, first appeared in the pages of various magazines. Collected for the first time are "O Ugly Bird!" "The Desrick on Yandro," "Vandy, Vandy," "One Other," "Call Me From the Valley," "The Little Black Train," "Shiver in the Pines," "Walk Like a Mountain," "On the Hills and Everywhere," "Old Devlins Was A-Waiting," "Nine Yards of Other Cloth," "Wonder As I Wander: Some Footprints on John's Trail," "Through Magic Mountains," "Farther Down the Trail," "Trill Coster's Burden," "The Spring," "Owls Hoot in the Daytime," "Can These Bones Live?" "Nobody Ever Goes There," "Where Did She Wander?" [Horror; Short stories]

1102.   Wellman, Manly Wade. **The Old Gods Waken.** New York: Berkley,
C   1984. 192 pp. ISBN 0-425-07015-8. (First published by Doubleday, 1979.)
        Sequels: *After Dark; The Lost and the Lurking; The Hanging Stories.*

This is the first of the Silver John novels. The scene is set on Walter Mountain in the peaceful rural South. A strange clash of cultures is due to erupt, however, as two Englishmen, ancient Druids, are determined to arouse the traditional Indian spirits who slumber on the mountaintop. Only John seems aware of their plan, and only John is willing to try to stop them. [Legends, Celtic; Legends, Native American]

1103.   Wellman, Manly Wade. **Twice in Time.** New York: Baen, 1988. 214 pp.
C   ISBN 0-671-69791-9.

The title novella is bound with "Leonardo Before His Canvas" and "The Timeless Tomorrow." [Short stories; Time travel]

1104.   Wells, H. G. **The Invisible Man.** Bound with *The Time Machine*, New
D   York: Signet, 1982. 320 pp. ISBN 0-451-51877-2. (First published in
        England in 1887.)
        Other works: *Lost Worlds.* Movie versions: *The Invisible Man*, 1933.
        Director: James Whale. Stars: Claude Rains, Gloria Stuart, and Una
        O'Connor. *The Invisible Man*, 1975. Director: Robert Michael Lewis.
        Stars: David McCallum, Melinda Fee, and Jackie Cooper.

Many of us have dreamed of the fun it would be if we were invisible, but the
adventures of the hapless hero show us that invisibility is really a curse.
[Transformation]

1105.   Wells, H. G. **The Island of Dr. Moreau.** New York: Magnum Lancer,
D   1968. 189 pp. (First published in England in 1896.)
        Movie versions: *The Island of Dr. Moreau*, 1977. Director: Don Taylor.
        Stars: Burt Lancaster, Michael York, and Nigel Davenport.

Edward Prendick is rescued from a shipwreck by a mysterious man in a small
boat headed for a distant island. When they reach the island, Edward is forced
ashore, where he discovers the terrible experiments of the mad Dr. Moreau.
[Science gone wrong]

1106.   Wells, William K. **Effigies.** New York: Dell, 1980. 442 pp. ISBN 0-440-
C   12245-7.

A corrupt and evil man is wandering, leaving death behind him. The man
believes in occult practices and worships evil powers. No one is safe when this
man comes to town. [Satanism]

1107.   Wender, Theodora. **Murder Gets a Degree.** New York: Avon, 1986.
C   150 pp. ISBN 0-380-75014-7.

College students often like to play around with new experiences and investigate new religions, but what might seem to be dabbling in magic to some turns to
serious business when death is the result. Glad Gold, a logical professor of
English, finds herself investigating death with a supernatural touch. [Occult
mystery/detective; Satanism]

1108.   Werlin, Marvin, and Mark Werlin. **The Savior.** New York: Dell, 1981.
C   480 pp. ISBN 0-440-17748-0. (First published by Simon & Schuster,
        1978.)

Christopher McKenzie has special powers, but in using them recklessly he
finds he can cause misery and pain to those he loves. [Paranormal abilities]

1109.   Wernick, Saul. **The Fire Ants.** New York: Charter, 1976. 310 pp. ISBN
C   0-441-23833-5.

Those who have ever been bitten by a fire ant know the sharp, fiery pain. But
those who are bitten by these mutant fire ants don't live to talk about it; nor do
their neighbors, because everybody's dead. [Monsters, insect-type]

1110. Wescott, Earle. **Winter Wolves.** New York: Bantam, 1989. 261 pp. ISBN
C   0-553-27923-8. (First published by Yankee Peddlar, 1988.)

A complex tale of shifting perspectives revolving around the revenge of a
pack of ghostly wolves. [Monsters]

1111. West, Lindsay. **Empire of the Ants.** New York: Ace, 1977. 180 pp. ISBN
C   0-441-20560-7.
       Movie versions: *Empire of the Ants*, 1977. Director: Bert J. Gordon.
       Stars: Joan Collins, Robert Lansing, Albert Salmi, and John David
       Carson.

Marilyn Fryser is an opportunist out to make fast and big bucks by developing a coastal island. On a trip designed to make suckers buy plots of land, she sees
an unexpected sight—giant rapacious ants. (Based on the original story "The
Empire of the Ants" by H. G. Wells; see entry 1298.) [Monsters, insect-type]

1112. West, Owen (pseud. of Dean Koontz). **The Mask.** New York: Jove,
C   1981. 305 pp. ISBN 0-515-05695-2.
       Other works: *The Funhouse.*

Carl and Paul are somehow touched by the lonely orphaned teenager who
appeals to them for friendship. Jane, however, doesn't really seem to come from
anywhere, and she is very elusive regarding the details of her life. Then the terrible things begin to happen in the night, things that cannot be controlled.
[Horror]

1113. Westall, Robert. **Break of Dark.** Harmondsworth, England: Puffin
A   Plus, 1984. 173 pp. ISBN 0-14-031581-0. (First published by Chatto &
       Windus, 1982.)
       Other works: *The Haunting of Chas McGee and Other Stories; Fathom
       Five; Futuretrack 5.*

Mysterious, eerie stories for teens, including "Hitch-hiker," "Blackham's
Wimpey," "Fred, Alice and Aunty Lou," "St. Austin Friars," "Sergeant Nice."
[Horror; Short stories]

1114. Westall, Robert. **The Cats of Seroster.** London: Piccolo, 1986. 278 pp.
A   ISBN 0-330-29239-0. (First published by Macmillan, 1984.)

The frightened boy is terrified of being found—and murdered—by those
who assassinated his father the duke. When he is found, he is lucky, for his
rescuer is Cam, a young English vagabond who decides to help the young duke.
Little does Cam realize, however, that he will soon be involved in sorcery. [Black
magic]

1115. Westall, Robert. **The Devil on the Road.** New York: Ace, 1985. 200 pp.
A   ISBN 0-441-14290-7. (First published by Greenwillow, 1978.)

What starts as an aimless summer vacation of John Webster roaming on a
motor bike becomes a strange and desperate quest in another time for him to save
a lovely young witch from death at the hands of dreaded Matthew Hopkins, the
Witchfinder General. [Time travel; Witchcraft]

1116. Westall, Robert. **Ghost Abbey.** New York: Scholastic, 1988. 169 pp.
A   ISBN 0-590-41693-6. (First published by Scholastic in hardcover, 1988.)

It's extra tough for Maggi when her mother dies, for not only must she deal with her own grief, but she's expected to take over her mother's role as homemaker for her father and brothers. Then Maggi's father takes a job renovating an old abbey, and Maggi discovers many secrets there. [Ghosts]

1117. Westall, Robert. **The Scarecrows.** Harmondsworth, England: Puffin
A   Plus, 1983. 160 pp. ISBN 0-14-031465-2. (First published by Chatto & Windus, 1981.)

Simon doesn't like his new stepfather, and he hates the idea of spending the summer at his stepfather's place in the country. He starts to explore in order to stay away from home as much as possible and discovers the old millhouse, scene of a former tragedy and full of an evil presence. The scarecrows in the nearby field are odd and also full of evil. Simon begins to feel trapped, and he doesn't know where to go for help. [Evil]

1118. Westall, Robert. **The Watch House.** Harmondsworth, England: Puffin
A   Plus, 1980. 204 pp. ISBN 0-14-031285-4. (First published by Macmillan, 1977.)

Anne, deserted by her father and unwanted by her mother, is sent to live with an old servant in a house next to a desolate old watchhouse. Lonely and unhappy, Anne explores her new home and finds in the old watchhouse an evil presence that soon makes itself known to her. [Ghosts]

1119. Westall, Robert. **The Wind Eye.** Harmondsworth, England: Puffin Plus,
A   1982. 159 pp. ISBN 0-14-031374-5. (First published by Macmillan, 1976.)

When Bertrand and Madeleine get married, their children have to face forming a blended family. At first they get on together well enough, then things start to happen. One day Madeleine accidently steps on the tomb of the dreaded and fabled St. Cuthbert and everything starts to go wrong. [Legends, Christian]

1120. Westlake, Donald, and Abby Westlake. **Translyvania Station.** Miami
C   Beach, Fla.: Dennis Miller, 1987. 122 pp. ISBN 0-939767-05-8.

This script for a famous Mohonk Mystery Weekend — where hotel visitors play assigned roles in a game — features vampires and Stephen King. [Vampires]

1121. Weverka, Robert. **Spectre.** New York: Bantam, 1979. 154 pp. ISBN
C   0-553-13302-0.
         Movie versions: *Spectre*, 1977. Director: Clive Donner. Stars: Robert Culp, Gig Young, John Hurt, Gordon Jackson, Ann Bell, James Villiers, and Majel Barrett.

Based on a script by Gene Roddenberry. A criminologist and his assistant investigate ghostly goings-on in an old English abbey. [Haunted houses]

1122. Whalen, Patrick. **Monastery.** New York: Pocket Books, 1988. 346 pp.
C   ISBN 0-671-66187-6.

A desolate island off the coast of Washington State hardly seems to be the place for occult evil. Yet there is an old abbey here, an abbey that guards many evil secrets. This evil cannot rest. [Vampires]

1123. Wharton, Edith. **The Ghost Stories of Edith Wharton.** New York: Popu-
C   lar Library, 1973. 320 pp.

A noted American writer turns to tales of the macabre, including "The Lady's Maid's Bell," "The Eyes," "Afterward," "Kerfol," "The Triumph of Night," "Miss Mary Pask," "Bewitched," "Mr. Jones," "Pomegranate Seed," "The Looking Glass," "All Souls." [Ghosts; Short stories]

1124. Wheatley, Dennis. **The Devil Rides Out.** London: Arrow, 1974. 320 pp.
C   ISBN 0-0990-7240-8. (First published by Hutchinson, 1956.) (Available in
      a simplified version by the same title for younger children, retold by
      Alison Sage; see entry 896.)
      Other works: *The Haunting of Toby Jugg; The Ka of Gifford Hillary;
      The Gateway to Hell; The Satanist.* Movie versions: *The Devil's Bride,*
      1968. Director: Terence Fisher. Stars: Christopher Lee, Charles Gray,
      Nike Arrighi, Patrick Mower, Sarah Lawson, and Paul Eddington.

Simon Aron seems to be in trouble, and his friends, the Duc de Richleau, Rex van Ryn, and Richard Eaton, decide to investigate. What they discover is a vile satanic plot that threatens to destroy all of them, including the beautiful young woman who is slated to be a human sacrifice. [Satanism]

1125. Wheatley, Dennis. **The Irish Witch.** London: Arrow, 1975. 446 pp. ISBN
C   0-09-910440-7. (First published by Hutchinson, 1973.)

The early years of the nineteenth century were turbulent times in England and Ireland. Roger Brook, a government agent deeply involved in the complex dealings of Napoleonic politics and war, finds to his dismay that his beloved son has joined a revival of the notorious satanic cult, the Hellfire Club. [Cults; Satanism]

1126. Wheatley, Dennis. **Strange Conflict.** New York: Ballantine, 1972. 320
C   pp. SBN 345-02988-7-150. (First published by Hutchinson, 1941.)

Wheatley's protagonists, a wise French duke, a sturdy American, and a brave English Jew, pit their skills against Nazi villains who practice in the occult. The climax of the book is set in Haiti where voodoo rites blend with adventures on the astral plane. Good triumphs, of course, in the end, leaving our heroes ready to take on further occult adventures in other books. [Black magic; Nazi occultism; Voodoo]

1127. Wheatley, Dennis. **To the Devil — a Daughter.** New York: Bantam, 1968.
C   329 pp. (First published in London by Hutchinson, 1953.)
      Movie versions: *To the Devil — a Daughter,* 1976. Director: Peter Sykes.
      Stars: Richard Widmark, Christopher Lee, Honor Blackman, and
      Natassja Kinski.

A beautiful young woman has been promised to the devil in order to give her father good fortune. As her twenty-first birthday approaches (the date she has been promised for the sacrifice), her father attempts to hide her. Well-meaning neighbor Molly Fountain uncovers these evil goings-on and joins in the effort to save Christina from her fate. [The devil; Satanism]

1128. White, T. H. **The Once and Future King.** New York: Berkley, 1983. 640
A   pp. ISBN 0-425-06310-0. (First published by Putnam, 1958.)
       Sequels: *The Book of Merlin.* Other works: *Mistress Masham's Repose.*

Used as the basis for Disney's animated feature, *The Sword and the Stone.*
King Arthur's story told with humor and style from the viewpoint of the insecure
young king called Wart. [Legends, Arthurian]

1129. Whitney, Phyllis A. **Mystery of the Mysterious Traveler.** New York:
A   Signet New American, 1974. 172 pp. ISBN 0-451-09847-1. (First pub-
       lished as *The Island of the Dark Woods* by Westminister, 1967.)

Laurie is excited, much more excited than her sister Celia about their visit to
Aunt Serena, and when she sees the huge gloomy house in Staten Island, she
suspects there's some kind of mystery going on. When she sees the phantom
stagecoach she knows that something very different is going to happen. [Ghosts]

1130. Whitten, Les. **The Alchemist.** New York: Zebra, 1986. 412 pp. ISBN
C   0-8217-1865-7. (First published by Charterhouse, 1973.)

Martin Dobecker seems to be a quiet, placid sort of fellow, quite satisfied
with his routine life. Little do people know, however, that he has a most peculiar
hobby, that of experimenting with black magic. [Alchemy; Black magic]

1131. Whitten, Leslie H. **Moon of the Wolf.** New York: Avon, 1975. 222 pp.
C   ISBN 0-380-22715-1. (First published by Doubleday, 1967.)

There's a savage killer stalking the moonlit bayou country, and although it
seems unlikely, Aaron Whitaker finally comes to the reluctant conclusion that the
killer is neither man nor beast. [Werewolves]

1132. Wilde, Kelley. **The Suiting.** New York: TOR, 1989. 245 pp. ISBN
C   0-812-50253-1. (First published by St. Martin's Press, 1988.)

When Victor Frankl comes into possession of a fabulously expensive hand-
tailored suit, he resolves to become the kind of man worthy to wear such a
garment. But the suit has a will of its own, and Victor learns that he is no longer
the master of his will or his fate. [Evil]

1133. Wilde, Oscar. **Complete Fairy Tales of Oscar Wilde.** New York: Signet,
B   1990. 221 pp. ISBN 0-451-52435-7.

These magical tales by a tortured genius include "The Happy Prince," "The
Nightingale and the Rose," "The Selfish Giant," "The Devoted Friend," "The
Remarkable Rocket," "The Young King," "The Birthday of the Infanta," "The
Fisherman and His Soul," "The Star-Child." [Fairy tales; Short stories]

1134. Wilde, Oscar. **The Picture of Dorian Gray.** New York: Laurel-Leaf,
D   1956. 224 pp. ISBN 0-440-36914-2. (First published by Ward Lock, 1891.)
       Movie versions: *The Picture of Dorian Gray*, 1945. Director: Albert
       Lewin. Stars: George Saunders, Donna Reed, and Angela Lansbury.

Staying young is granted to Dorian Gray, who remains youthful in
appearance while his portrait grows old and haggard. Gray's life of dissipation
seems to have no checks and controls, but he finds that even those who possess a
charmed life must eventually pay the price. [Eternal youth]

1135. Willard, Nancy. **Things Invisible to See.** New York: Bantam, 1986. 262
C   pp. ISBN 0-553-25563-0. (First published by Knopf, 1985.)

Ben Harkissian loves baseball, but little does he realize that the day will come when he must play his team against one drafted by Death, who has all the dead baseball greats on his side. [Heaven and hell]

1136. Williams, Charles. **Many Dimensions.** Grand Rapids, Mich.: Eerdmans,
C   1981. 269 pp. ISBN 0-802-281221-X. (First published by Victor Gollancz,
       1931.)
       Other works: *All Hallows' Eve; Descent into Hell; The Place of the Lion;*
       War in Heaven; The Greater Trumps.

A scientist is able to travel through time by use of a mysterious and ancient stone. [Legends, Christian; Time travel]

1137. Williams, Ursula Moray. **Gobbolino The Witch's Cat.** Harmondsworth,
B   England: Puffin, 1965. 150 pp. ISBN 0-14-030239-5. (First published by
       Harrap, 1942.)

The gentle story of a witch's cat who gets into a great deal of mischief on her own, not all of it dealing with magic. [Witchcraft]

1138. Williamson, Chet. **Lowland Rider.** New York: TOR, 1988. 342 pp.
C   ISBN 0-812-52722-4.
       Other works: *Ash Wednesday; McKain's Dilemma; Soulstorm.*

Jesse Gordon's wife has been brutally murdered, and Jesse has gone mad with grief. Determined to find his wife's killers, Jesse goes underground — literally — in New York City. Underneath the streets of the city Jesse investigates the dark world of subway tunnels, where he discovers a bizarre life-style and a strange, frightening figure dressed in white who seems to be pure evil. [Evil]

1139. Williamson, J. N. **Noon Spell.** New York: Leisure, 1987. 368 pp. ISBN
C   0-8439-2556-6.
       Other works: *The Houngan; The Tulpa; The Ritual; Death Coach;*
       Death-Angel; The Offspring; The Evil One; Playmates; Ghost Mansion;
       The Longest Night; Evil Offspring; Ghost; Brotherkind; Wards of Arma-
       geddon; The Black School; Hell Storm.

Grady Calhoun doesn't believe in the supernatural, and he certainly isn't worried when the old charlatan puts a curse on him, a curse that will cause him to die within forty-five days. What Grady doesn't fully realize at first is that others will suffer because of his disbelief; they will suffer horribly. [Curses]

1140. Williamson, J. N. **Premonition.** New York: Leisure, 1981. 287 pp.
C   ISBN 0-8439-0959-5.

Ingrid Solomon is a beautiful woman beset by frightening secrets. She is obsessed by the notion of eternal life and is dabbling in a scientific experiment that might help her dream come true. She has not reckoned on other powers, however, powers that will punish her for trying to discover arcane mysteries. [Eternal youth; Science gone wrong]

1141.   Willis, Connie. **Lincoln's Dreams.** New York: Bantam Spectra, 1988. 228
C   pp. ISBN 0-553-27025-7. (First published in hardback by Bantam, 1987.)

At first Jeff Johnston, a history researcher for a best-selling author, is not impressed with Annie's claims of vivid dreams — nightmares, really. Jeff decides that immersion in the Civil War will cure Annie of her nightly terrors, in which tragic Willie Lincoln seems to be a key. [Dreams]

1142.   Willis, Maud. **The Devil's Rain.** New York: Dell, 1975. 171 pp. ISBN
C   0-440-04553-1.
        Movie versions: *The Devil's Rain*, 1975. Director: Robert Feust. Stars:
        Ernest Borgnine, Ida Lupino, William Shatner, Tom Skerrit, Eddie
        Albert, Keenan Wynn, and Joan Prather.

Evil incarnate has come back to Stanville in the form of Satan's followers. Stanville used to be a perfect little midwestern town, but now it won't be, for everyone who lives there is in danger. [Satanism]

1143.   Wilson, Colin. **The Glass Cage.** New York: Bantam, 1973. 249 pp. ISBN
C   0-553-07636-1. (First published by Random House, 1967.)

Damon Reade is seeking isolation and quiet time for reflection. Instead, he finds himself embroiled in a horrifying morass of murder and occult secrets as well as a clairvoyant connection with a maniacal killer. [Evil]

1144.   Wilson, Colin. **The Schoolgirl Murder Case.** Chicago: Academy Chicago,
C   1982. 255 pp. ISBN 0-586-04232-6. (First published by Hart-Davis, 1974.)
        Other works: *God of the Labyrinth.*

The murder of a prostitute dressed like a schoolgirl leads Saltfleet of Scotland Yard into a world of occult evil and mysterious activity. [Satanism]

1145.   Wilson, David Henry. **The Coachman Rat.** New York: Baen, 1990. 218
C   pp. ISBN 0-671-72030-9. (Originally published as *Ashmadi* in West Ger-
        many, 1985. First published in the United States by Carroll & Graf,
        1989.)

Cinderella has long been a favorite fairy tale for many. Here is a fresh perspective on the whole story as related by Robert, the rat who is changed into the coachman for that now-famous evening. [Fairy tales]

1146.   Wilson, F. Paul. **The Keep.** New York: Berkley, 1982. 406 pp. ISBN
C   0-425-05324-5. (First published by William Morrow, 1981.)
        Sequels: *Reborn.* Other works: *Black Wind; The Touch.* Movie versions:
        The Keep, 1983. Director: Michael Mann. Stars: Scott Glenn, Ian
        McKellan, and Alberta Watson.

The awesome castle keep in the Carpathians is covered with mysterious symbols and shrouded in secrets. The Nazis cannot cope with the savage murders of their soldiers. A learned professor and his beautiful daughter are summoned to unravel the mystery, and they discover the original evil, Rasalom, a monster who feeds on human despair and misery. [Monsters; Vampires]

1147. Wilson, F. Paul. **Soft and Others.** New York: TOR, 1990. 306 pp. ISBN
C   0-812-50375-9.

Clever tales with many a twist, including "The Cleaning Machine,"
"Ratman," "Lipidleggin'," "To Fill the Sea and Air," "Green Water," "Be Fruitful
and Multiply," "Soft," "The Last 'One Mo' Once Golden Oldies Revival,'" "The
Years the Music Died," "Dat-Tay-Vao," "Doc Johnson," "Buckets," "Traps,"
"Muscles," "Ménage à Trois," "Cuts." [Horror; Short stories]

1148. Wilson, F. Paul. **The Tomb.** New York: Berkley, 1984. 404 pp. ISBN
C   0-425-07295-9. (First published by Whispers Press, 1984.)

Repairman Jack is a fixer — not of broken appliances as his father thinks, but
of misjustice. Jack can be hired to right wrongs, according to his morals. One day
he takes two unusual and (he thinks) unconnected jobs that lead him into a
horrifying fight to save a child from the terror of sacrifice to Kali, the rapacious
Indian goddess of destruction. [Legends, Indian; Monsters]

1149. Wilson, Mary. **The Changeling.** New York: Dell, 1975. 176 pp. ISBN
C   0-440-04510-0.

Edna wants to keep the family-run charity hospital in the tropics open
because the need of the natives is so great. But she hasn't reckoned with the power
of voodoo, a power that isn't interested in the advancements of medical science.
[Voodoo]

1150. Wilson, Robert C. **Icefire.** New York: Berkley, 1984. 533 pp. ISBN
C   0-425-10247-5. (First published by G. P. Putnam's Sons, 1984.)
       Other works: *Crooked Tree.*

Far away on an icebound island in Lake Michigan is a hospital for the
criminally insane. So far removed from authority, doctors can experiment as they
like with little regard for the surrounding awesome landscape, where ancient
powers reside. [Legends, Native American; Science gone wrong]

1151. Windsor, Patricia. **Killing Time.** New York: Laurel-Leaf, 1983. 188 pp.
A   ISBN 0-440-94471-6. (First published by Harper & Row, 1980.)

After his parents' divorce, Sam is dragged to the country. Life in the sticks
isn't as dull as Sam thinks at first, especially when he finds Druid worshippers up
to no good. [Cults; Legends, Celtic]

1152. Winston, Daoma. **A Sweet Familiarity.** New York: Critic's Choice, 1986.
C   254 pp. ISBN 1-55547-111-0. (First published by Interpub Communica-
       tions, 1981.)

Meadowville's two families of power were the Vickerys and the Paiges,
friends for many years until the tragedy occurred. Maggie is dead now, but when
Claude, who loved her years ago, returns to Meadowville, Maggie's spirit is ready
for revenge. [Ghosts]

1153. Winters, Mick. **Full Moon.** New York: Berkley, 1989. 327 pp. ISBN
C   0-425-11472-4.

The full moon is a beautiful thing to see, but it also can being great evil to
earth, as Professor Keith Ransom knows. He knows, also, that it's up to him to
save the world from the devastation that the power of the moon can initiate. [Evil]

1154.   Winthrop, Wilma. **Tryst with Terror.** New York: Lancer, 1972. 223
A   pp.

Denise has suddenly started being afraid. She has always been somewhat fearful of old Aunt Abigail, and now whispers are telling her that Aunt Abigail is the reincarnation of a medieval witch. Her aunt's house is no cozy cottage but a forbidding old mansion with many secrets that may be dangerous for Denise. [Legends, Celtic]

1155.   Wolf, Joyce. **White Spider.** New York: Leisure, 1987. 400 pp. ISBN
C   0-8439-2513-2.

Sample is a girl on the verge of womanhood. Her innocent world, however, is about to be destroyed, for her young flesh is needed for a horrible sacrifice to the dreaded white spider. [Horror]

1156.   Wolfe, Gene. **Peace.** New York: Berkley, 1982. 246 pp. ISBN 0-425-
C   04644-3. (First published by Harper & Row, 1975.)
        Other works: *Castleview.*

Alden Dennis Weer is not a typical old man in a midwestern town; he communicates with all manner of supernatural beings. [Ghosts]

1157.   Wolfe, Gene. **Soldier of the Mist.** New York: TOR, 1986. 335 pp. ISBN
A   0-812-55815-4.
        Sequels: *Soldier of Arete.*

The gods and goddesses of ancient Greece were very real to those who lived in that time and place. Latro is a man of his times, and his adventures make fine reading. [Legends, classical]

1158.   Wood, Bari. **The Tribe.** New York: Signet, 1981. 339 pp. ISBN 0-451-
C   11104-4.

Imaginary writings of horror pale when compared with the real facts of the Holocaust. Some did survive this horror, however, and they seek revenge from the living by using the dead. [Legends, Jewish]

1159.   Wood, Bari, and Jack Geasland. **Dead Ringers.** New York: Signet, 1978.
C   343 pp. ISBN 0-451-15989-6.
        Movie versions: *Dead Ringers*, 1988. Director: David Cronenberg. Stars:
        Jeremy Irons, Genevieve Bujold, Heidi Von Palleske, and Barbara
        Gordon.

Twin doctors share their lives, lovers, and personalities to the point that even they wonder who is who. [Altered states of consciousness]

1160.   Woodley, Richard. **"It's Alive!"** New York: Ballantine, 1977. 156 pp.
C   ISBN 0-345-25879-7.
        Movie versions: *"It's Alive!"* 1974. Director: Larry Cohen. Stars: John
        Ryan, Sharon Farrell, Andrew Duggan, Guy Stockwell, James Dixon,
        and Michael Ansara.

There's something very wrong with the Burns baby. From the moment it's born, the baby attacks and kills, starting with everybody in the delivery room. Then it escapes, and what really tears up Frank, the father, is that the baby seems to be heading home. [Monsters]

1161. Woodley, Richard. **Man from Atlantis.** New York: Dell, 1977. 204 pp.
A ISBN 0-440-15368-9.
Movie versions: *Man from Atlantis*, 1977. Director: Lee H. Katzin. Stars: Patrick Duffy, Belinda Montgomery, Art Lund, Dean Santoro, Victor Bruno, and Lawrence Pressman.

Mark Harris looks like other men, but in water he is extraordinary. As a man/creature from the legendary Atlantis, Mark Harris is able to help save the world from the power ploys of a mad genius. [Atlantis; Lost lands]

1162. Woods, Stuart. **Under the Lake.** New York: Avon, 1988. 281 pp. ISBN
C 0-380-70519-2. (First published by Simon & Schuster, 1987.)

The southern town is full of mysteries, and one of the biggest is the lights that some can see under the lake. Reporter John Howell tries to unravel the tangled stories from the past. [Ghosts; Paranormal abilities]

1163. Woolrich, Cornell. **Vampire's Honeymoon.** New York: Carroll & Graf,
C 1985. 223 pp. ISBN 0-88184-132-3.

Four stories about vampires by the author of *Rear Window*, including "Vampire's Honeymoon," "Graves for the Dead," "I'm Dangerous Tonight," "The Street of Jungle Death." [Short stories; Vampires]

1164. Wormser, Richard. **Thief of Baghdad.** New York: Dell, 1961. 191 pp.
A Movie versions: *Thief of Baghdad*, 1961. Director: Arthur Lubin. Stars: Steve Reeves, Giorgia Moll, Arturo Dominici, and Edy Vessel.

The dashing story of Karim, a lowly thief who perseveres in the trials of the Seven Gates, becomes the ruler of Baghdad, and wins the hand of beautiful Princess Amina. [Legends, Arabian]

1165. Worth, Valerie. **Gypsy Gold.** New York: Farrar, Straus & Giroux, 1986.
A 176 pp. ISBN 0-374-42820-4. (First published by Farrar, Straus & Giroux, 1983.)
Other works: *Curlicues; Fox Hill.*

When young Miranda's parents decide that her future must be that of wife to an elderly wealthy man, she revolts and runs away with the gypsies. There she discovers that fortune-telling is more than a con game, and during her new life she finds out new truths about herself. [Gypsy lore]

1166. Wright, Betty Ren. **Ghosts Beneath Our Feet.** New York: Scholastic,
A 1984. 137 pp. ISBN 0-590-33704-1.
Other works: *Secret Windows.*

Katie and her mother and stepbrother are spending the summer in a desolate old mining town in upper Michigan. One of Katie's new friends tells her stories about the trapped ghosts of miners who died years before. Are they truly trying to escape? And who is the strange, shadowy ghost girl who seems to be trying to tell Katie something? [Ghosts]

1167.   Wright, T. M. (see also F. W. Armstrong). **A Manhattan Ghost Story.**
C   New York: TOR, 1984. 381 pp. ISBN 0-812-52750-X.
        Sequels: *The Waiting Room; Boundaries.* Other works: *Carlisle Street;*
        The People of the Dark; The Woman Next Door; The Children of the
        Island; The Playground; The Island.

Ghosts don't always look transparent and dress in trailing white draperies.
Some seem as normal as other people, especially when the setting is New York
City. [Ghosts]

1168.   Wright, T. M. **Strange Seed.** New York: TOR, 1987. 309 pp. ISBN
C   0-812-52762-3. (First published by Everest, 1978.)

Rachel is not thrilled when her new husband drags her away from her
beloved New York to the deserted countryside of his boyhood home. The house
has been vandalized, requiring a great deal of work, and then they find the strange
child in the wood, one who comes from nowhere and will not communicate. An
evil of unknown origin is closing in on them. [Evil]

1169.   Wrightson, Patricia. **The Ice Is Coming.** New York: Ballantine Del Rey,
A   1981. 196 pp. ISBN 0-345-33248-2. (First published in the United States
        by Atheneum, 1977.)
        Sequels: *The Bright Dark Water; Journey Behind the Wind.*

Wirrum, a young aborigine of Australia, senses that something is wrong with
the land. Frost and ice have begun forming during the hottest summer months,
and the elusive spirits of the countryside seem restless. Then he discovers that the
Ninya, the ancient ice-spirits, are loose and must be brought back under control
or the country will become shrouded with a never-ending winter. [Legends,
Aboriginal]

1170.   Wrightson, Patricia. **A Little Fear.** Harmondsworth, England: Puffin,
B   1985. 111 pp. ISBN 0-14-031847-X. (First published in the United States
        by Atheneum, 1983.)

Mrs. Tucker decides that life in a senior citizen's home is not for her, so she
goes away to live on her own with her dog Hector. But her chosen home is already
inhabited by something dark and evil that wants Mrs. Tucker out of there.
[Legends, Australian]

1171.   Wyndham, John. **The Kraken Wakes.** Harmondsworth, England: Pen-
C   guin, 1955. 240 pp. ISBN 01400.10750. (First published by Michael
        Joseph, 1953.)
        Other works: *Day of the Triffids; The Midwich Cuckoos.*

Deep in the sea lie many strange wonders. For many centuries there have
been fearful whispers of the dreadful kraken, which sometimes wrecks havoc
when aroused. We can only hope that the dreaded kraken never wakes, for its
power is awesome. [Monsters]

1172.   Yarbro, Chelsea Quinn. **Firecode.** New York: Popular Library, 1987.
C   453 pp. ISBN 0-445-20229-7.
        Other works: *Cautionary Tales; Beastnights; False Dawn; Aristo; The*
        Godforsaken; Sins of Omission; Nomads; Dead & Buried.

The miracles of the technological age and of supernatural powers come together to create what seems to be an unbeatable evil. Anyone who dials a certain electronic code can summon the fire, but the summoning costs a high price. Carter Milne, a beautiful security expert, gets involved and quickly realizes this case may be more than she can handle. [Evil]

1173.   Yarbro, Chelsea Quinn. **A Flame in Byzantium.** New York: TOR, 1988.
C   470 pp. ISBN 0-812-52804-2. (First published by TOR Hardbacks, 1987.)
        Sequels: *The Crusader's Torch; A Candle for D'Artagnan.*

Beautiful Olivia, the friend and lover of St. Germain, is a fascinating woman. She is also a vampire, possessed with eternal life. Eternal life is not necessarily a wonderful thing, for those who have it must life through history's most tumultuous times. In ancient times, Olivia must flee from her beloved Rome to Byzantium, a city of intrigue and danger. [Vampires]

1174.   Yarbro, Chelsea Quinn. **Hotel Transylvania.** New York: Signet, 1979.
C   279 pp. ISBN 0-451-08461-6. (First published by St. Martin's Press, 1978.
        Series republished by TOR, 1988.)
        Sequels: *Blood Games; The Palace; Path of the Eclipse; Tempting Fate; The Saint-Germaine Chronicles; Out of the House of Life.*

Beautiful young women sometimes fall in love with fascinating older men. Madeleine, however, makes the mistake of falling in love with a vampire, who fortunately helps to save her from others more evil than himself. [Vampires]

1175.   Yarbro, Chelsea Quinn. **A Mortal Glamour.** New York: Bantam, 1985.
C   308 pp. ISBN 0-553-245887-2.

Strange, frightening things are happening in the fourteenth-century convent at Avignon. The gentle nuns seem tempted beyond belief as they are courted by a fascinating emissary of the devil who is determined to collect souls for his master. [The devil]

1176.   Yarbro, Chelsea Quinn. **Signs and Portents.** New York: Jove, 1987.
C   188 pp. ISBN 0-515-09345-9. (First published by Dream Press, 1984.)

Unsettling stories, including "Do Not Forsake Me, O My Darlin'," "Depth of Focus," "Space/Time Arabesque," "Savory, Sage, Rosemary, and Thyme," "Best Interest," "The Ghosts at Iron River," "Fugitive Colors," "Coasting," "The Arrows," "The End of the Carnival." [Horror; Short stories]

1177.   Yariv, Fran Pokras. **The Hallowing.** New York: Jove, 1980. 255 pp.
C   ISBN 0-515-05192-6.

Sharon Jenner seems to have a perfect life as wife, mother, and career woman, yet something strange is happening to her. At first it simply seems odd that she can do such things, for she never had psychic abilities before. Now Sharon wonders at her new powers and, even more, wonders who has bestowed these wonderful gifts. [Legends, Christian]

1178.   Yolen, Jane. **Merlin's Booke.** New York: Ace, 1986. 176 pp. ISBN
C   0-441-52552-0.
        Other works: *Cards of Grief; Dragonfield and Other Stories; The Magic Three of Salatia.*

The land of Camelot is a magical one, full of dragons, magic, and sorcerers. The most powerful sorcerer of all is Merlin, a wizard of skill and yet susceptible to human foibles. [Legends, Arthurian]

1179. York, Carol Beach. **Nights in Ghostland.** New York: Archway, 1987.
B   121 pp. ISBN 0-671-63793-2.
       Other works: *I Will Make You Disappear; The Ghost of the Isherwoods; When Midnight Comes; Where Evil Is.*

Laura and Douglas have plenty of spooky troubles. Most kids would think it hard enough to deal with one ghost, but Laura and Douglas have three to contend with, and one of them leads to Wood's End, where there are even more ghosts. [Ghosts]

1180. York, Carol B. **On That Dark Night.** New York: Bantam, 1985. 128
A   pp. ISBN 0-553-25207-0.

Allison Morley is determined to find out about the scary things that are frightening her friend Julie. Can Julie really be possessed by someone who lived eighty years ago? Allison and Julie's search becomes a terrifying journey into a frightening past. [Reincarnation]

1181. York, Carol Beach. **Revenge of the Dolls.** Middletown, Conn.: Xerox,
B   1980. 103 pp. (First published by Elsevier/Nelson, 1979.)

Old aunts Sarah and Grace hardly seem good hostesses for young Alice, Trissy, and Paulie. But Aunt Sarah does make dolls, odd, ugly talking dolls for herself. One day Paulie throws a doll in the fire, little suspecting that the other dolls will get revenge. [Monsters]

1182. Younger, Jack. **Claw.** New York: Manor, 1976. 219 pp. ISBN 0-532-
C   15177-1.

Some animals are just never truly domesticated, and many would claim that this includes cats. One summer the cats in New England go berserk, and anyone who sees them on the prowl would have to agree that the events described here just might be true. [Monsters]

1183. Zachary, Hugh. **The Revenant.** New York: Onyx, 1988. 239 pp. ISBN
C   0-451-40092-5.

Vicksburg, Mississippi, high above the Mississippi River, seems to be a wonderful place to bring up young children. But Jean and Vance Whitney soon discover to their horror that their perfect dream house is located next to an old Civil War battleground where the dead do not rest in peace. [Ghosts]

1184. Zaroulis, N. L. **The Poe Papers.** New York: Jove, 1978. 224 pp. ISBN
C   0-515-04457-1.

The acknowledged master of horror, Edgar Allan Poe, once had a passionate love affair with a lovely widow. But their love could not be blissful and serene, for Poe's raven invaded their happiness with supernatural power. [Horror]

1185. Zelazny, Roger, and Fred Saberhagen. **The Black Throne.** New York:
C   Baen, 1990. 278 pp. ISBN 0-671-72013-9.

Three children, Annie, Edgar Perry, and Edgar Allan Poe, meet on a timeless, placeless beach. Thereafter, their lives are mysteriously intertwined. Edgar Allan Poe is fated to live his life as a drunken, misunderstood author, and Edgar Perry is fated to live his life in the mad dreamworld created by the other Edgar. [Dreams; Transformation]

Anthologies

1186. Adams, Robert, Martin H. Greenberg, and Pamela Crippen Adams, eds.
C   **Hunger for Horror.** New York: DAW, 1988. 256 pp. ISBN 0-88677-266-4.

Hunger is a powerful incentive, and hunger for horror is even more of a compulsion, as witnessed in these stories: "The Feast in the Abbey" (Robert Bloch), "Pickman's Model" (H. P. Lovecraft), "Shaggy's Vengeance" (Robert Adams), "They Bite" (Anthony Boucher), "Share Alike" (Jerome Bixby and Joe E. Dean), "Oil of Dog" (Ambrose Bierce), "Beyond the Cleft" (Tom Reamy), "Gladys's Gregory" (John Anthony West), "The Same Old Grind" (Bill Pronzini), "The Enchanted Fruit" (Ramsay Campbell), "Elementals" (Stephen Vincent Benet), "The Cookie Lady" (Philip K. Dick), "The Malted Milk Monster" (William Tenn), "Rogue Tomato" (Michael Bishop), "The Iron Chancellor" (Robert Silverberg). [Horror; Short stories]

1187. Ashley, Mike, ed. **The Mammoth Book of Short Horror Novels.** New
C   York: Carroll & Graf, 1988. 518 pp. ISBN 0-88184-492-2.

Novellas about all sorts of scary stuff, including "The Monkey" (Stephen King), "The Parasite" (Arthur Conan Doyle), "There's a Long, Long Trail A-Winding" (Russell Kirk), "The Damned" (Algernon Blackwood), "Fengriffen" (David Case), "The Uttermost Farthing" (A. C. Benson), "The Rope in the Rafters" (Oliver Onions), "Nadelman's God" (T. E. D. Klein), "The Feasting Dead" (John Metcalfe), "How the Wind Spoke at Madaket" (Lucius Shepard). [Horror; Short stories]

1188. Aickman, Robert, ed. **The [numbered] Fontana Book of Great Ghost**
A   **Stories.** New York: Beagle, 1971. (Later books edited by Christine Bernard.)

Classic, scary stories, including "Playing with Fire" (Sir Arthur Conan Doyle), "Man-Size in Marble" (Edith Nesbit), "How Love Came to Professor Guildea" (Robert Hichens), "The Demon Lover" (Elizabeth Bowen), "A. V. Laider" (Sir Max Beerbohm), "The Facts in the Case of M. Valdemar" (Edgar Allan Poe), "Our Distant Cousins" (Lord Dunsay), "The Inner Room" (Robert Aickman), "Thurnley Abbey" (Perceval Landon), "Nightmare Jack" (John Metcalfe), "The Damned Thing" (Ambrose Bierce), "Afterward" (Edith Wharton). [Ghosts; Short stories]

1189. Asimov, Isaac, Martin H. Greenberg, and Charles G. Waugh, eds.
C   **Devils.** New York: Signet, 1987. 351 pp. ISBN 0-451-14865-7.
     Other similar anthologies by the editors: *Wizards; Witches.*

Delightful wicked tales of the dealings of Old Nick himself, including "I'm Dangerous Tonight" (Cornell Woolrich), "The Devil in Exile" (Brian Cleeve), "The Cage" (Ray Russell), "The Tale of Ivan the Fool" (Leo Tolstoy), "The Shepherds" (Ruth Sawyer), "He Stepped on the Devil's Tale" (Winston Marks), "Rustle of Wing" (Frederic Brown), "That Hell-Bound Train" (Robert Bloch), "Added Inducement" (Robert F. Young), "The Devil and Daniel Webster"

(Stephen Vincent Benet), "Colt .24" (Rick Hautala), "The Making of Revelation, Part I" (Philip José Farmer), "The Howling Man" (Charles Beaumont), "Trace" (Jerome Bixby), "Guardian Angel" (Arthur C. Clarke), "The Devil Was Sick" (Bruce Elliot), "Deal with the D.E.V.I.L." (Theodore R. Cogswell), "Dazed" (Theodore Sturgeon). [The devil; Short stories]

1190. Asimov, Isaac, Martin H. Greenberg, and Charles G. Waugh, eds.
C   **Young Monsters.** New York: Harper & Row, 1985. 213 pp. ISBN 0-06-020169-X.
     Other anthologies by the editors: *Young Ghosts.*

A collection of stories about some disgusting youngsters — all monsters, including "Homecoming" (Ray Bradbury), "Good-by, Miss Patterson" (Phyllis MacLennan), "Disturb Not My Slumbering Fair" (Chelsea Quinn Yarbro), "The Wheelbarrow Boy" (Richard Parker), "The Cabbage Patch" (Theodore R. Cogswell, "The Thing Waited Outside" (Barbara Williamson), "Red as Blood" (Tanith Lee), "Gabriel-Ernest" (Saki), "Fritzchen" (Charles Beaumont), "The Young One" (Jerome Bixby), "Optical Illusion" (Mack Reynolds), "Idiot's Crusade" (Clifford D. Simak), "One for the Road" (Stephen King), "Angelica" (Jane Yolen). [Monsters; Short stories]

1191. Asquith, Lady Cynthia, ed. **The Ghost Book.** New York: Beagle, 1971.
C   270 pp. SBN 8441-95155-095.
     Sequels: *The Second Ghost Book; The Third Ghost Book.*

A noted English occult author collects tales including "The Villa Desiree" (May Sinclair), "Chemical" (Algernon Blackwood), "The Duenna" (Mrs. Belloc Lowndes), "A Visitor from Down Under" (L. P. Hartley), "The Lost Tragedy" (Denis Mackail), "Spinsters' Rest" (Clemence Dane), "Mrs. Lunt" (Hugh Walpole), "Munitions of War" (Arthur Machan), "The Rocking-Horse Winner" (D. H. Lawrence), "'A Recluse'" (Walter de la Mare), "The Corner Shop" (C. L. Ray), "Two Trifles" (Oliver Onions), "Twelve O'Clock" (Charles Whibley), "The Amorous Ghost" (Enid Bagnold), "Mr. Tallent's Ghost" (Mary Webb), "Pargiton and Harby" (Desmond MacCarthy). [Ghosts; Short stories]

1192. Barker, Clive. **Night Visions: Hardshell.** New York: Berkley, 1988. 279
C   pp. ISBN 0-425-10975-5. (First published as *Night Visions 4* by Arbor House, 1987.)

Terrorizing and terrific tales by masters of prose including "Miss Attila the Hun" (Dean R. Koontz), "Hardshell" (Dean R. Koontz), "Twilight of the Dawn" (Dean R. Koontz), "Predators" (Edward Bryant), "The Baku" (Edward Bryant), "Frat Rat Bash" (Edward Bryant), "Haunted" (Edward Bryant), "Baggage" (Edward Bryant), "Doing Colfax" (Edward Bryant), "The Deep End" (Robert R. McCammon), "A Life in the Day Of" (Robert R. McCammon), "Best Friends" (Robert R. McCammon). [Horror; Short stories]

1193. Benedict, Stewart H., ed. **Tales of Terror and Suspense.** New York:
A   Dell, 1963, 288 pp.

A fine introduction to famous writers of supernatural horror stories, including "Mademoiselle de Scuderi" (E. T. A. Hoffmann), "Mateo Falcone" (Prosper Mérimée), "A Descent into the Maelstrom" (Edgar Allan Poe), "Mr. Justice Harbottle" (J. Sheridan LeFanu), "The Traveller's Story of a Terribly

Strange Bed" (Wilkie Collins), "The Squaw" (Bram Stoker), "The Hand" (Guy de Maupassant), "The Adventure of the Speckled Band" (Sir Arthur Conan Doyle), "The Strange Ride of Morrowbie Jukes" (Rudyard Kipling), "The Lodger" (Marie Belloc Lowndes), "The Escape" (Hereward Carrington), "The Vanishing Lady" (Alexander Woollcott), "The Small Assassin" (Ray Bradbury). [Horror; Short stories]

1194. Benford, Gregory, and Martin Harry Greenberg, eds. **Hitler Victorious.**
C   New York: Berkley, 1987. 323 pp. ISBN 0-425-10137-1. (First published by Garland, 1986.)

Stories based on the fascinating premise that Hitler won World War II. Speculations include "Two Dooms" (C. M. Kornbluth), "The Fall of Frenchy Steiner" (Hilary Bailey), "Through Road No Whither" (Greg Bear), "Weihnachtsabend" (Keith Roberts), "Thor Meets Captain America" (David Brin), "Moon of Ice" (Brad Linaweaver), "Reichs-Peace" (Sheila Finch), "Never Meet Again" (Algis Budrys), "Do Ye Hear the Children Weeping?" (Howard Goldsmith), "Enemy Transmissions" (Tom Shippey), "Valhalla" (Gregory Benford). [Nazi occultism; Short stories]

1195. Birkin, Charles, ed. **The Witch-Baiter.** New York: Paperback Library,
C   1967. 159 pp. (First published as *The Tandem Book of Horror Stories* by Tandem, 1965.)

A noted horror writer has collected the following demonic tales: "The Puppets" (Francis King), "Old Man's Beard" (H. R. Wakefield), "The Cyclops Juju" (Shamus Frazer), "Arabesque: The Mouse" (A. E. Coppard), "Thirty" (Guy Preston), "The Medicine Cupboard" (Charles Birkin), "Dorner Cordaianthus" (Hester Holland), "The Witch-Baiter" (R. Anthony), "Cold Blood" (George Langelaan), "The Fifth Mask" (Shamus Frazer), "Lord Mount Prospect" (John Betjeman). [Horror; Short stories]

1196. Bleiler, Everett F., ed. **A Treasury of Victorian Ghost Stories.** New York:
C   Scribners, 1983. 358 pp. ISBN 0-684-17823-0.

An expert on Gothic literature selected some scary tales including "To Be Read at Dusk" (Charles Dickens), "The Ghost in the Bride's Chamber" (Charles Dickens), "Nine O'Clock!" (Wilkie Collins), "The Dutch Officer's Story" (Mrs. Catherine Crowe), "Wicked Captain Walshawe, of Wauling" (J. S. Le Fanu), "A Curious Experience" (Mrs. Henry Wood), "Le Vert Galant" (Anonymous), "At Chrighton Abbey" (Mary E. Braddon), "The Man with the Nose" (Rhoda Broughton), "Ken's Mystery" (Julian Hawthorne), "A Terrible Vengeance" (Mrs. J. H. Riddell), "The Old Lady in Black" (Anonymous), "The Library Window" (Mrs. Margaret Oliphant), "The Empty Picture Frame" (Mrs. Alfred Baldwin), "A Grammatical Ghost" (Elia W. Peattie), "The Mystery of the Semi-Detached" (E. Nesbit), "My Enemy and Myself" (Vincent O'Sullivan), "Midday Magic" (Paul Heyse), "Witch In-Grain" (R. Murray Gilchrist), "A Stray Reveler" (Emma Dawson), "The Vanishing House" (Bernard Capes), "Bodies of the Dead" (Ambrose Bierce), "Death and the Woman" (Gertrude Atherton), "The Laird's Luck" (Arthur Quiller-Couch). [Ghosts; Short stories]

1197.   Campbell, Ramsey, ed. **Fine Frights; Stories That Scared Me.** New York:
C   TOR, 1988. 309 pp. ISBN 0-812-51670-2.

Horror stories collected by a major British author, including "Child's Play" (Villy Sorensen), "More Sinned Against" (Karl Edward Wagner), "Lost Memory" (Peter Phillips), "The Fifth Mask" (Shamus Frazer), "The Horror at Chilton Castle" (Joseph Payne Brennan), "The Clerks of Domesday" (John Brunner), "Thurnley Abbey" (Perceval Landon), "Cutting Down" (Bob Shaw), "The Necromancer" (Arthur Gray), "The Greater Festival of Masks" (Thomas Ligotti), "The War Is Over" (David Case), "Upon the Dull Earth" (Philip K. Dick). [Horror; Short stories]

1198.   Campbell, Ramsey, ed. **New Terrors II.** New York: Pocket Books, 1984.
C   256 pp. ISBN 0-671-45117-0. (First published by Pan Books, 1980.)

Grisly little stories to make you shiver and scream including "Sun City" (Lisa Tuttle), "Time to Laugh" (Joan Aiken), "Bridal Suite" (Graham Masterton), "The Miraculous Cairn" (Christopher Priest), "The Rubber Room" (Robert Bloch), "Drama in Five Acts" (Giles Gordon), "The Initiation" (Jack Sullivan), "Lucille Would Have Known" (John Burke), "The Funny Face Murders" (R. A. Lafferty), "Femme Fatale" (Marianne Leconte), "Can You Still See Me?" (Margaret Dickson), "One Way Out" (Felice Picano), "The Ice Monkey" (M. John Harrison), "Symbiote" (Andrew J. Offutt), "Across the Water to Skye" (Charles L. Grant). [Horror; Short stories]

1199.   Cantor, Hal, ed. **Ghosts and Things.** New York: Berkley, 1962. 160 pp.
C   SBN 425-00666-2.

Classic tales of spirits, including "The Romance of Certain Old Clothes" (Henry James), "Caterpillars" (E. F. Benson), "Markheim" (Robert Louis Stevenson), "The Ghost Ship" (Richard Middleton), "The Novel of the White Powder" (Arthur Machen), "The Night-Doings at 'Deadman's'" (Ambrose Bierce), "Running Wolf" (Algernon Blackwood), "The Music on the Hill" (Saki), "Phantas" (Oliver Onions), "The House" (Andrew Maurois), "The Lovely House" (Shirley Jackson). [Ghosts; Short stories]

1200.   Carter, Lin, ed. **Discoveries in Fantasy.** New York: Ballantine, 1972.
C   243 pp. ISBN 0-345-02546-6.

The ancient world and its fascinating civilizations have inspired many writers to create stories of these times, including "The Vision of Yin" (Ernest Bramah), "The Dragon of Chiang Tao" (Ernest Bramah), "The Poet of Panopolis" (Richard Garnett), "The City of Philosophers" (Richart Garnett), "The Bird with the Golden Beak" (Donald Corley), "The Song of the Tombelaine" (Donald Corley), "The Miniature" (Eden Phillpotts). [Legends, Chinese; Legends, classical; Legends, medieval; Short stories]

1201.   Carter, M. L., ed. **The Curse of the Undead.** New York: Fawcett,
C   1970. 223 pp. ISBN 0-449-02276-075.

Vampire stories, including "Excerpts from 'Justine'" (Marquis de Sade), "The Bleeding Nun" (Matthew Gregory Lewis), "The Vampyre" (John Polidori), "Morella" (Edgar Allan Poe), "Excerpts from 'Carmilla'" (J. Sheridan Le Fanu), "Excerpts from 'Dracula'" (Bram Stoker), "For the Blood Is the Life" (F. Marion

Crawford), "Softly While You're Sleeping" (Evelyn E. Smith), "The Bogey Man Will Get You" (Robert Bloch), "Blood" (Fredric Brown), "Vanishing Breed" (Niel Straum). [Vampires; Short stories]

1202.   Cerf, Bennett, ed. **Famous Ghost Stories.** New York: Random Vantage,
C   1956. 361 pp. ISBN 0-394-70140-2.

Some classic tales collected by a noted anthologist, including "The Haunted and the Haunters" (Edward Bulwer-Lytton), "The Damned Thing" (Ambrose Bierce), "The Monkey's Paw" (W. W. Jacobs), "The Phantom Rickshaw" (Rudyard Kipling), "The Willows" (Algernon Blackwood), "The Rival Ghosts" (Branden Matthews), "The Man Who Went Too Far" (E. F. Benson), "The Mezzotint" (Montague Rhodes James), "The Open Window" (Saki), "The Beckoning Fair One" (Oliver Onions), "On the Brighton Road" (Richard Middleton), "The Considerate Hosts" (Thorp McClusky), "August Heat" (W. F. Harvey), "The Return of Andrew Bentley" (August Derleth and Mark Schorer), "The Supper at Elsinor" (Isak Dinesen), "The Current Crop of Ghost Stories" (Bennett Cerf). [Ghosts; Short stories]

1203.   Chetwynd-Hayes, R., ed. **Cornish Tales of Terror.** London: Fontana,
C   1970. 190 pp.

Lovely, mysterious Cornwall is the site of many supernatural stories, including "The Roll-Call of the Reef" (Sir Arthur Quiller-Couch), "The Misanthrope" (J. D. Beresford), "The Botathen Ghost" (R. S. Hawker), "All Soul's Night" (A. L. Rowse), "The Narrow Way" (R. Ellis Roberts), "The Phantom Hare" (M. H.), "The Iron Pineapple" (Eden Phillpotts), "Wish Me Luck" (A. H. Manhood), "Mrs. Lunt" (Sir Hugh Walpole), "The Birds" (Daphne du Maurier), "The Spectre Bridegroom" (Robert Hunt), "The Bodmin Terror" (R. Chetwynd-Hayes). [Legends, Cornish; Short stories]

1204.   Child, Lincoln, ed. **Dark Company: The Ten Greatest Ghost Stories.**
C   New York: St. Martin's Press, 1984. 356 pp. ISBN 0-312-18232-5. (First
        published by St. Martin's Press, 1983.)

One collector's selection of the ten best ghostly goodies includes "Fall of the House of Usher" (Edgar Allan Poe), "Jolly Corner" (Henry James), "Green Tea" (Sheridan Le Fanu), "The Mezzotint" (M. R. James), "The Great God Pan" (Arthur Machen), "The Willows" (Algernon Blackwood), "The Shadow Out of Time" (H. P. Lovecraft). [Ghosts; Short stories]

1205.   Child, Lincoln, ed. **Tales of the Dark.** New York: St. Martin's Press,
C   1987. 184 pp. ISBN 0-312-90339-1.

Classic masterpieces of supernatural terror, including, "The Fall of the House of Usher" (Edgar Allan Poe), "The Signalman" (Charles Dickens), "Green Tea" (Joseph Sheridan Le Fanu), "The Squaw" (Bram Stoker), "Markheim" (Robert Louis Stevenson), "The Upper Berth" (F. Marion Crawford), "The Yellow Wallpaper" (Charlotte Perkins Gilman), "They" (Rudyard Kipling), "The Yellow Sign" (Robert W. Chambers), "The Voice in the Night" (William Hope Hodgson). [Horror; Short stories]

1206. Coffey, Frank, ed. **Modern Masters of Horror.** New York: Ace, 1982.
C   286 pp. ISBN 0-441-53507-0. (First published by Coward, McCann & Geoghegan, 1981.)

Wonderful stories sure to induce shivers, including: "The Monkey" (Stephen King), "The New Tenant" (William Hallahan), "In the Cards" (Robert Bloch), "Clay" (George A. Romero), "A Cabin in the Woods" (John Coyne), "Makeup" (Robert R. McCammon), "The Small World of Lewis Stillman" (William F. Nolan), "The Siege of 318" (Davis Grubb), "The Champion" (Richard Laymon), "The Power of the Mandarin" (Gahan Wilson), "Horror House of Blood" (Ramsey Campbell), "Absolute Ebony" (Felice Picano), "The Root of All Evil" (Graham Masterton), "Julian's Hand" (Gary Brandner), "The Face" (Jere Cunningham). [Horror; Short stories]

1207. Cramer, Kathryn, and David G. Hartwell, eds. **Christmas Ghosts.** New
C   York: Dell, 1988. 265 pp. ISBN 0-440-20217-5. (First published by Arbor House, 1987.)

It has long been an English tradition to tell ghost stories at Christmastime, and here are some choice selections, including "Their Dear Little Ghost" (Elia Wilkinson Peattie), "The Curse of the Catafalques" (F. Anstey), "The Story of the Goblins Who Stole a Sexton" (Charles Dickens), "Christmas Night" (Elizabeth Walter). "A New Christmas Carol" (Arthur Machen), "A Christmas Game" (A. N. L. Munby), "The Great Staircase at Landover Hall" (Frank R. Stockton), "The Water Ghost of Harrowby Hall" (John Kendrick Bangs), "Christmas Meeting" (Rosemary Timperly), "The Ghost" (William D. O'Connor), "Christmas Reunion" (Sir Andrew Caldecott), "The Ghosts at Grantley" (Leonard Kip), "The Christmas Banquet" (Nathaniel Hawthorne), "The Crown Derby Plate" (Marjorie Bowen), "A Strange Christmas Game" (Mrs. J. H. Riddell), "Calling Card" (Ramsey Campbell), "A Christmas Tree" (Charles Dickens). [Ghosts; Legends, Christian; Short stories]

1208. Cuddon, J. A., ed. **The Penguin Book of Ghost Stories.** Harmonds-
C   worth, England: Penguin, 1985. 512 pp. ISBN 0-14-006800-7.

Some delightfully scary stories, both old and new, including "The Beggarwoman of Locarno" (Heinrich von Kleist), "The Entail" (E. T. A. Hoffman), "Wandering Willie's Tale" (Walter Scott), "The Queen of Spades" (Alexander Pushkin), "The Old Nurse's Story" (Elizabeth Gaskell), "The Open Door" (Margaret Oliphant), "Mr. Justice Harbottle" (Sheridan Le Fanu), "Le Horla" (Guy de Maupassant), "Sir Edmund Orme" (Henry James), "Angeline, or the Haunted House" (Emile Zola), "The Moonlit Road" (Ambrose Bierce), "A Haunted Island" (Algernon Blackwood), "The Rose Garden" (M. R. James), "The Return of Imray" (Rudyard Kipling), "My Adventure in Norwalk" (A. J. Alan), "The Inexperienced Ghost" (H. G. Wells), "The Room in the Tower" (E. F. Benson), "One Who Saw" (A. M. Burrage), "Afterward" (Edith Wharton), "The Wardrobe" (Thomas Mann), "The Buick Saloon" (Ann Bridge), "The Tower" (Marghanita Laski), "Footsteps in the Snow" (Mario Soldati), "The Wind" (Ray Bradbury), "Exorcizing Baldassare" (Edward Hyams), "The Leaf-Sweeper" (Muriel Spark), "'Dear Ghost....'" (Fielden Hughes), "Sonata for Harp and Bicycle" (Joan Aiken), "Come and Get Me" (Elizabeth Walter), "Andrina" (George Mackay Brown), "The Axe" (Penelope Fitzgerald), "The Game of Dice" (Alain Danielou), "The July Ghost" (A. S. Byatt). [Ghosts; Short stories]

1209. Cuddon, J. A., ed. **The Penguin Book of Horror Stories.** Harmonds-
C   worth, England: Penguin, 1984. 607 pp. ISBN 0-14-006799-X.

A collection of fine tales of shivery horror, including "The Monk of Horror, or The Conclave of Corpses" (Anonymous), "The Astrologer's Prediction, or The Maniac's Fate" (Anonymous), "The Expedition to Hell" (James Hogg), "Mateo Falcone" (Prosper Merimee), "The Case of M. Valdemar" (Edgar Allan Poe), "La Grande Breteche" (Honore de Balza), "The Romance of Certain Old Clothes" (Henry James), "Who Knows?" (Guy de Maupassant), "The Body Snatchers" (Robert Louis Stevenson), "The Death of Olivier Becaille" (Emile Zola), "The Boarded Window" (Ambrose Bierce), "Lost Hearts" (M. R. James), "The Sea-Raiders" (H. G. Wells), "The Derelict" (William Hope Hodgson), "Thurnley Abbey" (Perceval Landon), "The Fourth Man" (James Russell), "In the Penal Colony" (Franz Kafka), "The Waxwork" (A. M. Burrage), "Mrs. Amworth" (E. F. Benson), "The Reptile" (Augustus Muir), "Mr. Meldrum's Mania" (John Metcalfe), "The Beast with Five Fingers" (William Fryer Harvey), "Dry September" (William Faulkner), "Crouching at the Door" (D. K. Broster), "The Two Bottles of Relish" (Lord Dunsany), "The Man Who Liked Dickens" (Evelyn Waugh), "Taboo" (Geoffrey Household), "The Thought" (L. P. Hartley), "Comrade Death" (Gerald Kersh), "Leningen Versus the Ants" (Carl Stephenson), "The Brink of Darkness" (Yvor Winters), "Activity Time" (Monica Dickens), "Earth to Earth" (Robert Graves), "The Dwarf" (Ray Bradbury), "The Portobello Road" (Muriel Spark), "No Flies on Frank" (John Lennon), "Sister Coxall's Revenge" (Dawn Muscillo), "Thou Shalt Not Suffer a Witch...." (Dorothy K. Haynes), "The Terrapin" (Patricia Highsmith), "Man from the South" (Roald Dahl), "Uneasy Homecoming" (Will F. Jenkins), "The Squarist" (J. N. Allan), "An Interview with M. Chakko" (Vilas Sarang). [Horror; Short stories]

1210. Curran, Ronald, ed. **Witches, Wraiths and Warlocks.** New York: Faw-
D   cett Premier, 1971. 354 pp. ISBN 0-449-30061-7.

The great tradition of American folk and literary tales of the supernatural including "Enchantments Encounter'd" (Cotton Mather), "Old Deb and Other Old Colony Witches" (William Root Bliss), "Gen. Andrew Jackson: The Great Soldier and Statesman's Visit to the Bell Witch" (M. V. Ingram), "The Cat-Witch" (Richard M. Dorson), "The Witch Dance on the Brocken" (Frederick Gottschalck), "The Leeds Devil" (Charles M. Skinner), "Stolen Fire" (Virginia Frazer Boyle), "Seeing the Devil in Three Shapes" (Richard M. Dorson), "Jonathan Moulton and the Devil" (Samuel Adams Drake), "Barney Oxman and the Devil" (Thomas Chandler Hailburton), "The Death Waitz" (Charles M. Skinner), "The Haunted House" (Richard Chase), "The Ghost" (Anonymous), "The Long Sleep" (Charles M. Skinner), "The Legend of the Pipe" (Launcelot), "Coffined Alive" (Anonymous), "The Castle of Costanzo" (Anonymous), "The Parricide Punished" (Anonymous), "The Wig and the Black Cat" (Anonymous), "The Witch" (Miss Elizabeth P. Hall), "The Veil" (E. E.), "The Midnight Voyage of the Seagull" (Mrs. Volney E. Howard), "The Sphinx" (Anonymous), "Tale of a Conjurer" (Anonymous), "The Enchanter Faustus and Queen Elizabeth" (Anonymous), "The Dream" (Anonymous), "The Captive's Dream" (Anonymous), "The Wooden-Legged Ghost" (John Waters), "A Ghost Story" (I. P. A.), "The Village Doctor" (Rudolph), "Young Goodman Brown" (Nathaniel Hawthorne), "The Legend of Sleepy Hollow" (Washington Irving), "The Black

Cat" (Edgar Allan Poe), "A Ghost Story" (Mark Twain), "Rappaccini's Daughter" (Nathaniel Hawthorne), "The Tartarus of Maids" (Herman Melville), "Ligeia" (Edgar Allan Poe), "Rip van Winkle" (Washington Irving), "The Fall of the House of Usher" (Edgar Allan Poe), "The Bell-Tower" (Herman Melville). (Short stories; Witchcraft]

1211.   Dalby, Richard, ed. **Dracula's Brood.** Wellingborough, England: Equa-
D   tion, 1989. 348 pp. ISBN 1-85336-120-8.

Nineteenth- and early twentieth-century vampire classics, including "The Last Lords of Gardonal" (William Gilbert), "The Fate of Madame Cabanel" (Eliza Lynn Linton), "The Man-Eating Tree" (Phil Robinson), "The Vampyre" (Vasile Alecsandrai), "A Mystery of the Campagna" (Anne Crawford), "Ken's Mystery" (Julian Hawthorne), "The Parasite" (Sir Arthur Conan Doyle), "Good Lady Ducayne" (Mary E. Braddon), "Let Loose" (Mary Cholmondeley), "Will" (Vincent O'Sullivan), "The Stone Chamber" (H. B. Marriott Waton), "The Vampire Maid" (Hume Nisbet), "The Old Portrait" (Hume Nisbet), "Marsyas in Flanders" (Vernon Lee), "An Unscientific Story" (Louise J. Strong), "A Dead Finger" (Sabine Baring-Gould), "The Feather Pillow" (Horacio Quiroga), "The Singular Death of Morton" (Algernon Blackwood), "Aylmer Vance and the Vampire" (Alice and Claude Askew), "The Sumach" (Ulric Daubeny), "Wailing Well" (M. R. James), "Another Squaw?" (E. Heron-Allen), "The Living Stone" (E. R. Punshon), "Prince of Darkness" (Frederick Cowles). [Short stories; Vampires]

1212.   Dalby, Richard, ed. **The Mammoth Book of Ghost Stories.** New York:
C   Carroll & Graf, 1990. 654 pp. ISBN 0-88184-590-6.

Fifty spine-tingling ghost stories from three centuries, including "The Unsettled Dust" (Robert Aickman), "How He Left the Hotel" (Louisa Baldwin), "Whessoe" (Nugent Barker), "The Shuttered Room" (E. F. Benson), "An Inhabitant of Carcosa" (Ambrose Bierce), "Is There Anybody There?" (Charles Birkin), "The Whisperers" (Algernon Blackwood), "Curfew" (L. M. Boston), "I'm Sure It Was No. 31" (A. M. Burrage), "The Guide" (Ramsey Campbell), "The Limping Ghost" (R. Chetwynd-Hayes), "Mrs. Zant and the Ghost" (Wilkie Collins), "The House by the Tarn" (Basil Copper), "In Kropfsberg Keep" (Ralph A. Cram), "The Ghost in all the Rooms" (Daniel Defoe), "The Bagman's Uncle" (Charles Dickens), "The Bully of Brocas Court" (Arthur Conan Doyle), "In the Confessional" (Amelia B. Edwards), "The Tune in Dan's Cafe" (Shamus Frazer), "Beyond the Bourne" (John S. Glasby), "The Valley of Lost Children" (William Hope Hodgson), "The Sand-Walker" (Fergus Hume), "The Real Right Thing" (Henry James), "The Haunted Dolls' House" (M. R. James), "The Wall-Painting" (Roger Johnson), "'They'" (Rudyard Kipling), "The Last Laugh" (D. H. Lawrence), "Robin's Rath" (Margery Lawrence), "The Dream" (J. Sheridan Le Fanu), "The Sundial" (R. H. Malden), "The Fifteenth Man" (Richard Marsh), "Brenner's Boy" (John Metcalfe), "Uncle Abraham's Romance" (Edith Nesbit), "What Was It?" (Fitz-James O'Brien), "The Next Room" (Vincent O'Sullivan), "The Footstep of the Aventine" (Roger Pater), "William Wilson" (Edgar Allan Poe), "Courage" (Forrest Reid), "The Last of Squire Ennismore" (Mrs. J. H. Riddell), "The Garside Fell Disaster" (L. T. C. Rolt), "The Tears of Saint Agathé" (David G. Rowlands), "The Soul of Laploshka" (Saki), "The Old Dining-Room" (Sapper), "The Between-Maid" (Montague Summers), "A Ghost Story" (Mark Twain), "The Folly" (Mark Valentine), "Out of the Wrack I Rise"

(H. Russell Wakefield), "In the Pines" (Karl Edward Wagner), "Where Angels Fear...." (Manly Wade Wellman), "The House of the Nightmare" (Edward Lucas White), "The Canterville Ghost" (Oscar Wilde), "The Spectre Spiders" (William J. Wintle). [Ghosts; Short stories]

1213. Danby, Mary, ed. **The [numbered] Armada Ghost Book.** London:
B   Armada Fontana, 197?- . (Books 1-13 in the series edited by Christine
       Bernard and Mary Danby.)

Book 14 contains representative examples of these primarily English stories for younger teens: "The Longest Journey" (Catherine Gleason), "The Junk Room" (Terry Tapp), "Under the Bedclothes" (David Langford), "Gibson's" (Ann Pilling), "The Ghost of Smeaton Hall" (Geoffrey Palmer and Noel Lloyd), "The Third Eye" (R. Chetwynd-Hayes), "In Flanders Fields" (Frances Thomas), "Can't Help Laughing" (Alison Prince), "The Train Watchers" (Sydney J. Bounds), "The Ghost Writer" (Mary Danby).

Contents of book 15 (published in 1983) include "Run for Your Life" (Philip Sidney Jennings), "Hallowe'en" (Rita Morris), "Who's a Pretty Boy, Then?" (Jan Mark), "The Patchwork Quilt" (August Derleth), "The Sound of Sirens" (Tony Richards), "Spirit of the Trail" (Sydney J. Bounds), "Christmas in the Rectory" (Catherine Storr), "The Servant" (Alison Prince), "Whoever Heard of a Haunted Lift?" (Alan W. Lear), "Mr. Jones" (Mary Danby). [Ghosts; Short stories]

1214. Danby, Mary, ed. **Nightmares.** London: Armada, 1983- .
A

Longer stories that build to nice scary endings such as these stories in *Nightmares 3* (ISBN 0-00-692551-0): "Clifftops" (Antony Bennett), "Barnacles" (Johnny Yen), "Dead Letter" (Alan W. Lear), "House of Horror" (Sydney J. Bounds), "The Diary" (Samantha Lee), "Shadow of the Rope" (Roger Malisson), "Joplin's" (Brian Mooney), "The Shaft" (Philip C. Heath), "Old Wiggie" (Mary Danby). [Horror; Short stories]

1215. Dann, Jack, and Gardner Dozois, eds. **Demons!** New York: Ace, 1987.
C   278 pp. ISBN 0-441-14264-8.
       Other anthologies by the editors: *Magicats!; Sorcerers!; Bestiary!*

Tales of devilish doings by denizens of the depths, including "Grail" (Harlan Ellison), "The Willow Platform" (Joseph Payne Brennan), "The Night of White Bhairab" (Lucius Shepard), "The Mangler" (Stephen King), "The Last Demon" (Isaac Bashevis Singer), "The Golden Rope" (Tanight Lee), "Basileus" (Robert Silverberg), "Twilla" (Tom Reamy), "The Purple Pterodactyls" (L. Sprague de Camp), "Goslin Day" (Avram Davidson), "Nellthu" and "Snulbug" (Anthony Boucher), "One Other" (Manly Wade Wellman), "An Ornament to His Profession" (Charles L. Harness). [Demons; Heaven and hell; Short stories]

1216. Dann, Jack, and Gardner Dozois, eds. **Mermaids!** New York: Ace Fan-
C   tasy, 1986. 260 pp. ISBN 0-441-52567-9.

Stories about mythical sea creatures of the watery depths, including "Nothing in the Rules" (L. Sprague de Camp), "She Sells Sea Shells" (Paul Darcy Boles), "The Soul Cages" (T. Crofton Croker), "Sweetly the Waves Call to Me" (Pat Murphy), "Driftglass" (Samuel R. Delany), "Mrs. Pigafetta Swims Well" (Reginald Bretnor), "The Nebraskan and the Nereid" (Gene Wolfe), "The Lady and the Merman" (Jane Yolen), "The White Seal Maid" (Jane Yolen), "The Fisherman's Wife" (Jane Yolen), "Till Human Voices Wake Us" (Lewis Shiner), "A Touch of Strange" (Theodore Sturgeon), "Something Rich and Strange" (Randall Garrett and Avram Davidson), "The Crest of Thirty-Six" (Davis Grubb), "The Shannon Merrow" (Cooper McLaughlin), "Fish Story" (Leslie Charteris), "In the Islands" (Pat Murphy). [Mermaids; Short stories]

1217.   Dann, Jack, and Gardner Dozois, eds. **Unicorns!** New York: Ace Fan-
C   tasy, 1982. 308 pp. ISBN 0-441-85444-3.

A collection of sixteen magical tales about a beloved beast, the unicorn, including "The Spoor of the Unicorn" (Avram Davidson), "The Silken Swift" (Theodore Sturgeon), "Eudoric's Unicorn" (L. Sprague de Camp), "The Flight of the Horse" (Larry Niven), "On the Downhill Side" (Harlan Ellison), "The Night of the Unicorn" (Thomas Burnett Swamm), "Mythological Beast" (Stephen R. Donaldson), "The Final Quarry" (Eric Norden), "Elfleda" (Vonda N. McIntyre), "The White Donkey" (Ursula K. Le Guin), "Unicorn Variation" (Roger Zelazny), "The Sacrifice" (Gardner Dozois), "The Unicorn" (Frank Owen), "The Woman the Unicorn Loved" (Gene Wolfe), "The Forsaken" (Bev Evans), "The Unicorn" (T. H. White). [Unicorns; Short stories]

1218.   **The Dark Dominion.** New York: Paperback Library, 1970. 158 pp.
C

Stories about vampires and werewolves, including "The Kill" (Peter Fleming), "The Refugee" (Jane Rice), "A Case of Irish Lycanthropy" (Theophile Gautier), "Jikininki" (Lafcadio Hearn), "The Werewolf" (Frederick Marryat), "Stubbe Peeter" (B. J. Hurwood, translater), "The Case of Ivan of Shiganska" (Elliott O'Donnell). [Short stories; Vampires; Werewolves]

1219.   Dawood, N. J., trans. **Tales from the Thousand and One Nights.** Har-
C   mondsworth, England: Penguin, 1954. 343 pp. ISBN 01400.90231.

All the magical fables and tales from Arabian lands, including "The Tale of King Shashriyar and His Brother Shahzaman," "The Fable of the Donkey, the Ox, and the Farmer," "The Tale of the Hunchback," "The Donkey," "The Young Woman and Her Five Lovers," "Sinbad the Sailor and Sinbad the Porter," "The Historic Fart," "Aladdin and the Enchanted Lamp," "The Tale of Kafur the Black Eunuch," "The Porter and the Three Girls of Baghdad," "The Tale of Khalifah the Fisherman," "The Dream," "The Tale of Judar and His Brothers," "The Tale of Ma'Aruf the Cobbler." [Legends, Arabian; Magic; Short stories]

1220.   Dozois, Gardner, and Susan Casper, eds. **Ripper!** New York: TOR, 1988.
C   427 pp. ISBN 0-812-51700-8.

Stories about Jack the Ripper, some with a supernatural twist, including "Jack's Decline" (Lucius Shepard), "Gentlemen of the Shade" (Harry Turtledove), "Dead Air" (Gregory Nicoll), "Street of Dreams" (John M. Ford), "Yours Truly, Jack the Ripper" (Robert Bloch), "Anna and the Ripper of Siam" (S. P. Somtow), "The Edge" (Pat Cadigan), "An Awareness of Angel" (Karl Edward Wagner), "Old Red Shoes" (Stephen Gallagher), "From Hell, Again" (Gregory Frost), "Spring-Fingered Jack" (Susan Casper), "The Sins of the Father" (Scott Baker), "A Good Night's Work" (Sarah Clements), "Knucklebones" (Tim Sullivan), "The Prowler in the City at the Edge of the

World" (Harlan Ellison), "The Lodge of Jahbulon" (Cooper McLaughlin), "Game in the Pope's Head" (Charles L. Grant), "Love in Vain" (Lewis Shiner). [Jack the Ripper; Short stories]

1221. Elwood, Roger, ed. **Demonkind.** New York: Avon, 1973. 192 pp. ISBN
A   0-380-14886-0.

Children can be more powerful than they appear, as evidenced in these stories: "Linkage" (Barry Malzberg), "Mud Violet" (R. A. Lafferty), "Bettyann's Children" (Kris Neville), "Child" (Joan C. Holly), "World of Gray" (Norman Spinrad), "Dandy" (Ted White), "A Proper Santa Claus" (Anne McCaffrey), "The Marks of Painted Teeth" (Jack Dann), "The Eddystone Light" (Laurence Yep), "From Darkness to Darkness" (Terry Carr), "Monologue" (Philip Jose Farmer). [Paranormal abilities; Short stories]

1222. Elwood, Roger, ed. **Vampires, Werewolves and Other Monsters.** New
C   York: Curtis, 1974. 205 pp. SBN 502-09260-095.

Stories about some terrible beasts, including "Problem Child" (Brian Lumley), "Moonglow" (Steve Barnes), "Night Riders" (Luc Scott), "The Student" (K. M. O'Donnell), "Diary of a Werewolf" (Joseph Payne Brennan,) "Inner Circle" (Barry N. Malzberg), "Litter" (Ramsey Campbell), "Who Is Sylvia?" (Thomas N. Scortia and Chelsea Quinn Yarbro), "Night of the Wolf" (Robin Schaeffer), "Grimjank" (W. T. Webb), "Cry Wolf" (Basil Copper), "Testify" (Barry N. Malzberg). [Monsters; Short stories]

1223. Elwood, Roger, and Vic Ghidalia, eds. **Young Demons.** New York:
C   Avon, 1972. 160 pp. ISBN 0-380-02434-075.

Terrible tales of diabolic children, including "Sredni Vahstar" (Saki), "Bettyann" (Kris Neville), "The Transcendent Tigers" (R. A. Lafferty), "Apple" (Anne McCaffrey), "The Small Assassin" (Ray Bradbury), "Shut the Last Door" (Joe Hensley), "Games" (Katherine MacLean), "Jamboree" (Jack Williamson). [Horror; Short stories]

1224. Etchison, Dennis. **Masters of Darkness II.** New York: TOR, 1988.
C   338 pp. ISBN 0-812-51764-4.

Weird and frightening tales by an assortment of fine modern horror writers, including "Up under the Roof" (Manly Wade Wellman), "The Other Room" (Lisa Tuttle), "A Garden of Blackred Roses" (Charles L. Grant), "Cottage Tenant" (Frank Belknap Long), "The Hounds" (Kate Wilhelm), "Zombique" (Joseph Payne Brennan), "Taking the Night Train" (Thomas F. Monteleone), "Black Corridor" (Fritz Leiber), "Strangers in Paradise" (Damon Knight), "Gemini" (Tanith Lee), "Glimmer, Glimmer" (George Alec Effinger), "Perverts" (Whitley Strieber), "On Ice" (Barry N. Malzberg), "The Monkey Treatment" (George R. R. Martin), "Casey Agonistes" (Richard McKenna). [Horror; Short stories]

1225. Furman, A. L., ed. **Ghost Stories.** New York: Archway, 1964. 163 pp.
A   ISBN 0-671-52525-5. (First published as *Teen-Age Ghost Stories* by Simon and Schuster, 1961.)

Good ghost stories for teenage readers, such as "Ghost Alarm" (Carl Henry Rathjen), "Ghost of Black John" (William MacKellar), "Dark Flowers" (Kay Hangaard), "The Ghost of Old Stone Fort" (Harry Harrison Kroll), "Valley of

No Return" (Willis Lindquist), "Mystery of the Ghost Junk" (James Benedict Moore), "The Haunted Pavilion" (Patricia McCune), "The Haunted Tumbler" (Diana Meyers). [Ghosts; Short stories]

1226. Galin, Mitchell, and Tom Allen, eds. **Tales from the Darkside.** New
C   York: Berkley, 1988. 248 pp. ISBN 0-425-11095-8.

The narrative version of stories for the popular dramatic television series, including "The Devil's Advocate" (Michael McDowell, based on a teleplay by George A. Romero), "The Word Processor of the Gods" (Stephen King), "A Case of the Stubborns" (Robert Bloch), "Inside the Closet" (Michael McDowell), "Printer's Devil" (Ron Goulart), "Levitation" (Joseph Payne Brennan), "Halloween Candy" (Michael McDowell), "The Satanic Piano" (Carl Jacobi), "Slippage" (Michael P. Kube-McDowell), "The Shrine" (Pamela Sargent), "In the Cards" (Michael McDowell, based on a teleplay by Carole Lucia Satrina), "The Bitterest Pill" (Frederik Pohl), "Hush!" (Zenna Henderson), "The Circus" (Sydney J. Bounds), "Distant Signals" (Andrew Weiner), "The Odds" (Michael McDowell, based on a teleplay by Carole Lucia Satrina). [Horror; Short stories]

1227. Gelb, Jeff, and Michael Garrett, eds. **Hotter Blood: More Tales of**
C   **Erotic Horror.** New York: Pocket Books, 1991. 336 pp. ISBN
        0-671-70149-5.
        Other works: *Hot Blood* edited by Jeff Gelb and Lonn Friend.

Tales of passion set within the horror genre, including "Nocturn" (John L. Byrne), "The Tub" (Richard Laymon), "The Picture of Health" (Ray Garton), "Change of Life" (Chet Williamson), "Demonlover" (Nancy A. Collins), "Confession" (Kurt Busiek), "Wolf in the Memory" (Stephen Gresham), "To Have and to Hold" (Gary Brandner), "Cruising" (Lisa W. Cantrell), "Dream on Me" (Mick Garris), "DeVice" (Stephen Gallagher), "The Best" (Paul Dale Anderson), "Something Extra" (J. N. Williamson and James Kisner), "Juice" (Kiel Stuart), "Surprise" (Rex Miller), "Rococo" (Graham Masterton), "Dear Diary" (Elsa Rutherford), "The Splicer" (Don D'Ammassa), "A Hard Man Is Good to Find" (R. Patrick Gates), "Bedroom Eyes" (Michael Newton), "Atrocities" (Lucy Taylor), "Pearldoll" (John Shirley), "The Kind Men Like" (Karl Edward Wagner), "The Braille Encyclopedia" (Grant Morrison). [Horror; Short stories]

1228. Godwin, Parke, ed. **Invitation to Camelot.** New York: Ace, 1988. 258
C   pp. ISBN 0-441-37200-7.

Stories from King Arthur's court, including "The Storyteller" (Jane Yolan), "Their Son" (Morgan Llywelyn), "The Minstrel's Tale" (Tanith Lee), "Two Bits of Embroidery" (Phyllis Ann Karr), "The Camelot Connection" (Elizabeth Ann Scarborough), "Uallannach" (Parke Godwin), "Seven from Caer Sidi" (Susan Shwartz), "The Vow that Binds" (Gregory Frost), "Nimue's Tale" (Madelein E. Robin), "Night Mare" (Chelsea Quinn Yarbro), "The Palace by Moonlight" (Sharan Newman), "Meditation in a Whitethorn Tree" (Jane Yolen), "Winter Solstice, Camelot Station" (John M, Ford). [Legends, Arthurian; Short stories]

1229. Gorman, Ed, and Martin H. Greenberg, eds. **Stalkers.** New York: ROC,
C   1990. 386 pp. ISBN 0-451-45048-5.

Novellas about the thrill of the chase, including "Trapped" (Dean R. Koontz), "Flight" (John Coyne), "A Day in the Life" (F. Paul Wilson), "Lizardman" (Robert R. McCammon), "Pilots" (Joe R. Lansdale and Dan Lowry), "Stalker" (Ed Gorman), "Getting the Job Done" (Rick Hautala), "Children of Cain" (Al Sarrantonio), "A Matter of Principle" (Max Allan Collins), "Miss December" (Rex Miller), "A Matter of Firing" (John Maclay), "The Sacred Fire" (Charles de Lint), "The Stalker of Souls" (Edward D. Hoch), "Darwinian Facts" (Barry N. Malzberg), "The Hunt" (Richard Laymon), "Mother Tucker" (James Kisner), "Jezebel" (J. N. Williamson), "What Chelsea Said" (Michael Seidman), "Riverenos" (Trish Janeshutz). [Horror; Short stories]

1230. Grant, Charles L., ed. **Fears.** New York: Berkley, 1983. 280 pp. ISBN
C   0-425-06066-7.
       Other anthologies in the series: *Horrors; Midnight; Terrors.*

Good scary stories selected by a master, including "Surrogate" (Janet Fox), "Coasting" (Chelsea Quinn Yarbro), "Spring-Fingered Jack" (Susan Casper), "Flash Point" (Gardner Dozois), "A Cold Day in the Mesozoic" (Jack Dann), "The Train" (William F. Nolan), "The Dripping" (David Morrell), "The Ragman" (Leslie Alan Horvitz), "Deathtracks" (Dennis Etchison), "Father Dear" (Al Sarrantonio), "As Old as Sin" (Peter D. Pautz), "Fish Night" (Joe R. Lansdale), "Remembering Melody" (George R. R. Martin), "The Pond" (Pat Cadigan), "The Beasts that Perish" (R. Bretnor), "Cassie, Waiting" (Julie Stevens), "High Tide" (Leanne Frahm). [Horror; Short stories]

1231. Grant, Charles L., ed. **Night Visions: Dead Image.** New York: Berkley,
C   1987. 309 pp. ISBN 0-425-10182-7. (First published as *Night Visions 2* by
       Dark Harvest, 1985.)

Frightening stories by three acknowledged master writers of modern horror, including "Black and White and Red All Over," "Mumbo Jumbo," "Dead Image" (David Morrell); "Wanderson's Waste," "Pick-Up," "Canavan Calling," "Oasis of Abomination," "Starlock Street," "The Haunting at Juniper Hill" (Joseph Payne Brennan); "Shrapnel," "Old Loves," "Blue Lady, Come Back" (Karl Edward Wagner). [Horror; Short stories]

1232. Grant, Charles L., ed. **Nightmares.** New York: Berkley, 1982. 256 pp.
C   ISBN 0-425-07693-8. (First published by Playboy, 1979.)

This acknowledged expert on horror is considered to be one of the best anthologists working today. Brought together here are "Suffer the Little Children" (Stephen King), "Peekaboo" (Bill Pronzini), "Daughter of the Golden West" (Dennis Etchison), "The Duppy Tree" (Steven Edward McDonald), "Naples" (Avram Davidson), "Seat Partner" (Chelsea Quinn Yarbro), "Camps" (Jack Dann), "The Anchoress" (Beverly Evans), "Transfer" (Barry N. Malzberg), "Unknown Drives" (Richard Christian Matheson), "The Night of the Piasa" (George W. Proctor and J. C. Green), "The Runaway Lovers" (Ray Russell), "Fisherman's Log" (Peter D. Pautz), "I Can't Help Saying Goodbye" (Ann Mackenzie), "Midnight Hobo" (Ramsey Campbell), "Snakes and Snails" (Jack C. Haldeman II), "Mass without Voices" (Arthur L. Samuels), "He Kilt It with a Stick" (William F. Nolan), "The Ghouls" (R. Chetwynd-Hayes). [Horror; Short stories]

1233. Grant, Charles L., ed. **The Greystone Bay Chronicles.** New York: TOR,
C   1988- .
        Series: *Greystone Bay; Doom City; The Seaharp Hotel.*

Stories about Greystone Bay, a place that seems to attract horror just like Oxrun Station and Castle Rock, including these in *The Seaharp Hotel:* "Ex-Library" (Chet Williamson), "The Coat" (Al Sarrantonio), "Beauty" (Robert R. McCammon), "Services Rendered" (Bryan Webb), "Aquarium" (Steve Rasnic Tem), "Three Doors in a Double Room" (Craig Shaw Gardner), "Revelations" (Melissa Mia Hall), "Room Service" (Les Daniels), "Evil Thoughts" (Suzy McKee Charnas), "Blood Lilies" (Robert E. Vardeman), "Interlude" (Wendy Webb), "A Muse for Mr. Kalish" (Leslie Alan Horvitz), "No Pain, No Gain" (Thomas F. Monteleone), "Old Friends Never Die" (Bob Booth), "Ami Amet Deli Pencet" (Nancy Holder). [Horror; Short stories]

1234. Grant, Charles L., ed. **Shadows.** (Numbered series 1-9.) New York:
C   Berkley, 1983-1987. (First published by Doubleday, 1982.)

A fine series of stories by leading contemporary writers of horror concluding with these in volume 9, "The Jigsaw Girl" (Stephen Gallagher), "The Lesson" (Christopher Browne), "On the Turn" (Leanne Frahm), "Moving Night" (Nancy Holder), "Sanctuary" (Kim Antieau), "Now You See Me" (Sherilee Morton), "The Fishing Village of Roebush" (Leslie Alan Horvitz), "Icarus" (Galad Elflandsson), "Ants" (Nina Kiriki Hoffman), "Nor Disregard the Humblest Voice" (Ardath Mayhar), "The Skins You Love to Touch" (Janet Fox), "Walk Home Alone" (Craig Shaw Gardner), "The Father Figure" (T. L. Parkinson), "An Ordinary Brick House" (Joseph Payne Brennan), "Overnight" (Lou Fisher), "The Last Time I Saw Harris" (Galad Elflandsson), "Tavesher" (Peter Tremayne), "Bloodwolf" (Steve Rasnic Tem). [Horror; Short stories]

1235. Green, Roger Lancelyn, ed. **A Book of Dragons.** Harmondsworth,
A   England: Puffin, 1973. 250 pp. ISBN 0-14-03-0606-4. (First published by
        Hamish Hamilton, 1970.)

Stories and poems about dragons, arranged in four sections—"Dragons of Ancient Days," "Dragons of the Dark Ages," "Dragons of Folklore," and "Dragons of Later Days" including "Jason and the Dragon of Colchis," "The Song of Orpheus" (Andrew Lang, translator), "The Boy and the Dragon," "The Dragon of Macedon," "The Fox and the Dragon," "The Dragon and the Peasant," "The Dragon's Egg," "Dragons and Elephants," "Sigurd the Dragon-Slayer," "Beowolf and the Dragon," "Ragnar Shaggy-Legs and the Dragons," "An Adventure of Digenes the Borderer," "The Red Dragon of Wales," "Sir Tristram in Ireland," "Sir Lancelot and the Dragon" (Sir Thomas Malory), "St. George and the Dragon," "The Mummers' Play," "Sir John Maundeville's Dragon" (Jean D'Outremeuse), "The Dragons of Rhodes, Lucerne, and Somerset," "The Laidly Worm" (Joseph Jacobs), "The Lambton Work" (Joseph Jacobs), "The Little Bull-Calf" (Joseph Jacobs), "The Dragon and His Grand-mother" (Mary Sellar), "The Dragon of the North," "The Master Thief and the Dragon," "Stam Bolovan and the Dragon," "The Prince and the Dragon," "The Cock and the Dragon," "The Chinese Dragons," "The Red Cross Knight and the Dragon" (Edmund Spenser), "The Shepherd of the Giant Mountains" (M. B. Smedley after Fouque), "Jabberwocky" (Lewis Carroll), "The Lady Dragonissa" (Andrew Lang), "The Fiery Dragon" (E. Nesbit), "The Dragon at Hide-and-Seek"

(G. K. Chesterton), "Conrad and the Dragon" (L. P. Hartley), "The Hoard" (J. R. R. Tolkien), "The Dragon Speaks" (C. S. Lewis), "Epilogue" (St. John the Divine). [Dragons; Short stories]

1236. Greenberg, Martin H., ed. **Mummy Stories.** New York: Ballantine,
C   1990. 225 pp. ISBN 0-345-36354-X.

Those mysterious shrouded figures from the distant past bring special shivers, as shown in "Masque" (Ed Gorman), "Lot No. 249" (Sir Arthur Conan Doyle), "Bones" (Donald A. Wollheim), "Monkeys" (E. F. Benson), "Asleep on the Job" (Scott Parson), "Remains to Be Seen" (Sharyn McCrumb), "The Man in Crescent Terrace" (Seabury Quinn), "Some Words with a Mummy" (Edgar Allan Poe), "Beetles" (Tarleton Fiske), "The Weekend Magus" (Edward D. Hoch), "The Curse of Amen-Ra" (Victor Rousseau), "Mummy No. 50" (D. R. Meredith), "The Eyes of the Mummy" (Robert Bloch), "Uncle Jack Eats a Mummy" (Alan Robbins). [Mummies; Short stories]

1237. Greenberg, Martin H., and Rosalind M. Greenberg, eds. **Phantoms.** New
C   York: DAW, 1989. 270 pp. ISBN 0-88677-348-2.

Stories of haunting mysterious figures, including "The Opera of the Phantom" (Edward Wellen), "The Phantom of the Soap Opera" (Henry Slesar), "The Other Phantom" (Edward D. Hoch), "Dark Muse" (Daniel Ransom), "Too Hideous to be Played" (J. N. Williamson), "The Final Threshold" (K. Marie Ramsland), "Marian's Song" (James Kisner), "The Light of Her Smile" (Karen Haber), "Time-Tracker" (Barry N. Malzberg), "Dark Angel" (Gary Alan Ruse), "The Unmasking" (Steve Rasnic Tem), "The Grotto" (Thomas Millstead), "Comfort the Lonely Light" (Gary A. Braunbeck). [Ghosts; Short stories]

1238. Greenberg, Martin Harry, Richard Matheson, and Charles G. Waugh,
C   eds. **The Twilight Zone: The Original Stories.** New York: Avon, 1985.
       550 pp. ISBN 0-380-89601-X.

Tales from the popular television series written by authors other than Rod Serling (see entry 931). Movie versions: See entry 96. Contents include "Preface" (Carol Serling), "Introduction" (Richard Matheson), "One for the Angels" (Anne Serling-Sutton), "Perchance to Dream" (Charles Beaumont), "Disappearing Act" (Richard Matheson), "Time Enough at Last" (Lynn A. Venable), "What You Need" (Lewis Padgett), "Third from the Sun" (Richard Matheson), "Elegy" (Charles Beaumont), "It's a *Good* Life" (Jerome Bixby), "The Valley Was Still" (Manly Wade Wellman), "The Jungle" (Charles Beaumont), "To Serve Man" (Damon Knight), "Little Girl Lost" (Richard Matheson), "Four O'Clock" (Price Day), "I Sing the Body Electric!" (Ray Bradbury), "The Changing of the Guard" (Anne Serling-Sutton), "In His Image" (Charles Beaumont), "Mute" (Richard Matheson), "Death Ship" (Richard Matheson), "The Devil, You Say?" (Charles Beaumont), "Steel" (Richard Matheson), "Nightmare at 20,000 Feet" (Richard Matheson), "The Old Man" (Henry Slesar), "The Self-Improvement of Salvadore Ross" (Henry Slesar), "The Beautiful People" (Charles Beaumont), "Long Distance Call" (Richard Matheson), "An Occurrence at Owl Creek Bridge" (Ambrose Bierce). [Horror; Short stories]

1239. Greenberg, Martin H., and Charles G. Waugh, eds. **Cults of Horror.**
C   New York: DAW, 1990. 350 pp. ISBN 0-88677-437-3.

A primary purpose of cults through the ages has been to take advantage of the belief that great power can be derived through the concentration of individual wills, as illustrated in "The Feast of Saint Dionysus" (Robert Silverberg), "Devils in The Dust" (Arthur J. Burks), "The Questing Tycoon" (Leslie Charteris), "The Peacemaker" (Gardner Dozois), "The Legend of Gray Mountain" (Emily Katharine Harris), "Sword for a Sinner" (Edward D. Hoch), "The Shaker Revival" (Gerald Jonas), "The Red One" (Jack London), "The House of Eld" (Robert Louis Stevenson), "Sticks" (Karl Edward Wagner), "Overkill" (Edward Wellen), "In the Abyss" (H. G. Wells), "Fear Is a Business" (Theodore Sturgeon). [Cults; Short stories]

1240. Greenberg, Martin, and Charles G. Waugh, eds. **Devil Worshippers.** New
C   York: DAW, 1990. 348 pp. ISBN 0-88677-420-9.

Stories of those who follow the powers of darkness, including "Sweet Sixteen" (Robert Bloch), "The Missing Item" (Isaac Asimov), "The Compleat Werewolf" (Anthony Boucher), "No News Today" (Cleve Cartmill), "The Night Train to Lost Valley" (August Derleth), "The Sacrifice" (Perceval Gibbon), "Young Goodman Brown" (Nathaniel Hawthorne), "The Vicar of Hell" (Edward D. Hoch), "The Words of Guru" (C. M. Kornbluth), "The Power" (Murray Leinster), "The Stranger from Kurdistan" (E. Hoffman Price), "The Globe of Memories" (Seabury Quinn), "School for the Unspeakable" (Manly Wade Wellman), "Such Nice Neighbors" (Chelsea Quinn Yarbro), "The New People" (Charles Beaumont). [The devil; Short stories]

1241. Greenberg, Martin, and Charles G. Waugh, eds. **House Shudders.** New
C   York: DAW, 1987. 332 pp. ISBN 0-88677-223-0.

Haunted houses are full of fearful stories, including "The House and the Brain" (Edward Bulwer-Lytton), "The Yellow Wallpaper" (Charlotte Perkins Gilman), "The Judge's House" (Bram Stoker), "The Rats in the Walls" (H. P. Lovecraft), "The Cat Jumps" (Elizabeth Bowen), "The Thing in the Cellar" (David H. Keller), "'Lizzie Borden Took an Axe....'" (Robert Bloch), "The Moon of Montezuma" (Cornell Woolrich), "The House in Bel Aire" (Margaret St. Clair), "The School Friend" (Robert Aickman), "One of the Dead" (William Wood), "The Bogeyman" (Stephen King), "Dark Winner" (William F. Nolan), "No Hiding Place" (Jack L. Chalker), "Teeth Marks" (Edward Bryant), "The Tearing of Greymare House" (Michael Reaves), "The Children, They Laughed So Sweetly" (Charles L. Grant). (Haunted houses; Short stories]

1242. Greenberg, Martin, and Charles G. Waugh, eds. **Vamps: An Anthology**
C   **of Female Vampire Stories.** New York: DAW, 1987. 365 pp. ISBN
       0-88677-190-0.

The ultimate seductress, the vampire, in tales including "One for the Road" (Stephen King), "She Only Goes Out at Night" (William Tenn), "Heredity" (David H. Keller), "Clarimonda" (Theophile Gautier), "The Cloak" (Robert Bloch), "For the Blood Is the Life" (F. Marion Crawford), "The Last Grave of Lill Warran" (Manly Wade Wellman), "The Girl with the Hungry Eyes" (Fritz Leiber), "Ken's Mystery" (Julian Hawthorne), "Restless Souls" (Seabury Quinn), "The Drifting Snow" (August Derleth), "When It Was Moonlight" (Manly Wade

Wellman), "Luella Miller" (Mary Wilkins Freeman), "Dress of White Silk" (Richard Matheson), "Red as Blood" (Tanith Lee), "Carmilla" (Sheridan LeFanu). [Vampires; Short stories]

1243. Haining, Peter, ed. **The Ghost's Companion: Stories of the Supernatural.**
A   Harmondsworth, England: Puffin, 1978. (First published by Victor Gollancz, 1975.)

An occult researcher and writer collects some goodies for teens, including "A School Story" (M. R. James), "The Red Lodge" (H. R. Wakefield), "The Furnished Room" (O. Henry), "A Haunted Island" (Algernon Blackwood), "My Own True Ghost Story" (Rudyard Kipling), "The Boy Who Drew Cats" (Lafcadio Hearn), "The Monstrance" (Arthur Machen), "Escort" (Daphne du Maurier), "South Sea Bubble" (Hammond Innes), "Hallowe'en for Mr. Faulkner" (August Derleth), "The Ghost" (Richard Hughes), "The Case of the Red-Headed Women" (Dennis Wheatley), "Smoke Ghost" (Fritz Leiber), "Aunt Jezebel's House" (Joan Aiken), "Fever Dream" (Ray Bradbury). [Ghosts; Short stories]

1244. Haining, Peter, ed. **The Ghouls.** New York: Stein and Day, 1971. 380
A   pp. ISBN 0-8128-8144-3.

A history of horror films that uses the stories on which the films were based to trace various themes, including "The Devil in a Convent" (Francis Oscar Mann), "The Lunatics" (Edgar Allan Poe), "Puritan Passions" (Nathaniel Hawthorne), "Phantom of the Opera" (Gaston Leroux), "The Magician" (Somerset Maugham), "Freaks" (Tod Robbins), "Most Dangerous Game" (Richard Connell), "Dracula's Daughter" (Bram Stoker), "All That Money Can Buy" (Stephen Vincent Benet), "The Body Snatcher" (Robert Louis Stevenson), "The Beast with Five Fingers" (W. F. Harvey), "The Beast from 20,000 Fathoms" (Ray Bradbury), "The Fly" (George Langelaan), "Black Sunday" (Nikolai Gogol), "Incident at Owl Creek" (Ambrose Bierce), "Monster of Terror" (H. P. Lovecraft), "The Skull" (Robert Bloch), "The Oblong Box" (Edgar Allan Poe). [Horror; Short stories]

1245. Haining, Peter, ed. **The Lucifer Society: Macabre Tales by Great Modern**
C   **Writers.** New York: Signet, 1973. 256 pp. (First published by Taplinger, 1972.)

Terrifying stories about strange happenings of a supernatural nature, such as "Man Overboard" (Sir Winston Churchill), "Timber" (John Calsworthy), "The Angry Street" (G. K. Chesterton), "The Call of Wings" (Agatha Christie), "The Cherries" (Lawrence Durrell), "A Man from Glasgow" (Somerset Maugham), "Earth to Earth" (Robert Graves), "The Grey Ones" (J. B. Priestley), "The Man Who Didn't Ask Why" (C. S. Forester), "All but Empty" (Graham Greene), "Animals or Human Beings" (Angus Wilson), "Something Strange" (Kingsley Amis), "The Post-Mortem Murder" (Sinclair Lewis), "The Dance" (F. Scott Fitzgerald), "A Rose for Emily" (William Faulkner), "The Bronze Door" (Raymond Chandler), "A Man Who Had No Eyes" (MacKinlay Kantor), "The Affair at 7 Rue de M---" (John Steinbeck), "The Snail Watcher" (Patricia Highsmith), "Inferiority Complex" (Evan Hunter), "The Terrible Answer" (Paul Gallico), "Miriam" (Truman Capote), "Exterminator" (William Burroughs), "During the Jurassic" (John Updike). [Monsters; Short stories]

1246.   Hammett, Dashiell. **Creeps by Night.** New York: Belmont, 1961. 141 pp.
C   (First published by John Day, 1931.)

Horror stories collected by the noted detective story writer, including "A Rose for Emily" (William Faulkner), "The House" (Andre Maurois), "The Spider" (Hanns Heinz Ewers), "The Witch's Vengeance" (W. B. Seabrook), "Mr. Arcularis" (Conrad Aiken), "The Strange Case of Mrs. Arkwright" (Harold Dearden), "The King of the Cats" (Stephen Vincent Benet), "Beyond the Door" (Paul Suter), "Perchance to Dream" (Michael Joyce), "A Visitor from Egypt" (Frank Belknap Long). [Horror; Short stories]

1247.   Hitchcock, Alfred, ed. **Alfred Hitchcock's Monster Museum.** New York:
A   Random House, 1965. 213 pp. ISBN 0-394-84899-3.

The "master of the macabre" selects some personal favorites, including "Introduction: A Variety of Monsters" (Alfred Hitchcock), "Slime" (Joseph Payne Brennan), "The King of the Cats" (Stephen Vincent Benet), "The Man Who Sold Rope to the Gnoles" (Idris Seabright), "Henry Martindale, Great Dane" (Miriam Allen deFord), "Shadow, Shadow on the Wall" (Theodore Sturgeon), "Doomsday Deferred" (Will F. Jenkins), "The Young One" (Jerome Bixby), "The Desrick on Yandro" (Manly Wade Wellman), "The Wheelbarrow Boy" (Richard Parker), "Homecoming" (Ray Bradbury). [Horror; Short stories]

1248.   Hitchcock, Alfred, ed. **Alfred Hitchcock's Supernatural Tales of Terror**
A   **and Suspense.** New York: Random House, 1983. 213 pp. ISBN
        0-394-85622-8.

Strange tales with mysterious elements woven into the plots, including "Attention, Suspense Fans!" (Alfred Hitchcock), "The Triumph of Death" (H. Russell Wakefield), "The Strange Valley" (T. V. Olsen), "The Christmas Spirit" (Dorothy B. Bennett), "The Bronze Door" (Raymond Chandler), "Slip Stream" (Sheila Hodgson), "The Quest for 'Blank Cleveringi'" (Patricia Highsmith), "Miss Pinkerton's Apocalypse" (Muriel Spark), "The Reunion After Three Hundred Years" (Alexis Tolstoy), "The Attic Express" (Alex Hamilton), "The Pram" (A. W. Bennett), "Mr. Ash's Studio" (H. Russell Wakefield). [Horror; Short stories]

1249.   Hitchcock, Alfred, ed. **Alfred Hitchcock's Witch's Brew.** New York:
A   Random House, 1983. 183 pp. ISBN 0-394-85911-1. (First published by
        Random House, 1977.)

A nice mixture of terrible, really nasty happenings, including "To Whet Your Appetite...." (Alfred Hitchcock), "The Wishing Well" (E. F. Benson), "That Hell-Bound Train" (Robert Bloch), "As Gay as Cheese" (Joan Aiken), "Madam Mim" (T. H. White), "Blood Money" (M. Timothy O'Keefe), "His Coat So Gay" (Sterling Lanier), "They'll Never Find You Now" (Lord Dunsany), "In the Cards" (John Collier), "Strangers in Town" (Shirley Jackson), "The Proof" (John Moore). [Horror; Short stories]

1250.   Hoopes, Ned E. **Speak of the Devil.** New York: Dell, 1967. 205 pp.
A

The Old Boy is up to his never-ending tricks in "The Devil and Tom Walker" (Washington Irving), "The Devil and Daniel Webster" (Stephen Vincent Benet), "The Painter's Bargain" (William Makepeace Thackery), "The Devil and the Old

Man" (John Masefield), "The Devil and the Deep Sea" (Rudyard Kipling), "Satan and Sam Shay" (Robert Arthur), "The Friendly Demon" (Daniel Defoe), "The Devil in the Belfry" (Edgar Allan Poe), "Young Goodman Brown" (Nathaniel Hawthorne), "The Lightning-rod Man" (Herman Melville), "The Devil" (Guy de Maupassant), "Madam Lucifer" (Richard Garnett), "The Demon Pope" (Richard Garnett), "Little St. Michael" (Laurence Housman), "The Demon Lover" (Elizabeth Bowen), "The Devil George and Rosie" (John Collier), "Dance with the Devil" (Betsy Emmons). [The devil; Short stories]

1251. Ireson, Barbara, ed. **Ghostly and Ghastly.** London: Beaver Arrow, 1977.
A   222 pp. ISBN 0-09-942710-9.
       Other anthologies by the editor: *Creepy Creatures; Fantasy Tales; Ghostly Laughter; Fearfully Frightening.*

Old and new favorites by English and American authors, such as "The Emissary" (Ray Bradbury), "The Thing in the Cellar" (David H. Keller), "A Pair of Hands" (Sir Arthur Quiller-Couch), "The House of the Nightmare" (Edward Lucas White), "Miss Jemima" (Walter de la Mare), "The Devil's Cure" (Barbara Softly), "The Earlier Service" (Margaret Irwin), "Linda" (Joan Mahe), "Billy Bates' Story" (Geoffrey Palmer and Noel Lloyd), "Remembering Lee" (Eileen Bigland), "Jack-in-the-Box" (Ray Bradbury), "The Canterville Ghost" (Oscar Wilde). [Horror; Short stories]

1252. Ireson, Barbara, ed. **Spooky Stories.** Ealing, England: Carousel, 1978- .
A

Macabre stories by women writers including these scary jewels from *Spooky Stories 6*: "Finders Keepers" (Joan Aiken), "Guess" (Philippa Pearce), "Witchcraft Unaware" (Rosemary Timperley), "The Figure" (Margaret Biggs), "Tea at Ravensburgh" (Joan Aiken), "The Empty Schoolroom" (Pamela Hansford Johnson), "The Girl in the Bedroom" (Margaret Biggs), "Can't Help Laughing" (Alison Prince). [Horror; Short stories]

1253. Jones, Stephen, ed. **The Mammoth Book of Terror.** New York: Carroll
C   & Graf, 1991. 587 pp. ISBN 0-881844-622-8.

Top contemporary horror writers provide gulps in "The Last Illusion" (Clive Barker), "Bunny Didn't Tell Us" (David J. Schow), "Murgunstrumm" (Hugh B. Cave), "The Late Shift" (Dennis Etchison), "The Horse Lord" (Lisa Tuttle), "The Jumpety-Jim" (R. Chetwynd-Hayes), "Out of Copyright" (Ramsey Campbell), "The River of Night's Dreaming" (Karl Edward Wagner), "Amber Print" (Basil Copper), "The House of the Temple" (Brian Lumley), "The Yugoslaves" (Robert Bloch), "Firstborn" (David Compton), "The Black Drama" (Manly Wade Wellman), "Crystal" (Charles Grant), "Buckets" (F. Paul Wilson), "The Satyr's Head" (David A. Riley), "Junk" (Stephen Laws), "Pig's Dinner" (Graham Masterton). [Horror; Short stories]

1254. Kahn, Joan, ed. **Some Things Strange and Sinister.** New York: Avon,
A   1973. 223 pp. ISBN 0-380-0084-9.
       Other anthologies by the editor: *Handle with Care; Frightening Stories; Some Things Dark and Dangerous.*

Some unusual stories about some very odd happenings, including "The Lamp" (Agatha Christie), "Nerves" (Guy de Maupassant), "Thus I Refute Beelzy"

(John Collier), "Keeping His Promise" (Algernon Blackwood), "The House" (Andre Maurois), "The Call of the Hand" (Louis Golding), "The Dream Woman" (W. Wilkie Collins), "The Story of the Late Mr. Elvesham" (H. G. Wells), "The Strange Occurrences Connected with Captain John Russell" (Neil Bell), "The Book" (Margaret Irwin), "Dracula's Ghost" (Bram Stoker), "The Cocoon" (John B. L. Goodwin), "The Empty Schoolroom" (Pamela Hansford Johnson), "The Ghost of Washington" (Anonymous). [Horror; Short stories]

1255.   Lansdale, Joe R., and Pat LoBrutto, eds. **Razored Saddles: Macabre**
C   **Western Tales.** New York: Avon, 1990. 285 pp. ISBN 0-380-71168-0.
        (First published by Dark Harvest, 1989.)

Terror rides through the dusty West, striking horror in the hearts of everyone in stories such as "Black Boots" (Robert R. McCammon), "Thirteen Days of Glory" (Scott Cupp), "Gold" (Lewis Shiner), "The Tenth Toe" (F. Paul Wilson), "Sedalia" (David J. Schow), "Trapline" (Ardath Mayhar), "Trail of the Chronium Bandits" (Al Sarrantonio), "Dinker's Pond" (Richard Laymon), "Stampede" (Melissa Mia Hall), "Razored Saddles" (Robert Petitt), "Empty Places" (Gary L. Raisor), "Tony Red Dog" (Neal Barrett, Jr.), "The Passing of the Western" (Howard Waldrop), "Eldon's Penitente" (Lenore Carroll), "The Job" (Joe R. Lansdale), "I'm Always Here" (Richard Christian Matheson), "'Yore Skin's Jes's Soft 'n Purty....' He Said." (Chet Williamson). [Horror; Short stories]

1256.   McCauley, Kirby, ed. **Dark Forces.** New York: Bantam, 1981. 544 pp.
C   ISBN 0-553-14801-X. London: Future, 1981. 551 pp. ISBN
        0-7088-1979-6.

Horror stories by contemporary writers who explore the corners of hell in "The Late Shift" (D. Etchison), "The Enemy" (I. B. Singer), "Dark Angel" (E. Bryant), "The Chest of Thirty-Six" (D. Grubb), "Mark Ingestre: The Customer's Tale" (R. Aickman), "Where the Summer Ends" (K. E. Wagner), "The Bingo Master" (J. C. Oates), "Children of the Kingdom" (T. E. D. Klein), "The Detective of Dreams" (G. Wolfe), "Vengeance Is" (T. Sturgeon), "The Brood" (R. Campbell), "The Whistling Well" (C. D. Simak), "The Peculiar Demesne" (R. Kirk), "Where the Stones Grow" (T. Tuttle), "The Night Before Christmas" (R. Bloch), "The Stupid Joke" (E. Gorey), "A Touch of Petulance" (R. Bradbury), "Lindsay and the Red City Blues" (J. Haldeman), "A Garden of Blackred Roses" (C. L. Grant), "Owls Hoot in the Daytime" (M. W. Wellman), "Where There's a Will" (R. Matheson and R. C. Matheson), "Traps" (G. Wilson), "The Mist" (S. King). [Horror; Short stories]

1257.   MacEwen, Mary E., ed. **Stories of Suspense.** New York: Scholastic,
A   1963. 220 pp.

Scary stories selected especially for teens, including "The Birds" (Daphne du Maurier), "Of Missing Persons" (Jack Finney), "Midnight Blue" (John Collier), "Flowers for Algernon" (Daniel Keyes), "Taste" (Roald Dahl), "Two bottles of Relish" (Lord Dunsay), "Charles" (Shirley Jackson), "Contents of the Dead Man's Pockets" (Jack Finney), "The Perfectionist" (Margaret St. Clair). [Horror; Short stories]

1258.   Martin, George R. R., ed. **Night Visions: The Hellbound Heart.** New
C   York: Berkley, 1988. 278 pp. ISBN 0-425-10707-8. (First published by
         Dark Harvest, 1986.)

A collection of frightening stories including "In the Trees" (Ramsey
Campbell), "This Time" (Ramsey Campbell), "Missed Connection" (Ramsey
Campbell), "Root Cause" (Ramsey Campbell), "Looking Out" (Ramsey
Campbell), "Bedtime Story" (Ramsey Campbell), "Beyond Words" (Ramsey
Campbell), "Riding the Nightmare" (Lisa Tuttle), "From Another Country" (Lisa
Tuttle), "The Dragon's Bride" (Lisa Tuttle), "The Hellbound Heart" (Clive
Barker). [Horror; Short stories]

1259.   Masterton, Graham, ed. **Scare Care.** New York: TOR, 1990. 400 pp.
C   ISBN 0-812-51097-6. (First published for the Scare Care Trust, 1989.)

An anthology compiled for children's charities. Stories include "Mommy"
(Kit Reed), "Things Not Seen" (James Robert Smith), "The Ferries" (Ramsey
Campbell), "Good Night, Sweet Prince" (D. W. Taylor), "Printer's Devil"
(Celeste Paul Sefranek), "Mommy and the Flies" (Bruce Boston), "The Tourists"
(John Burke), "The Wish" (Roald Dahl), "Monstrum" (J. N. Williamson),
"Breakfast" (James Herbert), "Clocks" (Darrell Schweitzer), "The Strangers"
(Steve Rasnic Tem), "Table for None" (William Relling, Jr.), "Little Miss
Muffett" (Peter Valentine Timlett), "Night Watch" (C. Dean Andersson), "The
Last Gift" (Peter Tremayne), "Manny Agonistes" (James Kisner), "Family Man"
(Jeff Gelb), "A Towpath Tale" (Giles Gordon), "Mars Will Have Blood" (Marc
Laidlaw), "My Name Is Dolly" (William F. Nolan), "The Night Gil Rhys First
Met His Love" (Alan Rodgers), "Models" (John Maclay), "Crustacean Revenge"
(Guy N. Smith), "Sarah's Song" (Roderick Hudgins), "The Avenger of Death"
(Harlan Ellison), "Cable" (Frank Coffey), "Spices of the World" (Felice Picano),
"Down to the Core" (David B. Silva), "Junk" (Stephen Laws), "The Woman in
the Wall" (John Daniel), "Loopy" (Ruth Rendell), "Time Heals" (Gary A.
Braunbeck), "David's Worm" (Brian Lumley), "The Pet Door" (Chris B. Lacher),
"By the Sea" (Charles L. Grant), "Changeling" (Graham Masterton), "In the
West Wing" (Roland Masterton). [Horror; Short stories]

1260.   Molin, Charles, ed. **Ghosts, Spooks and Spectres.** Harmondsworth,
A   England: Puffin, 1971. 185 pp. ISBN 0-14-031485-7. (First published by
         Hamish Hamilton, 1967.)

A fine selection of various kinds of terror tales to keep the reader riveted:
"Teeny-Tiny" (Anonymous), "The Signal-Man" (Charles Dickens), "The Strange
Visitor" (Anonymous), "A Ghostly Wife" (Anonymous), "Legend of Hamilton
Tighe" (Richard Bartram), "The Phantom Ship" (Captain Marryat), "The Brown
Hand" (Sir Arthur Conan Doyle), "The Ghost-Brahman" (Anonymous), "The
Ghost-Ship" (Richard Middleton), "The Water Ghost of Harrowby Hall" (John
Kendrick Bangs), "The Inexperienced Ghost" (H. G. Wells), "The Buggane and
the Tailor" (Dora Broome), "Laura" (Saki), "The Betrayal of Nance" (R.
Blakeborough), "The Ghost Who Was Afraid of Being Bagged" (Anonymous),
"The Beast with Five Fingers" (W. F. Harvey), "The Night the Ghost Got In"
(James Thurber), "The Story of Glam" (Andrew Lang). [Ghosts; Short stories]

1261. Monteleone, Thomas F., ed. **Borderlands.** New York: Avon, 1990. 334
C   pp. ISBN 0-380-75924-1.

Previously unpublished stories selected by an accomplished writer, including "The Calling" (David B. Silva), "Scartaris, June 28th" (Harlan Ellison), "Glass Eyes" (Nancy Holder), "The Grass of Remembrance" (John DeChancie), "On the Nightmare Express" (Francis J. Matozzo), "The Pounding Room" (Bentley Little), "Peeling It Off" (Darrell Schweitzer), "The Raw and the Cooked" (Michael Green), "His Mouth Will Taste of Wormwood" (Poppy Z. Brite), "Oh, What a Swell Guy Am I" (Jeffrey Osier), "Delia and the Dinner Party" (John Shirley), "Suicide Note" (Lee Moler), "Stillborn" (Nina Kiriki Hoffman), "Ladder" (T. E. D. Klein), "Muscae Volitantes" (Chet Williamson), "The Man in the Long Black Sedan" (Ed Gorman), "His Frozen Heart" (Jack Hunter Daves, Jr.), "Evelyn Grace" (Thomas Tessier), "By the Light of the Silvery Moon" (Les Daniels), "A Younger Woman" (John Maclay), "But You'll Never Follow Me" (Karl Edward Wagner), "Stephen" (Elizabeth Massie), "Alexandra" (Charles L. Grant), "The Good Book" (G. Wayne Miller), "By Bizarre Hands" (Joe R. Lansdale). [Horror; Short stories]

1262. Morris, Janet, ed. **Rebels in Hell.** New York: Baen, 1986. 308 pp. ISBN
C   0-621-65577-9.

The bad never stop trying; so what do they have to lose, as shown in "Undercover Agent" (Chris Morris), "Hell's Gate" (Bill Kerby), "Gilgamesh in the Outback" (Robert Silverberg), "Marking Time" (C. J. Cherryh), "Table with a View" (Nancy Asire), "There Are No Fighter Pilots down in Hell" (Martin Caidin), "'Cause I Served My Time in Hell" (David Drake), "Monday Morning" (C. J. Cherryh), "Graveyard Shift" (Janet Morris). [Heaven and hell; Short stories]

1263. Moskowitz, Sam, and Alden H. Norton, eds. **Ghostly by Gaslight.** New
C   York: Pyramid, 1971. 223 pp. ISBN 0-515-2416-7.

Unusual stories hard to locate elsewhere. Included are "The Friend of Death" (Pedro Antonio de Alarcon), "Who Knows?" (Guy de Maupassant), "The Story of a Ghost" (Violet Hunt), "The Spider of Guyana" (Erckmann-Chatrian), "The Moon-Slave" (Barry Pain), "The Spell of the Sword" (Frank Aubrey), "The Man Who Lived Backwards" (Allen Upward), "The God Pan" (Huan Mee), "The Mystery of the Bronze Statue" (W. B. Sutton), "Doctor Armstrong" (D. L. B. S.), "The Enchanted City" (Hubert Murray). [Ghosts; Short stories]

1264. Norton, Alden H., ed. **Masters of Horror.** New York: Berkley, 1968.
C   192 pp.

Weird and terrible tales, including "The Were-Wolf" (Clemence Housman), "Dracula's Guest" (Bram Stoker), "The Transformation" (Mary Wollstonecraft Shelley), "The Yellow Sign" (Robert W. Chambers), "The Women of the Wood" (A. Merritt), "Blind Man's Bluff" (H. R. Wakefield), "A Piece of Linoleum" (David H. Keller), "Before I Wake" (Henry Kuttner), "The Candy Skull" (Ray Bradbury). [Horror; Short stories]

1265.   Owen, Betty, ed. **Nine Strange Stories.** New York: Scholastic, 1974.
C   155 pp.

Classic chilly stories, including "The Rocking-Horse Winner" (D. H. Lawrence), "Heartburn" (Hortense Calisher), "The Snail-Watcher" (Patricia Highsmith), "Manuscript Found in a Police State" (Brian Aldiss), "The Man Who Sold Rope to the Gnoles" (Idris Seabright), "The Mark of the Beast" (Rudyard Kipling), "The Summer People" (Shirley Jackson), "The Leopard Man's Story" (Jack London), "The Garden of Forking Paths" (Jorge Luis Borges). [Horror; Short stories]

1266.   Owen, Betty, ed. **Stories of the Supernatural.** New York: Scholastic,
A   1967. 224 pp.

Good stories to make some good shivers, including "The Willows" (Algernon Blackwood), "The Vertical Ladder" (William Sansom), "The Dancing Doll" (Gerald Kersh), "Sir Dominick's Bargain" (J. Sheridan Le Fanu), "The Cocoon" (John B. L. Goodwin), "The Madwoman" (Gerald Kersh), "The Fly" (George Langelaan). [Horror; Short stories]

1267.   **The [numbered] Pan Book of Horror Stories.** London: Pan, 1959- .
A   Over twenty collections have been published to date.

These stories may seem gentle at first, but when you think about them.... Contents of book 13: "The Man Whose Nose Was Too Big" (Alan Hillery), "Flame!" (Norman Kaufman), "The Twins" (Harry Turner), "The Swans" (Carl Thomson), "The Revenge" (David Farrer), "Window Watcher" (Dulcie Gray), "Spinalonga" (John Ware), "Aggrophobia" (L. Micallef), "Awake, Sleeping Tigress" (Norman Kaufman), "The Dead End" (David Case). [Horror; Short stories]

1268.   Parry, Michel, ed. **Ghostbreakers.** London: Dragon Grafton, 1986.
B   128 pp. ISBN 0-583-30913-5. (First published by Grafton, 1985.)

A very enjoyable collection of ghost stories, including "The Gateway of the Monster" (William Hope Hodgson), "The Story of Konnor Old House" (E. & H. Heron), "The Warder of the Door" (L. T. Meade and Robert Eustace), "The Sussex Vampire" (Arthur Conan Doyle), "The Story of Yand Manor House" (E. & H. Heron), "The Horse of the Invisible" (William Hope Hodgson). [Ghosts; Short stories]

1269.   Parry, Michel, ed. **The Rivals of Frankenstein.** London: Corgi, 1977.
A   222 pp. ISBN 0-552-10465-5.

Stories of monsters less well known than Frankenstein's beast, but none the less awesome, including "The Colossus of Ylourgne" (Clark Ashton Smith), "The Last of the Daubeny-Fitzalans" (Arnold Harvey), "The Dancing Partner" (Jerome K. Jerome), "Moxon's Master" (Ambrose Bierce), "Dr. Karnstein's Creation" (Donald F. Glut), "Almost Human" (Robert Bloch), "Count Szolnok's Robots" (D. Scott-Moncrieff), "Herbert West, Reanimator" (H. P. Lovecraft), "Pithecanthropus Rejectus" (Manly Wade Wellman), "The Dead Man" (Fritz Leiber), "The Iron Man" (Eando Binder). [Monsters; Science gone wrong; Short stories]

1270.   Pattrick, William, ed. **Duel**. London: Star, 1987. 223 pp. ISBN 0-352-
C   32164-4.
        Movie versions: *Duel*, 1971. Director: Stephen Spielberg. Stars: Dennis
        Weaver, Tim Herbert, Charles Peel, and Eddie Firestone. *Maximum*
        Overdrive ("Trucks"), 1986. Director: Stephen King. Stars: Emilio
        Estevez, Pat Hingle, Laura Harrington, and Yeardley Smith.

        Horror stories of the open road, including "The Car with the Green Lights"
(William LeQueux), "The Dust-Cloud" (E. F. Benson), "How It Happened" (Sir
Arthur Conan Doyle), "The Last Trip" (Archie Binns), "The Demon Lover"
(Elizabeth Bowen), "Jaywalkers" (H. Russell Wakefield), "The Ghost of the
Model T" (Betsy Emmons), "The Ghost Car" (Ken Batten), "New Corner" (L. T.
C. Rolt), "'Just like Wild Bob'" (William F. Nolan), "Auto Suggestion" (Charles
Beaumont), "Duel" (Richard Matheson), "Second Chance" (Jack Finney),
"Trucks" (Stephen King), "The Hitch-Hiker" (Roald Dahl). [Horror; Short
stories]

1271.   Pattrick, William, ed. **Mysterious Sea Stories**. New York: Dell, 1987.
C   246 pp. ISBN 0-440-16088-X. (First published by Salem House, 1985.)

        Scary and mysterious tales of the ocean deep, including "Ms. Found in a
Bottle" (Edgar Allan Poe), "The Legend of the Bell Rock" (Captain Frederick
Marryat), "Hood's Isle and the Hermit Oberlus" (Herman Melville), "A
Bewitched Ship" (W. Clark Russell), "J. Habakuk Jephson's Statement" (Sir
Arthur Conan Doyle), "The Benevolent Ghost and Captain Lowrie" (Richard
Sale), "Make Westing" (Jack London), "The Black Mate" (Joseph Conrad), "A
Matter of Fact" (Rudyard Kipling), "The Finding of the Graiken" (William Hope
Hodgson), "Davy Jones's Gift" (John Masefield), "In the Abyss" (H. G. Wells),
"Undersea Guardians" (Ray Bradbury), "The Turning of the Tide" (C. S.
Forester). [Horror; Short stories]

1272.   **Playboy's Stories of the Sinister & Strange**. Chicago: Playboy Press,
C   1969. 217 pp.

        Selections from the pages of *Playboy* magazine by its editors include "The
Mannichon Solution" (Irwin Shaw), "The Dark Music" (Charles Beaumont),
"Somewhere Not Far From Here" (Gerald Kersh), "The Investor" (Bruce Jay
Friedman), "Ripples" (Ray Russell), "The Dispatcher" (Gerald Green), "Wise
Child" (John Wyndhand), "Welcome to the Monkey House" (Kurt Vonnegut,
Jr.), "Room 312" (G. L. Tassone), "The Golden Frog" (Ken W. Purdy), "The
Annex" (John D. Mac Donald). [Horror; Short stories]

1273.   Pronzini, Bill, ed. **Midnight Specials**. New York: Avon, 1987. 261 pp.
C   ISBN 0-380-01941-8. (First published by Bobbs-Merrill, 1977.)
        Other anthologies by the editor: *Dark Sins, Dark Dreams; Tricks and*
        Treats.

        Train stories involving the macabre and mysterious, including "The Signal-
Man" (Charles Dickens), "The Shooting of Curly Dan" (John Lutz), "The
Invalid's Story" (Mark Twain), "A Journey" (Edith Wharton), "The Problem of
the Locked Caboose" (Edward D. Hoch), "Midnight Express" (Alfred Noyes),
"Faith, Hope and Charity" (Irvin S. Cobb), "Dead Man" (James M. Cain), "The
Phantom of the Subway" (Cornell Woolrich), "The Man on B-17" (August
Derleth), "The Three Good Witnesses" (Harold Lamb), "Snowball in July"

(Ellery Queen), "All of God's Children Got Shoes" (Howard Schoenfeld), "The Sound of Murder" (William P. McGivern), "The Train" (Charles Beaumont), "Hell-Bound Train" (Robert Bloch), "Inspector Maigret Deduces" (Georges Simenon), "Sweet Fever" (Bill Pronzini), "The Man Who Loved the Midnight Lady" (Barry N. Malzberg). [Horror; Short stories]

1274.   Pronzini, Bill, ed. **Werewolf!** New York: Perennial, 1980. 229 pp. ISBN
C   0-06-080504-8. (First published by Arbor House, 1979.)

That furry beastie roams in many locations in these stories: "Loups-Garous" (Avram Davidson), "The Were-Wolf" (Clemence Housman), "The Wolf" (Guy de Maupassant), "The Mark of the Beast" (Rudyard Kipling), "Dracula's Guest" (Bram Stoker), "Gabriel-Ernest" (Saki), "There Shall Be No Darkness" (James Blish), "Nightshapes" (Barry N. Malzberg), "The Hound" (Fritz Leiber), "Wolves Don't Cry" (Bruce Elliott), "Lila the Werewolf" (Peter S. Beagle), "A Prophecy of Monsters" (Clark Ashton Smith), "Full Sun" (Brian W. Aldiss). [Short stories; Werewolves]

1275.   Ptacek, Kathryn, ed. **Women of Darkness.** New York: TOR, 1988. 306
C   pp. ISBN 0-812-52443-8.

Stories by women horror writers, including "Baby" (Kit Reed), "Ransom Cowl Walks the Road" (Nancy Varian Berberick), "True Love" (Patricia Russo), "In the Shadows of My Fear" (Joan Vander Puttin), "The Spirit Cabinet" (Lisa Tuttle), "Hooked on Buzzer" (Elizabeth Massie), "Little Maid Lost" (Rivka Jacobs), "Mother Calls but I Do Not Answer" (Rachel Cosgrove Payes), "Nobody Lives There Now. Nothing Happens." (Carol Orlock), "The Baku" (Lucy Taylor), "The Devil's Rose" (Tanith Lee), "Midnight Madness" (Wendy Webb), "Monster McGill" (Cary G. Osborn), "Aspen Graffiti" (Melanie Tem), "Sister" (Wennicke Eide Cox), "Samba Sentado" (Karen Haber), "When Thunder Walks" (Conda V. Douglas), "Slide Number Seven" (Sharon Epperson), "The Unloved" (Melissa Mia Hall), "Cannibal Cats Come Out Tonight" (Nancy Holder). [Horror; Short stories]

1276.   Russell, Jean, ed. **The Magnet Book of Sinister Stories.** London: Mag-
B   net, 1986. 127 pp. ISBN 0-416-46120-4. (First published by Methuen, 1982.)

A selection of very unsettling tales, such as "The Dollmaker" (Adele Geras), "Dangleboots and the Day After Tomorrow" (Dennis Hamley), "Black Dog" (Joan Phipson), "Miss Hooting's Legacy" (Joan Aiken), "Spring-Helled Jack" (Gwen Grant), "The Parrot" (Vivien Alcock), "Welcome Yule" (Jan Mark), "Mister Mushrooms" (Robert Swindells), "The Passing of Puddy" (Gene Kemp), "Remember Remember the Fourth of November" (Marjorie Darke), "The Pelican" (Ann Pilling), "The Book of the Black Arts" (Patricia Miles). [Horror; Short stories]

1277.   Russell, Jean, ed. **The Magnet Book of Strange Tales.** London: Mag-
B   net, 1981. 144 pp. ISBN 0-416-21190-9. (First published by Methuen, 1980.)

Weird and uncanny happenings that couldn't really happen — or could they? Included are "Moths" (Robert Swindells), "The Birthday Present" (Marjorie Darke), "Just a Guess" (Dick King-Smith), "The Demon Kite" (Farrukh Dhondy),

"The Boy's Story" (Catherine Storr), "When the Grey Horses Trot" (Gareth Lovett Jones), "Exit" (Patricia Miles), "Mr. Hornet and Nellie Maggs" (Alison Morgan), "Billy's Hand" (Adele Geras), "She Was Afraid of Upstairs" (Joan Aiken), "A Quiet Yippee" (Chris Powling), "The Shadow" (Joan Phipson), "The Whistling Boy" (John Gordon), "The Promise" (Tony Ross). [Horror; Short stories]

1278. Ryan, Alan, ed. **Halloween Horrors.** New York: Charter, 1987. 245 pp.
C ISBN 0-441-31607-7.

Stories about that favorite day of all are collected here, including "He'll Come Knocking at Your Door" (Robert R. McCammon), "Eyes" (Charles L. Grant), "The Nixon Mask" (Whitley Strieber), "The Samhain Feis" (Peter Tremayne), "Trickster" (Steve Rasnic Tem), "Miss Mack" (Michael McDowell), "Hollow Eyes" (Guy N. Smith), "The Halloween House" (Alan Ryan), "Three Faces of the Night"(Craig Shaw Garner), "Pumpkin" (Bill Pronzini), "Lover in the Wildwood" (Frank Belknap Long), "Apples" (Ramsey Campbell), "Pranks" (Robert Bloch). [Halloween; Short stories]

1279. Ryan, Alan, ed. **Haunting Women.** New York: Avon, 1988. 210 pp.
C ISBN 0-380-89881-0.

Horror stories by women writers, including "The Renegade" (Shirley Jackson), "The Villa Désirée" (May Sinclair), "The House of the Famous Poet" (Muriel Spark), "Loopy" (Ruth Rendell), "The Yellow Wallpaper" (Charlotte Perkins Gilman), "The Foghorn" (Gertrude Atherton), "The Ghost" (Mrs. Henry Wood), "Simon's Wife" (Tanith Lee), "Hell on Both Sides of the Gate" (Rosemary Timperley), "The Shadowy Third" (Ellen Glasgow), "The Sound of the River" (Jean Rhys), "Robbie" (Mary Danby), "Heartburn" (Hortense Calisher), "The Cloak" (Isak Dinesen). [Horror; Short stories]

1280. Salmonson, Jessica Amanda, ed. **Tales by Moonlight.** New York: TOR,
C 1983. 286 pp. ISBN 0-812-52552-3.

An uneven collection with some really fine stories such as "Introduction" (Stephen King), "The Nocturnal Visitor" (Dale C. Donaldson), "Flames" (Jeffrey Lant), "An Egg for Ava" (Richard Lee-Fulgham), "See the Station Master" (George Florance-Guthridge), "A Tulip for Eulie" (Austelle Pool), "Cobwebs" (Jody Scott), "The Toymaker and the Musicrafter" (Phyllis Ann Karr), "Witches" (Janet Fox), "A Night Out" (Nina Kiriki Hoffman), "Jaborandi Jazz" (Gordon Linzner), "A Wine of Heart's Desire" (Ron Nance), "Spring Conditions" (Eileen Gunn), "The Sky Came Down to Earth" (Steve Rasnic Tem), "Joan" (Mary Ann Allen), "The Night of the Red, Red Moon" (Elinor Busby), "Toyman's Name" (Phyllis Ann Karr), "Dog Killer" (William H. Green), "The Mourning After" (Bruce McDonald), "The Hill Is No Longer There" (John D. Berry), "The Inhabitant of the Pond" (Linda Thornton). [Horror; Short stories]

1281. Salmonson, Jessica Amanda. **What Did Miss Darrington See?** New York:
C The Feminist Press, 1989. 263 pp. ISBN 1-55861-006-5.

Little-known stories of the supernatural by women writers, including "The Immortal" (Ellen Glasgow), "The Long Chamber" (Olivia Howard Dunbar), "A Ghost Story" (Ada Trevanion), "Luella Miller" (Mary E. Wilkins Freeman), "What Did Miss Darrington See?" (Emma B. Cobb), "La Femme Noir" (Anna

Maria Hall), "A Friend in Need" (Lisa Tuttle), "Attachment" (Phyllis Eisenstein), "Dreaming the Sky Down" (Barbara Burford), "The Sixth Canvasser" (Inex Haynes Irwin), "An Unborn Visitant" (Vita Sackville-West), "Tamar" (Lady Eleanor Smith), "There and Here" (Alice Brown), "The Substitute" (Georgia Wood Pangborn), "The Teacher" (Luisa Valenzuela), "The Ghost" (Anne Sexton), "Three Dreams in a Desert" (Olive Schreiner), "The Fall" (Armonia Somers), "Pandora Pandaemonia" (Jules Faye), "The Doll" (Vernon Lee), "The Debutante" (Leonora Carrington), "The Readjustment" (Mary Austin), "Clay-Shuttered Doors" (Helen R. Hull), "Since I Died" (Elizabeth Stuart Phelps), "The Little Dirty Girl" (Joanna Russ), "Envoi: For Emily D." [Horror; Short stories]

1282. Sammon, Paul M., ed. **Splatterpunks.** New York: St. Martin's Press,
C   1990. 346 pp. ISBN 0-312-04581-6.

No-holds-barred explosions of nastiness, including "Night They Missed the Horror Show" (Joe R. Lansdale), "The Midnight Meat Train" (Clive Barker), "Film at Eleven" (John Skipp), "Red" (Richard Christian Matheson), "A Life in the Cinema" (Mick Garris), "Less Than Zombie" (Douglas E. Winter), "Rapid Transit" (Wayne Allen Sallee), "While She Was Out" (Edward Bryant), "Meathouse Man" (George R. R. Martin), "Reunion Moon" (Rex Miller), "I Spit in Your Face: Films that Bite" (Chas. Balun), "Freaktent" (Nancy A. Collins), "Crucifax Autumn: Chapter 18 – The Censored Chapter" (Ray Garton), "Goosebumps" (Richard Christian Matheson), "Goodbye, Dark Love" (Roberta Lannes), "Full Throttle" (Philip Nutman), "City of Angels" (J. S. Russell), "Outlaws" (Paul M. Sammon). [Horror; Short stories]

1283. Saunders, Elizabeth A. **When the Black Lotus Blooms.** Atlanta: Unname-
C   able Press, 1990. 322 pp. ISBN 0-934227-05-5.

Brooding stories and poems, including "Ninfea" (Kay Marie Porterfield), "The Rift in Autumn" (Thomas E. Fuller), "A Scene Like Silver" (Susan MacTabert), "The Grey Smudge" (Joseph Payne Brennan), "A Case Study" (Donald M. Hassler), "Marine Passage" (Jane Yolen), "Skeleton Key" (Scott H. Urban), "The Pursuit of Happiness" (Michael N. Langford), "Siren Strains" (Jame A. Riley), "Door Closing" (Wendy Webb), "Midnight Visit" (Carlton Grindle), "The Lon Chaney Factory" (Brad Linaweaver), "Ballad of the Faithful Wife" (Millea Kenin), "Marker" (Joseph Payne Brennan), "Dancer in the Dark" (Thomas E. Fuller), "Strange High Armadillo in the Mist" (Gerald W. Page), "Dream" (Bobby G. Warner), "Drifting Atoms" (Mary Elizabeth Counselman), "Dream People" (John Grey), "Late Bloomer" (Janet Fox), "A Trick of the Night" (S. K. Epperson), "On the Blue Guillotine" (Gregory Nicoll), "Red Rover" (Glen Egbert), "The Wind Has Teeth" (G. Warlock Vance and Scott H. Urban), "Graveyards in the Dark" (S. K. Epperson), "For Ray" (Michael N. Langford), "Pinto Rider" (Charles L. Grant), "Snow Dove" (Brad Strickland), "Carousel" (S. K. Epperson), "The Window" (Elizabeth Conklin), "Armada Moon" (Thomas E. Fuller), "Waygift" (Gerald W. Page), "La Belle Dame" (Jack Massa), "Precurser" (Donald M. Hassler), "The Egret" (Michael Bishop), "Grey Men" (Joseph Payne Brennan), "Gothic" (Jame A. Riley), "Not by Blood Alone" (Millea Kenin), "Moving" (James Robert Smith). [Horror; Short stories]

1284.	Schiff, Stuart David, ed. **Whispers IV.** New York: Jove, 1987. 240 pp.
C	ISBN 0-515-09482-X. (First published by Doubleday, 1983.)

Some of the best stories culled from the pages of *Whispers* magazine, including "A Night on the Docks" (Freff), "Into Whose Hands" (Karl Edward Wagner), "Out of Copyright" (Ramsey Campbell), "Elle est Trois. (La Mort)" (Tanith Lee), "Come to the Party" (Frances Garfield), "The Warrior Who Did Not Know Fear" (Gerald W. Page), "Fair Trade" (William F. Nolan), "I Never Could Say Goodbye" (Charles L. Grant), "The Devil You Say!" (Lawrence Treat), "Diploma Time" (Frank Belknap Long), "Tell Us about the Rats, Grandpa" (Stephen Kleinhen), "What Say the Frogs Now, Jenny?" (Hugh B. Cave), "The Beholder" (Richard Christian Matheson), "Creative Coverage, Inc." (Michael Shea), "The Dancer in the Flames" (David Drake), "The Reflex-Man in Whinnymuir Close" (Russell Kirk). [Horror; Short stories]

1285.	Schmidt, Stanley, ed. **Unknown.** New York: Baen, 1988. 304 pp. ISBN
C	0-671-69785-4.

Collected tales from a noted fantasy pulp, including "The Compleat Werewolf" (Anthony Boucher), "The Coppersmith" (Lester del Rey), "A God in a Garden" (Theodore Sturgeon), "Even the Angels" (Malcolm Jameson), "Smoke Ghost" (Fritz Leiber), "Nothing in the Rules" (L. Sprague de Camp), "A Good Knight's Work" (Robert Bloch), "The Devil We Know" (Henry Kuttner), "The Angelic Angleworm" (Frederic Brown). [Horror; Short stories]

1286.	Schow, David J., ed. **Silver Scream.** New York: TOR, 1988. 500 pp.
C	ISBN 0-812-52555-8.

Movies as a theme for horror, including "Introduction" (Tobe Hooper), "Preflash" (John M. Ford), "Cuts" (F. Paul Wilson), "The Movie People" (Robert Bloch), "Sinema" (Ray Garton), "Son of Celluloid" (Clive Barker), "The Answer Tree" (Steven R. Boyett), "Night They Missed the Horror Show" (Joe R. Lansdale), "More Sinned Against" (Karl Edward Wagner), "Return of the Neon Fireball" (Chet Williamson), "Night Calls the Green Falcon" (Robert R. McCammon), "Bargain Cinema" (Jay Sheckley), "Lifecast" (Craig Spector), "Double Feature/Sirens and Hell" (Richard Christian Matheson), "A Life in the Cinema" (Mick Garris), "Splatter: A Cautionary Tale" (Douglas E. Winter), "Film at Eleven" (John Skipp), "The Show Goes On" (Ramsey Campbell), "The Cutter" (Edward Bryant), "Pilgrims to the Cathedral" (Mark Arnold), "Endsticks" (David J. Schow). [Horror; Short stories]

1287.	Serling, Rod, ed. **Triple W: Witches, Warlocks and Werewolves.** New
C	York: Bantam, 1963. 181 pp. SBN 553-07142-075.

A collection of stories from "The Twilight Zone", including "The Amulet" (Gordon Dickson), "The Story of Sidi Nonman" (Anonymous), "The Final Ingredient" (Jack Sharkey), "Blind Alley" (Malcolm Jameson), "Young Goodman Brown" (Nathaniel Hawthorne), "The Chestnut Beads" (Jane Roberts), "Hatchery of Dreams" (Fritz Leiber), "The Mark of the Beast" (Rudyard Kipling), "And Not Quite Human" (Joe L. Hensley), "Wolves Don't Cry" (Bruce Elliott), "The Black Retriever" (Charles G. Finney), "Witch Trials and the Law" (Charles Mackay). [Werewolves; Witches; Short stories]

1288. Shwartz, Susan, ed. **Arabesques: More Tales of the Arabian Nights.**
C   New York: Avon, 1988. 258 pp. ISBN 0-380-75319-7.
      Sequels: *Arabesques II.*

Wonderful new stories full of genies, giants, and flying carpets, including "The Tale of the Djinni and the Sisters" (Larry Niven), "The Tale of the Rose and the Nightingale (And What Came of It)" (Gene Wolfe), "Foolish, Wicked, Clever and Kind" (Tanith Lee), "Memoirs of a Bottle Djinni" (Jane Yolen), "An Eye for the Ladies" (Esther M. Friesner), "Truthseeker" (Nancy Springer), "The Dowery of the Rag Picker's Daughter" (Andrew Norton), "Kehailan" (Judith Tarr), "The Elephant In-Law" (Elizabeth Scarborough), "The King Who Was Summoned to Damascus" (Melissa Scott), "The Truthsayer" (William R. Forstschen), "The Banner of Kaviyan" (Harry Turtledove), "The Lovesick Simurgh" (M. J. Engh). [Legends, Arabian; Short stories]

1289. Shepard, Leslie, ed. **The Dracula Book of Great Horror Stories.** Secaucus,
C   N.J.: Citadel, 1981. 288 pp. ISBN 0-8065-0765-9.
      Other anthologies by the editor: *The Dracula Book of Great Vampire Stories.*

Classic tales by the all-time great writers, such as "Captain Murderer" (Charles Dickens), "The Pit and the Pendulum" (Edgar Allan Poe), "The Haunted and the Haunters: or, The House and the Brain" (Sir Edward Bulwer-Lytton), "The Inn" (Guy de Maupassant), "The Dancing Partner" (Jerome K. Jerome), "The Cone" (H. G. Wells), "The Monkey's Paw" (W. W. Jacobs), "Caterpillars" (E. F. Benson), "The Judge's House" (Bram Stoker), "The Voice in the Night" (W. H. Hodgson), "The Festival" (H. P. Lovecraft), "County Magnus" (M. R. James), "The Travelling Grave" (L. P. Hartley), "The Wendigo" (A. Blackwood). [Horror; Short stories]

1290. Singer, Kurt, ed. **The [numbered] Target Book of Horror.** London:
A   Target, 1983?- .

Timeless tales of terror and fear including these in book 2 of the series: "The Man Who Cried Wolf!" (Robert Bloch), "The Nameless Mummy" (Arlton Eadie), "The Man They Couldn't Hang" (Judge Marcus Kavanagh), "Legal Rites" (Isaac Asimov and James MacCreagh), "The Devil and Sharon Tate" (Michael Ballentine), "The Exorcist—New York Style" (Kurt and Jane Singer), "Not According to Dante" (Malcolm Jameson).
     Contents of book 4 are "The Haunted and the Haunters" (Lord Lytton), "The 'Ouanga' Charm" (W. B. Seabrook), "Green Jewel of Death" (Princess Catherine Radziwill), "The Phantom Coach" (Elma B. Edwards), "Ghosts Come to Hell" (Pat Scholer), "Wages of Envy" (Mark Bartholomeusz), "White Lady of the Hohenzollerns" (Clyde Clark). [Horror; Short stories]

1291. Skipp, John, and Craig Spector, eds. **Book of the Dead.** New York:
C   Bantam, 1989. 390 pp. ISBN 0-553-27998-X.

Two masters of splatterpunk have collected some ghoulish tales including "Blossom" (Chan McConnell), "Mess Hall" (Richard Laymon), "It Helps If You Sing" (Ramsey Campbell), "Home Delivery" (Stephen King), "Wet Work" (Philip Nutman), "A Sad Last Love at the Diner of the Damned" (Edward Bryant), "Bodies and Heads" (Steve Rasnic Tem), "Choices" (Glen Vasey), "The Good Parts" (Les Daniels), "Less Than Zombie" (Douglas E. Winter), "Like Pavlov's

Dogs" (Steven R. Boyett), "Saxophone" (Nicholas Royle), "On the Far Side of the Cadillac Desert with Dead Folks" (Joe R. Lansdale), "Dead Giveaway" (Brian Hodge), "Jerry's Kids Meet Wormboy" (David J. Schow), "Eat Me" (Robert R. McCammon). [Zombies; Short stories]

1292. Spector, Robert D., ed. **The Candle and the Tower.** New York: Warner,
D   1974. 272 pp. ISBN 0-446-76395-0.

Stories from the early days of gothic literature, including "Edeliza" (E. W.), "The Clock Has Struck!!!" (William Farrow), "The Castle of Costanzo" (William Farrow), "The Friar's Tale" (Anna Seward), "Rodriguez and Isabella, or The Terrors of Conscience, a Tale" (Anna Seward), "Retribution, a Tale Founded on Facts" (Thomas Bellamy), "Sir Bertrand, a Fragment" (Anna Laetitia Barbauld), "Henry Fitzowen" (Nathan Drake), "Ramond, a Fragment" (Juvenis), "The Nun" (S. P.), "The Cave of St. Sidwell, a Romance" (E. F.), "Schabraco, a Romance" (E. F.), "The Castle of De Warrenne, a Romance" (E. F.). [Gothic romance, Short stories]

1293. Stone, Idella Purnell. **14 Great Tales of ESP.** New York: Fawcett, 1969.
C   301 pp. SBN 449-02164-075.

Stories of people with most unusual powers, including "The Foreign Hand Tie" (Randall Garrett), "The Leader" (Murray Leinster), "What Thin Partitions" (Mark Clifton and Alex Apostolides), "Project Nightmare" (Robert Heinlein), "Preposterous" (Frederic Brown), "Modus Vivendi" (Walter Bupp), "Belief" (Isaac Asimov), "I'm a Stranger Here Myself" (Mack Reynolds), "The Man on Top" (R. Bretnor), "False Image" (Jay Williams), "Ararat" (Zenna Henderson), "These Are the Arts" (James H. Schmitz), "The Garden in the Forest" (Robert F. Young), "And Still It Moves" (Eric Frank Russell). [Paranormal abilities; Short stories]

1294. Sullivan, Tim, ed. **Tropical Chills.** New York: Avon, 1988. 258 pp. ISBN
C   0-380-75500-9.

Horror can be found in any climate. Included are "Houston, 1943" (Gene Wolfe), "Mama Doah's Garden" (Susan Lilas Wiggs), "Grim Monkeys" (Steve Rasnic Tem), "The Flowers of the Forest" (Brian W. Aldiss), "White Socks" (Ian Watson), "Chrysalis" (Edward Bryant), "Night Fishing on the Caribbean Littoral of the Mutant Rain Forest" (Robert Frazier and Bruce Boston), "Dead Meat" (Charles Sheffield), "Where Do You Live, Queen Esther" (Avram Davidson), "Talking Heads" (George Alec Effinger), "Getting Up" (Jack Dann and Barry N. Malzberg), "It Was the Heat" (Pat Cadigan), "A Part of Us" (Gregory Frost), "Graveyard Highway" (Dean R. Koontz). [Horror; Short stories]

1295. Summers, Montague, ed. **The Penguin Supernatural Omnibus.** Har-
C   mondsworth, England: Penguin, 1976. 573 pp. ISBN 0-1400-7297-7.
        (First published by Victor Gollancz, 1931.)

A weighty collection of mysterious stories collected by a mysterious occult personage. The stories include "Narrative of the Ghost of a Hand" (J. Sheridan Le Fanu), "An Account of Some Strange Disturbances in Aungier Street" (J. Sheridan Le Fanu), "Man-size in Marble" (Evelyn Nesbit), "The Judge's House" (Bram Stoker), "Perceval Landon" (Thurnley Abbey), "The Story of the Spaniards" (E. and H. Heron), "The Phantom Coach" (Amelia B. Edwards),

"Brickett Bottom" (Amyas Northcote), "The Cold Embrace" (Miss Braddon), "How the Third Floor Knew the Potteries" (Amelia B. Edwards), "Not to Be Taken at Bed-time" (Rosa Mulholland), "To Be Taken with a Grain of Salt" (Charles Dickens), "The Signal-man" (Charles Dickens), "The Compensation House" (Charles Collins), "The Engineer" (Amelia B. Edwards), "When I Was Dead" (Vincent O'Sullivan), "The Story of Yand Manor House" (E. and H. Heron), "The Business of Madame Jahn" (Vincent O'Sullivan), "Amour Dure" (Vernon Lee), "Oke of Okehurst" (Vernon Lee), "Eveline's Visitant" (Miss Braddon), "John Charrington's Wedding" (Evelyn Nesbit), "De Profundis" (Roger Pater), "The Dream Woman" (Wilkie Collins), "Singular Passage in the Life of the Late Henry Harris, Doctor in Divinity" (Richard Barham), "The Spirit of Stonehenge" (Jasper John), "The Seeker of Souls" (Jasper John), "The Astrologer's Legacy" (Roger Pater), "My Brother's Ghost Story" (Amelia B. Edwards), "Sir Dominick's Bargain" (J. Sheridan Le Fanu), "The Bargain of Rupert Orange" (Vincent O'Sullivan), "Carmilla" (J. Sheridan Le Fanu), "The White Wolf of the Hartz Mountains" (Frederick Marryat), "A Porta Inferi" (Roger Pater), "Jerry Jarvis's Wig" (Richard Barham), "The Watcher o' the Dead" (John Guinan), "The Story of Konnor Old House" (E. and H. Heron), "Toussel's Bride" (W. B. Seabrook). [Horror; Short stories]

1296. Volumes 1-3, edited by Richard Davis; volumes 4-7 edited by Gerald
C   Page; volumes 8- edited by Karl Edward Wagner.
        Volumes 1-3, edited by Richard Davis; volumes 4-6 edited by Gerald
        Page; volumes 7-   edited by Karl Edward Wagner.

Good selections of stories published in scattered sources picked out by an expert in the field. Volume 18 (1990) includes "Kaddish" (Jack Damn), "The Gravedigger's Tale" (Simon Clark), "Meeting the Author" (Ramsey Campbell), "Buckets" (F. Paul Wilson), "The Pit-Yakker" (Brian Lumley), "Mr. Sandman" (Scott D. Yost), "Renaissance" (A. F. Kidd), "Lord of Infinite Diversions" (T. Winter-Damon), "Rail Rider" (Wayne Allen Sallee), "Archway" (Nicholas Royle), "The Confessional" (Patrick McLeod), "The Deliverer" (Simon MacCulloch), "Reflections" (Jeffrey Goddin), "Zombies for Jesus" (Nina Kiriki Hoffman), "The Earth Wire" (Joel Lane), "Sponge and China Tea" (D. F. Lewis), "The Boy with the Bloodstained Mouth" (W. H. Pugmire), "On the Dark Road" (Ian McDowell), "Narcopolis" (Wayne Allen Sallee), "Nights in the City" (Jessica Amanda Salmonson), "Return to the Mutant Rain Forest" (Bruce Boston and Robert Frazier), "The End of the Hunt" (David Drake), "The Motivation" (David Langford), "The Guide" (Ramsey Campbell), "The Horse of Iron & How We Can Know It & Be Changed by It Forever" (M. John Harrison), "Jerry's Kids Meet Wormboy" (David J. Schow). [Horror; Short stories]

1297. Waugh, Carol-Lynn Rossel, Martin Harry Greenberg, and Isaac Asimov,
C   eds. **13 Horrors of Halloween.** New York: Avon, 1983. 175 pp. ISBN
        0-380-81814-7.

Stories for that most magical night of the year such as "Halloween" (Isaac Asimov), "Unholy Hybrid" (William Bankier), "Trick-or-Treat" (Anthony Boucher), "The October Game" (Ray Bradbury), "Halloween Girl" (Robert Grant), "Day of the Vampire" (Edward D. Hoch), "Night of the Goblin" (Talmage Powell), "The Adventure of the Dead Cat" (Ellery Queen), "Pumpkin Head" (Al Sarrantonio), "The Circle" (Lewis Shiner), "All Souls" (Edith Wharton), "Yesterday's Witch" (Gahan Wilson), "Victim of the Year" (Robert F. Young). [Halloween; Short stories]

1298. Waugh, Charles G., Martin H. Greenberg, and Frank D. McSherry, Jr.,
C   eds. **Cinemonsters.** Lake Geneva, Wis.: TSR, 1987. 319 pp. ISBN
       0-88038-504-9.

Stories and novellas on which some favorite horror movies have been based,
including "Who Goes There" (John W. Campbell, Jr.) filmed as *The Thing*,
"Masque of the Red Death" (Edgar Allan Poe), "Casting the Runes" (M. R.
James) filmed as *Night of the Demon*, "The Foghorn" (Ray Bradbury) filmed as
The Beast from 20,000 Fathoms, "The Skull of the Marquis de Sade" (Robert
Bloch) filmed as *The Skull*, "Mother by Protest" (Richard Matheson) filmed as
The Stranger Within, "The Empire of the Ants" (H. G. Wells), "Herbert West,
Reanimator" (H. P. Lovecraft) filmed as *Re-Animator*, "Killdozer!" (Theodore
Sturgeon), "The Exchanged Kiss" (O. Henry), "Dracula's Ghost" (Bram Stoker)
filmed as *Dracula's Daughter*, "There Shall Be No Darkness" (James Blish)
filmed as *The Beast Must Die*. [Monsters; Short stories]

1299. Weinberg, Robert E., ed. **The Eighth Green Man & Other Strange**
C   **Folk.** Mercer Island, Wash.: Starmont, 1989. 171 pp. ISBN
       1-55742-066-1.

This collection culled from the pages of the old pulp magazine *Weird Tales*
includes "The Eighth Green Man" (G. G. Pendarves), "The Nightwire" (H. F.
Arnold), "The House of the Worm" (Mearle Prout), "The Gray Death" (Loual B.
Sugarman), "Norn" (Lireve Monet), "His Brother's Keeper" (Major George
Fielding Eliot), "The Dead Wagon" (Greye LaSpina), "The Floor Above" (M. L.
Humphreys), "The Cavern" (Manly Wade Wellman), "The Wolf-Woman"
(Bassett Morgan), "Jorgas" (Robert Nelson). [Horror; Short stories]

1300. Williamson, J. N., ed. **The Best of Masques.** New York: Berkley, 1988.
C   228 pp. ISBN 0-425-10693-4.

Wonderful stories by wonderful writers, including "Nightcrawlers" (Robert
R. McCammon), "Buried Talents" (Richard Matheson), "Soft" (F. Paul Wilson),
"Second Sight" (Ramsey Campbell), "Everybody Needs a Little Love" (Robert
Bloch), "The Yard" (William F. Nolan), "The Substitute" (Gahan Wilson),
"Maurice and Mob" (James Herbert), "Angel's Exchange" (Jessica Amanda
Salmonson), "Hidey Hole" (Steve Rasnic Tem), "Long After Ecclesiastes" (Ray
Bradbury), "The Night Is Freezing Fast" (Thomas F. Monteleone), "The Old Men
Know" (Charles L. Grant), "Splatter" (Douglas E. Winter), "Czadek" (Ray
Russell), "Wordsong" (J. N. Williamson), "Down by the Sea near the Great Big
Rock" (Joe R. Lansdale), "Outsteppin' Fetchit" (Charles R. Saunders),
"Somebody Like You" (Dennis Etchison), "Third Wind" (Richard Christian
Matheson), "The Boy Who Came Back from the Dead" (Alan Rodgers), "Popsy"
(Stephen King). [Horror; Short stories]

1301. Wilson, Gahan. **Favorite Tales of Horror.** New York: Tempo, 1976.
A   186 pp. ISBN 0-448-12627-3.

Noted cartoonist and critic of horror books and movies edits a collection of
spooky tales for teens, including "Kitty Fisher" (Charles Birkin), "The Treader of
the Dust" (Clark Ashton Smith), "The Horror of the Heights" (Sir Arthur Conan
Doyle), "The Sea Was Wet as Wet Could Be" (Gahan Wilson), "Luella Miller"
(Mary Wilkins Freeman), "The Idol with Hands of Clay" (Sir Frederick Treves),

"My Favorite Murder" (Ambrose Bierce), "The Clock" (William Fryer Harvey), "The Harbor-Master" (Robert W. Chambers), "Rats" (M. R. James). [Ghosts; Short stories]

1302. Windling, Terri, ed. **Faery!** New York: Ace, 1985. 308 pp. ISBN
C   0-441-22564-0.

A collection of charming stories about the strange inhabitants of the shadowy secret world of inhuman beings, such as "A Troll and Two Roses" (Patricia A. McKillip), "The Thirteenth Fey" (Jane Yolen), "Lullaby for a Changeling" (Nicholas Stuart Gray), "Brat" (Theodore Sturgeon), "Wild Garlic" (William F. Wu), "The Stranger" (Shulamith Oppenheim), "Spirit Places" (Keith Taylor), "The Box of All Possibility" (Z. Greenstaff), "The Seekers of Dreams" (Felix Marti-Ibanez), "Bridge" (Steven R. Boyett), "Crowley and the Leprechaun" (Gregory Frost), "The Antrim Hills" (Mildred Downey Broxon), "The Snow Fairy" (M. Lucie Chin), "The Five Black Swans" (Sylvia Townsend Warner), "Thomas the Rhymer" (traditional Scottish ballad), "Prince Shadowbow" (Sheri S. Tepper), "The Erlking" (Angela Carter), "The Elphin Knight" (traditional Scottish ballad), "Rhian and Garanhir" (Grail Undwin), "The Woodcutter's Daughter" (Alison Uttley), "The Famous Flower of Serving Men" (traditional Scottish ballad), "Touk's House" (Robin McKinley), "The Boy Who Dreamed of Tir Na N-og" (Michael M. McNamara). [Fairies; Short stories]

1303. Winter, Douglas E., ed. **Prime Evil.** New York: Signet, 1989. 380 pp.
C   ISBN 0-451-15909-8. (First published by New American Library, 1988.)

Thirteen never-before published stories by modern masters, including "The Night Flier" (Stephen King), "Having a Woman at Lunch" (Paul Hazel), "The Blood Kiss" (Dennis Etchison), "Coming to Grief" (Clive Barker), "Food" (Thomas Tessier), "The Great God Pan" (M. John Harrison), "Orange Is for Anguish, Blue for Insanity" (David Morrell), "The Juniper Tree" (Peter Straub), "Spinning Tales with the Dead" (Charles L. Grant), "Alice's Last Adventure" (Thomas Ligotti), "Next Time You'll Know Me" (Ramsey Campbell), "The Pool" (Whitley Strieber), "By Reason of Darkness" (Jack Cady). [Horror; Short stories]

1304. Winter, Douglas E., ed. **The Skin Trade.** New York: Berkley, 1990.
C   329 pp. ISBN 0-425-12003-1. (First published as *Night Visions V* by Dark
       Harvest, 1988.)

Terrifically terrible tales of terror, including "The Reploids" (Stephen King), "Sneakers" (Stephen King), "Dedication" (Stephen King), "Metastasis" (Dan Simmons), "Vanni Fucci Is Alive and Well and Living in Hell" (Dan Simmons), "Iverson's Pits" (Dan Simmons), "The Skin Trade" (George R. R. Martin). [Horror; Short stories]

Books in Series

Books in series are listed in the publisher's series order. Not all titles are annotated earlier. Selection of titles to be annotated was based on availability rather than quality.

Alfred Hitchcock & the
Three Investigators Series
[Category B]

A spin-off of the Three Investigators Series that deals with more occult themes than the original series. Three adventurous boys investigate odd happenings. Published by Random House.

Crooked Cat.
Deadly Double.
Flaming Footprints.
Green Ghost.
Haunted Houseful.
Headless Horse.
Laughing Shadow.
Moaning Cave.
Monster Mountain.
Mystery of the Cranky Collector.
Screaming Clock.
Shark Reef.
Silver Spider.
Sinister Scarecrow.
Skeleton Island.
Terror Castle.
Vanishing Treasure.
Whispering Mummy.

Birthstone Gothic Series
[Category C]

A series of twelve gothic romances, each dealing with a different birthstone. Published by Ballantine.

Ross, Marilyn. *The Ghost and the Garnet.*
Ross, Marilyn. *The Amethyst Tears.*
Tower, Diana. *Stone of Blood.*
Ross, Marilyn. *Shadow over Emerald Castle.*
DeWeese, Jean. *The Moonstone Spirit.*
Alexander, Jan. *Blood Ruby.*
DeWeese, Jean. *The Carnelian Cat.*
Tower, Diana. *A Gleam of Sapphire.*
Kent, Fortune. *Opal Legacy.*
Toombs, Jane. *A Topaz for My Fair Lady.*
Wagner, Sharon. *Turquoise Talisman.*

Dark Forces Series
[Category A]

A series dealing with the dark side of occult themes. Written for teens with strong stomachs. Published by Bantam.

Logan, Les. *The Game.*
Bridges, Laurie, and Paul Alexander. *Magic Show.*
Sparger, Rex. *The Doll.*
Bridges, Laurie, and Paul Alexander. *Devil Wind.*
Sparger, Rex. *The Bargain.*
Bridges, Laurie, and Paul Alexander. *Swamp Witch.*
Logan, Les. *Unnatural Talent.*
Siegel, Scott. *The Companion.*
Coville, Bruce. *Eyes of the Tarot.*
Siegel, Scott. *Beat the Devil.*
Coville, Bruce. *Waiting Spirits.*
Bridges, Laurie. *The Ashton Horror.*
Weinburg, Larry. *The Curse.*
Scott, R. C. *Blood Sport.*
Polcovar, Jane. *The Charming.*
Gonzalez, Gloria. *A Deadly Rhyme.*

Dark Shadows Series
[Category C]

All books in this series, based on the very successful daytime soap opera, were written by Marilyn Ross, pseudonym of W. E. D. (Dan) Ross. The stories are gothic in nature, centered around Barnabas Collins, a vampire. Published by Paperback Library.

Barnabas, Quentin and the Vampire Beauty.
Barnabas, Quentin and the Hidden Tomb.
Barnabas, Quentin and the Mad Magician.
Barnabas, Quentin and the Sea Ghost.
Barnabas, Quentin and the Grave Robbers.
Barnabas, Quentin and Dr. Jekyll's Son.
Barnabas, Quentin and the Body Snatchers.
Barnabas, Quentin and the Magic Potion.
Barnabas, Quentin and the Serpent.
Barnabas, Quentin and the Scorpio Curse.
Barnabas, Quentin and the Frightened Bride.
Barnabas, Quentin and the Haunted Cave.
Barnabas, Quentin and the Witch's Curse.
Barnabas, Quentin and the Crystal Coffin.
Barnabas, Quentin and the Nightmare Assassin.
Barnabas, Quentin and the Avenging Ghost.
Barnabas, Quentin and the Mummy's Curse.
Barnabas, Quentin and the Gypsy Witch.
Barnabas Collins and Quentin's Demon.
Barnabas Collins and the Mysterious Ghost.
The Peril of Barnabas Collins.
Barnabas Collins Versus the Warlock.
The Phantom and Barnabas Collins.
The Foe of Barnabas Collins.
The Secret of Barnabas Collins.
The Demon of Barnabas Collins.
The Curse of Collinwood.
Strangers at Collins House.
The Mystery of Collinwood.
Victoria Winters.
Dark Shadows.
Barnabas Collins.

Dennis Wheatley Library of the Occult
[Category C]

A series of fiction and nonfiction selected by Dennis Wheatley, an acknowledged authority on the occult and author of a number of occult novels. Published by Sphere.

Stoker, Bram. *Dracula.*

Endore, Guy. *The Werewolf of Paris.*

Crowley, Aleister. *Moonchild.*

Blavatsky, Helena. *Studies in Occultism.*

Hodgson, William Hope. *Carnacki the Ghost-Finder.*

O'Donnell, Elliott. *The Sorcery Club.*

Tabori, Paul. *Harry Price: The Biography of a Ghost-Hunter.*

Crawford, F. Marion. *The Witch of Prague.*

Wheatley, Dennis, ed. *Uncanny Tales 1.*

Mason, A. E. W. *The Prisoner in the Opal.*

Brodie-Innes, J. W. *The Devil's Mistress.*

Cheiro. *You and Your Hand.*

Bowen, Marjorie. *Black Magic.*

Bonewits, Philip. *Real Magic.*

Goethe. *Faust.*

Wheatley, Dennis, ed. *Uncanny Tales 2.*

Hodgson, William Hope. *The Ghost Pirate.*

Leroux, Gaston. *The Phamtom of the Opera.*

Williams, Charles. *The Greater Trumps.*

Magre, Maurice. *The Return of the Magi.*

Wheatley, Dennis, ed. *Uncanny Tales 3.*

Eaton, Evelyn. *The King Is a Witch.*

Shelley, Mary. *Frankenstein.*

Dunsany, Lord. *The Curse of the Wise Woman.*

Rohmer, Sax. *Brood of the Witch Queen.*

McGregor, Pedro. *Brazilian Magic: Is It the Answer?*

Buchan, John. *The Gap in the Curtain.*

Zolar. *The Interpretation of Dreams.*

Metrux, Alfred. *Voodoo.*

Benson, R. H. *The Necromancers.*

Whealey, Dennis, ed. *Satanism and Witches.*

Grant, Joan. *The Winged Pharaoh.*

Huysmans, J. K. *Down There.*

Lewis, Mathew. *The Monk.*

Dumas, Alexandre. *Horror at Fontenay.*

McCormick, Donald. *The Hell-Fire Club.*

Corelli, Marie. *The Mighty Atom.*

Mossiker, Frances. *The Affair of the Poisons.*

Lewis, Hilda. *The Witch and the Priest.*

Franklyn, Julian. *Death by Enchantment.*

Prangley, Ida. *Fortune Telling by Cards.*

Saxon, Peter. *Dark Ways to Death.*

Double Fastback Horror Stories
[Category B]

Written for readers with low reading ability, the series is full of high interest. Published by Fearon.

Gersdorf, A. G. *The Bird.*

Liberatore, Karen. *Coming Home.*

Lorimer, Janet. *Deadly Rose.*

Lorimer, Janet. *The Dollhouse.*

Brandner, Gary. *The Experiment.*

Greene, Janice. *Fast Forward.*

Girard, Ken. *Fun House.*

Laymon, Richard. *The Halloween Heart.*

Brandner, Gary. *Mind Grabber.*

Girard, Ken. *Weekend Vacation.*

Find Your Fate Series
[Category B]

Multiple-ending choice books based on the character of Indiana Jones from the hit movie. The reader makes decisions for Indiana along the way in each adventure. Written for younger teens. Published by Ballantine.

Stine, Robert L. *Indiana Jones and the Curse of Horror Island.*

Estes. Rose. *Indiana Jones and the Lost Treasure of Sheba.*

Stine, Robert L. *Indiana Jones and the Giants of the Silver Tower.*

Wende, Richard. *Indiana Jones and the Eye of the Fates.*

Helfer, Andrew. *Indiana Jones and the Cup of the Vampires.*

Wenk, Richard. *Indiana Jones and the Legion of Death.*

Stine, Robert L. *Indiana Jones and the Cult of the Mummy's Crypt.*

Stine, Megan, and H. William Stine. *Indiana Jones and the Dragon of Vengeance.*

Weiss, Ellen. *Indiana Jones and the Gold of Genghis Khan.*

Fleshcreepers Series
[Category B]

A series of simplified occult novels originally published for adults and rewritten for young children. See main entries for original authors and authors of the simplified versions. Published by Beaver.

Poldari, John. *The Vampyre.*

Stoker, Bram. *Blood from the Mummy's Tomb.*

Stevinson, Robert Louis. *Dr. Jekyll and Mr. Hyde.*

Wheatley, Dennis. *The Devil Rides Out.*

Night Visions Series
[Category C]

Originally published in hardcover and reissued in paperback with distinct titles. The contents are short stories, generally by the three well-known horror writers. Published by Dark Harvest Press.

Night Visions: Dead Image ed. by Charles L. Grant.

Night Visions: The Hellbound Heart ed. by George R. R. Martin.

Night Visions: In the Blood ed. by Alan Ryan.

Night Visions: Harshell ed. by Clive Barker.

Night Visions: The Skin Trade ed. by Douglas E. Winter.

Three Investigators Series
[Category B]

The tales of three daring young sleuths who search for solutions (sometimes logically explained) to odd goings-on in many strange places. Written by M. V. Carey using characters developed by Robert Arthur. Published by Random House for younger readers.

The Secret of Terror Castle.
The Mystery of the Stuttering Parrot.
The Mystery of the Whispering Mummy.
The Mystery of the Green Ghost.
The Mystery of the Vanishing Treasure.
The Secret of Skeleton Island.
The Mystery of the Fiery Eye.
The Mystery of the Silver Spider.
The Mystery of the Screaming Clock.
The Mystery of the Moaning Cave.
The Mystery of the Talking Skull.
The Mystery of the Laughing Shadow.
The Secret of the Crooked Cat.
The Mystery of the Coughing Dragon.
The Mystery of the Flaming Foot-prints.
The Mystery of the Nervous Lion.
The Mystery of the Singing Serpent.
The Mystery of the Shrinking House.
The Secret of Phantom Lake.
The Mystery of Monster Mountain.
The Secret of the Haunted Mirror.

The Mystery of the Dead Man's Riddle.
The Mystery of the Invisible Dog.
The Mystery of Death Trap Mine.
The Mystery of the Dancing Devil.
The Mystery of the Headless Horse.
The Mystery of the Magic Circle.
The Mystery of the Deadly Double.
The Mystery of the Sinister Scarecrow.
The Secret of Shark Reef.
The Mystery of the Scar-Faced Beggar.
The Mystery of the Blazing Cliffs.
The Mystery of the Purple Pirate.
The Mystery of the Wandering Cave Man.
The Mystery of the Kidnapped Whale.
The Mystery of the Missing Mermaid.
The Mystery of the Two-Toed Pigeon.
The Mystery of the Smashing Glass.
The Mystery of the Trail of Terror.
The Mystery of the Rogues' Reunion.
The Mystery of the Creep-Show Crooks.
The Mystery of Wreckers' Rock.

Time Machine Series
[Category B]

Choose-your-own-ending series that permits the reader to make choices based on preferences and historical facts. For that reason, the majority of the books are set in the past rather than in the future. Published by Bantam.

Gasperini, Jim. *Secret of the Knights.*
Bischoff, David. *Search for Dinosaurs.*
Smith, Mark. *Sword of the Samurai.*
Gasperini, Jim. *Sail with Pirates.*
Perry, Steve. *Civil War Secret Agent.*
Cover, Arthur Byron. *Rings of Saturn.*
Dixon, Dougal. *Ice Age Explorer.*
Gasperini, Jim. *Mystery of Atlantis.*
Overholser, Stephen. *Wild West Rider.*

Cover, Arthur Byron. *American Revolutionary.*
Nanus, Susan, and Marc Kornblatt. *Mission to World War II.*
Walker, Robert W. *Search for the Nile.*
Gaskin, Carol. *Secret of the Royal Treasure.*
Cover, Arthur Byron. *Blade of the Guillotine.*

Kornblatt, Marc. *Flame of the Inquisition.*

Glatzer, Richard. *Quest for the Cities of Gold.*

Reit, Seymour. *Scotland Yard Detective.*

Stevenson, Robin. *Sword of Caesar.*

Gaskin, Carol, and George Guthridge. *Death Mask of Pancho Villa.*

Bailey, Nancy. *Bound for Australia.*

Gaskin, Carol. *Caravan to China.*

Lerangis, Peter. *Last of the Dinosaurs.*

Twilight Series
[Category A]

A series of books for teens dealing with occult themes. Less gruesome than the Dark Forces books. Published by Dell.

Cowan, Dale. *Deadly Sleep.*

Haynes, Betsy. *The Power.*

Brunn, Robert. *The Initiation.*

Howe, Imogen. *Fatal Attraction.*

Francis, Dorothy Brenner. *Blink of the Mind.*

Haynes, James. *Voices in the Dark.*

Veley, Charles. *Play to Live.*

Armstrong, Sarah. *Blood Red Roses.*

Daniel, Colin. *Demon Tree.*

Stevenson, E. *The Avenging Spirit.*

Laymon, Carl. *Nightmare Lake.*

Smith, Janet Patton. *The Twisted Room.*

Howe, Imogen. *Vicious Circle.*

Callahan, Jay. *Footprints of the Dead.*

Coville, Bruce. *Spirits & Spells.*

Selden, Neil. *Drawing the Dead.*

Netter, Susan. *Storm Child.*

Trainor, Joseph. *Watery Grave.*

Kassem, Lou. *Dance of Death.*

Trainor, Joseph. *Family Crypt.*

Cusick, Richie Tankersley. *Evil on the Bayou.*

Blake, Susan. *The Haunted Dollhouse.*

Byron, Amanda. *The Warning.*

Gonzalez, Gloria. *A Deadly Rhyme.*

Bicknell, Arthur. *Scavenger's Hunt.*

Zodiac Club Series
[Category A]

A series with female protagonists dealing mainly with romance. Astrology plays a part in all the books, since the young heroines are members of an astrology club. Published by Pacer/Berkley.

Daniels, Gail. *The Stars Unite.*

Godfrey, Sarah. *Aries Rising.*

Nichols, Lynn J. *Taurus Trouble.*

Rees, E. M. *Libra's Dilemma.*

Palatini, Margie. *Capricorn & Co.*

Kroll, Joanna. *Sagittarius Serving.*

Lawrence, S. J. *Aquarius Ahoy!*

Rees, E. M. *Gemini Solo.*

Daniels, Gail. *Cancer, the Moonchild.*

Rees, E. M. *Pisces Times Two.*

Palatini, Margie. *Scorpio's Class Act.*

Glossary

Abominable snowman. A legendary creature — half-man, half-beast — inhabiting mountainous areas of the world. Also called: Big Foot; Yeti.

Alchemy. Use of primative chemical and/or magical spells to change substances, particularly base metals, into gold. Most prevalent belief was in the Philosopher's Stone, rumored to produce the change into gold.

Altered states of consciousness. Deliberate and accidental changes in personality such as mind-altering experiments through conditioning, drugs, etc.

Angels. Heavenly beings usually depicted as the messengers of the creator, or the supreme being.

Astrology. A pseudoscientific system that uses the position of the sun, moon, planets, and stars to analyze human personalities, coming events, etc.

Atlantis. A legendary island that sank beneath the sea.

Bathody, Countess Elizabeth. A sixteenth-century, central European historical figure who murdered virgins in order to bathe in their blood, her "beauty secret" for eternal youth.

Big Foot. *See* Abominable snowman.

Black magic. Secret powers, thought to be derived from the devil and the demons of hell, used for evil purposes.

Cults. Intensely close-knit groups devoted to often-secret purposes, sometimes the followers of a charismatic leader.

Curses. Evil wishes.

Dragons. Mythical beasts symbolic of evil in many legends.

ESP (extrasensory perception). Those senses beyond the ordinary used in such activities as clairvoyance, levitation, precognition, etc., currently controversial, particularly in scientific circles.

Exorcism. Religious ceremony to drive out or expel demons possessing a human and purify the person.

Fairies. Legendary creatures in British folklore believed to be semihuman, magical beings who live just under the earth's surface.

Fantasy games. Role-playing entertainments, such as Dungeons and Dragons, that employ the use of mythical creatures and magical powers.

Frankenstein. Mary Shelley's fictional creation; a famous monster created from dead body parts.

Ghosts. The spirits of the dead who have not yet found a final resting place.

Golem. A robot-like monster supposedly created in sixteenth-century Prague by Rabbi Loew, a real-life scholar.

Gothic romance. A genre of literature, first written in England in the eighteenth century, that employs such conventions as spooky settings, endangered maidens, sinister characters, and generally eerie occurrences.

Gypsy lore. Superstitions about the Romany people, Irish tinkers, and other nomadic cultures.

Halloween. The last day of October, an old pagan holiday, that is still celebrated as an evening of superstition, a time for ghosts, and masquerading. Believed by many to be an important day, or sabbat, for satanists. Originally, All Hallow's Eve, the day before All Saints' Day.

Jack the Ripper. A now-legendary murderer who brutally killed prostitutes in London a hundred years ago. Never captured nor identified, Jack remains a popular mystery.

Knights Templars. A military and religious society of celibate knights in medieval Europe that originated in Jerusalem during the crusades; one of many legends proports that they worshiped the devil in return for secret powers.

Laveau, Marie. A famous voodoo queen in nineteenth-century New Orleans.

Legerdemain. Sleight of hand and optical illusions created by stage magicians.

Lost lands. Legendary continents, countries, or islands usually inhabited by strange beasts and magical people with untold wealth and knowledge.

Magic. The use of spells and prayers to nonconventional dieties in order to obtain desired results.

Manimals. Part-beast, part-human creatures such as werewolves and cat people. *See also* werewolves.

Mermaids. Beautiful, mythical sea creatures that are half-human, half-fish.

Mummies. In supernatural terms, ancient Egyptian mummies (corpses wrapped in cloth) endowed with motion and "life."

Nazi occultism. Modern legends arising from Hitler's known interest in astrology and other supernatural ideas.

Nostradamus. A sixteenth-century French physician who wrote a series of mysterious predictions for the future of the world.

Obeah. A syncretic religious system combining Christianity with African beliefs.

Paranormal abilities. Human abilities not generally accepted by science, such as second sight or clairvoyance. *See also* ESP.

Possession. Taking over the personality and mind of a human being, such as a ghost possessing a living person.

Powwow. A syncretic belief system combining Christianity with superstitious spells and charms reputedly still practised by the Pennsylvania Dutch.

Reincarnation. The belief that a soul passes from one body or life to another after death.

Santeria. An umbrella term for Christian/African religions. *See also* Obeah; Syncretic religions.

Satanism. A religious belief based on the worship of Satan, or the devil, that is geared to obtaining personal power for often evil purposes.

Shamanism. A religious belief focused on magic and mythology as explained and practiced by a shaman, or medicine man.

Spiritualism. A popular alternative belief in nineteenth-century France which spread throughout the world and is still practiced today; includes the belief in being able to communicate with spirits of the dead.

Syncretic religions. The combination or melding of two or more different religions, such as those derived from African slaves who practiced their masters' Christian religion publicly while secretly practicing their own beliefs within the structure of Christianity. Examples: voodoo, macumba, etc. *See also* Obeah; Powwow; Santeria.

Time travel. Scientific or magical means of transportation to another time period, past or future.

Unicorns. Mythical beasts, usually portrayed as white horses with a single horn, often endowed with magical powers.

Vampires. Legendary beings, either monsters or once-living humans, who maintain eternal life by sucking blood from humans.

Vanishings. Disappearances of humans who are never heard of again. Reappearances may also occur mysteriously. In contemporary belief, such vanishings and reappearances are often related to abductions and releases by creatures from outer space in UFOs.

Voodoo. *See* syncretic religions.

Werewolves. The most common kind of "manimal," a legendary creature who lives primarily in human form but turns into a wolf during a full moon. *See also* Manimals.

Witchcraft. Often confused with satanism. In medievel Europe the term was used synonymously with heresy; witches were frequently executed for being worshippers of Satan. In today's world, witchcraft is considered to be a survival of old pagan beliefs, often based on ancient Druid customs of Britain, and generally considered to be practiced for good rather than evil.

Yeti. *See* Abominable snowman.

Zombies. Originally defined as the "walking dead," corpses returned to a souless existence through voodoo spells. Today's zombies are often the result of atomic/toxic disasters, such as the flesheaters of Romero's famous movie, *Night of the Living Dead.*

Movie Index

Numbers refer to entry number.

Title Index

Numbers following the title refer to entry number.

Subject Index